W9-CAN-303

ASTRAL WEEKS

ASTRAL WEEKS

A

SECRET HISTORY

of

1968

RYAN H. WALSH

NEW YORK | PENGUIN PRESS | ·· 2018 ··

PENGUIN PRESS

An imprint of Penguin Random House LLC
375 Hudson Street
New York, New York 10014
penguin.com

Image credits appear on page 347.

ISBN: 9780735221345 (hardcover)
ISBN: 9780735221352 (e-book)

Printed in the United States of America
1 3 5 7 9 10 8 6 4 2

Designed by Marysarah Quinn

FOR MARISSA

CONTENTS

ASTRAL WEEKS

In the Beginning

YOU KNOW THIS STORY. At the 1965 Newport Folk Festival, twenty-three-year-old singer-songwriter and future Nobel laureate Bob Dylan defiantly led his band through a decibel-pushing, distortion-heavy electric set, including "Maggie's Farm" and "Like a Rolling Stone," shocking folk purists. "If I had an axe, I'd chop the microphone cable right now," Pete Seeger grumbled. Fans booed, organizers were aghast, and Dylan had turned himself into someone else. It's one of the true culture-shifting moments in rock 'n' roll history. But what else happened that night?

Though other acts followed Dylan, the evening was enveloped by a confused, mournful feeling: The festival was now a funeral. One musician was so upset by Dylan's set that he performed an unscheduled coda. On the empty, unlit Newport stage, a skinny, twenty-seven-year-old harmonica player named Mel Lyman closed out the proceedings.

"I wanted to save the world with music . . . I still do, but I was more naive at that time," Lyman told a reporter in 1971. "I kept having this fucking recurring image in my sleep, of playing 'Rock of Ages.' Every night I'd toss around in bed, I'd say, 'Don't make me do it. Don't make me do it.' Finally I said, 'OK, if it's gotta be done, I'll do it.'" Lyman was at Newport as part of Jim Kweskin's Jug Band, but their performance had ended long before Dylan's heretical set. As crowds streamed toward the exit, Lyman pushed out a eulogy through his instrument.

"I played 'Rock of Ages.' The people heard it as they were leaving, but it was more for the musicians than the people," Lyman explained. "The musicians were spellbound. They were hearing what they should've been doing. Some of the musicians were crying—I was told that later. I must've lost ten pounds during that song. The sweat was just pouring down. The spirit was so strong I could barely get it out—you know, the harmonica, that's a pretty tiny hole for all that spirit to go through, that little tiny reed." According to some reports, his rendition of "Rock of Ages" went on for half an hour.

Within eighteen months of this performance Mel Lyman would commandeer an entire neighborhood of run-down houses in the Fort Hill area of Roxbury, an impoverished part of Boston, issue cuss-laden pronouncements through an influential underground newspaper, and declare he was God to anyone who would listen. By early 1968, more than a hundred people lived with Mel in his Fort Hill Community. Their stated goal was ever changing and hard to pin down, but on several occasions Lyman "Family" members spoke to the press about creating "the most beautiful music the world has ever known"—and it seemed that they were hell-bent on making this music in a style that was in direct opposition to Dylan's Newport act. The Lymans rejected electric instruments, embracing traditional American folk stylings as a way to transform their lives.

The most beautiful music the world has ever known. Some of the music that emerged from Fort Hill was certainly lovely. But this story starts with a man who undeniably made good on a similar ambition, at the same time and in the same place. He came to the idea himself, by way of a dream.

. . .

IN EARLY 1968, seven miles from Mel Lyman's Fort Hill Community and across the Charles River, a twenty-one-year-old Van Morrison had just found himself the holder of a lease for an apartment on Green Street in Cambridge, Massachusetts. He was about to make a masterpiece.

Born in 1945 in Belfast, Ireland, George Ivan Morrison started writing poetry as a child, "before I knew what poetry was." His father's vast record collection, acquired during a trip to the States, introduced Van to the mysterious world of American blues through artists like Leadbelly and Jelly Roll Morton. Beginning his music career as a teenager, he played saxophone and guitar for several acts before finding acclaim as the front man of R&B act Them, who first toured America in 1966. A stint at the Whisky a Go Go in Los Angeles led to the band jamming with Jim Morrison, sharing a bill with Captain Beefheart, and despite a 50 percent alcohol discount, running up a $2,600 tab. Another anecdote involved Van borrowing a guitar, smashing it onstage, then casually telling the sobbing ex–ax owner, "That's art, man."

On June 23, Them appeared in San Francisco, where Morrison met Janet Rigsbee, a nineteen-year-old Bay Area model and aspiring actress. "I looked at him, he looked at me, and it was alchemical whammo," she said. "I had never been to a rock concert before. We really connected in a very spiritual way, so we tried to spend as much time together as we could while he was touring up and down California."

"One night he would perform well, and the next night he would just glower at the audience," Them guitarist Jim Armstrong recalled. Between shows Morrison was putting together the lyrics for "Ballerina," an ode to Janet and one of the first pieces of *Astral Weeks* to be written. When Them's work visas were not extended, the band returned to Ireland, where Van abruptly left the group. He spent part of his tour earnings on a reel-to-reel tape recorder, planted it at his parents' house, and laid down countless hours of song ideas. He pined for Janet, trying to figure out what would come next.

Described by one biographer as reeking of "Pall Malls, cheap cologne, and hit records," producer Bert Berns was no one's idea of a savior, but in 1967 Van Morrison wasn't in a position to be choosy. Berns had been the first American producer to work with Them; Morrison had been immediately enamored when he learned that Berns had written "I Don't Want to Go On Without You" for the Drifters. Berns introduced Them to overdubs and a song of his called "Here Comes the Night." Their version went to #2 in the United Kingdom, and #24 in the United States.

Berns could have attached himself to one of the several post-Morrison versions of Them, but he knew to bet on the talented but currently aimless singer. Berns hoped that Morrison could become a "rock and roll version of the Irish poet Brendan Behan"—a unique vision, to say the least. He offered $2,500 to sign a contract that a desperate Morrison barely reviewed.

Arriving in New York in 1967, Morrison was puzzled by what he found in the studio. "I showed up for the session, and forty people are there," he later explained to a Warner Brothers executive. "Four guitar players, four keyboard players, five singers, four entire rhythm sections. It was bizarre." In banter heard before one outtake, Morrison wishes it could be freer, remarking, "at the minute, we have a choke thing going, know what I mean?" No one did. One photo reveals an exhausted Morrison, head in his hands. Bert Berns was calling most of the shots at these sessions; he changed the lyrics and title of "Brown-Skinned Girl" at the last minute to the version we all know so well today. When Morrison was finally allowed to lay down "T.B. Sheets" in the style and arrangement he was comfortable with, he ended up sobbing in the vocal booth. "He was just torn apart," engineer Brooks Arthur recalled. "He was sitting on the floor in a heap like a wrung-out dishcloth, completely spent emotionally." After two days, Berns sent him back to Belfast; the producer would bring Morrison back to the States only if one of the songs became a hit. The singer told Janet that if she heard him on the radio, it meant he was on his way to find her.

Luckily, "Brown Eyed Girl" spent sixteen weeks on the *Billboard* charts, peaking at #10. Berns flew Morrison back to New York. Looking for more hits, Berns was agitated when the singer played him stream-of-consciousness demos he had recorded in Belfast. Ilene Berns, the producer's young wife, said that Morrison was out of control, even after Janet joined him in New York. Morrison would sabotage press showcases and studio sessions without warning. At a show at the Bottom Line, his onstage behavior caused the backup singers to flee mid-set. During one recording session, he flung his guitar at a wall and screamed at the musicians, who couldn't sort out the particular issue through his Irish accent.

On December 30, 1967, not long after an intense argument between Berns and Morrison, the producer died of a heart attack at the age of thirty-eight. Ilene was not shy about blaming Morrison. Van and Janet did not attend the funeral, which they later admitted was a terrible mistake. In early 1968, the couple relocated to Cambridge, Massachusetts. Morrison biographies tend to gloss over this pivotal moment. I wanted to find out why he came here, and why he left.

ASTRAL WEEKS IS my favorite record of all time. Like its eloquent champion Lester Bangs, I also believe the record to be some kind of "mystical document," despite the decidedly gritty circumstances around its creation. When I discovered it at twenty-two, I was experiencing my first true heartbreak—I felt like a shell of myself, carved out by loneliness. In my final year at Boston University, I'd fallen madly in love with someone, but she was torn between me and her longtime hometown boyfriend. Enter my upstairs neighbor, a palm reader whom I only knew as "Grandmother." (She called me "Grandson.") Studying our hands in the dim light of her apartment, she concluded that a cosmic accident had allowed us to meet—but that didn't mean we would stay together. Grandmother turned out to be right; the woman I loved moved to San Francisco, and something held me back. I stayed in Boston, where I was born and raised.

I had never heard of *Astral Weeks*; I was indifferent to Van Morrison. But something about seeing the cover, there in a record-store rack in Newton, commanded me to slap down eleven bucks and take it home. From the very first notes, the music seemed to serve as some kind of protection for the part of me that held on to hope and the idea of real love. A force field grew around me with each listen, as songs like "Sweet Thing" and "Madame George" helped beat back any encroaching cynicism. The album had presented itself in a moment when I needed to hear it, promising that I was not alone in my despair. Years later, I met a woman who put on *Astral Weeks* at the end of our first date. As the title track began and she held up the vinyl album cover, smiling, I can only assume my jaw hit the floor; I recalled all that talk about cosmic accidents and wondered if I was in the middle of another one. (Reader, I married her.)

At some point I learned that part of the album's origin story lay in my own backyard—which struck me as beyond coincidence. Over the years, I came to believe that if I could piece together the story of Van Morrison's time on my native soil, in those months before the album came out, I would understand something vital about the music that had buoyed me in those dark days. While researching the album's half-buried local connections, my curiosity about Boston in the late sixties grew into obsession. The music scene from which Van Morrison stocked his band, and the deeply strange tale of Mel Lyman's Fort Hill Community, suggested an incredibly rich artistic past forgotten by all but a few present-day residents.

As a musician myself, with a band operating out of Boston for more than ten years, I'd spent a good chunk of my life immersed in the city's music scene. So why hadn't these stories been passed around like legends at the Silhouette Lounge or the Middle East? Why was I blown away to learn that proto-punk and Natick native Jonathan Richman thought of Boston when he listened to *Astral Weeks?*

Legendary groups like Aerosmith sprouted up in the city in the seventies, but I was more interested in what came before. Dylan's electrified set at Newport, it seemed, had served as the inciting action for a sea change in Boston's counterculture—literally driving people mad, and making others treat the divisions between folk and rock like lines on a battlefield. Van Morrison and Mel Lyman embodied these struggles, and nearly everyone I spoke to had a story about one of them.

In a piece about the Pixies, *Pitchfork* sniffed, "Boston: a famous place but fiercely provincial, with all the reticence of small-town New England and almost no cosmopolitan sheen. We can always depend on Boston for more sports and software engineers." This is a story about Boston before tech innovation and athletic dominance became the city's calling cards— back when LSD and the occult, protest and serial murders were the subjects of most national news stories about life inside the Cradle of Liberty. From the comedy of errors that was MGM Records' attempt to launch the "Boston Sound," to the Velvet Underground's near constant, formative residency at the Boston Tea Party, to the groundbreaking weirdness being aired weekly on WGBH—looking back on Boston in 1968 is like catching a glimpse of an upside-down, hallucinogenic version of the thriving metropolis that stands today.

During the 1950s, Boston lost more residents than any other major city in America. Redevelopment efforts stalled in the early sixties; neighborhoods seen today as highly desirable were all but abandoned. When Mayor Kevin White was sworn into office on January 1, 1968, he spoke of a "New Boston," with plans to fill the city of forty-eight square miles with people of exceptional talent. He could never have imagined the group of eccentrics who would, almost instantly, make his public pledge a reality.

The story of the late-sixties counterculture in America has been told before, especially in regard to the drama unfolding in San Francisco, Chicago, and New York. But what happened in Boston has gone largely unremarked. Perhaps it has to do with the city's Puritan roots, a natural inclination to sweep anything but victories under the rug. This is the secret history of Boston in 1968, about people desperately hunting for something intangible and incandescent, many of whom referred to that *something* as God. Some found it, embodied it, or impersonated it; others were crushed by it. As Marilyn French wrote in *The Women's Room*, her bestselling novel inspired by her time at Harvard in 1968, "That year itself was an open door, but a magical one; once you went through it, you could never return."

ONE

Against Electricity

JOHN SHELDON WAS SEVENTEEN YEARS OLD when a frowning, baby-faced Irish man showed up at the door of his parents' house in Cambridge, Massachusetts. Sheldon, a guitar prodigy, had recently auditioned for the songwriter. Now here the guy was on his porch, all five-foot-five of him, with a local upright bass player looming over his shoulder.

The teenager didn't know what to make of him. "He didn't say very much. We played for a while, and the first thing I remember him saying was, 'Are you available for gigs?'"

And that was how John Sheldon became the guitarist for Van Morrison during the summer of 1968.

Morrison was still riding the buzz of "Brown Eyed Girl," but he certainly wasn't a household name. His adopted hometown didn't pay him special attention. "I remember one gig at the Boston Tea Party," Sheldon said, "but we had no drummer." With Van and the bass player, Tom Kielbania, they drove by Berklee School of Music and "saw this guy on the sidewalk. Tom said, 'Hey, it's Joe. Joe, do you want to play drums?' This is the kind of level that things were happening at then."

Morrison became a constant presence in the Sheldon household. He would tie up the family phone, carrying on epic arguments with Ilene Berns over royalties for "Brown Eyed Girl." "My parents would come down for breakfast on Sunday," Sheldon recalls, "and it would be a bunch of people they didn't know." Morrison even tried to convince Sheldon's mother to let him move into one of the rooms, along with his wife, Janet, and her son from a previous relationship, Peter. Mrs. Sheldon firmly said no, but not because she was a square. "You have to remember, this is the same house that James Taylor and other musicians would just hang out at," Sheldon says. (Taylor had become a family friend after dating John's older sister, Phoebe, which is how he ended up teaching Sheldon the basics on a red Duo-Sonic Fender he sold him for $100.) His parents sometimes complained about the flurry of musicians, "but I think that they liked it more than they didn't," Sheldon says. "It was something that was good for me. I didn't have much else going—I wasn't doing well in school or anything."

According to Sheldon, one day Morrison showed up at rehearsal with some news: he had a dream in which there were no more electric instruments. It was unclear to Sheldon if Morrison's overnight vision was specifically about the band or the world at large, but the singer proceeded to translate his dream into a reality. Kielbania played a stand-up bass; Sheldon moved to acoustic guitar. There would be no more drums. "That's when we started playing songs like 'Madame George,'" Sheldon says. But he was perplexed: "Van had taken me to see Jeff Beck and introduced me, and I thought Jeff Beck was awesome. I wanted to do *that* kind of music. I didn't want to go back to playing acoustic guitars." Sheldon didn't have a philosophical stance on electric versus folk; he just knew what excited him. Even strangers would judge his allegiance harshly. "I got off the subway in Harvard Square with my first electric guitar sticking out of a paper bag, and a guy said, 'Oh, another one for the other team.'"

After a long summer of hitting the New England circuit hard with dozens of live shows, Van Morrison was summoned to meet a record producer named Lewis Merenstein at Ace Recording Studios, across from Boston Common at 1 Boylston Place, a wide commercial alley off the busy main road. It was hard to miss, with its neon sign and a blinking arrow pointing to the front door. Owned by brothers Milton and Herbert Yakus, Ace was a four-track facility whose specialty was recording jingles and song-poems. Someone would bring a poem in, and for a fee, Milton would compose a song around the words, while Herbert arranged a recording with session players. The author would then own a song he or she had "written," amusing friends and family upon playback.

Accounts vary about whether Morrison and his band came to Ace just to audition for Merenstein, or if they had already been holed up for a few days to record some demos. (Merenstein was familiar with the studio, having worked freelance there in the past.) Now Morrison sat before him, and began strumming a new song.

> *If I ventured in the slipstream*
> *Between the viaducts of your dreams*

Thirty seconds in, "my whole being was vibrating," Merenstein said in 2008. "I knew he was being reborn . . . I knew I wanted to work with him at that moment."

John Sheldon remembered the producer telling Morrison, "I think you're a genius, and I want you to make a record for Warner Brothers." It was clear to the young guitarist that Merenstein wasn't talking to any of the other band members.

The song Van Morrison played that day, the one that so unhinged the producer, was called "Astral Weeks," and it would become the title track on the album that would redefine Morrison's career. That audition at Ace was the last time Sheldon was involved with the singer. His hunch had been correct: When Morrison left to record *Astral Weeks* in New York soon after, he didn't take Sheldon with him.

These days, the guitarist holds on to a "shining memory" from that summer, of Morrison sitting in his parents' yard in Cambridge, playing those songs from *Astral Weeks*. "He's out in the sun, and they're very melancholy. They're mournful songs." Sheldon wanted to *rock*, though; his ouster would lead him back to his beloved electric guitar and a new band called Bead Game. "Maybe ten years later, a friend of mine got me stoned and put on *Astral Weeks*, and I went, 'Hey, man, this *is* good!'"

Lauded as one of the greatest albums in the rock 'n' roll canon, *Astral Weeks* feels less like rock, more like a benediction, a song cycle of rebirth. Martin Scorsese claims the first fifteen minutes of *Taxi Driver* are based on it. Philip Seymour Hoffman quoted it in his Oscar acceptance speech. Elvis Costello called it "the most adventurous record made in the rock medium"; part of the late Jeff Buckley's own myth is tied with his choice to cover "The Way Young Lovers Do." The critic Lester Bangs claimed it contained "the quality of a beacon." Joni Mitchell was so taken aback by the album that she badgered one of Van's guitarists for information about him before finally meeting him: "What is he actually like?"

Morrison once told an interviewer that the songs on *Astral Weeks* were "just channeled. They just came through." The mystical layer adds to its allure, though the details of its origin are full of incidents that are anything but. It's an album that was planned, shaped, and rehearsed in Boston and Cambridge. This fact has been a secret kept in plain view. The first clue is right on the album sleeve, a poem filled with Bay State references:

> *I saw you coming from the Cape, way from Hyannis Port all*
> *the way . . .*
> *I saw you coming from Cambridgeport with my poetry*
> *and jazz . . .*

The reasons that Van Morrison lived in the Boston area in 1968 are, to say the least, unexpected. *Astral Weeks*, it turns out, was born out of sheer desperation, conceived at a time when Morrison was trapped in a uniformly terrible recording contract and evading music-industry thugs during a year when America seemed hell-bent on ripping itself apart.

Despite being the author of that lousy contract, producer Bert Berns had genuine affection for the moody singer from Belfast; their working relationship was made up of both confrontations and victories. "Bert loved and identified with the rebel in Van, but wanted to keep him closer to the center when making records," engineer Brooks Arthur recalled to biographer Clinton Heylin. "Van was obsessed with feel. Bert had great commercial sense." In the pursuit of hits, Berns latched on to trends quickly. This is how the late-sixties wave of psychedelia became forever tied to Morrison's debut solo album, *Blowin' Your Mind!* without the singer's knowledge in 1967— complete with a cover sporting trippy fonts and a photograph of a visibly sweaty Morrison, clearly meant to convey that *the drugs* had just kicked in. The liner notes double down on the concept: "And Van blows and Van sings and Van screams and Van listens and Van says 'up them all' and becomes Van and what the hell that's his friend and now he can live with himself. This LP is Van Morrison. We won't explain it to you. With this one, go for yourself."

Morrison was furious, but he didn't have much time to yell at Berns; the producer died three months later. If Morrison found Berns difficult to deal with, what came next was worse. At a certain point in the sixties, Bert Berns became fascinated by people associated with the mob. Fascination became friendship, and friendship turned to business. Now that Berns was dead, Morrison's main contact at Bang Records was Carmine "Wassel" DeNoia, whose father was the inspiration for the character Nicely-Nicely in *Guys and Dolls*. Wassel was an even less forgiving boss than Berns. While the FBI classified him as only a "low level" mobster, he was still a scary menace. In 1975, Wassel was convicted of payola—bribing radio DJs in exchange for heavy rotation of a record—which might not sound like rough work until you hear how Wassel described a typical day. "So here's this disc jockey," Wassel said in 2001. "I throw open the window, pick him up, flip him, shake him out by the ankles. Ninth floor. All the change fell out of his pockets. Some friends of mine picked it up."

Even today, Wassel hasn't lost any of his tough-guy shtick; when I ring him up one night, he answers, "Hello, City Morgue." He's lived for more than fifty years on West Seventy-second Street in Manhattan. When I arrive, he's wearing a loose white undershirt, blue pajama pants, and thick-rimmed black glasses. He's friendly, forthcoming, and a little scattered. "I helped that guy out," Wassel insists about Morrison. "If he ever sees me again, he better stand up and salute me!"

Wassel says he "got Bert Berns started in the music business." Of course, Berns had been involved in the music business long before they met, so what he actually meant was that he introduced Berns to full-blown gangsters like Genovese family member Patsy Pagano—and to the quick results that brute force yielded when applied to the creative industries. Back in Berns's day, this included everything from bullying performers back into studios, dismantling local record-bootlegging operations with a sledgehammer, and finding ways to borrow money that didn't require a credit check. These connections gave Berns and Bang Records an advantage that could level the playing field against more-established labels.

In August 1967, Berns organized a belated record-release party for "Brown Eyed Girl" on a boat that departed from Fiftieth Street in Manhattan. Van attended with his new love Janet Rigsbee. There's a picture from this evening hanging on Wassel's wall. The framed photo shows the singer sporting a rare smile. Janet looks happily taken aback by the fanfare, Berns is glancing at Janet, and Wassel is in back, a giant cigar stuffed in his mouth, with eyes closed and head tilted back. Performer Tiny Tim tried to join the festivities that night, I learn, but Wassel says he threw him overboard into the Hudson River. "They had to fish him out of there," Wassel tells me, laughing. "He was soaked." At some point in the evening, Morrison delivered a soulful solo set for the revelers.

I ask Wassel to tell me more about what happened with Van Morrison right before the singer fled New York. For a moment he looks stumped. "Oh," Wassel remembers, "I broke his guitar on his head."

This is true. Here's what happened:

One night, Wassel visited the singer at the King Edward Hotel, where Morrison and Janet were staying. They were already anxious: Morrison's immigration papers were not wholly in order, and he was worried about being deported; his last visit to an office trying to correct the work permit issue ended with an official telling him, "You're now deported, bye-bye." During the encounter with Wassel, Morrison was severely intoxicated. Wassel asked about a radio he had given Morrison, which now appeared to be broken. Morrison's temper flared up, worsened by booze, so Wassel put an end to his incomprehensible string of expletives by smashing the singer's acoustic guitar over his head. Morrison would later tell others that he and Janet once returned from dinner to find their hotel door full of bullet holes. Neil Diamond, Berns's other poised-to-make-it act at the time, reported similar calamities. "The unholy hell that was unleashed upon [Van] when Bert died was really horrible," Janet recalls, noting another instance where Wassel banged on their door, screaming, "You're finished in the business. D'you hear me?"

All of this may have had something to do with why, in early 1968, Van Morrison and Janet Rigsbee hastily got married and moved to Cambridge, Massachusetts.

BY AUGUST 1968, shortly before his audition with Lewis Merenstein, but after literally dreaming up his new acoustic sound, Morrison booked several shows under the name "The Van Morrison Controversy" to hone his new material and sound. What the titular brouhaha referred to was never specified, but the fact that his record contract led to bullet holes in a hotel door might be a good starting point. These shows took place at a nightclub called the Catacombs, at 1120 Boylston Street in the Fenway, two floors below a pool parlor. (Today, it's a stack of rehearsal studios beneath a pizza joint.) Hieroglyphics decorated the walls. The club mostly hosted jazz, but Morrison's poet-rock fit right in.

At this point, the band had dwindled down to Morrison on guitar and bassist Tom Kielbania. John Sheldon, the guitar wunderkind, had been ditched, and drummer Joey Bebo had left of his own volition. At a jam session near the docks of Lewis Wharf in Boston, Kielbania recruited a flute player named John Payne. Payne was twenty-two, on one of many leaves of absence from his studies at Harvard, stuck editing high school math books for Houghton Mifflin. Kielbania excitedly talked to Payne about what lay on the horizon: "We're recording an album! We're going to Europe!" Though Payne was strictly into jazz, the gig sounded better than staring at equations all day.

Payne remembers meeting Morrison in the back of the Catacombs: "This guy comes out, a short guy with a pageboy, a blank look on his face. Tom says, 'Van, this is the guy I was telling you about.' He goes, 'Uh, eh,' and gives me a limp hand. He was just in his own world."

As Payne watched from the audience, Morrison and Kielbania began to play. "I listened to the first set and I didn't like it," Payne says. "I thought, *The guy doesn't seem like he wants me to be here, maybe the bass player is forcing me on him.* And until I'm on the stage with him, I don't get it." Then Payne joined the pair for the second set. "I started playing a little and I could tell he had heard everything I had played and he was reacting to it. His phrasing was not independent of what I was doing, and I had *never* experienced that. This was alive. Then he starts the next song and it's 'Brown Eyed Girl.'" Payne was shocked: He was playing with the man whose voice he'd been hearing on the jukebox for months. "I could still play, but it was like, *Oh my God*."

In the audience, Eric Kraft was spellbound. He'd been assigned to cover Morrison's string of Catacombs shows for an underground weekly called

Boston After Dark. Decades later, he still recalls it in vivid detail. "It was so amazing," he says. "It changed my life, actually." The following night, Kraft managed to get the taciturn Morrison talking. Sitting on the kitchen floor of the club, Morrison spoke of his label troubles, the songs he was writing, his hopes for himself. In turn, Kraft revealed his own dream. It was the first time he had told anyone that he wanted to be a fiction writer. Morrison told him to go for it. "The fact that it interested him was very propulsive for me," says Kraft, who has since published eleven books in a multivolume novel about the life of his alter ego, Peter Leroy. "It pushed me forward." That night, he went home and woke up his wife to tell her what he had just seen.

In his review, Kraft conveys the evening's power. Van "winces and strains to bring the song up from far within him, producing at times a strangely distant sound that carries a lyric of loss and disillusionment. . . . He has total control over the number and, by now, over most of the audience as well." Bassist Kielbania is "weaving and rocking as though there were a string tying him to Morrison's hand. It looks like the flute player is going to work out—he improvises a fine solo. When the number ends, the applause is long and heartfelt; Karen [*sic*] is smiling; everybody is smiling. Christ it's going to be beautiful. When the album comes out in October or November, buy several."

I mention a rumor I'd heard a while back: that Peter Wolf made an audio recording of one of these nights at the Catacombs. Kraft gasps at the possibility that one of the most important moments of his life has been preserved, and might be accessed again. If they exist, Wolf's tapes would have historic importance: Morrison reportedly performed much of *Astral Weeks* these nights with the Boston trio, a lineup that never received any substantial credit for helping shape songs that would end up on the album. Peter Wolf, of course, went on to be the charismatic singer for the hit-making J. Geils Band, not to mention the husband of actress Faye Dunaway, but he currently lives alone in Boston. I had to find out whether those tapes were real—and if I could hear them.

. . .

BACK AT THE CATACOMBS, Van Morrison also met the man who would extricate him from Bang Records' mob ties.

His savior was a former Boston DJ turned Warner Brothers executive named Joe Smith. In the 1950s, Smith recalls being "the first guy who played real rock 'n' roll on Boston radio." In 1968, he was at the Catacombs on a tip from a colleague. Plenty of people were interested in signing Morrison, but the singer's lack of social graces, coupled with the Bang Records baggage, wasn't helping his cause. Smith wasn't impressed with Morrison's personality: "He was a hateful little guy," he recalls. "His live performance? He may as well have been in Philadelphia. There's no action from him. But his voice! I still think he's the best rock 'n' roll voice out there." Smith set the wheels in motion right away, asking producer Lewis Merenstein to travel to Boston to audition the singer. Merenstein would narrowly beat Bob Dylan and Velvet Underground producer Tom Wilson to Boston by a matter of days. Meanwhile, Smith also needed to figure out a way to erase Morrison's ties with the unsavory side of Bang Records. "There was a guy in town named Joe Scandore, who was Don Rickles's manager. And he was *connected*," Smith says. "I had to go to him and say, 'How can I get this deal through so I can release this guy?' And he set up the arrangement."

The arrangement sounds completely terrifying. At six p.m. on Ninth Avenue in Manhattan, Joe Smith entered an abandoned warehouse with a sack containing $20,000 in cash. Smith remembers how it went down: "I had to walk up three flights of stairs, and there were four guys. Two tall and thin, and two built like buildings. There was no small talk. I got the signed contract and got the hell out of there, because I was afraid somebody would whack me in the head and take back the contract and I'd be out the money."

Did he ever hear from these people again?

"No," Smith deadpans. "They weren't in the music business."

Regardless, the transaction was a success; the moment that Smith dropped that sack of money on the warehouse floor, a clear path toward the creation of *Astral Weeks* opened up before him. Van Morrison was now signed to Warner Brothers.

WITH ITS ROOTS IN TEMPERS, outbursts, gangsters, and violence, it's ironic that *Astral Weeks* ended up being an album completely preoccupied with notions of transcendence and the sublime. But the love story at its core was just as significant to Morrison's reality in 1968.

Morrison began calling his new wife Janet Planet, "probably because it rhymed," she says. In a mad rush, they moved into an apartment in a disheveled little building on Green Street in Cambridge. "It was not a wonderful place to live. What more than made up for the unpleasant surroundings, though, was the astonishingly fertile creative period we found ourselves in," she remembers. The couple was broke, hungry, and hunted. But it was there, sitting at their tiny kitchen table, strumming an acoustic guitar, that Morrison wrote and refined much of *Astral Weeks*. "We both absolutely believed that once people heard this music Van would be back on track, career-wise," Janet says. "I'm very thankful that the world has at length caught up with what we both knew in 1968."

Janet Planet kept track of Morrison's songs and lyrics for him, listened to the demos, and helped him revise. "Van liked to work in a sort of stream-of-consciousness way back then," she says, "letting the tape recorder continue to run while he just sort of played guitar and improvised, trying various things for twenty minutes or so at a time. Then we would go back, listen, and decide what was good, what to keep, tidy up rhyme scheme, and then try it out again. It was a fascinating process, both to witness and to be part of." The end result of Janet's organizational assistance would be a binder of Van's new songs, a tome he would later flip through during the sessions trying to find a tune to close the album that satisfied Merenstein.

From the outside, the years immediately following *Astral Weeks* seemed like a fairy tale for the couple: Morrison and Janet moved to Woodstock, New York, and then to California. They had a daughter named Shana. As Morrison's muse, Janet appeared in several press photos; she even wrote the liner notes for a few albums. "We were finally really LIVING in a dreamland," Janet Planet said, remembering the scant blissful period the couple found post–*Astral Weeks*. She sits atop a horse on the cover of *Tupelo Honey*, with a grounded Morrison proudly at her side. Her original liner notes for *Moondance*, titled "A Fable," quite literally translated their story into a fairy tale. But as the myth of Van Morrison grew, his relationship with Janet shattered irreversibly. Even before California, she said, "our life was very traumatic and horrible. I couldn't stand any more of his rage as my daily reality." In Morrison's account, Janet wanted too much socializing, which didn't leave enough room for all the work he wanted to complete. "I was confusing the music with the man," Planet recalled. "The music was everything you could hope for as a romantic. The man was a prickly bear." In 1973, Janet left, filing for divorce a few months later.

When I find her via her Etsy shop, Lovebeads by Janet Planet, she's listed as Janet Morrison Minto out of Sherman Oaks, California. She can no longer bear to hear her ex-husband's music.

"Being a muse is a thankless job, and the pay is lousy," she says. "I suppose it could be considered unfortunate that hearing the intro to 'Brown Eyed Girl' come over the grocery store's speaker system is my signal to hit the checkout counter and get out, ASAP."

Imagine a world in which your memory of an early, intense, turbulent relationship gets constantly triggered by a pop song nearly as ubiquitous now as it was during its heyday fifty years ago. What mechanisms might you put in place to protect yourself from repeatedly reexperiencing that pain? To this day, however, Janet still recalls the small window of happiness the two found, and the music he conjured during their time together. "I'm sure that no one loved his artistry more or believed in his greatness more than me."

As for the songwriter himself, his personal thoughts on *Astral Weeks* change from interview to interview. He's said it was originally planned as an opera, and also that it's just a random assortment of songs. That the arrangements are "too samey," and—incredibly—that it's not a personal record. "It's not about me," he told NPR in 2009. "It's totally fictional. It's put together of composites, of conversations I heard—you know, things I saw in movies, newspapers, books, whatever. It comes out as stories. That's it. There's no more."

If Janet Morrison Minto has to walk out of a store when "Brown Eyed Girl" starts playing, perhaps Morrison's claim that these songs have nothing to do with his own life is *his* strategy for dealing with the painful memories. After all, Morrison earns his living by singing those songs into a microphone every night. What would you do?

PETER WOLF is a difficult man to get ahold of.

I'm in touch with a friend of Wolf's who sometimes facilitates meetings and interviews. The initial phone calls establish that Wolf is hesitant to share stories right now. Months pass. More calls and demurrals. Out of the blue one day I receive a phone call from a blocked number.

"Hi, this is Peter."

We arrange to meet that weekend. Wolf's friend advises me to bring some pastries or my favorite book to the interview. "I can't tell you what it is exactly," he instructs me, "just that it come from the heart." The day of the interview, Wolf delays it by a few hours in the afternoon. Then I'm instructed to sit in the lobby of a nearby hotel and wait. Peter calls again, shortly after. He's not ready to meet yet, but he asks me a dozen questions about Van Morrison that he already knows the answers to. It's one last level of vetting, which I think I pass. Thirty minutes later I'm told that maybe Peter would like to meet at my apartment instead. I'm starting to think this is all some sort of elaborate prank.

Wolf is Boston rock royalty, but the levels of clearance and foreplay are getting excessive. I consider returning back home when my voice mail lights up with an address and a time.

IT'S 10:15 P.M. on a Saturday night and I'm walking down the hallway of a downtown high-rise toward Peter Wolf's place carrying a box of fancy mini cheesecakes. He opens the door before I even knock. He's wearing a dark suit and one of his signature hats. He welcomes me in and offers me a drink. The living room is set up for consuming music. For example, where you might place a television, there is a coffee table stacked with a turntable, CD deck, and receivers, flanked by two deluxe tower speakers. The walls are lined with LPs and books. I scan the room thinking I might spot the boxes that house the tapes of Morrison performing in '68. No such luck. He returns with two tumblers of whiskey and compliments me on my choice of pastries.

I motion to my tape recorder and tell him, "I'm going to start rolling now." Wolf shakes his head. He hands me a pencil and a piece of paper, insisting he made Keith Richards's biographer do the same.

"My band then was called the Hallucinations," Wolf begins, as I scribble to keep up. "A kind of neo-punk thing. We practiced at the Boston Tea Party on Berkeley Street. One day during rehearsal, this guy came into the club looking for a gig. He was speaking real funny."

The singer was already a fan of Morrison's work. "At the time, Them's 'Gloria' was like the national anthem for every garage band in the country," Wolf says. "Even so, the gigs and opportunities in Boston weren't coming easy. We became friends quickly. He'd come over to use my telephone, because he and Janet barely had anything at the time."

Meanwhile, Wolf had an overnight shift DJing at 104.1 WBCN, Boston's new free-form radio station, where he'd take on a persona he called the Woofa Goofa. Wolf committed to doing all his on-air talking as the

Woofa character, emitting a hyperfast stream-of-consciousness combination of total jive and rock 'n' roll minutiae. Shortly after Morrison moved to town, Wolf began receiving postcards at the station requesting a myriad of obscure blues artists. As they continued to run into each other, Morrison began telling Wolf about this great Boston DJ he was listening to late at night. Wolf revealed his on-air identity, Morrison copped to being the correspondent, and the two were bonded for life.

Morrison would come by WBCN and play records with Woofa Goofa all night long. Wolf introduced Morrison to musicians in town. They hung out after hours at clubs, partied with bands that rolled through Boston. Wolf opens a small drawer in front of him and pulls out a stack of photographs, all related to his friendship with Morrison. He hands me a picture of the two of them, so happy and soused that I almost get drunk just looking at it. Wolf tells me you get really close with someone once you've thrown up on each other.

Did Wolf pick up a copy of *Astral Weeks* right when it came out? "There's a test pressing of it somewhere here," he says, motioning to his wall of records. He found the album "so unexpected, almost baroque." As he pulls various Van records off the shelf, he scans the liner notes and offers his memories of days gone by. Eventually I bring up the live recordings from 1968. "When is the last time you've listened to that recording from the Catacombs, Peter?"

Wolf stares at me, trying to remember. "Not for . . . a very, very, very long time."

Neither of us says anything.

"We'd have to bake the tapes," Wolf finally adds.

When a reel of magnetic tape has been left alone for decades, deterioration occurs in a way that if you simply played the tapes again it might sound fine, but you'd be forever destroying the recording as you went, with layers of the reel shedding off as it passes through the machine. One solution to prevent this outcome is to place the reels in an oven and bake them before playback. I have a vision of the both of us donning aprons and putting the legendary recordings inside Wolf's stove right then and there. That, of course, doesn't happen. He mentions a specialist up in Maine who could do the transfer properly.

I excuse myself to use the bathroom. When I return he's staring at something on the bookshelf. "Here they are," he says, pointing to a spot that had been right behind my head the entire time. It's surreal to finally lay eyes on something you've been imagining for so long, to see what it looks like rather than what your imagination insisted it would be. Here are two slender tape boxes, faded and worn, tiny labels affixed to both with Wolf's notations in faded ink. "VAN MORRISON TRIO—THE CATACOMBS—1968."

"Would you ever let me hear these?"

"Sure," Wolf says. "If we got them transferred, sure."

When I close my notebook, he becomes visibly more relaxed. He sits down in front of his table of stereo equipment and cues something up. I hear the hiss of an unmastered recording and a riff played on an acoustic guitar. After five seconds, Wolf hits pause, raises his eyebrows, and asks, "What is it?"

I know the riff, but after having seen what I consider the Holy Grail of musical artifacts I'm absolutely useless. Wolf hits play, revealing a demo recording of Morrison's song "Domino." He shows me old postcards Van sent from Fairfax, California, then recites a poem called "The Cold Heart of the Stone," about their time together in 1968. What I had interpreted as rock diva behavior with the day's earlier delays had actually been Wolf taking the time to prepare a proper presentation of his Morrison-related memories.*

Wolf walks me to his building's front door, and we end up talking for another thirty minutes. He tells me about seeing Woody Guthrie as a child, and how he was in the audience the night Bob Dylan recited the poem "Last

---

* It's easy to take this too far: I pick up a little jar from the table of snacks and hold it up to him. "Did you put this out on purpose?" I ask, showing him the brand name: Tupelo Honey. Wolf laughs and says no.

Thoughts on Woody Guthrie." As we chat, a steady stream of older, well-dressed partygoers exit the building, headed home. Just as another pack walks by, I swear I hear one of them say, "Van the Man." I must be imagining things; I decide not to bring it up. Wolf continues with his story for a moment longer, then pauses and points outside. "Did that guy just say 'Van the Man'?" I nod. "That's *really* weird," Wolf says, a mischievous smile on his face.

SOMEWHERE, in the middle of that night I spent in Wolf's apartment, he told me a story about one of the times Van Morrison came back to town. He wouldn't clarify the date or give me any additional context. All he told me was this:

It's late at night. Van Morrison is exhausted after his concert in Boston, but there's one thing he still wants to do while he's here. He gets into a car with Wolf and picks a destination. Wolf drives down Mass. Ave., heading into Cambridge. Nothing looks like it did in 1968, but then again, neither do the two men in the car. They turn onto a series of side streets. As they approach the address, Wolf slows down to a crawl, because neither of them has been here in a long, long time, and it looks barely familiar. Just past the intersection of Bay and Green streets, Wolf points out the window, to the left, where Van and Janet—his Planet, cosmic partner, entire world—lived in 1968. Morrison sits there for a moment, gazing into the past. And then, without a word, they drive off.

TWO

God's Underground
Newspaper

WHILE VAN MORRISON toiled in Cambridge trying to jump-start his career, another musician in Boston was preparing to do the opposite. The signs had been clear for the last few years, but now in 1968 Jim Kweskin was truly ready to walk away from his life in music. By anyone's measure, the Jim Kweskin Jug Band was on the rise, enjoying the kind of industry breaks that Van Morrison was hoping for. The band was signed to Warner Brothers' imprint Reprise and shared a manager with Bob Dylan, the formidable Albert Grossman. They had their audiences warmed up by legends like Janis Joplin and appeared on *The Tonight Show*, where they flummoxed Johnny Carson by passing him a kazoo while they played. They were influential, too; the unfortunately named Mother McCree's Uptown Jug Champions—the precursor to the Grateful Dead, featuring Jerry Garcia and Bob Weir—straight-up cribbed set lists and song arrangements directly from the Jim Kweskin Jug Band. In 1961, Bob Dylan listed Kweskin as one of his favorite singers. When rock historian Ed Ward compiled a list of the most influential artists of the decade, he included Kweskin alongside the Beatles and the Stones. "It's not like we were Elvis Presley or anything," band member Geoff Muldaur later explained, "but we got to do almost anything we wanted to do."

Kweskin's good-time music was inspired by an early-twentieth-century fad in which bands deployed household items like combs, washboards, and, of course, jugs to fashion a goofy, jubilant sound. The grim realities of the Great Depression put an end to the genre's popularity, but in the late fifties, young musicians introduced to the anachronistic genre by Harry Smith's influential *Anthology of American Folk Music* revived it. Kweskin embraced the sound as his own while at Boston University. He was a tall, talented, happy-go-lucky guy with a Woody Guthrie obsession and an oversized mustache to match his irreverent personality. He might have remained that way too, if his original banjo player, Bob Siggins, didn't quit the band in 1963.

In what has to be one of the less common reasons for leaving a band, Siggins was headed to BU to get his PhD in molecular neurophysiology; the Kweskin crew needed a quick replacement. That replacement was named Mel Lyman.

"When Mel joined the Jug Band he needed a job, and I needed a banjo player," Kweskin explains. *Rolling Stone* reported that the job was in fact a legal requisite after Lyman was arrested for marijuana in Tallahassee, Florida—that is, a steady, paid music gig that would keep Lyman out of trouble. Kweskin was happy to employ the man, who was a multi-instrumentalist and a genuine musical talent. "Mel was a far better harmonica player than banjo player," Kweskin says, "but he didn't even let us know that he played harmonica at first."

Lyman's personal influence over Kweskin emerged around the same time he discovered Lyman's hidden harmonica expertise, at a local show in 1964 when the usual blower, David Simon, didn't show up. Kweskin thought, "Oh my God. That's the most beautiful harmonica playing I've ever heard in my life." Little miracles followed Lyman around daily. "He never made a telephone call when the line was busy, he never called anybody and they weren't home," Kweskin said. "And you'd say it was a coincidence, maybe [if it happened] once or twice. But it happened every day."

From that point on, Lyman felt the freedom to behave strangely on-stage. He regularly refused to perform if he wasn't in the mood, and soon Kweskin embraced the same spirit. "Sometimes you have to create an embarrassing or painful or angry situation just so that everybody's in the same place at the same time," Kweskin later remarked about the intent of these bizarre concert confrontations.

In 1964, the Jim Kweskin Jug Band comprised Kweskin on guitar, Lyman on harmonica, Bill Keith on banjo, Geoff Muldaur on mandolin, guitar, and vocals, Maria D'Amato on vocals and tambourine, and Fritz Richmond on jug. They open *Festival!*, Murray Lerner's 1967 documentary about the early-sixties installments of the Newport Folk Festival—a sign of the Jug Band's dominance, given that the slate also included Johnny Cash, Son House, Mississippi John Hurt, and Bob Dylan. *Festival!* contains some of the only available footage of Lyman. The Jug Band performs about a minute of the lovelorn "Hannah" before the cameraman calls cut. "Are you telling me you cut in the middle of that song?" Kweskin angrily inquires. "If we had *really* been blowing," Lyman interjects, "he couldn't have helped but listen." The decision to cut meant the band had failed, according to Mel. Here, he comes off as a bright young man who has developed his own philosophy about life and art.

While Kweskin may have been the front man, the *Festival!* footage makes it blazingly clear who commanded the attention of the room when the music stopped. After the band playfully gangs up on Lerner, Lyman goes on an earnest rant: "We're trying to take our perception, our understanding of the truth and put it in a form, so you can hear it sensually, with your ears, just like a painter takes what he knows of the truth and puts it on a canvas so the people can dig it in a sensual way with their eyes. Our thing happens to be an ear-thing, that's all." Lyman pauses, smiles. Lerner cuts to the title card. The movie starts.

A folk music virtuoso, Lyman was also present at the birth of the America psychedelic revolution. In the early sixties, he had followed his girlfriend, Judy Silver, a Kansas native, from New York City to Waltham, Massachusetts, where they lived with some of her Brandeis University friends. One town over, in Newton, professors Timothy Leary and Richard Alpert had begun expanding their Harvard Psilocybin Project—in which they administered psychoactive chemicals to graduate students on a large scale—to include off-campus, unofficial research conducted in their respective homes. Their quiet, suburban houses quickly became a test site for the prominent commune they would soon establish in Millbrook, New York. Artists, writers, and musicians crashed at Leary's 47 Homer Street place and Alpert's home on 23 Kenwood. The intake of psychedelics was Olympian, trading sexual partners commonplace, and the residents' children ran around unsupervised. No one can recall exactly how Mel Lyman found his way to Richard Alpert's house, but he soon became a fixture, grinding up morning glory seeds when the LSD ran out, and performing "This Land Is Your Land" for wide-eyed mental cosmonauts by candlelight.

Leary emphasized the importance of "set and setting" for psychedelic exploration—the idea that your mental state and physical surroundings would be the most significant predictor of the type of trip you'd experience. In other words, almost all bad trips could be avoided with the proper precautions and preparation. But according to Lyman's friend Charles Giuliano, Mel purposely subverted these guidelines to work to his advantage. He'd dose a group of friends, then show them an alarming movie, or wait for people to enter the apex of their trip and then present both a problem and the solution, making Lyman a hero in their eyes. At some point Lyman's girlfriend Judy became mentally unhinged, in part due to taking acid in a fragile state, and she fled back home to Kansas. "He worshipped Judy, really loved her," Giuliano surmised. "Then she split. She couldn't help it—she was totally freaked out."

Soon, Leary would help define a generation by coining the phrase "Turn on, tune in, drop out" and Richard Alpert would travel to India, transforming himself into Ram Dass, one of the most prominent spiritual leaders of the twentieth century. Meanwhile, a heartbroken Mel Lyman moved into Jim Kweskin's attic in Huron Village, a neighborhood right outside Harvard Square.

Kweskin and Lyman had problems with the growing folk music scene in New England. They formed a twenty-man committee called United Illuminating to address certain issues they felt were beginning to ruin the Newport Folk Festival. "There are 26 performing groups on this Saturday night. That means eight minutes for each performer," Kweskin declared in the summer of 1966. "How can Chuck Berry or The Lovin' Spoonful be expected to do anything in that amount of time?" Joan Baez, Lyman said, was invited to join the discussion but had refused to come. She darkly remarked that Lyman and Kweskin were bringing "hate" to everything they touched.

"Every year, they build on the ruins of last year's festival," Lyman complained to a reporter. "There is an attitude here of fall in, do your gig and split." In Lyman's ideal world, the feeling that the Newport Folk Festival evoked, at its best, was something to aspire to as a way of life: community, music, and teamwork in service of the attempt to make something unique. Sometime during the summer of '66, it must have become apparent to Lyman that instead of trying to fix a faltering fellowship like the Newport Folk Festival, he could just as easily build his own from scratch.

Back in Boston, he took note of a set of crumbling houses in a crime-ridden part of Roxbury known as Fort Hill. Fort Ave. Terrace abutted a public park, formerly the grounds of a Revolutionary War fort. In the middle stood a seventy-foot Gothic tower right out of a fairy tale, albeit one that had gone very, very wrong. From afar, it looks as if the iconic Disney World castle has crumbled save for one remaining turret. The Cochituate Standpipe, built to provide water to the growing Roxbury neighborhood in 1868, had fallen out of use by 1880. Fifteen years later, landscape architect Frederick Law Olmsted was commissioned to replicate the success of his work with New York's Central Park and the connected string of green spaces in

Boston known as the Emerald Necklace, and turn the fort into an eye-pleasing public space, incorporating the defunct structure. He added an iron balcony on the top, an attendant's office on the ground. The Cochituate Standpipe would serve as an observatory with a stunning view of a growing city; it can be spotted from countless locations all over Boston.

As the city grew, Roxbury fell into decline. In the fall of 1966, Lyman, his wife, and a few friends moved into some run-down houses on Fort Ave. Terrace and began slowly renovating them. His new Family was about to move in.

AT ONE POINT the Lyman Family owned every house on Fort Ave. Terrace and even a couple on Fort Avenue, forming an L-shaped territory hugging the southwest corner of Highland Park. Though the Cochituate Standpipe belonged to the city of Boston, the Lymans cut the lock off the tower, replaced it with their own, and began to fix up the spooky-looking relic as well as the weedy, broken-glass-covered park that surrounded it.

Throughout 1967 and 1968, Mel Lyman and the Fort Hill Community were treated as a curiosity in the press, with reporters and TV producers trudging up the hill to capture a human interest piece in step with the times. But after Charles Manson and his family went on their killing spree in Los Angeles in 1969, the public regarded the idea of communal living under the direction of a charismatic leader with greater alarm. David Felton, the editor of Hunter S. Thompson's *Fear and Loathing in Las Vegas*, had covered the Manson story for *Rolling Stone*, and in 1971 went to Boston to investigate the Lymans for the magazine. His story spanned two back-to-back issues and landed Mel Lyman on the cover. The article identifies many Family members by full name, investigates Lyman's media company, United Illuminating, Inc.,*

* Lyman borrowed the name from a Connecticut power company whose neon sign he spotted one night on a drive between Boston and New York. The company's motto—"Eternally at Your Service"—was Lyman's creation: He had it painted onto the side of the community's VW Bus.

and interviews devotees and defectors. It's filled with larger-than-life details and startling quotes, such as this one from Jim Kweskin, the man who, five years earlier, was famous for making music with kazoos and washboards: "The Manson Family preached peace and love and went around killing people. We don't preach peace and love and we haven't killed anyone. Yet."

In the spring of 1968, Lyman had a dream whose imagery he felt was prescriptive. The next day he ordered his followers to construct a formidable, protective wall around his house. Like Van Morrison across the river, Lyman was now commanding people based on what he saw when he was sleeping.

Now, driving down Fort Ave. Terrace, the wall was the only thing I could focus on. As I got close to the door they built into the wall, I noticed a green mailbox affixed to the structure. On a piece of paper taped to the mailbox was a list of the current residents of the house: Jim Kweskin, United Illuminating, and half a dozen other names associated with the Lyman Family. I looked up in shock at the house behind the wall and saw the silhouettes of some people through the main bay window. Mel Lyman has been gone since 1978, but in that moment I realized that his Family was alive and well, and were still living together up on Fort Hill.

THE LYMAN FAMILY attracted followers of a pedigree far more impressive than that of your run-of-the-mill sixties commune. During its ascent, the Fort Hill Community attracted the likes of Jessie Benton, daughter of the painter Thomas Hart Benton; Mark Frechette, troubled star of the film *Zabriskie Point*; Paul Williams, founder of the groundbreaking music magazine *Crawdaddy*; two children of the novelist Kay Boyle; David Gude, a musical influence on James Taylor and Carly Simon back on Martha's Vineyard; and Owen deLong, a Harvard graduate who had been a speechwriter for Robert Kennedy. David Felton was curious why they would hand over their freedom so casually in exchange for what he considered to be neofascism. "It did raise questions for me that they were all from liberal, artistic, creative families," Felton says. "It crossed my mind: did these kind of people make bad parents?"

What was daily life on Fort Hill like in the late sixties and early seventies? A current resident might describe a happy community, where hard work paid off and people revealed their unconscious intentions through continued personal confrontations. But even those members would agree that there could be extreme tactics of control. "He does manipulate us, but he doesn't manipulate us for evil," Lyman's third wife, Jessie Benton, once admitted. "He manipulates us to be what we truly are."

A former member of the Lyman Family, however, might have a darker take. One ex-member, Norman Truss, told Felton, "The only rules were the ones Mel made up as he went along, and he changed them from day to day." These involved everything from when one should sleep and shower, who could be romantically involved with each other, and even whether sexual intercourse was currently allowed. According to some FHC exiles, members who needed help following these rules could be mercilessly ridiculed, placed inside a windowless basement (known as the Vault), or given a guided LSD trip by Mel himself to help adjust to the Hill's way of life. A deep interest in astrology was a requisite, and serious decisions were often made based on a singular reading. If it helped them control somebody, one former member reported, these readings would be rigged. They all loved Mario Puzo's *The Godfather*, playing basketball, and watching televised football games. Occasionally, they'd record music too.

Felton's article "The Lyman Family's Holy Siege of America" opens with the escape of Paul Williams, the founder of *Crawdaddy*. But it was long after the story was published that Felton learned exactly why he fled the Hill. According to Felton, Williams had a private session with Mel—an acid session. "And during the time, Paul told him that he was in love with him," Felton says. "The next night, Mel, who had tape-recorded the whole session, played it publicly for the whole house at the dinner table, and turned him into a vegetable, basically. Now, that is a pretty cruel mind-fuck."

The piece also dives into the rise and fall of *Avatar*, a popular underground newspaper, which was the subject of multiple controversies in 1968. "Lyman got on this trip of wanting to take over the world through media," Felton explains. Inspired by the early success of the *Los Angeles Free Press* and the sudden availability of cheap offset printing, new branches of the underground press were sprouting up weekly all over the United States in the mid-sixties. Antiwar screeds, counterculture poetry, and deliberate tests of the limits of free speech were all typical of the type of content plastered all over the abundant page counts found in these underground tabloids; the Lyman Family wanted to join the party. Or as Mel put it, "Once the basic requirements of survival had been met we were able to devote some time to other things . . . we had something good and something can only stay good if it is shared."

There was only one problem. They didn't know how to print and distribute a newspaper.

Luckily for them, Dave Wilson, the founder of *Broadside of Boston*, had grown tired of covering the increasingly quiet Cambridge folk scene and wanted to turn his publishing talents toward something more political. Just like Kweskin before him, the Boston/Cambridge folk scene had somehow drawn a dotted line directly from guitar ballads to communes, from tradition to counterculture. In July 1967, after much insisting from the residents of Fort Hill, everyone agreed on the newspaper's name: *Avatar*. Derived from a Sanskrit word, an avatar is a deity who takes on a human form to walk the Earth; a bold title for a newspaper, certainly.

Looking at old issues is a pure dose of sixties madness. Across several editions from 1968, there are fetishistic photo spreads of the Cochituate Standpipe tower, the Family's most visible symbol of their growing power, and columns with titles like "Diary of a Young Artist" and "Journals of John the Wasted." Astrological discussions share the page with diatribes against the war in Vietnam. Each issue is tied together with mystical, elegant drawings by Lyman Family artist Eben Given, and the presentation on the whole is impressively cool and enigmatic. It's easy to see why the paper was a hit with the student population. At its peak, *Avatar* was published biweekly, running anywhere from sixteen to twenty-four pages and packed with ads.

Most striking is the amount of real estate dedicated to photos of Mel, collages of photos of Mel, quotes by Mel placed on top of even larger photographs of Mel. There's a "letters to the editor" section in the front of each issue—but it's dwarfed by the "Letters to Mel" section in the back. On page 11 of December 1967's "Woman Issue" is a half-page drawing of an open mouth with one of Mel's poems placed inside.

> *I am going to fuck the world*
> *I am going to fill it with hot sperm*
>
> *Mmm mmm, I can't wait*
>
> *I am a giant erection*
> *I am ALL COCK*
> *. . . and the world*
> *is ALL CUNT*

This, again, is from "The Woman Issue," in which the Lyman Family women are finally allowed to represent themselves with their own words. Elsewhere, Jessie Benton declares, "To live for Man is the highest expectation."

Responding to a letter writer with a hopeless outlook on life, Mel Lyman replies, "Why don't you just try and let yourself DIE and see what happens." Such aggression wouldn't be out of place in a YouTube comment, and indeed some of *Avatar*'s features predict the current social media landscape. All-caps, troll-style replies to genuine calls for help? You can see that both on Twitter and in *Avatar*. Hundreds of photos of yourself all collected in one place? That's on Facebook right now and in the March 29, 1968, issue of the paper. (And of course, on most social platforms, your profile picture is referred to as your "avatar.") Seen today, *Avatar* sometimes resembles a printed-out collection of Internet memes and rants, published words that garnered Lyman literal "followers." But it's also a reminder of how difficult it once was to find an audience for provocative self-expression. For those with a vested interest in keeping things civil, the language and philosophy printed in *Avatar* were truly upsetting. When issue 11 came off the presses in October 1967, Family members who sold it on the streets of Boston began getting arrested on obscenity charges.

It started in Cambridge. Throughout the first ten months of 1967, Mayor Daniel J. Hayes Jr. had grown increasingly fed up with a scourge that was spreading along the banks of the Charles River and, alarmingly, into the main streets of his great city. The problem? Hippies. "The great unwashed are creating an intolerable situation in our City by the widespread use of drugs and other anti-social practices such as boys and girls living together under the guise of 'Free Love' and without any benefit of clergy," Hayes declared. Two days after his announcement of a "War on Hippies," there was a televised police raid of 183 Columbia Street, a house in a slum of Cambridge, yielding narcotics arrests for the seventeen people inside. "I never saw such a filthy situation. There are terms which I could use but I would not use in public," the mayor told reporters, proud of his self-censorship.

Hayes was up for reelection in less than a month, and the purge was a way of grabbing headlines. One bizarre profile in *The Harvard Crimson* featured Hayes gleefully sipping a chocolate shake, smoking Newports, and expounding on his hot new term for hippies. "It's not the hippie, it's the hip-bo." Come again? "Hip-bo comes from three things. First, hobo. Second, the combination of hippie and bum. Third, from Life Buoy soap. Remember that commercial with the foghorn blowing B-O, B-O?" The term did not catch on.

Hayes had no idea that Lyman, the mastermind behind *Avatar*, hated the very concept of "the hippie" just as he did, but it wouldn't have mattered: He knew filth when he saw it. At first, Hayes figured he could shut the underground rag down on a technicality. "The editors were warned that their offices would be condemned unless they installed 'separate bathrooms for men and women,'" *Boston Magazine* reported. "Rather than bow to what they felt was patent harassment, the paper moved itself to 37 Rutland Street in Boston's South End."

The next issue of *Avatar* featured a mock obituary of Mayor Hayes.

At the mayor's behest, an anonymous city council member spread word to three of Cambridge's biggest newspaper stands that continued sales of *Avatar* would result in prosecution; all capitulated. Mel Lyman retaliated by sending hordes of Hill people into Harvard Square to hawk the newspaper the old-fashioned way. *Extra! Extra! God is a harmonica player with a commune in Roxbury and this is his cool underground newspaper!*

Next came a strategy of minutiae. Hayes declared the sellers needed permits. *Avatar* obtained one. Cambridge then told *Avatar* they had to renew it every month. City Manager Joseph A. DeGuglielmo then revoked the permit anyway, citing "obscene literature," and denied their request for a new permit. It was all but an official ban on the sale of *Avatar* achieved through an endless roll of red tape, the latest episode in the city's rich tradition of censorship. The phrase "Banned in Boston" was coined in the 1890s in response to moral crusader Anthony Comstock's fiery speeches on obscene and lewd creations; his followers in turn founded the New England Watch and Ward Society, a censorship advocacy group. Under the society's influence, banning books became commonplace; the Boston Public Library relocated its sinful titles to a locked room that became known as the Inferno. Distasteful plays were edited in advance of local performances; these censored cutups became known as the "Boston Version." In fact, this mind-set was so embedded into the fabric of the city, Boston still had an official city censor until 1982; the last man to hold the job, the aptly named

Richard Sinnott, spent most of the sixties and seventies trying to police the content of rock concerts and the musical *Hair*. The reasons why Boston became Censorship Central are complex, but its Puritan heritage, reinforced by subsequent generations of conservative Catholic citizens, partly explains it. Over the years, city censors banned everything from *Leaves of Grass* to "Wake Up Little Susie" by the Everly Brothers.

Lyman was livid, but also instantly knew what many book publishers had gleaned during the peak of Boston's banning efforts: A certain audience would see this as the paper's strongest selling point. For the next issue, Lyman had Eben Given design a lush, hand-drawn center spread, featuring four words that spelled it out pretty clearly:

FUCK

SHIT

PISS

CUNT

"I'll rent a goddamn airplane and drop them all over the goddamn motherfucking state," Lyman wrote in the next issue. "This is just a polite warning, you're playing with dynamite, don't fuck with me." The following week, someone started throwing bricks through the windows of establishments that sold or helped publish *Avatar*. Police raided the new offices, confiscating issues 11, 12, and 13. The War on Hippies was looking more and more like a direct attack on free speech. In response, thirty *Avatar* vendors were deployed to Harvard Square to hand out two thousand free issues to passersby. By the time vendor John Rogers and staff artist Ed Beardsley were arrested, the *Avatar* crew decided it was finally time to get a lawyer.

"I was a typical Boston College grad. I thought booze was great and grass was bad," attorney Joe Oteri told his alma mater's newspaper in 1967. "It's taken time to build up empathy for these people." His clientele gave him the reputation as the city's preeminent "pot lawyer." An Italian-American native of South Boston, he was also a close family friend of future organized crime boss Whitey Bulger, and, eventually, host of *The Joe Oteri Show* on local TV.

In court, before Judge Elijah Adlow, Oteri claimed that Beardsley's possession of thousands of copies of the newspaper did not prove he intended to distribute it. The *Crimson* captured the dynamic that was developing in the courtroom:

"You're falling back on a technicality," admonished Adlow. "This is first and foremost a question of morality."

"I'm a lawyer," said Oteri. "And I thought this was a court of law."

The Joe Oteri Show, indeed.

Avatar was well represented in the courtroom, though Lyman and Kweskin were nowhere to be found, and the paper's coverage of the trial wavered from straight-up journalism to crass reactionary parody. In the next issue they facetiously quoted Judge Adlow as stating, "Shut up you c— and let's get this f— show on the road." When Adlow was made aware he was quoted as such, the judge responded, "The reporter for the paper needs a hearing aid, I use those words only in select conversations."

Among Oteri's witnesses for the defense was a forty-five-year-old professor of government from Boston University named Howard Zinn. Zinn is now revered as the author of *A People's History of the United States* and a lifelong defender of civil rights, but his presence at the trial did not cause any particular stir. In fact, he was treated as if he were part of the problem. Zinn testified that "a remarkably large proportion of the material [in *Avatar*] has had to do with issues of social importance." *Avatar* reported that the prosecution attorney, Mr. Day, then proceeded to attack Zinn himself as someone "without redeeming social value." Zinn's outspoken protest of the draft and the Vietnam War would soon make some Bostonians feel the same way about the BU professor.

In his closing argument, Oteri told Judge Adlow he would take the case to the Supreme Court if necessary.

"Who's getting excited about the Supreme Court?" Adlow replied. "When they look at this, they're going to crawl out of their black pajamas and censor it."

Beardsley and Rogers were found guilty.

THAT FALL, the chocolate-shake-drinking Daniel J. Hayes Jr. lost the Cambridge mayoral election to Walter J. Sullivan. Suddenly, everyone was willing to compromise. In February 1968, the two parties agreed that there would be no more arrests of *Avatar* salesmen, no more confiscation, and, likewise, that *Avatar* would never have more than seven vendors in Harvard Square nor "aggressively sell" an issue to anyone, especially if they were under eighteen. Hayes and City Councilor Alfred E. Vellucci claimed that the War on Hippies had nothing to do with their reelection campaigns.

Avatar's legal team, however, knew that wasn't the case, and felt confident appealing the guilty sentences in a higher court to prove it. Harvey Silverglate, first under the employment of Joe Oteri and then on his own, pursued justice for *Avatar* and the Fort Hill Community even after the paper stopped being published later that year. "I knew certain things that suggested we would win," Silverglate explained. "I knew police officers had sent their children to buy *Avatar*s simply so they could charge vendors with distributing obscenity to minors. I knew the police had met with politicians to plan the harassment of *Avatar* vendors. I even knew of one instance where a judge involved with the case had met police officers to discuss the matter. Very illegal. And we were prepared to subpoena everyone involved. The Supreme Judicial Court knew we knew all of this, and the guilty verdicts were reversed."

The highest legal opinion on the matter is *The Commonwealth v. Faith Gude*, a decision which has served as a precedent for numerous free speech cases tried in the intervening years. The court statement reads, "[*Avatar*'s] authors seem to take pride in the rediscovery of certain four letter words old in Chaucer's day and widely but covertly employed until recently. We cannot say that their use violates the statute. Any lapse was not one of morals but rather one of manners."

"Things have never been better for *Avatar*," Lyman commented on the entire ordeal in 1968. "Look at all the free publicity we're getting."

I THOUGHT MY RESEARCH into Fort Hill, *Avatar*, and Mel Lyman had been proceeding under the radar, but shortly after requesting some information about the Cochituate Standpipe from the Roxbury Historical Society, I was contacted by a member of the Lyman Family. Over e-mail, Dick Russell, who identified himself as a writer and a part-time Fort Hill resident, suggested we meet up. I was about to be vetted by the Fort Hill Community.

Russell functions as the historian of the Fort Hill Community. His writing career includes coauthoring some of ex–Minnesota governor Jesse Ventura's conspiracy-theory books and championing environmental causes. Though he isn't mentioned in Felton's 1971 exposé, that feature did have a hand in how he became a member: As a young journalist at the University of Kansas, he read the *Rolling Stone* piece, and was unsettled by the fact that the Family had purchased a farm nearby.

Over coffee and sandwiches, Russell explains how the Fort Hill crew came west: In the late sixties, Lyman was getting tired of traveling long distances from city to city to check on the various new outposts of his community. His solution was as bizarre as you might imagine. One former Family member recalled that Mel consulted a map of the United States, drew lines between Boston, Los Angeles, San Francisco, and New York—the cities where the FHC had outposts—and "decided to find land where the lines crossed, very near the geographical center of the forty-eight contiguous states, in northeastern Kansas."

Russell first visited the Kansas farm in the hopes of writing an exposé on the Family himself; he didn't like the idea of the type of people described in Felton's article setting up camp in his home state. "I still haven't written the article," Russell tells me as he smiles. "I fell in love with everyone there. All of those nasty tactics described in the article? I never saw any of it." Russell contends that Mel Lyman didn't feel he had accomplished all that he had set out to do, and by the time of his death he was "very, very despondent about it."

We talk about some of the negative angles to the Fort Hill story, as well as the importance of *Avatar*'s free speech victory. "I liked 'the cut of your jib' as the old pirate expression goes, and I think others would, too," Russell e-mails me later. He goes on to explain that some of the community is interested in talking about the legacy of the Family, but others just want to quietly live out their golden years. He passes along some contact information for a few community members possibly willing to talk. Meanwhile, I made plans to see Jim Kweskin perform live at Club Passim in Harvard Square.

David Felton says that after his piece appeared, Kweskin and some others visited the *Rolling Stone* offices in San Francisco and demanded to see cofounder and editor Jann Wenner. "Jann snuck out the back door. They were really upset about the story. I said we were going to call the police. They broke open the doors and came after me. Kweskin was yelling, 'You pissant!' Now sometimes they *did* beat people up, but mainly they just tried to make you scared. And if you weren't scared they just left you alone. So finally, they just left us alone."

In 1972 or so, Felton was covering a Maria Muldaur concert; Kweskin happened to be the opener. Felton said hello, sparking a heated exchange. The journalist continued smiling until Kweskin smacked him across the face, drawing blood. "That'll be good for your story," the musician said. As he walked away, he told Felton, "If you ever say 'hi' to me again, I'll kill you." According to Felton, it was the last time the two men have spoken to each other. Jim Kweskin, however, claims he never saw Felton again after the *Rolling Stone* piece was published.

. . .

JIM KWESKIN PULLS UP to Club Passim in a black Ford Econoline van with an extended cab. He's the only one in the van. He brings some guitars into the club. When he comes back out, I greet him. He invites me into the van.

We do a slow drive around Harvard Square, waiting for the clock to strike six so he can get cheaper parking for the van in a nearby lot. We double-park on Church Street and he pulls out his phone to show me videos of his recent tour of Japan. Kweskin is vice president of the Fort Hill Construction Company—a family-run contracting business headquartered in Los Angeles since 1971—and he often makes a point in interviews to state how he enjoys Jug Band reunion tours now that it isn't his full-time job.

Club Passim is where Club 47 existed for a chunk of the sixties; it's a room that holds a lot of memories for Jim Kweskin. Inside, he muses on the dissolution of his original band in 1968. "There was a TV show on Channel 2 in Boston, and Mel did an interview on it," Kweskin says. "The TV show was just Mel and [host] David Silver. It was so moving. So powerful and beautiful. Mel was so strong. Then a few weeks later the Jug Band was on a nationally broadcasted variety show. It was hosted by Jonathan Winters. He would do his comedy and then he'd bring musical artists out. They had us in costume, it was all staged. And I watched this thing a few weeks later and it just seemed so *silly* to me. I was looking at myself thinking, 'What the fuck am I doing?' Here Mel Lyman could go on a little local TV show and be so beautiful and meaningful by talking, and then there's the Jug Band on TV looking so silly."

That was the last straw for Kweskin. He told his bandmates that he couldn't do it anymore. For many in the Cambridge folk scene, the 1968 breakup of Jim Kweskin's Jug Band was the death knell for a community already in long decline. But Kweskin didn't care. He had work to do. "We were building and fixing up houses," Kweskin recalls of his daily life after the Jug Band. "I was the best *Avatar* salesman among the bunch. The first time I went out I sold thirty-five papers. Basically, I was living the life of the Fort Hill Family."

It's puzzling to get inside the mind-set of someone who shared a bill with the Doors just twelve months earlier, now happily selling newspapers around Harvard Square, but Kweskin is genuinely happy recollecting the life change. He's so open and friendly that it's hard to reconcile him with the short-tempered Lyman acolyte from the late sixties and seventies.

What was Mel Lyman's message? Kweskin makes an attempt to answer but gets flustered.

"Mel was very anti–peace and love of the hippie flower child. To him, life was hard work. We could all do it together, but it wasn't playing around. It wasn't just smoking pot. It was serious business. That's one of the messages. There were many messages that went very deep into spiritualness. God was a personal thing that's internalized, not organized religion. There were so many different levels of Mel's message. I feel others are more qualified, I should be, I suppose, but . . ." The sentence trails off into a hearty laugh.

Listening to him warm up for the show, I think how odd it is that jug music, which he declared ridiculous and unrewarding in 1968, is something he travels around the world doing blissfully today. I sit at a table up front with a couple who seem to be friends of Jim's. I say hello and they introduce themselves. Their last name is Lyman.

Just as my head starts to spin, the band begins playing the goofiest feel-good music I've ever heard. The whole show is so sweetly upbeat that it sometimes borders on parody, like an outtake from Christopher Guest's film *A Mighty Wind*. At one point, Maria Muldaur takes out a balloon filled with helium and uses it to make Geoff Muldaur's voice sound like a small child's. Jim Kweskin is hard to read onstage. He doesn't particularly look like he's having fun, but then again, he doesn't even need to play these gigs—on some level he must want to be here.

Near the end of the show, Maria Muldaur—who admonished Kweskin and Lyman for being on a bad trip back in 1968—croons a song entitled "He Calls That Religion." It's a takedown of a hypocritical religious leader that starts out amusing and winds up serious. It's hard to look into Kweskin's blank stare and listen to Muldaur's intense delivery and not draw a few conclusions.

In the summer of 2015, the Peabody Essex Museum in Salem hosted the Thomas Hart Benton exhibit "American Epics." It was the first major re-evaluation of the paintings by the so-called enemy of modernism since the 1980s. After seeing Benton's large-scale work in person, I became fascinated by a particular piece, *The Sources of Country Music*, in which some of his son-in-law's followers—all members of the Fort Hill Community—stood in as the models. Examining a reproduction of the mural, I took a hard look at the painting's dancing couple at an outdoor hootenanny. *Is that Jim Kweskin?*

Benton came out of retirement to paint the piece for the Country Music Hall of Fame in 1973, at age eighty-four. The previous year, *Life* magazine reported:

> He is also resigned to the fact that he has had little influence on contemporary American painting. What does still intrigue him is the whimsy of youth—in particular his 33-year-old daughter, Jessie, who married a controversial figure in the youth culture named Mel Lyman. Lyman, 34, is the spiritual leader of a network of communes in Boston, New York, Los Angeles and San Francisco. Benton has given the group some property in Martha's Vineyard and recently bought them a 281-acre farm in Kansas to grow their own food.
>
> "They've got some crazy ideas," Benton says, "like conducting their lives by the stars. Mel's a guru. He's full of crap of course, but we get along. I never argue with the young.

"His success is that he represents the revolt against the assembly lines. Not that a commune would suit me, but they have found a solution to the greatest problem of youth: loneliness. They live like artists, separate from society but with a sense of communion. We've got to have alternatives to the life we're living, so I'll hold my criticism in abeyance."

On January 19, 1975, Benton spent the day going back and forth about whether he should research and replace the locomotive seen in the background of *The Sources of Country Music*. In the end, he decided the painting was finished and went out to his studio to sign the mural, marking its completion. But before he could put his name to it, he experienced a massive heart attack. He died in his studio, his final mural forever unsigned. "He died so beautifully," Jessie Benton told filmmaker Ken Burns in his 1988 documentary about the painter. Mel may have been full of crap, but after Benton's death, the property that the painter bequeathed to the Lyman Family, as well as the sales of some of his art, would only strengthen Lyman's empire. There were plenty of American communes and cults in the late sixties and seventies, but none that were financially floated by the estate of a legendary American artist.

Post–Jug Band, Jim Kweskin and Mel Lyman kept recording and making music, but the tone and content of the songs changed from goofy to serious, ebullient to contemplative. On some bootlegs of recordings made during this period by the Fort Hill Community, the music is understated and melancholy, just about as far from Jug Band music as you can get. Some of the songs are downright eerie, like a cover of "I'm So Lonesome I Could Cry" that sounds straightforward, save for the fingers drifting all over the piano without regard to key or melody, placing a fog of menace over the tune.

According to his contract, Kweskin still owed one album to Warner/ Reprise, even though the Jug Band had broken up. After becoming friendly with label president Mo Ostin, Kweskin convinced him to visit Fort Hill to see his new way of life and hear his new sound. Ostin reportedly dug the songs and liked Mel Lyman; a deal was struck. The result, elaborately titled *Richard D. Herbruck Presents Jim Kweskin's America Co-starring Mel Lyman and the Lyman Family* (1971), is the only official Kweskin/Lyman collaboration recorded and commercially released post–Jug Band. It also happens to be fantastic—the sort of record you might make a bar-stool argument for as a classic. Like *Astral Weeks*, there isn't an electric instrument to be found on the recording. In the liner notes, Kweskin boldly declared, "I am singing America to you and it is Mel Lyman. He is the new soul of the world." When I ask one of the session musicians about the LP's credits insisting he had "come down from Alaska to play the dobro," Mayne Smith tells me, "I was living in North Oakland and have never been to Alaska." All of this aside, *America* remains an engaging album to experience. Upon release, sales were scant and reviews were often just excuses to trash the cult mentality surrounding the whole affair. Ostin couldn't do much; he had his hands full with a short-tempered Van Morrison, who was insisting that the label president "promise him" a #1 single off *Tupelo Honey*. After *America* fizzled and Felton's exposé was published, Ostin declined to comment on anything related to Mel Lyman.

In the years following the 1971 *Rolling Stone* piece, things became very quiet on Fort Hill. Lyman became more reclusive. The community, once so publicity hungry, no longer honored most press requests. By that point, Mel Lyman had been written about by such New Journalism deities as Hunter S. Thompson (Mel's mentioned in *Fear and Loathing in Las Vegas*), Tom Wolfe, and Lester Bangs, but none of the exposure had been positive. The Family now focused on growing their Fort Hill Construction Company in Los Angeles; its success, together with the Benton inheritance and their pooled-resources ethos, transformed the group from the kind of people who used to dig through Dumpsters for food to those who could live comfortably in any one of their many homes across the United States. In the long run, being a part of the Fort Hill Community turned out to be financially rewarding for those who stuck with it and kept their sanity intact.

It was a surprise when, in the mid-eighties, the Fort Hill Community revealed to the public that Mel Lyman had passed away in April 1978. They never presented a death certificate, provided details about how he went, or disclosed what they did with his remains. There was no legal investigation. The information put a weird spin on some earlier articles, such as the *Boston Herald American* piece from late March 1978 claiming that "even in the ephemeral state, Mel still holds the power over a large family of talented, intelligent and educated people."

Family member George Peper called Felton a decade after his piece and invited him to dinner. "He told me Mel had died in France. He didn't say much more about it, and nothing has been written about it, and it is kind of a mystery. I think there's two possibilities. One: He did die of failing health, his health was never too good, that's what they claim. But his death certificate has never been shown or anything like that. The other possibility is that he didn't want the responsibility of being God anymore." He considers. "He may be living somewhere in Europe. He could still be alive!"

IT'S CURIOUS THAT THE LYMAN FAMILY wouldn't leverage an event like Mel's death in an attempt to rehabilitate their beloved leader's reputation. If Lyman's message was important and beautiful to them, why wouldn't they try to set the record straight, to publish something that *did* make his message clear? Did they realize he was just a flawed human being who had momentarily dazzled them? Maybe they were still following Mel's marching orders—this time, by telling everyone he was dead.

After interviewing Jim Kweskin, I purchase a complete collection of *Avatar*s from the Fort Hill Community—the twenty-three issues still available (there were twenty-five issues altogether, but there are no more physical copies of issue 2 and what happened to issue 25 is a story all its own) plus all four issues of *American Avatar*, its short-lived glossy magazine successor. Seen today, it perfectly captures Boston's late-sixties counterculture. From the ads for area thrift shops, to the coverage of local antiwar demonstrations, to the notices of upcoming concerts by groups like Peter Wolf's Hallucinations, *Avatar* is much more than an altar laid out for Mel Lyman.

Studying the old mastheads, it's curious to note how many names are still on the Fort Ave. Terrace mailbox. Trying to see how the *Avatar* staff ended up becomes a kind of hobby for me over the next few weeks. I often end up on Facebook, where I pore through profiles for any indication that these folks might be the same upstarts who shook up Boston fifty years earlier. On one such profile, among a sea of digital shots of family and grandchildren, is a lone, scanned-in picture of a man who looks strangely familiar. Then it hits me: He's the spitting image of an older Mel Lyman.

Could Felton be right? Or am I seeing things?

THREE
The Silver Age of Television

IF YOU WERE WATCHING WGBH on February 7, 1968, in a house with two TVs, you were in luck.

That Wednesday night, without warning, viewers were invited to take part in a radical experiment. Instructions appeared on the screen: "Gather two television sets in the same room. Place them six feet apart. Turn one to Channel 2. Turn the other to Channel 44."

On the left screen appeared a young British man named David Silver, who proceeded to interview theater director Richard Schechner. This footage was in black and white. On the right television, tuned to Channel 44, David Silver materialized in full color, adding commentary to the interview unfolding on the other screen, putting himself down as a phony. Elsewhere in the show, home viewers watched agog as the young British invader played Ping-Pong across screens, the tiny white ball magically zipping between two unconnected boxes in their living room.

The show's creators tried to keep the left program comprehensible without the aid of the other screen, "so that our audience wouldn't freak out and turn it off." Up on Fort Hill in Roxbury, the experiment impressed the impossible-to-freak-out mystic of *Avatar*, Mel Lyman. "I was only able to view the half that was shown on Channel 2 but that was sufficient to produce a wholly positive and enthusiastic response in me," Lyman wrote in an open letter to Silver published in the paper's next issue. "By God Dave you really ARE a pioneer in television, your show is without a doubt the most real, the most alive, the most IMPORTANT thing happening in the TV medium . . . I want the word to get around. WATCH THE SILVER SHOW ON TELEVISION!"

For two years, twice a week, *What's Happening, Mr. Silver?* transformed home televisions into portals for a psychedelic fever dream, uninterrupted by commercials or common sense.

WHEN HE WAS GROWING UP in East Lancashire, England, David Silver's first love was Shakespeare. He attended the University of Birmingham's Shakespeare Institute, and saw every play put on by the Royal Shakespeare Company for four years. At the same time, he was enchanted by the raw power of the Rolling Stones and Bob Dylan. He stayed for two degrees, writing his postgraduate thesis not on the Bard but on a contemporary American author: Saul Bellow. Silver's tutor sent it to Sylvan Barnet, a Shakespeare scholar at Tufts University, who was so impressed he invited Silver to come teach in Boston. Silver soon moved into his new home on Brattle Street in Cambridge. At twenty-two, he was the youngest "instructor professor" the school ever had.

With heaps of UK bands making inroads on the pop charts, David Silver instantly became a popular figure on the Tufts campus. Karen Thorne clearly remembers his arrival. "He looked like a dead ringer for Mick Jagger," she says of her teacher who was only a year older. "He took one look at me and I became his girlfriend. I can't explain it any other way." With a word of caution, Tufts was willing to let young love bloom between a student and a professor. The couple fell for each other and the city at the same time, shopping for records at the COOP in Harvard Square and attending concerts at the Boston Tea Party.

One evening in April 1967, the couple was watching TV with mounting boredom. Thorne complained that nothing on the tube resembled "our lives or our culture or our desires." She told Silver he should change that: "You're English, you're trendy, you look the right way."

Silver recalls that a poetry professor at Tufts knew a producer at WGBH and set up a meeting for him. Thorne, on the other hand, is certain that they walked into the WGBH offices off the street, telling a receptionist, "We have an idea for a show. Who should we talk to?" Whatever the case, Silver got a meeting with director Fred Barzyk.

Barzyk came from Wisconsin to WGBH in 1958. The nonprofit station had only been on air for four years, employing fifty people at its Massachusetts Avenue headquarters near MIT in Cambridge. Though Barzyk had aspired to a career in theater, not television, the $85 a week was hard to turn down. Shortly after arriving, Barzyk had a series of arguments with two WGBH producers about their coverage of the Boston Symphony Orchestra—the station's most popular offering. "I felt there was more to do visually than cut from the oboe to the trombone at the right moment," he says. "Why couldn't we make abstractions timed to the music revealing a visual understanding of the music?"

Barzyk kept looking for a way to take the avant-garde sensibility he had fallen in love with in college and apply it to television. On the wall of his apartment off Beacon Street, he chalked his new motto on the wall. It read "ETV IS DEAD," referring to "Educational Television," WGBH's bread and butter. He thought educational television had an identity crisis: "Was it high-minded talking heads or how-to shows? Was it Julia Child or strong political documentaries? Or was it to reach to the young audience we had in Boston?"

The old guard at WGBH wanted to hold the line, but six years later, the burgeoning popularity of the Canadian theorist Marshall McLuhan gave

Barzyk what he needed to push for change. McLuhan's 1964 book *Under-standing Media: The Extensions of Man* introduced the concept of "the medium is the message." "I never even finished one of his books," Barzyk confesses. But it didn't matter. To the leadership team at WGBH, Barzyk looked like an expert on a developing zeitgeist. A few years after McLuhan's rise, Barzyk got another lucky break when the Rockefeller Foundation and the National Endowment for the Arts provided artists with a chance to try out their talents on the small screen. Experimental television labs popped up in San Francisco, New York, and Boston. The funding removed the lingering hesitations at WGBH. It was finally time to do something more than just cut from the oboe to the trombone.

David Silver recalls Barzyk's vague but exciting proposal from their first meeting: "We're gonna set up a situation in Studio A and you're just going to . . . do things, and hopefully they'll like you." One day in May 1967, David Silver entered the studio and found a table full of magazines waiting for him as his only prompt. Silver riffed on an issue of *Cosmopolitan*. It wasn't good. But six weeks later, Barzyk told him they were scheduled to do a five-part series, one hour each with the possibility of more. Another program director had seen it and decided Silver was the man for the job.

Management who assumed that Barzyk would simply throw together something quaint hadn't considered his love of offbeat theater. The show would be the equivalent of a video happening, "a scrambled exploration of nonsense and critical info," he says.

Silver did press before a single episode had aired. "It makes me angry to see television not getting anywhere near its potential after all this time," he wrote in the August 1967 issue of *New England Teen Scene*. "We have color, satellites, instant replays—yet the vast majority of television programming drags years behind its own space age technology. How long must we, the public, wait for this to change?"

Only about twenty minutes of scattered clips exist online. David Silver has agreed to show me a few of the full episodes. "God knows what this is," he says softly, squinting as he scrolls through a video player on a laptop. "This was just craziness."

The show is about to begin.

IT GOES LIKE THIS: A swarm of inkblots. Cut to a circular logo bouncing across the screen. A child announces the title of the show, then looks confused. A Jim Kweskin song plays as the inkblots return. A half-second clip of a woman in a red dress, staring off into the distance. Edits happen without warning and truncate sentences throughout. Host David Silver sits on the floor and asks the woman a question, but her answer goes unheard—cut to stock footage of a man talking about producing high school yearbooks. Cut back to the woman telling Silver about an impending "cataclysmic event." Microcuts to old commercials. Aretha Franklin's "Respect" starts to play.

Behind Silver and the lady in the red dress, a dozen young people dance wildly. Seated to their left and right are an extremely old man and woman, watching. Backward sequence of Silver eating a banana. Stock footage run through an effects module rendering it new in an array of psychedelic color patterns. Black-and-white scene of samurais fighting. The editing pace quickens. Four distinct audio tracks play at once, often at odds with one another. Silver, all in black, fences with a woman dressed all in white. Inkblots overlay the duel. A woozy pattern spins as we hear news reports on the Vietnam War.

"You could be frozen for several hundred years," a woman in a floral pattern dress tells Silver while the dancers clap in time behind them. "That would break up the monotony of eternity." The elderly pair looks confused. Dave Wilson, an *Avatar* founder, drives his motorcycle onto the set and does loops around the whole scene, the exhaust thickening. "Mustang Sally" by Wilson Pickett plays. Silver lies down with the woman on the floor, the dancers keep swaying, and Wilson continues to circle everything with his hog. With no fanfare, the end credits appear. The sound fades out. You're left in total silence, watching the elderly pair's reactions. They do not understand what just happened. Do you?

The episode, "Madness and Intuition," won a National Educational Television award.

Barzyk used every film chain and videotape machine he could find to create it. "I had groups of thousands of slides being projected," he recalls. He said that whenever anyone got bored, they should just yell out, so that he could cut to something else, without rhyme or reason. He assumed that everything would make sense in the end. Twenty-two minutes into the half-hour show, he got up and left; the episode had taken on a life of its own and no longer required a director.

"I asked video engineers to ignore the idea of perfectly matched cameras," Barzyk says. "I told them to do 'mistakes': oversaturate the colors, flip to negative, wash over the real picture with artificial colors from their electronic controls." Sometimes they'd sit in the control room after a live airing, waiting for viewer feedback. "Some woman called the station complaining that she hated the show and that the cuts were too quick," Karen Thorne says. "She said the show was giving her brain cancer. Fred loved that. He told *everybody* that the show was giving this woman brain cancer."

Silver says "Madness and Intuition" was probably inspired by a mutual appreciation for Allan Kaprow, who had helped developed the concept of performance art in the late fifties and early sixties, culminating with his instructional record released in 1966 entitled *How to Make a Happening*. Kaprow would have enjoyed the episode and its aftermath. From his rules for a happening: "Give up the whole idea of putting on a show for audiences. A happening is not a show. Leave the shows to the theatre people and discotheques. A happening is a game with a high, a ritual that no church would want because there's no religion for sale."

There were certainly experimental films around that approached the level of absurdity found in Silver and Barzyk's creation, but the difference was that this program snuck into people's homes twice a week. And it wasn't just Boston airing the madness. *What's Happening, Mr. Silver?* appeared on thirteen partner stations across the United States. Andy Warhol may have been the superstar of the experimental film world, but even he had to convince you to seek out his movies. For Barzyk and Silver's form of madness and intuition, you didn't even have to leave your couch.

Silver and Barzyk owed a debt to Warhol's pioneering work, and the British TV host was ecstatic when, in 1967, he learned that Warhol was coming to town with the Velvet Underground and wanted to be on the show. They shot the segment in an upstairs room at 53 Berkeley Street, the home of the Boston Tea Party, where the Velvets were headlining that night. Warhol and VU chanteuse Nico, director Paul Morrissey, and another regular from the Factory sit around while Silver tries to coax genuine information out of the group.

SILVER: Would you call yourself a director?

WARHOL: No, the people I cast usually direct the movie.

SILVER: What do you do, just watch?

WARHOL: Yes, I get my thrills that way.

SILVER: What would your reaction be to a critic or person who looked at one of your films and just said, "Rubbish. Trite nonsense. Boring"?

WARHOL: Well, that's the way we feel about it. [*Everyone laughs*]

SILVER: You really do? You're not putting me on?

WARHOL: Yes.

SILVER: Are you interested in making more conventional type of movies?

WARHOL: Oh yes. That's all we're gonna do right now. Is make conventional movies.

SILVER: Will you continue your artwork?

WARHOL: No, we're just gonna make conventional movies.

NICO: Bow-tie movies. [*Laughter*]

WARHOL: What's a bow-tie movie?

NICO: Bow-tie movies. [*Displays an imaginary bow tie on her neck*]

SILVER: This is a conventional movie?

MORRISSEY: It's what all the kids are doing nowadays.

WARHOL: I think any camera that takes a picture comes out all right.

Something like this aired every Wednesday and Sunday at 10:30 p.m. *Newsweek* loved the show. Gregory Mcdonald, who went on to write a popular series of novels about a smart-ass detective named Fletch, called it a "weekly half-hour mind blower" in his *Boston Globe* piece, which appeared on New Year's Eve 1967.

> By the end of the more-or-less half-hour program (so far it's run anywhere from 25 to 41 minutes) you're a beat-up mess on the floor, hand groping for the Off switch while the title credits count ten over your bloody, bowed head.
>
> "I never miss it," said a lady who hates the program. "I never can believe it makes me as mad as it does."
>
> "If we're going to be radically new," Barzyk says, "we ought to disturb people, rather than satisfy them. If we ever get too much good comment on anything, we know we have failed. If we ever leave the audience knowing what we think, we fail. Our idea is to make the audience think."

The piece gave *What's Happening, Mr. Silver?* a huge boost. More episodes were ordered for 1968, and WGBH allocated a $200,000 budget for the show.

David Silver, the accidental English professor, was suddenly a celebrity. "I couldn't walk anywhere in Boston or Cambridge without being stopped," Silver remembers with a smile. "I would go places and give talks. I talked to the Harvard Club. I talked to the American Association of Psychologists and Psychiatrists. People couldn't get enough."

"I was literally a groupie," Peter Simon recalls. "It was the first TV show that spoke to the stoned generation, ever." Simon, the younger brother of singer-songwriter Carly Simon, was *BU News* photo editor at the time. He would host a potluck dinner where everyone would get fed, stoned, and then watch "as if God was speaking from the heavens." Meanwhile, due to Silver's work visa, he had to continue teaching at Tufts, though they reduced his workload to one class a semester. "I was a star teacher for two years," Silver says. His thirty-odd students would critique every show in class, until at last he'd tell them it was time to return to Herman Melville.

In the *Globe*, WGBH program director Michael Rice called *What's Happening, Mr. Silver?* "the *Mister Rogers* of the 18 to 25 generation." Barzyk had a different take: "I'm trying to create noise in the system, because I think noise itself is good." Understandably, tension was mounting between station leadership and the show's far-out creators. But at the start of 1968, Barzyk and Silver were untouchable. "They could not step on Fred's toes," Thorne says. "He got away with *everything*."

"Your program and you have annoyed me quite regularly," one letter read. "If Mr. Silver is a symbol of the youth of today, preserve me from them."

As the show's popularity grew, it booked bigger guests, including Frank Zappa, William F. Buckley, the Maharishi Mahesh Yogi, and Bill Cosby. But the boldface names didn't distract from the creators' devotion to the unpredictable. Silver says that Barzyk "knew more than I did. It was a show about how I reacted to this stuff." Karen Thorne adds, "As soon as the cameras started rolling, David was electrifyingly entertaining."

One week, Silver would be delving into "warlocks and spiritualists"; the next, he'd be interviewing adolescents on how they consumed and created media. "Hey kids, your eyes see farther than mine do," Silver's voice-over announces, over B-roll of teens messing with radios. "They scan the world, don't they? All those stations on the dial. An endless pattern of extension. Sense extension. The third eye. Twenty-one inches. The third ear. AM and FM. Stereo. They aren't wasting any time. They've started already. The radio stations are already being built. Meet Deni Choi, 14 years old, man of the media."

CHOI: They say on the packaging that legally you can only broadcast up to ten feet, legally. But they put the legally part in quotes. So they know you're not going to stick to the ten feet.

SILVER: What do you hope to broadcast?

CHOI: Music. Continuous music. Especially a group called A Twist of Time.

SILVER: That's a local group?

CHOI: Uh huh.

SILVER: What are you going to call the station?

CHOI: WLSD. On the high end of the band.

Back to Silver's voice-over: "Sorry kids, but the FCC says you can't transmit quite like that. That's a no-no. Big brother's listening. Go back to your Tinker Toys."

"I wanted to do parties as episodes," Silver says. After some misfires, Barzyk and Silver put together the "most outrageous" bash they could imagine: an episode framed as a party for Vietnam War veterans and protesters. Barzyk decorated Studio A with all manner of military props: trunks and swords, cannons and guns. Some of it was theatrical, some of it actual equipment from the army. Approximately twenty-five collegiate draft resisters and twenty uniformed servicemen were on set, getting tipsy on complimentary booze before the cameras rolled.

The tape of the episode has been wiped, but Silver re-creates it. He sat between the protesters and the servicemen. There was little hostility, but both groups started out fairly quiet. "At some point one of the resisters moved over to the other side and just sat with the military guys," and Silver encouraged people to cross lines and sit anywhere they wanted, as a Stones record played. By the end, a small bit of mutual understanding was achieved. "We're getting it," a twenty-three-year-old corporal said to Silver on air. "We knew there were protests but it's hard to understand it when you're out there in a paddy field getting shot at." Later the director learned that this episode had made the show a target of army intelligence surveillance—the curious onlookers allowed to watch from the control booth, many snapping photographs, weren't just fans, as it turned out.

Meanwhile, at home, Karen and David's life outside of the public eye was becoming just as surreal as their fan-filled strolls down Mass. Ave. "I remember being with David and I closed my eyes and opened my eyes," says Thorne, now a professional psychic. "I saw our Egyptian bodies kind of astrally floating in the air. I saw our spirit bodies, the Ka and Ba. I woke David up and told him and he said, 'Don't even tell me because you're starting to freak me out with this shit.'" This retelling jogs her memory. She recalls a chilling episode with a local personality.

"I don't remember his last name. But it was Mel. Who was a guru. In . . . Roxbury?"

"Mel Lyman," I say.

"That's right. . . . Mel was not a nice guy."

THE *AVATAR* EPISODE of *What's Happening, Mr. Silver?* was shot entirely on film and preedited for airing on WGBH. There is no live studio footage, nor any of Silver's usual direct addresses to the camera. It's basically a twenty-five-minute documentary, opening with footage of *Avatar* hawkers in Harvard Square. This was late January or early February 1968, just as the obscenity arrests and trials were winding down.

"Would you like an *Avatar?*" Paula Press, a recent teenage addition to the Fort Hill Community, asks a young man walking by.

"No, I think all boring papers should be censored. *Avatar* is *so* boring."

"Well, that's only a personal opinion," Press counters.

"Mel Lyman couldn't be God because he doesn't write well enough."

"Boston's underground newspaper *Avatar* was busted," explains Silver in voice-over, "like all good underground newspapers should."

The camera crew visits *Avatar*'s production office, located at 37 Rutland Street in Boston's South End, to meet the team dedicated to bringing the paper to the people.

Like the *Rolling Stone* piece, the episode is structured the way the Fort Hill Community intended it to be structured. That is, they purposely keep the interviewer away from Mel at first, introducing him to assorted members who, by design, inflate the legend of Mel so that by the time the interview happens, the audience is practically dizzy with anticipation.

"'Avatar,' as far as I know, means the bringer of new messages or a kind of spiritual rebirth. What is *Avatar*?" Silver asks a staffer.

"It's like the spirit of God manifested on Earth. This is a tangible manifestation of spirit. That's exactly what the paper is."

"You have something, though, that draws you all together, I've noticed," Silver cautiously proceeds. "What is that?"

"It's mostly embodied in Mel."

Upon each subsequent mention of Mel, the footage is interrupted by a photograph of the Fort Hill guru looking messianic, and accompanied by the sound effect of a camera clicking.

An unidentified young man tells Silver, "Mel is putting himself up on a pedestal telling people, 'I am the truth.' He's trying to get a reaction from people and I think the reaction he'd like to get is people saying, 'No, you're not the truth. You're not God.'"

Next, Silver trekked up to Fort Hill where he was given a tour of the community by Eben Given, the artist whose work adorns most of the *Avatar* covers, and who Silver describes in the episode as "Guru #2." Karen Thorne, who usually accompanied her beau for the taping of every episode, abandoned the film crew once they arrived on the Hill. "They heard I was psychic," she recalled. "They were kind of afraid of me. And I was afraid of them."

Set to a recording of Mel's banjo music, Eben Given and Faith Gude unlock the Hill's tower and bring Silver up to the top viewing deck. Given points out which houses the community owns, which one he lives in, and which one is Mel's. Silver is impressed with the view of the city. Given says it's been two years since the Fort Hill Community got their first house.

Silver does his best to make sense of who's who during his tour of the Hill, but is never quite sure. Showing footage of some kids playing indoors, Silver adds, "These definitely, I think, are some of Mel's children." One of the kids reads a poem from *Avatar*, written by Jackie Lyman, Mel's daughter. After establishing that Mel loves candy and that the community publishes a newspaper, Jackie's poem perfectly captures the duality of life inside the Fort Hill Community in the space of two lines.

We are a big funny family.
The hill is good and bad.

Another unnamed man eloquently explains that Mel is "our theologian. He is reminding us of our spiritualism. That's his job in the evolutionary scale of man. Your job, David, is finding out what's happening and bringing it to the people."

The Fort Hill Community finally led Silver and the camera unit into the kitchen to meet Mel Lyman. The community, anticipating some kind of misrepresentation by the show, documented the interview themselves too. About fifteen people were crammed inside the kitchen of 4½ Fort Ave. Terrace. A galaxy of Family member John Kostick's star sculptures hung from the ceiling. George Peper photographed the scene; a tape recorder was rolling in the corner as well. Paranoia was running so high they didn't even wait for the show to air before publishing the entire interview transcript in the next issue of *Avatar*. Besides private footage belonging to the community, this is the only known film of Lyman in full-on guru mode. He stares at Silver with the intensity of a supernova, takes forty-second pauses to answer questions, and remains eerily contrarian at every turn. Compared with the Lyman seen in Murray Lerner's *Festival* documentary, this incarnation is almost unrecognizable. Like a bizarro counterculture version of the Frost/Nixon interviews, Silver chain-smokes and interrogates the man who claims to be God.

> SILVER: When you've said you're God in the *Avatar*, what are the different ways in which this has affected people?
>
> LYMAN: A lot of people want to tell me that they're God, too. I get a lot of letters saying, "Well, if you're God, I'm gonna be God too, man." That's all right. I arouse *something*. At least somebody wanted to be part of what I said I was part of, or wanted to be what I said I was. It's very strong.
>
> SILVER: If people resented the fact, and people do, of one individual calling himself God and using that word, why do you think they resent it?
>
> LYMAN: 'Cause they haven't the courage to call themselves that and then live up to it. That's the hard part.
>
> SILVER: What's the initial step?
>
> LYMAN: Birth.
>
> SILVER: Why birth?
>
> LYMAN: 'Cause it's first.
>
> SILVER: You mean that existence—
>
> LYMAN: Boy, you sure got a mind. Whew, how can you stand it?
>
> SILVER: Well, I'm trying to, I'm trying to think. Um—
>
> LYMAN: (interrupting) I mean if you get all these things explained to yourselves, do you feel any better?

The whole affair has the air of Alice being taunted by the Cheshire Cat. Silver's usual confidence and brash sense of humor are nowhere to be found

in this footage. In fact, halfway through, the host is so stressed out he starts
to feel ill.

SILVER: Sorry, I'm sick to my stomach. Could I have some milk?
GEORGE PEPER: Here, have some Pepsi, it's better for you.
LYMAN: We all use Pepsi up here.

Lyman can even make a brand of soda sound ominous. The episode
aired with the title "Mel Lyman and the Avatar." In the last few minutes,
Silver coaxes a series of concrete beliefs out of Lyman, including his insistence that a change was coming to planet Earth in 1968. Later in the year,
Lyman would declare the precise start date of the Age of Aquarius—an
astrological period of two thousand–plus years promising an evolution of
consciousness and newfound unity on Earth—and mark its arrival with
his followers from the Hill.

SILVER: Do you think 1968 is a holy year? Do you think we're in a
    holy age? Do you think we're entering the new second coming era?
LYMAN: Yes.
SILVER: What evidence can you give me? What are the signs, what are
    the manifestations of this, around us?
LYMAN: This community, it's the most obvious one.
SILVER: And outside this community?
LYMAN: The *Avatar.* You know what the word Avatar means?
SILVER: Uh huh. Are you the Avatar, or is the Avatar more than you?
LYMAN: It's not more than me, no, and sometimes I'm the Avatar, and
    sometimes I'm asleep.

At one point he asks Mel, "How real do you think I'm being with you?"
To which Lyman replies, "You're being realer all the time."
It was this interview that caused Jim Kweskin to dissolve the Jug Band

and move permanently to the Hill. Fifty years on, David Silver refuses to comment on this episode, or anything related to Lyman and the Fort Hill Community.

BY EARLY 1968, David Silver knew that his future lay not in academia but in some form of show business. A talent agent named Richard wanted to represent Silver, who demurred. One day Richard called the TV host and said there was someone he wanted him to meet. An hour later, Silver heard a knock on the door. It was Van Morrison. Unlike many people in Boston at the time, Silver knew exactly who Morrison was without hearing him sing "Brown Eyed Girl." Silver made tea, and when they finished, they switched to beer. He told the singer, "I'm a Rolling Stones fanatic, a Yardbirds fanatic, and the only other band in the same league is Them."

Morrison humbly accepted the compliment and said he enjoyed Silver's show. They spent the next few hours talking about being the same age and trying to make it in the United States. "We had a lot in common!"

Despite Silver's lavish praise, Morrison expressed fears about his faltering career. Massachusetts hadn't exactly embraced him. Silver was encouraging. He told Morrison that Cambridge—now his home as well—was exactly the right place to be, even if the storied local folk scene was now on life support. The endorsement of Cambridge, in particular Club 47, by artists like Joan Baez, Bob Dylan, and Dave Van Ronk was hugely important to Morrison—it was one of the reasons that Morrison chose to flee there. But the scene's last gasp was during Morrison's Massachusetts residency, and his transition from rock-band front man to the pastoral, acoustic sound of *Astral Weeks* reverses what was happening in Boston's music scene at the time.

That afternoon, Morrison confessed to Silver about being scared no one would take notice of him in Boston. Maybe he should leave. Silver, incredulous that he was offering career pointers to one of his favorite singers, told him to stick around. He would end up as one of the greats. Morrison thanked the TV host for the advice and headed back to Green Street.

MEANWHILE, BARZYK AND SILVER were playing with different episode formats. Why not, Barzyk wondered, try to do the show live?

"Good evening," says an oddly agitated Silver on a WGBH set made to appear as a busy newsroom. "The reason you saw that bit of fakey film there to start off the show is that it's a parody of a news show. I'm *sick* and tired of ordinary news shows and *this* one is *my* thing!" Silver throws to a pretaped interview with Bill Cosby. Silver tries to gloss past the stale jokes his co-broadcaster, Russell Connor, offers in between segments. Silver smokes. Silver reviews the new Bob Dylan album, *John Wesley Harding*, comparing Dylan to Yeats. The "Apartment of the Week" segment just consists of footage of a run-down house in Somerville. "If you're a hippie in Cambridge who's being busted," Silver says, "go and live in that place." Behind him, people can be seen answering phones and bashing on typewriters. It's not clear if anything they're doing is real.

Silver reads an article about a motion from the United Nations to ban LSD. "For God's sake, there's a lot going on in North Korea," Silver ad-libs. "What the hell are they doing talking about LSD?" Barzyk throws to a prerecorded segment where the host visits a head shop selling pipes and underground newspapers: *Ramparts*, *Image*, *Inner Space*, *Avatar*. Back in the studio, a woman holds up a record of "Some Velvet Morning" and tries to smash it with a hammer. Barzyk cuts to footage of two kids dancing to the music.

"That was by Nancy Sinatra," Silver explains. "I *say* it was by Nancy Sinatra, but it's not really by Nancy Sinatra, because she's got false hair, false nose, she had her cheek bones shaved, and she's got false boobs! How false can you get?"

Fifty years later, Silver notes, "And that's why they took my show off the air."

"That moment?" I ask.

"Yes, well, and maybe what happened next."

Cohost Russell Connor admonishes Silver for being hard on Sinatra. Silver shrugs it off and introduces Professor Howard Zinn for a "guest editorial." The show cuts to a pretaped speech by Zinn in which he vividly rails against the Vietnam War. It was unheard of to feature this kind of direct antiwar sentiment anywhere on television, and even for those viewers used to the surreal rhythms of the David Silver show, it must have been a shock.

"How can we justify giant, powerful America bombarding the peasants of a small Asian country to force them to accept a corrupt and cruel government which they themselves are unwilling to fight for?" Zinn asks. "How can we justify this? Only by lying to ourselves or having our leaders lie to us."

Zinn concludes with support and admiration for those who refuse "to cross the sea to make war on the people of Vietnam."

"Thank you, Professor Zinn," Silver says. "I agree with every word you said."

Skip Ascheim hailed the episode in the next issue of *Avatar*: "For one hour, television actually woke up and lived a little, breathed real air from the outside world almost completely unfiltered." But the mood inside WGBH was grim. D.C. and Boston had seen the episode live; program director Michael Rice told Barzyk that what they'd done was unacceptable. "We're embarrassed," he said. "This may be the end of the show." Barzyk feigned mild concern. The two colleagues had a love-hate relationship, and Barzyk knew how to push Rice's buttons. Now he wondered how to respond.

"This is an experimental show and you can't *win* if you don't *lose*!" he cajoled. "You have to have disaster so you can do something better!"

Rice called his bluff. He proposed having their sit-down conversation about the appropriateness of the show's content on the air as a live, new episode—maybe the finale—of the series.

"Let's do that," Barzyk said, his eyes lighting up.

· · ·

"THE FACT THAT I HAVE THIS is a miracle," Silver tells me, cuing up the episode that would decide the fate of the show. "I would've thought they would've wiped this one."

The *WHMS?* logo appears, but without any psychedelic rock playing over it. There's no music at all.

"*What's Happening, Mr. Silver?* has been seen at this time for about sixteen weeks. Today we're going to talk about what in fact *has* happened, especially to last week's program. I'm Howard Spergel of WGBH's *Unit One*. We're in the Boston studio where *What's Happening, Mr. Silver?* has originated from the start. Joining me is Fred Barzyk, who has produced and directed the programs, Michael Rice, who is responsible for deciding whether WGBH will continue the Silver series, Robert Smith, program manager of WETA in Washington, and of course, David Silver himself. Michael, would you like to begin?"

Rice asks both Barzyk and Silver if they have any feelings about the previous episode; both pretend he's just asking about its artistic merits. "I think experiments never succeed totally," Silver deadpans. "They can't."

Barzyk and Silver execute this sort of masterful ballet dance around Rice's questions throughout the sixty minutes, intentionally misunderstanding the intent of the queries. In fact, the duo had conferred beforehand and even developed a strategy that included the director, David Atwood. Barzyk told him that "every time they even get close to the concept of shutting the show down, or even making us look bad, just cut to one of us, either Silver or myself, and we'll radiate the idea that we were being censored."

Rice looks annoyed. "I must confess that the questions of artistic success or failure of that particular show are of less importance to me just now, but rather specific things or attitudes that were said or displayed on it."

Silver goes for the "it wouldn't have been controversial in the UK" defense, but Rice cuts him off. "You draw no distinction between yourself, how you handle yourself personally on camera, and the extent to which you do so in private with your friends?"

"One shouldn't divide the two so totally that there's no relation to the two. The question of swearing on camera. I don't know whether or not I swore last week. But, uh . . . why shouldn't we use these words on television? What's wrong with it, really? We use them in private life!"

"Well, there was a devastating attack on a public entertainment figure, for example," Rice says, moving through his list of the episode's crimes. At the twelve-minute mark, the elephant in the room is finally addressed. The entire controversy, it seems, hinges on the authenticity of Nancy Sinatra's breasts.

"Well," Silver squirms, finally cornered with the direct charge, "what do you want me to say about that?"

"Well, let's say that a good number of people found that gratuitously insulting."

"Well, a good many found that it was perhaps telling it like it is."

Barzyk interjects with a smoke screen. "David was performing a function not only as an individual who was trying to say something, but also as an interlocutor for the format. In other words, David and I had rehearsed in the afternoon, and the kind of presentation of the material we had was unsatisfactory to me. We found that one of the things that would give it a certain amount of vitality was to make David mad, as a performer."

"But on the other hand he wasn't acting a part. He *was* David Silver," Rice counters. The hand on the meta-meter is going in circles at this point: Here is a show that's airing an episode in which the show itself is on trial— and within that episode is a serious investigation into whether the host of said TV show is a real person or a character.

Silver suggests the idea of ending future shows with a note about his opinions not reflecting the station's beliefs, to which Rice replies that the issue is "whether we want anything to do with you in the first place." WETA manager Robert Smith is even harsher, comparing the content of the show to "more like what we'd get on skit night at a summer boys' camp."

The issue of Howard Zinn's brutal anti-Vietnam editorial is an after-thought, addressed near the end of the debate. Smith believes it should have been followed by an opposing opinion, while Rice calls it an eloquent presentation of a point of view.

Then Rice sums up: Whether he likes it or not, David Silver is now a public persona. Silver, he contends, has commandeered WGBH for trivial purposes.

"I think that's a melodramatic way of looking at it," Silver protests.

"I think it is significant that we end this discussion on what is basically a point of disagreement," Spergel concludes. "Thank you for being with us."

I ask Barzyk if having his professional credentials questioned by his superior on television was awkward for him. "To me it was the height of the entire series!" he says. "All drama is conflict. This episode was theater."

Letters in support of Silver flooded the station; *Avatar* mocked Rice for being hypocritical and full of "newspeak." In the end, Michael Rice let the show remain on the air, with the proviso that they never broadcast live again.

SILVER STAYED, and the next episode, on February 7, was the brain-bending double-TV-set experiment—the show's wildest installment yet. In *Avatar*, Skip Ascheim described how, during the interview sequences, "Channel 2 closed in on [Richard] Schechner's face and 44 showed you Silver listening, but you couldn't be sure the two images came from the same time or place. . . . Here the technology ran far beyond my neurology. The only thing missing was a picture of yourself watching."

You can practically see Ascheim's mind floating away.

"I never quite felt it before, but television is made of electricity," he wrote. "You really can't even touch it."

Silver hung on for a while. But in the aftermath of Martin Luther King Jr.'s assassination, WGBH found itself playing a key role in keeping Boston calm. Pressure mounted on Michael Rice to make room for programming for and by the African-American community. Whether or not funding for Silver and "black television" truly became an either-or choice for WGBH, they certainly used it as a way to wrap up the Silver circus.

Rice told Barzyk that WGBH was going to take the money from the Silver show to develop a program called *Say Brother*—with Barzyk as consultant. "The Love Revolution, the hippies, the drugs—our show was a good way to reflect all that on television," Barzyk says. "Civil rights was clearly going to take center stage, so it made total sense to create room on air to address it."

The final episode of *What's Happening, Mr. Silver?* was a "masterpiece of camp," according to the *Globe*, featuring "a gang of sweet old ladies dashing about the city with violin cases trying to gun down Silver. In an ending similar to *Bonnie and Clyde* or that other pop-show of violence this year, the Democratic National Convention, they succeeded."

Somewhere inside that swan song was a sequence in which Silver and Karen Thorne are sitting up in bed. She's naked, her breasts exposed. WGBH aired the scene unedited, and Thorne believes hers was one of the first nude bodies on television. This small milestone aside, David Silver was devastated that the show had come to an end. "There was something there in Boston for me that was completely unique in my life," he reflects. "Not just being famous for a little while or having a little bit of power. There was something about the camaraderie and the community in the late sixties. I was a part of this community. I was awed by it. I loved being there. It was like a total joy to be in the United States. It felt like home to me."

Silver and Thorne got married in 1969 and had a daughter together, but split up a few years later. Thorne is now a professional psychic; Silver's varied career includes writing the documentary *The Compleat Beatles*, working at Warner Brothers, and hosting a mindfulness podcast. In 2000, *The New York Times* credited the Silver show as a key influence in the birth of video art. Silver agrees that he had an active role in the counterculture, adding, "I constantly felt like I was in a dream."

Fred Barzyk can still remember one incident that might have contributed to his partner's surreal feeling. In a Christmas episode, Silver walks through Boston Common, past trees lit up for the holidays. Two young women approach, recognizing him from somewhere.

"You're not real," one of the women says. "You're supposed to be on television."

David Silver answers curtly, "I'm real."

FOUR

Paul Revere Is Shamed; Being a Brief History of the Bosstown Sound

THE MEMBERS OF BEACON STREET UNION were taken aback by how quickly things were moving for them in late 1967. The band had formed less than a year before, and none of them had expected much to come of it. After recording an album with a well-known producer and hearing rumblings that the LP would be released on a label, they would periodically leaf through *Billboard* magazine at a newsstand in Harvard Square to learn how the music industry worked.

One day, drummer Dick Weisberg opened to a full-color ad announcing "The Sound Heard 'Round the World: Boston!!" The woodcut illustration depicted Revolutionary War soldiers with a mushroom cloud on the horizon:

Where the new thing is making everything else seem like yesterday.
Where a new definition of love is helping to write the words and music
    for 1968.

Three incredible groups.

Three incredible albums.

The best of The Boston Sound on MGM Records.

The ad listed three bands: Beacon Street Union, Orpheus, and Ultimate Spinach. "This was not making sense to us," Weisberg says. "It was like we were going crazy. We were like, 'Is this us?'"

This was how Beacon Street Union learned the name of their album, and that it was coming out on MGM Records. They had never heard of the other two bands.

Soon, A&R men from major labels would try and sign their own Boston Sound band. But within a year of the *Billboard* ad, the acts associated with the "Sound" would sport a spectacularly bruised reputation, and MGM's marketing campaign became an evergreen lesson in how *not* to sell new music to fans. The members of the various Boston Sound bands were hardly to blame: Unless you happened to know someone who had dealt with the record industry, there was just no way to educate yourself on the potential pitfalls. And with the threat of the Vietnam War draft looming, the kids of the Boston Sound glimpsed a dream and tried to grab it.

BEFORE WARNER BROTHERS' Joe Smith descended the narrow stairs of the Catacombs to hear Van Morrison perform in Boston in the summer of 1968, he had been hard at work on the opposite coast. RCA Victor had signed Jefferson Airplane in 1965, and Columbia had just snatched the rights to re-release Big Brother and the Holding Company's debut album. In 1967, Smith was sent to sign the Grateful Dead for Warner Brothers. "They did so much acid that it was very hard to separate reality from make-believe with them," Smith recalled. Jerry Garcia told him he wouldn't understand the music unless he dropped acid with them, but he took a pass. "I wouldn't breathe around them," he later explained. "Wouldn't drink anything. Wouldn't eat anything." Smith left San Francisco with his psyche intact and a deal with the Dead.

There was little doubt that these three acts belonged to an organic, homegrown scene, a community of fans and bands that epitomized Flower Power. In March 1967, the *San Francisco Chronicle* hailed the city as the "Liverpool of America," an impression deepened four months later when George Harrison spent one August day walking around Haight-Ashbury. Where connections to the Beatles could be found, there was money to be made. But the Bay Area's talent pool had already been fished clean by the major labels. You can picture A&R reps gazing at a map of the United States, wondering: *Where next?*

During the mid-sixties, Boston was home to two acts that seemed poised to break out: Barry and the Remains, who had toured with the Beatles and released their debut on Epic, and the Lost, who were briefly signed to Capitol and toured with the Beach Boys. Both groups had recently folded, though, and no other area act looked like their obvious successors. At the same time, the lines between popular-music genres were blurring; styles of songwriting were falling in and out of favor on an almost weekly basis.

The changing lineups at George Papadopoulos's Unicorn Coffee House on Boylston Street traced the path from Dylan's rebellious act at Newport to the spring of 1967: collegiate folk giving way to garage rock, then morphing into something harder to define. A local DJ, WBZ's Dick Summer, hosted a night of live music every Monday at the Unicorn. He invited WBZ's program director, Al Heacock, to come by. Heacock dubbed the new psychedelic sound "liquid rock" and instructed Summer to play one liquid rock song per hour on his show. ("The name was the only thing he got wrong," Summer said.)

Meanwhile, Ray Paret, who had studied aeronautical engineering at MIT, and David Jenks, a cabbie who daydreamed about designing album covers, started Amphion, a music management agency, in a building owned by the *Christian Science Monitor*, directly across from Symphony

Hall. One night, Paret and Jenks stopped at the Unicorn to hear a band that Heacock would have definitely classified as liquid rock. They were called Underground Cinema.

Clad in a white robe and sporting a pageboy haircut, the front man delivered cryptic instructions in a monotone over a bed of ambient noise:

> See the glazed eyes . . .
> And know the warmth of the hip death goddess.

The band kicked into a lazy, hypnotic groove as a rail-thin eighteen-year-old named Barbara Hudson approached the mic to sing the lines written by her bandmate Ian Bruce-Douglas, creating a kaleidoscopic portrait of the titular deity. Like a New England Nico, Hudson sang about the illusion of reality and how she was the mysterious girl of your dreams.

"We didn't like the name that much but they had a certain chemistry," Paret says. "Ian Bruce-Douglas was well spoken, talented. The rest of the group was a bunch of hicks from the Cape." That night, Amphion found its first band.

AT SIXTEEN, Ian Bruce-Douglas Wise enrolled at Berklee School of Music in Boston on a *DownBeat* magazine scholarship, but soon transferred to the University of Virginia. In Virginia, Ian started to write music, inspired by Dylan and Richard Fariña, whose performances back in Boston had made a deep impression on him; suicidal, he left school and moved back to his parents' house on Cape Cod, where his band Underground Cinema was born.

After seeing the band at the Unicorn, Jenks reached out to a man named Alan Lorber, whom he had met through a friendship with Lorber's brother. Lorber was a successful New York producer and arranger, of a mainstream kind: think Brill Building, not Haight-Ashbury. He'd later boast that his previous hits had garnered $50 million in record sales and that he was by Phil Spector's side when the "Wall of Sound" was born. (In his varied career, he had once written a handful of songs with Brooks Arthur, future engineer of the *Astral Weeks* sessions.) Lorber agreed to check out the Boston band. Dressed in jacket and tie, Lorber was impressed by their live show, but like Paret, he didn't care for the name either.

Bruce-Douglas and Lorber arrived at a verbal agreement that night at the Unicorn. Could anything be done about the . . . name? The singer had an idea. A few months earlier, he had obtained some pure LSD and had taken a solo trip alone in his bedroom. "I started looking at myself in the mirror and my face was doing funny things," Bruce-Douglas recalled. "I had a bunch of colored markers I used to draw with. I grabbed a green one and started drawing all these psychedelic designs on my face. When I was done, I looked at myself and said 'Whoa! I am ultimate spinach. Ultimate spinach is me!'"

Bruce-Douglas was Ultimate Spinach, and Ultimate Spinach was him, sure, but all together he, Lorber, Paret, Jenks, and the hicks from Cape Cod would work together to formulate "The Sound Heard Round the World." All they needed now was a record label.

BRUCE ARNOLD AND JACK MCKENES were booked at the Carousel on Cape Cod for a string of gigs, performing as the Villagers. The owner had offered to let them sleep over in the restaurant. During the day, Arnold and McKenes were expected to fill in as short-order cooks; at night, they'd shower off and perform live music for the patrons. When they were excused from their daytime duties for consistently burned burgers, they also lost a place to bed down. The Villagers didn't mind sleeping on the beach as long as it wasn't raining.

By 1967, the Villagers were playing Boston venues like Club 47 and the Unicorn, and had won "Best Folk Duo" in *Broadside of Boston*'s reader poll.

Arnold once played a show with Jim Kweskin's Jug Band before it disbanded. "I know this sounds odd," Arnold says, "but Mel Lyman was sitting in a lotus position . . . upside down. He didn't say a word the whole time he was in there and, of course, people have said that he ascended, that he was one of the ascended masters." Run-ins with possible ascended masters aside, the energy at folk shows was dwindling. Friends advised Arnold and McKenes to form a British Invasion–style band, but Bruce Arnold wasn't interested in mimicking English hit makers. "I wanted it to be a new modern American music," Arnold says. They added Eric Gulliksen on second guitar, and found a drummer in Harry Sandler, who cut his teeth with a surf rock outfit called the Mods.

The new lineup immediately caused a stir. "Over a period of two days we talked to nine different record companies and every one of them offered us some sort of a deal," Arnold recalled. One suitor, producer and songwriter Wes Farrell, liked their earthy, surging "Can't Find the Time" in particular. ("Write more songs like *that*!" he instructed.)

On the ride home the band landed on a name: Orpheus, the poet and musician in Greek mythology who traveled into hell to save his wife, Eurydice. Back in Boston, Amphion told the band that Alan Lorber wanted to audition them right away. "We showed up the next day and upon completing our set, Alan presented us with contracts," Bruce Arnold recalls. "We were told that MGM would be putting up a quarter of a million dollars to market us." That sum was accurate, but it turned out that the money would be spread out among all of the Boston bands included in the ad campaign. Drummer Harry Sandler remembers an immediate kinship with Lorber, something they weren't feeling with anyone they auditioned for in New York.

"We're going to work together on making Orpheus into a *great* pop group," Lorber told them confidently as they signed.

He set up the band in a suite at the Park Sheraton, across the street from Carnegie Hall in New York, while they recorded their debut. In the studio,

Lorber would have Bruce Arnold sit down next to him at the piano and play through the Orpheus songs on guitar. Arnold recalled, "I would play the chords and he would go find each note and then not only, to my delight, did he take care to use that exact chord I had discovered on the guitar, but also he had a name for it!"

"That's not a B minor, that's a B minor eleventh with a double flatted third," Lorber would say to an impressed Arnold. Lorber's main strength was arranging, and much more than any of the other Boston Sound bands, Orpheus is where his arranging talents had room to flourish. When it came time to record members of the New York Philharmonic on top of Orpheus's basic tracks, Lorber didn't want the whole band at the sessions. "While at the hotel, I would get confidential telegrams from Alan asking me to come to the studio to hear mixes or work on arrangements," says Arnold, who strategically remained in New York after his bandmates went back to Boston. Arnold had to tell a white lie to quell the others' suspicion, but hey, it was worth it to see orchestra members perform his compositions, right?

TODAY, BOSTON'S BEACON STREET is a vision of immaculate brownstones with astronomical price tags. But in the mid-sixties, it was a reasonably priced location to set up your kid while he or she attended Emerson or BU. Beacon Street was "the epicenter of the college scene," Dick Weisberg says, explaining his band's name.

Beacon Street Union followed up a series of successful local gigs—including opening for Jerry Lee Lewis and backing up Chuck Berry—with a trip to New York. After a show at Steve Paul's Scene on West Forty-sixth Street, they met producer Wes Farrell. Like Lorber, he was a seasoned industry hand. He had composed "Hang On Sloopy" with Bert Berns and penned the theme to the 1966 monster flick *Gammera the Invincible*. Walking into the Scene, Farrell bowled over the Beacon Street Union with his silk suit and Frankie Avalon hairdo. Over meals at Manhattan's fanciest restaurants, Farrell would order for the whole table while telling the boys he was looking for bands who had "fresh material and knew how to play in the contemporary style."

Back in Boston, word got around quickly. Weisberg remembers the Hallucinations' Peter Wolf asking if they had indeed signed with Farrell to make a record. Weisberg asked if there was something sketchy about Farrell, but it wasn't that.

"You can't make a good record if you haven't paid your dues," Wolf said.

THE FIRST THING you hear when you put on *The Eyes of the Beacon Street Union* is a voice intoning, with horror-movie gravitas:

> *Look into the land of the prophet. Look past the living streets of Boston. Look finally, into the eyes of the Beacon Street Union.*

This faux-profound Bay State poetry was written by a Boston College friend of the band's and mailed to Wes Farrell while he was mixing the album in New York. They were intended as the liner notes, but for some reason, Farrell put Tom Wilson in the vocal booth and had him read. Wilson was most famous for producing Bob Dylan's first electric album and his breakout hit, "Like a Rolling Stone." His orchestral overdubs on Simon & Garfunkel's "The Sounds of Silence" helped turn the forgotten song into a #1 radio hit in 1966. And although Andy Warhol is credited as producer of *The Velvet Underground and Nico* in 1967, it was Wilson who was in the studio, shaping the band's beautiful dark twisted fantasy. But his pedigree didn't lessen the Beacon Street Union's horror as the needle worked through the opening salvo.

"We finally get our hands on the album, and we can't wait to hear like what it sounds like," drummer Dick Weisberg says. "All of a sudden this spooky voice comes on and starts reading the liner notes. Our first reaction was: *This is not cool. This is not cool at all.*"

Even so, tracks like "Sadie Said No" and "Mystic Mourning" can still mesmerize, half a century later. It's by no means the train wreck that Weisberg implies, though you can understand his annoyance. "We were like this counterculture, weird thing that Farrell experimented with. But he did it his way, not ours." The band was embarrassed, and started to get on each other's cases. "It was a bad thing."

The initial reviews of the three Boston Sound albums were positive. *Broadside* covered them all in early 1968. *The Eyes of the Beacon Street Union* is "a fine album which makes it good listening," and *Orpheus* possessed "the magic that separates great from orgasmic." The eponymous Ultimate Spinach LP, hailed as the most unique of the bunch, overflows with ingenuity and humor. But like the Beacon Streeters, the Spinach front man wasn't thrilled with how the producer took control, mixing the album without consulting him. "He never was interested in my vision of these songs," Bruce-Douglas complained. "With all the grace and style of a bull in a china shop, he slapped those albums together." Almost as bad, in the liner notes Alan Lorber heaped praise on . . . Alan Lorber: "This first Ultimate Spinach LP is a result of the creative genius of producer Alan Lorber. The ever-changing fabric of sound and unique concept of the album is a highpoint in the Lorber career which has been dotted with numerous successes." To this day, Bruce-Douglas will often still sarcastically refer to Lorber as "the creative genius."

WITH THE JANUARY 29, 1968, *Newsweek*, the Boston Sound hit the national radar, acquiring a spelling variation that would stick. "At first only the names seem changed," the article begins.

> The scene is right from San Francisco as the psychedelic blobs
> assault the nerves and the raucous music hounds the dancers crowded
> hip to hippie in squirming abandon. Instead of the Jefferson Airplane

or the Grateful Dead, the music is by Ultimate Spinach, Earth Opera, Phluph and Butter. And instead of the Fillmore Auditorium, the scene is in the cavernous Psychedelic Supermarket, The Catacombs or The Boston Tea Party. The place, astonishingly, of this latest outbreak in the pop revolution is puritanical Boston. What has happened is more than just a new rock word—Bosstown. . . .

By February 1968, everyone under thirty in Boston had an opinion on the article and the bands named therein. *The Boston Globe* tirelessly covered the topic, noting gamely if stiffly, "What has happened is a 'pop' explosion with our beloved old Beantown square in the middle." More bands were forming practically overnight: Puff, Quill, Ill Wind, the Improper Bostonians, the Apple Pie Motherhood Band, Eden's Children, Phluph, A Warm Puppy, Bead Game, Bo Grumpus, Listening, Butter, the Cambridge Electric Opera Co., the Ford Theatre, One, the Freeborne, the Orphans, Cambridge Concept of Timothy Clover, Fort Mudge Memorial Dump, Groundspeed, Good Tymes.

By the time writer Richard Goldstein arrived from New York, on assignment from *Vogue*, everyone knew that "the word is out: Boston is 'in.'" His lengthy feature sways between praise and fair criticism:

> Fledgling Boston groups have been signed, sealed, and delivered like birthday Candygrams . . . these musicians know that the record industry has selected Boston to be the Florence of American rock. "Sometimes," explained a public-relations man, "you can make something happen by pushing hard enough," and the push is definitely on.

MGM president Mort Nasitir gets scholarly about it, remarking, "Some of this music is so intellectual that it is a little like the poet T. S. Eliot with his seven layers of ambiguity in each line."

Next, Goldstein sets his journalistic focus on a fascinating, new Boss-town group named Earth Opera. "There's actually a much stronger under-ground situation here than in Frisco, precisely because Boston is one of the most up-tight cities in America," singer Peter Rowan explained to the *Vogue* writer. Rowan, twenty-five, was already a music veteran, having re-corded his first song (as part of the Cupids) at age fourteen. Gravitating toward bluegrass music, in 1963 he started playing mandolin for legendary picker Bill Monroe. Rowan moved to Nashville to play guitar in Monroe's Blue Grass Boys; he recalls watching Dylan bang out most of *Blonde on Blonde* during that Tennessee residency. "We worked on the big repertoire night after night, playing the Grand Ole Opry, and stuff like that," Rowan recalls. "Monroe saw me getting too close to *his* style, so he used to stand behind me onstage and shout at me, 'Sing it like Pete Rowan! Tell 'em it's Pete Rowan!'"

Back in Boston, Rowan took Monroe's advice. He formed Earth Opera with David Grisman, and they proceeded to make some of the strangest music to be associated with the Bosstown Sound, flavored with dramatic lyrics, inventively sparse arrangements, and prog-rock leanings, most mem-orably on the genre-hopping enigma entitled "The Red Sox Are Winning."

Today, Rowan is a soft-spoken, practicing Buddhist, and he recalls that era with a smile. In 1967, he and Grisman first began working on songs that he thought of as "bluegrass slowed down," performing them at Club 47 and elsewhere. At one gig he came upon Mel Lyman backstage soaking his harmonicas in a jar of liquid, a common practice to a get a richer tone from a blues harp. When Rowan asked what was in the jar, Lyman said it was LSD.

He laughs at the recollection. "The scary thing is, he could've been tell-ing me the truth!"

But neither the developing rock scene nor the strange community form-ing up on Fort Hill piqued Rowan's interest. Instead he holed up in Brookline with Grisman, perfecting their "slow arpeggiated music." Elektra Records signed Earth Opera, who defied all their advice on how their debut record should sound. To the label's credit, "they let us form a band, put us up in L.A., and let *us* figure out what the fuck we were doing." The self-titled debut's mix of styles was distinctive enough in itself, but out of all the Boston Sound acts, Rowan's lyrics stand alone in directly addressing the Vietnam War. The leadoff song, "The Red Sox Are Winning," was no feel-good sports anthem, but instead a damning indictment of a city that would rather celebrate a baseball team than protest a generation of young men dying in a foreign war. Inside a fragmented, collage-style song structure, the singer embodies the apathy he saw in the people of Boston in the summer of 1967:

> *Should I turn off the TV*
> *or go to the race track*

The Red Sox were, in fact, winning. Rowan wrote the song in the middle of the season baseball fans would come to call "The Impossible Dream," where the team climbed out of a nine-year slump, clinching the American League pennant.

"I thought I picked up on the vibe pretty good at that time," Rowan says. "That was the summer when the Red Sox were winning but the gloom and doom of the whole Vietnam thing . . ." Rowan pauses, before mentioning a childhood friend who went to fight and didn't return.

Rowan was proud to express his anger on record. "I had a platform. I could say what I wanted. I was sympathizing with the warriors who had gone to Vietnam." "The Red Sox Are Winning" ends with the sound of an audience going rabid at Fenway, as an announcer goes berserk: "Let's make Boston America's #1 baseball city! Kill the hippies! Kill the hippies!"*

---

* Earth Opera wasn't the only Boston Sound band affected by the Red Sox' miraculous 1967 season. Dick Weisberg remembers a multi-night string of Beacon Street Union gigs at the Rathskeller in Kenmore Square, right next to Fenway Park. They had made a giant plywood sign that the club manager let them lean against the front, saying "NOW APPEARING,

Elektra sent Earth Opera on tour with the Doors in the spring of 1968. Jim Morrison would frequently be MIA moments before their scheduled time, and Earth Opera would be asked to extend their set. It warped Rowan's mind. "You're in front of an audience that wants to see a freak show," he says. "It's not that Jim himself was a freak so much, but that he knew how to touch that freak aspect in people." *The Great American Eagle Tragedy*, Earth Opera's follow-up, doubled down on the antiwar sentiment. The title track is a ten-minute opus that ends with Rowan shredding his vocal cords, screaming, "I can't stand it anymore!" After a long tour that unceremoniously ended in Huntington Beach, California, the band broke up in front of Rowan's eyes.

"We had no idea what the Bosstown Sound was," he adds.

AS THE BOSTON SOUND ads and promotion rolled out, Ultimate Spinach commenced their first tour in San Francisco, playing the Fillmore two weekends in a row. They now featured a second female singer, Priscilla DiDonato—an occasional cartoonist for *Broadside*—to match the layered sound on their recorded debut.

Amphion's Paret says Ian Bruce-Douglas "became an egomaniac, especially after he saw all the promotions. But they *were* a good live band!" Bruce-Douglas said that his bandmates turned against him on subsequent tours, claiming he caught wind of plans to accidentally attack him with a guitar in the middle of a show. He was still having disagreements with Lorber as well, who "wanted to market us as G-rated psychedelic bubblegum" and never forgave the group for acting like feedback-happy mad acid hatters on *The Pat Boone Show*.

Over in the Beacon Street Union camp, the guys had lobbied their colleges for a year off in order to tour behind their major-label debut. Their

BEACON STREET UNION—ALBUM COMING THIS JANUARY!" The drummer was home watching the news when he saw the eight-foot sign being carried through Kenmore Square by ecstatic Red Sox fans. Then they smashed it to pieces.

first show was on February 5 in Detroit's Grand Ballroom; the owner of the venue gave a tour, proudly pointing out bullet holes from the previous summer's riots. The opening act was the hometown MC5. "We get an endorsement deal from Custom Amplifiers, because we're MGM recording artists now," drummer Dick Weisberg recalls. "The only problem was, all the new gear was gonna meet us in Detroit when we got there." The band found the new equipment bewildering, perhaps explaining why they lost control over their usual tight live show that first night: A shriek from Tartachny's amp brought the guitarist to his knees, as though he'd been knifed in the skull.

In Los Angeles MGM Records threw a release party, but no one in Beacon Street Union was of drinking age yet, so the musicians had to stay in another room adjacent to the one with full bar service. Occasionally an executive would pop his head in to congratulate them. "It just kept getting weirder and weirder," Weisberg says. When the band played the following night, the crowd filled up with identical-looking waifs with floral wreaths on their heads, many carrying violin cases. Weisberg felt like he was in a Fellini movie.

Meanwhile, Orpheus was getting significant radio play, first with "I've Never Seen Love Like This," followed by the soft-rock precursor "Can't Find the Time," which peaked at #80 on *Billboard*'s Hot 100. With their mellow strum-a-thons and harmonizing, it's hard to imagine Orpheus opening for the Who, Led Zeppelin, and Cream, but they held their own, even without the orchestral sounds that enhanced their debut record. *Orpheus* was doing well in Boston and New York, in Bakersfield, California, in Hawaii—and that was about it, as those were the only places that were carrying the record in stores. Orpheus didn't know it, but MGM hadn't paid the pressing plant and according to Arnold was "basically going into bankruptcy" at the time.

The band was ecstatic when they were named #10 in the 1968 *Playboy* Jazz and Pop Reader Poll, between Hendrix and the Beatles, but were disillusioned to learn it was due to voter fraud. "We went into every magazine store in New York City and we posed as being from *Playboy*," an industry insider eventually explained to Arnold. "We told them that there was a typographical error on the ballot in this month's issue and [we] were going to take all of them, and that new ballots would be in the next issue." After collecting thousands of ballots, they wrote Orpheus on every single one of them, mailed them to multiple locations around the country, and then had them mailed to *Playboy* from those outposts. It's unclear if Alan Lorber knew this poll was rigged or not, but he would later cite the group's position on the *Playboy* list as proof that the critics had been wrong all along—and that audiences across the country adored them.

It got stranger. A friend of Arnold's returned from a visit to California with a few of the region's best underground newspapers. He pointed out an ad for a band called Orpheus set to appear live in San Francisco later that week. Orpheus—the band Arnold had founded—had never played, and were not scheduled to play, anywhere on the West Coast. The ad used the same distinctive font that adorned their album cover. The night of the San Francisco performance, his friend called the club and asked to speak to someone in the band.

"Hey man, I'm so glad Orpheus is playing there tonight," Arnold's friend said to the musician at the club. "Are you the same Orpheus who does that song, 'Can't Find the Time'?"

"Yeah, that's us!" the young man happily answered. Bruce Arnold was beyond bewildered. Why was there another Orpheus? When he confronted Alan Lorber, the producer denied having anything to do with it.

"THE COUNTRY IS NOW LOOKING TOWARD the East Coast because flower music is dying," Beacon Street Union drummer Dick Weisberg told *New England Teen Scene*, a comment all too typical of the scene. With so many Boston Sound musicians putting down the opposite side of the continent, it comes as no surprise that the first major piece of criticism about the scene came from the West Coast. The real surprise is that they found a local to pull the trigger.

Jon Landau is best known as the music critic who saw Bruce Springsteen perform in a club in Cambridge, wrote that he had seen the future of rock 'n' roll, and soon found himself to be the Boss's manager. But the lesser-known fact is that Jon Landau—born in Lexington, site of the original "Shot Heard Round the World"—was right there at the birth of rock criticism. In January 1966, Paul Williams published the inaugural issue of *Crawdaddy*, which *The New York Times* later called "the first magazine to take rock and roll seriously"; Landau tore through it cover to cover, thinking, *I can do better than this.**

"I was overcome with the vibrations emanating from Cambridge's folk revival," Landau wrote of his Lexington upbringing. "I started going to the Boston clubs, especially the old Club 47, as often as school and parents would allow. During a good week it wouldn't be surprising to see Eric Von Schmidt, Rolf Cahn, Tom Rush, Geoff Muldaur, Bobby Neuwirth, Jim Kweskin, the Charles River Valley Boys, Bill Keith, and Jim Rooney all up on stage at one point or another."

In his first *Crawdaddy* piece, Landau eulogizes the Remains ("They were how you told a stranger about rock 'n' roll"); his byline graces the debut issue of *Rolling Stone* in November 1967. By April 1968, the Boston Sound had incited such a heavy press cycle that *Rolling Stone* wanted it for the cover. Who better to get the facts right than a Bay Stater? Landau was no fan of the West Coast's musical output, having gone on record that the "San Francisco shit corrupted the purity of the rock that I loved and I could have led a crusade against it." But the first target for his lance would be home.

Under the headline "THE SOUND OF BOSTON: 'KERPLOP,'" Landau

---

* If Williams sounds familiar, it's because he was also a follower of Mel Lyman. The editor's eventual rejection of and escape from the Fort Hill Community is the first thing described in David Felton's 1971 exposé.

wrote, "The very real problem that Boston faces at the moment is that the hype may boomerang and hurt what has been a slowly developing situation. The first wave of albums is likely to give Boston a black eye with people genuinely interested in music." The piece retraced what happened in Boston and Cambridge in the previous five years, explaining the rise and fall of the folk scene, as well as mid-sixties garage rock bands such as the Lost, whom he considered "far superior to anything the city has now."

Though Landau was harshly critical of Lorber's grand scene scheme, the article is largely informational, with the headline and captions doing most of the name-calling ("PAUL REVERE IS SHAMED: 'BOSSTOWN SOUND' A DUD"). He highlighted the nightclubs and underground newspapers that made the scene more vibrant, pointing out that *Avatar*'s struggles with censorship had only made the paper stronger. "Nonetheless," he concluded, "one good club and two publications don't make a scene." The final word in the piece went to Jim Kweskin, who declared that geography is irrelevant—and that there is no Bosstown Sound. The next time Kweskin was quoted in the pages of *Rolling Stone*, he'd be explaining why he broke up his band to follow Mel Lyman.

In hindsight, Landau admits that he might have been too rough on some of the musicians, and that the whole debacle wasn't their fault. But most of all he remembers Kweskin's talent. "He was the best damn performer—you almost can't imagine how good he was," says the man who discovered Springsteen. "And Mel was great! Then *Avatar* arrived and I couldn't put the two things together.

"The real Boston Sound," Landau adds, "was Club 47 at the height of its existence."

PER LANDAU, it was true that the Lost had broken up before the Boston Sound went national, but the members of the band were all connected to this new development. In fact, every single member of the Lost appeared in one or more Boston Sound bands.*

Lost singer Ted Myers had watched some of his wildest dreams come true in the mid-sixties. In 1965 his band was signed to Capitol Records and toured with the Beach Boys; the following year, he married his girlfriend, Eve. One advertisement for the band in 1965 declared, "Five Americans from Boston—making the most British sound heard since the Tea Party." But botched distribution, recalled 45s, and substance use hampered their momentum, and in 1967 Myers announced the band was over.

For Myers, keeping his marriage together with his wife, Eve, proved to be just as hard as unifying his rock band. "We would break up every two or three months and ultimately get back together again," Myers explained. He had never been up to Fort Hill before, but when she joined up with Mel Lyman for a few days he finally drove up there to get her back. Lyman wasn't around, but Myers found the place unsettling, with what looked like a dozen or more Lyman "wives" and children milling about the houses on Fort Ave. Terrace. Eve gladly left with him.

Relocating to New York, Myers did a double take as his hometown suddenly exploded in the press as the chosen new music-industry ground zero. Since Alan Lorber was now looking to Ray Paret at Amphion for Boston musician recommendations, it was only a matter of time before Paret connected his old friend Myers with Lorber. "He offered me a publishing deal, which provided a small weekly stipend," Myers recalls. The $75 a week was enough for him to live on. Lorber said he would make an album with Myers if he put a band together. Thus was born Chamaeleon Church.

Personnel included his former Lost bandmate Kyle Garrahan, co-songwriter and bass player Tony Schueren, and on the drums, future *Saturday Night Live* star Chevy Chase. They met in the fall of '63, at the funeral

---

* Lost bassist Walter Powers even auditioned to be a member of Van Morrison's band, losing the spot to Berklee's Tom Kielbania.

of a mutual friend who had died in a motorcycle accident during Myers's first semester at Goddard College. Chase was eager to join the new band. "He was sort of straighter than us," Kyle Garrahan remembers. "But soon enough he became a freak." "Remember the Boston Sound?" Chase once asked a reporter. "Really heavy on violins."

Lorber sorted through all of Myers's new compositions, either declaring them suitable for recording or throwing them in the trash. "Lorber was not an easy person to deal with," Myers says. For instance, he insisted the singer change the line "kids on a bench getting high" to "kids on a bench getting by," which Myers unsuccessfully protested as not making a lick of sense. "He was a suit," guitarist Garrahan says of Lorber. "Suits are suits."

Before the photo shoot for the back cover, the image-conscious Myers took the band clothes shopping. They decided on long Edwardian morning coats. "Chevy's had a Nehru collar and looked like it was made out of brocaded upholstery fabric," he writes. In one of the few public comments Chevy Chase has ever made about Chamaeleon Church (to music writer Steve Simels), Chase goes beyond uncharitable—he's downright offensive: "They wore faggy little suits, they wrote faggy little songs, and they were all junkies and they're probably dead."

The band recorded their basic tracks in New York, after which Lorber assured Myers that he'd be looped in for the orchestral overdubs and mixing. But a few weeks later, the producer told him it was finished. "Don't complain until you've heard it," Lorber said, calling it "the best work I've ever done."

The musicians huddled around Myers's turntable and put the acetate test pressing on. "What we heard made us all physically ill," Myers wrote in his memoir. "There were weird, repeating echo effects and backwards envelopes—Lorber's idea of psychedelic effects. . . . To us, it just sounded like mush."

Lukewarm reviews greeted *Chamaeleon Church*; radio ignored it, and so did MGM. Amphion's Paret convinced the band that if they relocated to Boston he could get them live gigs. They played three shows to little fanfare, the last of which was at a high school football stadium in Waltham. At one point Chase walked to the front of the stage and started a filthy improv as the band vamped—the last sermon from Chamaeleon Church.

After the band's brief run, Alan Lorber suggested guitarist Kyle Garrahan go solo. Garrahan agreed and recorded a single, an original titled "Shame." Lorber set him up with a booking agent, who casually mentioned, "You know, if you got a full band together, you could go do some of Orpheus's gigs." The agent explained that sometimes other bands would learn a few Orpheus songs and tour regions that the actual band was too busy to hit. Initially repelled by the offer, Garrahan came around. The booking agent assured him that the real Orpheus knew about it. Garrahan recruited Chevy Chase and a few other musicians, learned how to play the breakout single "Can't Find the Time," and hopped in a van. "This band shows up for these gigs looking nothing like Orpheus, sounding nothing like Orpheus, and doing zero Orpheus tunes except that one hit single," Garrahan says. Chase remembered performing in a gym at the University of Kentucky when people started to notice.

"You're not Orpheus!" an audience member screamed.

"Yes, we are!" Chase yelled back.

These escalating audience encounters got back to the booking agent, and the fake southern U.S. Orpheus sham was over after just a few gigs. Later, when Bruce Arnold from Orpheus figured out what happened, it made a lot of sense to him why their booking agent only had the band tour the East Coast—there were Orpheus clones to cover the rest of the country. To this day, Arnold isn't certain how many fake versions of his band were on tour in the late sixties.

A MONTH AFTER *Rolling Stone* covered the Boston Sound, a *Wall Street Journal* feature printed dollar figures and marketing tactics so baldly that it seemed designed to turn a rock 'n' roll fan off music forever. "MGM sells each Ultimate Spinach album to the distributor for $2.03 (the retail list price is $4.79). It gives 49 cents of this to producer Alan Lorber, who gives an undisclosed share of this to performers."

Ed Abramson, however, the new manager for Ultimate Spinach and Orpheus, makes the article's most repellent remark. Abramson was Alan Lorber's accountant and head of a nascent artist management company called International Career Consultants. He explained to the *Journal* how he was enjoying his newfound power over the bands' creative instincts. "Ian [Bruce-Douglas] has a conception in his mind that anything he wants to say or do is fine. My job is to control that aspect. I had a meeting with him recently. It had to do with his overall attitude. On solos, for example, Ian might feel he wants to take a guitar solo and go on forever. I tell him he has to limit himself." It doesn't get any cooler than accountants telling musicians how long their guitar solos should be, does it?

"These articles and others were enough to overboil the outraged 'underground press,'" Lorber noted. He was likely referring, in part, to *Avatar.* Ken Emerson, a Harvard student who frequently wrote about music for the paper, started commenting on the Boston Sound in *Avatar* in late March 1968. Up until then, non-MGM Boston bands were bending over backward to associate themselves as part of the so-called Sound. Apple Pie Motherhood Band's 1968 debut on Atlantic, for instance, declares on the back cover that the band hails from Boston. "They made their first impact on the pop scene in Boss Town and they've been spreading the gospel of the Boston Sound throughout the length and breadth of the East Coast and the Mid-West."

Now, though, bands were becoming far less enthusiastic. Rusty Marcus, bassist for Eden's Children, shared his grim point of view with *Avatar.* "Just look at Boston," Marcus said. "Look at the colors, grey, brown, black. Everything's dirty, even the sky. In San Francisco there are pinks, whites, and yellows. . . . Boston could never support a music scene. You can't enjoy yourself if your body's sick, and Boston's sick, physically, psychologically sick.

"We're glad we're not lumped together with the rest of the Boston Sound," he concluded. "I mean, MGM's trying to buy its way on the charts. . . ."

IAN BRUCE-DOUGLAS ESCALATED his ego-fueled reign of terror. He hired Karyl Lee Britt to replace Priscilla DiDonato, and immediately began to pressure her to drop LSD with him. At a show in Central Park, the Spinach singer went berserk, throwing a piano bench onstage that nearly knocked Britt over.

Behold & See, the second album by Ultimate Spinach, arrived in August. Britt was already gone. It stalled at #198 on the *Billboard* chart. "Spinach must now abandon its eclecticism," *Broadside of Boston* wrote in its review. "They must stop borrowing indiscriminately and develop and do 'their own thing' or else they will find that whatever they do will really be nothing at all."

Bruce-Douglas seemed to agree. "I fired myself," he recalled, though his bandmates remember it the other way around. They last saw him in September 1968, going down the lift at the Amphion Management building, shouting obscenities up the elevator shaft. An Ian-less Ultimate Spinach was of little consequence to Lorber, who built an entirely new lineup around remaining original member Barbara Hudson almost instantly after Ian's departure. He still had Ted Myers and Tony Schueren, of the defunct Chamaeleon Church, under contract, so he installed the pair as the new leaders of Ultimate Spinach. "It felt weird," Myers says. For the first time, he had no say in the personnel. "The songs Tony and I wrote were not remotely like the rather bombastic stuff that Ian had written, so it was, for all intents and purposes, a whole other band."

Myers thought the album should be called *A New Leaf* (a clever nod to the big spinach leaf that graced the cover of the first LP). "But, in their infinite wisdom," Myers writes in his memoir, "Lorber and MGM Records decided to simply call the album *Ultimate Spinach*, which was the same title as the first album. Maybe they were hoping that people would buy this one by mistake."

During the subsequent tour, no one seemed to notice Ian wasn't in Ultimate Spinach anymore. "I guess my counterfeit Spinach fared better," Myers says in regard to the faux-Orpheus. After the Spinach tour, most of the new lineup was caught in a Back Bay drug raid. Myers took it as his cue to split. His wife, Eve, had just run off again, all the way to California, and he decided to chase her down one last time.

AKIN TO THE FAUX-SPINACH LP, the Lyman Family too released a record around this time whose origins were dubious. If you take the cover at face value, *Love Comes Tumbling Down* (Reprise 6353) is a record by—deep breath—"American Avatar: The Lyman Family with Lisa Kindred." The front cover shows Lyman in profile, standing in front of a gorgeous sunset on Fort Hill. The band name unfurls in a Tolkien-esque font designed by Eben Given.

But that's not the *real* title of this LP, which Reprise Records, a Warner subsidiary, released in 1969. It's actually supposed to be *Kindred Spirits*, an album that blues singer Lisa Kindred made for Vanguard in 1964. The Lyman Family stole it, renamed it, repackaged it, and resold it to a major record label, which in turn released it, oblivious to its origins.

David Gude, the Lyman Family member and Vanguard engineer on the project, explained what happened to David Felton in 1971. Kindred had a Vanguard contract, and Mel, an old friend, asked if he could back her up. "Lisa loved Melvin and she said sure." The band featured Fort Hill Community members Lyman, Kweskin, and Terry Bernhard, as well as Bruce Langhorne, a musician whose predilection for playing a giant "wagon wheel" tambourine inspired Bob Dylan to write a song about him.

Gude's boss at Vanguard didn't like the results. "He thought the harmonica was too loud, there was too much Melvin and not enough Lisa." In the end, Lyman had Gude steal the master tapes, thereby ending his employment at the record company. Then the guru of Fort Hill sat on the tapes for years. "At that time there was no such thing as the Lyman Family," Lisa Kindred told Felton. "At that time it was still my album."

Upon seeing the record for the first time, Kindred exclaimed, "I know Mel is an Aries with a God complex, but this is too much!" (Everyone who performs on the album is listed inside the gatefold with their astrological sign printed next to their name.) Lyman wrote the sententious liner notes: "The force that drew us together to record this music is the same force that is always evidenced in great works of art, and like all great works of art this music was created to elevate men, we were merely the instruments." This kind of note might have been appropriate if it were one of the greatest recordings of all time. As it stands, it's a pleasant-sounding blues record with loudly mixed harmonica all over it.

"I ended up being a sideman on my own album!" Kindred lamented.

The name of the record isn't the only fiction here. The intimidating photo of the Fort Hill Community on the back cover, showing twenty-two Family members arrayed in front of the tower, is in its own way false too. Amid the crowd, one person in the back row sticks out. For one, he's the only person smiling, and—even more strikingly—he's the only African American in the entire group. But look a little closer and you'll notice something strange. His shoulder seems to defy the rules of physics and exists, partially, on top of the person next to him. It almost seems as if he's been pasted into the group photo. It turns out the community had provided the same exact photo for an earlier *Globe* article about the commune. That time, though, the smiling man wasn't there. Someone had cut and pasted him into the group shot used for the album sleeve.

Why would they do this? Was it an ill-advised attempt at faking racial diversity? Was this their way of taunting the community around Fort Hill, whose neighborhood they invaded in 1966?

Why, from stolen tapes to inserted man, would they do *any* of this?

IN HINDSIGHT, Dick Weisberg agrees that Peter Wolf was right: The Beacon Street Union *hadn't* paid their dues yet when they scored a record deal in 1967. And in a cruel twist of fate, now that they *had* paid their dues, listeners labeled them a cookie-cutter product of MGM. Producer Wes Farrell promised that their second album, *The Clown Died in Marvin Gardens*, would put them back on track, but it tanked. Original members quit. The band tried to reform as the Eagles; Wes Farrell said they should call it the Silver Eagles. They settled on Eagle, releasing one album that no one heard. There were times in the next few years when they couldn't get a booking as Eagle, so they'd revert to their old Beacon Street Union name to score a gig.

Out of the three original Boston Sound bands, Orpheus was the least affected by the negative press and record company schemes, like fake versions of their band or music-reader-poll ballot stuffing. Maybe that's what they had in mind when they titled their second album *Ascending*. For singer Bruce Arnold, the only downside to their growing fame in New England was the way locals pronounced the band name: "*Ahhh*-fee-us."

Arnold's private belief that *he* was Orpheus and that the rest of the guys were simply his backing band was becoming harder to conceal. Tensions rose. Harry Sandler's showy live drumming was getting a lot of attention; Jack McKenes was doing a lot of drinking. After a sold-out show at Arlington High School in December 1969, a full-blown screaming match erupted in the dressing room. "Are we a band? Or are we just your sidemen?" Sandler fumed. Arnold didn't have to say it out loud. McKenes and Sandler quit that night.

In classic Alan Lorber fashion, a changing lineup wasn't a problem, as long as the band name could still be capitalized upon. Orpheus continued to release new music, but the first two albums undoubtedly represent their commercial peak. If you want to find out if Harry Sandler and Bruce Arnold eventually buried the hatchet, you don't need to look very far to get your answer. There's an Orpheus website where Bruce Arnold's name and likeness are conspicuously removed from all photographs and the band's biography. Stranger still, the website states that it was done at Arnold's request.

IN THE SUMMER OF 1969, *Fusion* magazine's Robert Somma published a cover story about what went wrong with the Boston Sound. Two balloons depict the scene in '68 and '69, with the latter completely deflated and flaccid.

In the fall of 1970, twenty-five-year-old Michael Curb became president of MGM Records. On his first day, he fired the entire A&R staff. Curb was just getting started. In November, he announced he was going to rid the label of any act that sang about hard drugs or promoted heavy substance use. Curb dropped eighteen bands, describing how the alleged miscreants "wipe out your secretary, waste the time of your promotion people, abuse the people in your organization, show no concern in the recording studio, abuse the equipment, and then to top things off, they break up." President Richard Nixon praised Curb, stating, "Your forthright stand against drug abuse is a responsible contribution to the welfare of your country." The young record exec denied the policy could turn into a witch hunt, magnanimously assuring *Billboard* readers that MGM wouldn't be making the specific list of dropped bands public.

The bands, of course, knew: They suddenly no longer had record contracts. Bruce Arnold from Orpheus, now operating the band with an entirely new lineup, was shocked to learn that his innocuous act was part of the druggy

MGM 18. "I had to think back what lyric it could possibly be," Arnold says. "Then I remembered: 'Baby, I remember when we turned on to a rainy day,' from 'I've Never Seen Love Like This.' The track was actually about getting turned on to a rainy day, cannabis optional." To this day, Arnold believes if the band had actually been busted for drugs, they would have been a lot more popular. When Curb was asked to comment on the Boston Sound, he dismissed his own label's recent back catalog as "just a bunch of junk."

Things got worse at the label. In 1972, MGM's Lenny Scheer, who had been instrumental in the marketing of the Boston Sound, was indicted for tax evasion related to unreported income he made by selling returned, unsold LPs from stores to discount houses and pocketing a portion for himself. Later that year, an MGM executive leaked stories to syndicated columnist Jack Anderson, who ran an ongoing investigation on payola in the music business. For the first time since the early sixties, the FCC started paying attention again. In 1975, a series of federal indictments ensnared everyone from low-level private record sellers like Bang Records associate Carmine "Wassel" DeNoia to big shots like Clive Davis, the president of CBS Records.* The party was over. Polydor absorbed MGM Records in 1976. Alan Lorber later trademarked the titles "Boston Sound" and "Bosstown Sound," just in case.

I'M AT A TINY CAMBRIDGE CLUB called Toad to see a local band, Fandango, do their regular Wednesday night slot. The packed room brims with joy, the crowd dancing as the band rips through a repertoire of classic soul covers. Fred Griffeth, the seventy-four-year-old lead singer, belts out a version of Ernie K-Doe's "A Certain Girl" as if he were half a century younger, looking for love.

Afterward, we talk in his camper van across the street. Griffeth was one

---

* Clive Davis was fired and legally fined $10,000, but given no prison time. DeNoia was convicted in 1976.

of three lead singers in the Bagatelle, the only band associated with the Boston Sound to feature black performers. He'd been recruited by Lee Mason, ex-drummer for the Lost, to join a large soul band he was assembling. The Bagatelle ballooned into a nine-person outfit, featuring three African-American singers trading off on lead vocals and backing each other up with tight harmonies. Opening for national acts like Richie Havens and the Peanut Butter Conspiracy, the band earned a reputation for putting on a hot live show—occasionally literally incorporating the talents of a fire-eating mime. In *Rolling Stone*, Landau raved about their "hip kind of soul music," judging them the best performing band in the city.

The Bagatelle landed a deal with ABC Records. Tom Wilson—fresh from his surprise Beacon Street Union incantation—was on board to produce. He promised the Bagatelle they would "figure out how to make it happen together," Griffeth says. "We went in the studio, recorded it, and next thing we knew, you know, they had put it out with strings and blah, blah, blah. We never got to say *a word* about what happened." At one point, to test if Wilson was paying more attention to their music or the model sitting on his lap, the mighty Bagatelle horn section purposely played off key during a take. "Great, guys," Wilson said, simultaneously flirting with women in the control room, "it's great!"

11pm SATURDAY arrived in the early summer of 1968. One review optimistically predicted that the album "ought to do a lot to wipe out the bad taste of the 'Boston Sound.'" The Bagatelle hit the road: nine men, two vans. Despite the critical praise, tempers were already running high by the time the band arrived in Chicago for an August show—just as the Democratic National Convention was under way at the International Amphitheatre. Ten thousand protesters filled the streets, chanting "The Whole World Is Watching!" and clashing with cops.

After the gig, Griffeth and a local friend went to check out if the riots were as bad as the TV coverage made it seem. Griffeth watched in shock as the police rushed a crowd, bashing them with batons. A white man stumbled away, holding his bloodied head and yelling, "Oh my God—they're hitting us like we're niggers."

The Bagatelle did not survive Chicago. Half the band decided to go to New York to try and start under a new name, while the other half headed for California. All of them were tired—not just of the Boston Sound, but of Boston itself. Griffeth went with the California crew. "When you get outta Chicago the whole landscape just blows out and opens you up," he says. The band drove west through Iowa and Nebraska, then decided to visit New Mexico. West and then south, the Bostonians kept driving, farther and farther from home. "Everybody was still, like, a little uptight because we had experienced some bad vibes and racial shit in the Midwest. But then that sign for New Mexico comes up: *The Land of Enchantment.* You pass over the border, man, and it was like that knot in your stomach went away. Everything relaxed. We get into Santa Fe and everybody said, *This is it. This is it for me.*"

FIVE

The White Light Underground

My other big record of the day was *White Light/White Heat.*

—LESTER BANGS, "Astral Weeks"

BUT WHAT IF THERE REALLY *WAS* A BOSTON SOUND? Something truly revolutionary, a music evocative of the city from which it sprang?

Critic Wayne McGuire believed it existed. In August 1968, he published a manifesto in *Crawdaddy*, arguing that two musicians were actually creating it.

It is irrelevant that the Velvet Underground first received significant exposure in their home city New York with Andy Warhol's Exploding Plastic Inevitable. It was in Boston, through record sales and Boston Tea Party performances, that they began to find some acceptance and meaningful response (like getting their equipment stolen). It is irrelevant that Mel Lyman's present instrument is *Avatar* and film, not music. What is relevant is that these two voices best express the character and spirit of the forces at work in Boston, home of the first American Revolution. It is a character and spirit which in the near future will make Boston the center of the second American Revolution, a revolution of the spirit.

The Velvet Underground's Lou Reed and the guru of Fort Hill would seem to be polar opposites, but in strange articles like McGuire's and a rock palace called the Boston Tea Party, the two briefly converged. At 53 Berkeley Street, the Velvets found a second life as a band, playing the club forty-three times between 1967 and 1970 (versus only three shows in their home base, New York). There, the band transformed from an Andy Warhol Factory novelty into a musical force. One night, after a chaotic MC5 set in which someone urged the crowd to tear down the hall, Reed took the stage and pledged his allegiance: "This is our favorite place to play in the whole country and we would hate to see anyone even try to destroy it!"

The Velvet Underground's favorite venue would never have existed had it not been for Mel Lyman and the Fort Hill Community.

JESSIE BENTON WAS BORN in Kansas City, Missouri, in 1939. The daughter of painter Thomas Hart Benton, Jessie enjoyed an artistic, celebrity-filled upbringing. When a certain movie star stayed at the Benton residence for a time, posing for her father, she fell head over heels. "I stayed in love with Marlon Brando for the rest of my life," Benton said. "Who wouldn't? He noticed me, and liked my father."

Both Thomas and his wife, Rita, revered traditional American music, and Jessie learned guitar at an early age; her first job was singing at the Ocean View Hotel on Martha's Vineyard, where the family spent their summers. When Edward R. Murrow brought his *Person to Person* interview program to the painter's house in 1955, a nineteen-year-old Jessie performed "The Turtle Dove Song" on dulcimer for a national TV audience.

Jessie Benton recalled an idyllic upbringing, especially those summers on Martha's Vineyard, where none of the island's residents made a fuss about her father's controversial public persona or batted an eye when the family skinny-dipped in the ocean.* As a child, Jessie immersed herself in Greek mythology, and for several years believed she was secretly Persephone, Zeus's daughter, the beautiful queen of the underworld (and also the subject of one of her father's most revered paintings). Showing a reporter around the Bentons' island property in 2012, she dreamily gazed over the landscape and declared, "This was our world."

With her striking looks and confidence, she exerted a powerful force. "We engaged Jessie to sit with our two four-year-olds," said one Vineyard resident. "It was strange that both fathers awoke early on the days Jessie was to come and soon appeared shaved and sporting combed locks." She attended Radcliffe College in the late fifties, just as Harvard Square's folk scene was blossoming. On Martha's Vineyard, she met David Gude, a recording engineer who exerted an influence on other young island musicians like James Taylor and Carly Simon. Gude and Benton married on New Year's Eve 1962, at St. Francis Xavier's Church in Kansas City. They had a son, Anthony, and though it would be years before she obtained a divorce, Jessie freely dated other men throughout the early sixties.

One such suitor was Robert Peter Cohon, who would become a successful character actor as Peter Coyote. In 1964, he was an artistic young man with interests in everything from political activism to mime work—to Jessie Benton.

> She was a natural aristocrat, haughty and achingly beautiful, blessed by her Italian mother with dark, tangled hair and a Caravaggio mouth. Her unerring instinct for the first-rate and the precision of her dismissive ridicule invigorated any room she entered, charging the atmosphere and alerting people to impending

---

* A self-declared "enemy of modernism," Benton was criticized for the ethnic stereotypes in some of his murals in the 1930s, and was fired in 1941 from his teaching position at the Kansas City Art Institute for homophobic remarks.

adventure or disgrace. Her behavior was restless and bold, and her natural incandescence made others pale by comparison. Her gifts were so abundant that her peers (the best and the brightest of Radcliffe and Harvard) seemed to accept as just her uncontested status as reigning queen.

Coyote persuaded her to move to San Francisco with Anthony, but Benton returned east every summer to Martha's Vineyard to be with her family. One night during the summer of 1965 she tried LSD for the first time. It was the same night Gude brought Mel Lyman to the Benton house.

Lyman walked into the living room and confidently assessed the huge portrait of an eighteen-year-old Jessie holding a guitar, painted by her father. "That doesn't look anything like you," Mel bluntly told Jessie. "That looks like a frog." Jessie had never cared for the portrait herself and was immediately fascinated by the first person to ever criticize it. "He was like something I had never seen or known ever," Benton says. "He really was like something from another planet." Jessie's first LSD trip was a bad one, but Mel stayed by her side throughout the forty-eight-hour psychedelic breakdown, singing and reading her his poetry. When she finally came out of it, she promptly called Peter Coyote and told him to send her things. "I've found God and I'm moving in with him," she said.

The new couple moved into their first home on Fort Hill in early 1966. Securing a divorce from Gude to marry Lyman would take some doing. She was going to need a good lawyer.

Now in his eighties, the accidental architect of Boston's alternative-media landscape currently lives in Lawrence, Kansas. "At the time I was one of the most famous people in Boston," Ray Riepen crows. "Riepen would say 'hello,' and voila! A 400-word feature," *The Boston Globe* noted, tongue in cheek. In the late sixties, Riepen was known as the "hippie entrepreneur" because he opened the Boston Tea Party, started the free-form phase of radio station WBCN, and bankrolled the pioneering alternative weekly *The Cambridge Phoenix*. Though all three institutions are now defunct, Riepen's business moves in the late sixties and early seventies resonated in Boston for decades.

How did a thirty-year-old Kansas City lawyer trigger a cultural transformation 1,400 miles away? The chain of events started when he went out on a few dates with fellow Kansas City native Jessie Benton; the evenings would end with Riepen bringing Jessie home and getting drunk on bourbon with her father.

In the summer of 1966, Riepen and Benton connected again, as she was trying to figure out how to legally split from David Gude. According to Benton, things with her estranged husband were amicable, but Riepen suggested that manufacturing a record of ill will would expedite the legal proceedings.

Lacking an actual "indignity," Riepen staged one. He had Benton dial Gude and ask if he was interested in getting back together; Gude unloaded, counting the ways she had hurt him. "Most people are too busy socializing to read the law anymore, but indignities *can* occur by the phone, and that was the grounds we used to file," Riepen explains.

Benton got her divorce. But she and David didn't drift physically far from each other. In fact, shortly after Benton and Lyman married and moved up to Fort Hill, Gude settled in next door with his new love interest, Faith Franckenstein. The four of them would constitute the founding members of the Fort Hill Community, a number that would steadily rise. ("20 or more adults, 9 to 12 children, some cats, two houses, seven apartments, lots of cars, a badly battered Revolutionary War monument . . . and one of the loveliest views of the city," read the first *Globe* profile, the following year.) With a new wife and free of his musical duties in Jim Kweskin's Jug Band, Mel turned his attention to what he believed would be his great artistic medium: experimental films.

Lucky for Mel, he had briefly roomed with one of the titans of the form: Jonas Mekas. A Lithuanian immigrant, Mekas had helped publish an anti-German newsletter back home. After his typewriter disappeared from its hiding place inside a stack of firewood, he fled to the United States, and within weeks of arriving, he and his brother Adolfas rented a Bolex 8mm camera. In 1964, he established the Film-Makers' Cinematheque, a peripatetic Manhattan institution that built its fan base and notoriety with artists like Stan Brakhage, Jack Smith, and Andy Warhol.

Ronna Page, who acted in Warhol's *Chelsea Girls* and later joined the Fort Hill Community, introduced Mekas to Mel Lyman. They met at her favorite hangout in Manhattan: the Paradox Restaurant, New York City's first macrobiotic eatery, where you could sit and watch Yoko Ono and others climb into a bag as conceptual art. When he learned that Lyman needed a place to stay, Mekas put him up for a few weeks. ("I'm not one of those people that asks too many questions about where you've come from," Mekas says.) During that time, Lyman saw how Mekas was always filming something, often with no expressed purpose or endgame.

"You just do it!" Mekas told Lyman, who was worried that filmmaking was too complicated. "That opened their eyes to possibilities," he says. "They got a camera and started fooling around." Fort Hill Community member George Peper felt inspired by the burgeoning DIY genre as well, and itched to start a Boston offshoot of the Cinematheque. "I will help with films, and suggest programming, but you do everything else," the busy Mekas told Peper. "It's your baby."

At the precise time Peper was searching for a way to open a Boston Cinematheque, he picked up a skinny hitchhiker in Cambridge named David Hahn. A twenty-two-year-old MIT dropout just back from a business venture in Honduras, Hahn wanted to construct an experimental light show to see what happened when the mind is overloaded with stimuli—a vision that fit with Peper's. They scouted locations, landing on the Magna building at 53 Berkeley Street in the South End, most recently home to a coffeehouse called the Moondial. It seemed perfect, but the lease was much more than they could afford. Jessie Benton knew someone from back home, now in Boston to attend Harvard, who might be able to help. She called Ray Riepen with some exciting news: Warhol and Mekas wanted to do a Boston division of the Film-Makers' Cinematheque. According to Benton, the two notorious filmmakers had a location, but they couldn't tie it up just yet. Would Ray help them secure the property?

After five years practicing law in Kansas City, Riepen had just come to Harvard for a master's degree, living in Somerville. "She told me the Ford Foundation was backing the Film-Makers' Cinematheque, and they were about to make a decision to come to Boston," he recalls. Therefore, Riepen's monetary investment would be temporary, but he'd be permanently connected to something *très chic*. He picked up a shirt off the floor, put on one of his three-piece suits, and drove without a license down to 53 Berkeley Street to check the place out. Riepen walked around the building with George Peper and Hahn. To this day you'll hear people involved with the Boston Tea Party, Riepen included, identify the place as a former synagogue, due to the prominent Star of David–shaped window. This is incorrect; the building was constructed in the early 1870s as a Unitarian Meeting House, and the stellar glass likely symbolizes the unity of all religions. Up a steep flight of stairs, inside the main room, was an altar/stage, behind which was a phrase written in the shape of a rainbow on the wall: "PRAISE YE THE LORD."

For reasons he still doesn't fully understand, Riepen put up his own money to secure the lease. Two weeks later, Benton called Riepen with some bad news. The grant money had fallen through. (Mekas recalls the Ford Foundation grant in question, but doesn't believe it was ever slated for anything in Boston. Jessie Benton doesn't recall the grant at all.) Riepen now held the lease to an "abandoned synagogue." This was not an ideal situation for a frugal man from Kansas City, attending grad school without a current source of income. After meeting Peper's new hitchhiker friend, he felt he had found someone he could work with; Riepen made David Hahn a co-owner of the operation. There were rumors that Hahn had driven up from Honduras with a trunk of gold bricks he had "acquired" in South America, but regardless of what his actual source of disposable income was, Hahn was able to make up the other half of the money needed to keep the Tea Party's doors open.

Under Fort Hill guidance, the Boston Cinematheque was ready to roll, but Riepen knew ticket sales to kooky flicks wouldn't cover costs, especially if Warhol wasn't actually involved. Riepen thought he could "give some dances" to help pay the rent, and Benton came up with the idea of opening a store as well. The Fort Hill contingent went to work, opening a shop on the second floor called Moon in Leo that dispensed "hodgepodge hippie" wares. Eben Given hand-painted names of FHC heroes on the wall next to the street-level staircase. Visitors passing names like Prometheus, Edison, and Lao Tzu must have wondered what exactly they were walking into.

Riepen came up with the club's name while sitting at Jim Kweskin's kitchen table ("Tea is code for 'dope,'" he points out), then aww-shucksed his way through the straitlaced city's entertainment licensing process. "I just want to give a dance or two for the kids on the weekends," he'd tell the person behind every desk with a manufactured air of naivete. He pretended to stumble through the process, and made under-the-table payments when required. ("Everybody in Boston was on the take," Riepen claims.) In the coming years, Riepen tried to mark these payments down on his tax returns. "You can't put $78,000 a year down for 'police payoffs,'" his accountant said, aghast. "You'll end up in the trunk of your car!"

AT FIRST, the schedule was fairly simple: The Fort Hill Community would screen films at the Cinematheque all week long, then turn the reins over to the Tea Party for the weekend.

Lyman immediately started making soundtracks for some of the silent pictures and adding live-action flourishes to others, such as when the Fort Hill gang sat at a table and ate a full meal while Warhol's *Harlot* played behind them, to the director's delight. Despite being the connection that made the Cinematheque possible, Jessie Benton went to only one screening, whereupon she watched a long close-up of a vagina for twenty minutes before deciding these films weren't for her.

In the first *Globe* story on the venue, the entire endeavor is presented as the work of the Fort Hill Community; Riepen's name isn't even mentioned. "The wedding of the Cinemateque [*sic*] and the Boston Tea Party was almost a happenstance thing. But the people involved in the two projects, imbued as they were with astrological astuteness and a sensitivity to the cosmic forces of the stars, are not surprised." This version of the story wouldn't last long. Within a few months, Riepen would dominate every Tea Party story, and the Cinematheque would fade out of the picture completely. But in those early days, Ray and the FHC were unlikely collaborators; he recalled occasionally visiting Fort Ave. Terrace to see what life was like up there. "That was not my scene," he says. "Mel Lyman would organize his group by giving them acid at dinner and then taking them up in the attic and telling them how much he loved them. He did that with a lot of people, and a lot of people who were fairly bright stayed with him. I was very paranoid about it. I practically took my own taster to dinner there."

When an interviewer asked Lyman why the Cinematheque closed, he claimed it was because the Tea Party contingent was "out to make money. We'd like to make money too, but we don't want to stop doing what we love to do, we don't put that first." He then revealed what was really taking up most of Fort Hill's time: an underground newspaper that had just published its first issue, under the name *Avatar*.

On January 20, 1967, the Boston Tea Party held its first rock 'n' roll concert—or, as Riepen had presented it to city officials, "a dance for the kids." Local legends the Lost, on the verge of splintering into three different Bosstown Sound units, were the triumphant headliners. For *Rolling Stone*, it was "without a doubt the most important date in Boston Rock and Roll history."

David Hahn had hired all manner of local freaks and geeks to produce a psychedelic atmosphere inside. Scott Bradner, who worked at Harvard, came across an old sensory deprivation chamber on campus—a giant hemisphere that would enclose a human from the waist up. He "borrowed" it and built the venue's all-important strobe light inside. The strobe, in combination with overhead projectors and color organs, transformed the Tea Party from a cavernous church room into a disorienting, hallucinogenic playground. One visual technician at the club recalled how attendees would come in and say, "Turn on the strobes!," then "whirl around and fall on the floor. This was a safe place to temporarily lose your mind; the city had never seen anything like it."

The Boston Tea Party's concert room had an otherworldly ambience, according to the employees, musicians, and audience members who were there. By all accounts, it was a space where people from all walks of life could mix without tension. According to Fred Griffeth of the Bagatelle, "At that time if you went to South Boston, you could get your ass kicked. But people were getting together at the Tea Party from all over the city. I *never* saw a fight there. MIT students were becoming friends with members of biker gangs. Even with my pessimism, I was saying, 'Wow, maybe, maybe, maybe people can get along.' I thought it was the future."

Press coverage was generous and steady. "Harvardians, hippies, cyclists, stray sailors, tuned-up insurance company drones all gyrate with the bliss of children," the *Globe* drooled. By the time city officials realized that Riepen was doing a lot more than throwing weekend dances "for the kids," it was too late: The club was a phenomenon. Riepen now wondered how he might make some real money off the place. With the hefty rent and his partner David Hahn taking home half the profits, he wasn't exactly raking it in. A few months into 1968, Riepen bought out Hahn and became the sole owner of the Boston Tea Party.

"The last time I saw David was on top of Fort Hill," George Peper says. "After we talked, he ran back down toward his house but turned back to me and said, 'Tell everyone that I love them so much.'" Hahn returned to Honduras. In 1976, he dove under his ship, the *Olive Oyl*, had a heart attack, and never resurfaced.

VAN MORRISON FIRST appeared on the Tea Party stage during a Hallucinations set. In late May 1968, Peter Wolf's band opened for John Lee Hooker three nights in a row. On the third night, Wolf invited his new friend to sing with the band. "We'd been doing 'Gloria' for some time, even before it was a popular thing to do," Wolf explained in 1973. When an inebriated Morrison joined the Hallucinations to perform the song he wrote, the audience was aghast. "Up comes Van Morrison doing this whole crazed show, talking Japanese for thirty-five minutes into the microphone," Wolf said. He recalled an unintentional mash-up, Morrison singing "Mean Ole' World" as the Hallucinations played "Gloria." Wolf admonished the confused audience: "Don't you know who this man is? He wrote the song!"

Later that night, Tea Party manager Steve Nelson drove Wolf, Morrison, and Hooker home in the club's VW Bus. The trio had a lot to talk about, but between the booze and the accents, Nelson couldn't make out a single word.

Getting drunk rock stars home safely was one of Nelson's easier Tea Party tasks; keeping the police and licensing commission from shutting the club down turned out to be far more laborious. For the opening weekend of 1968, the Harvard Law School grad had booked a strong bill of locals, and word of mouth helped make the Saturday crowd double the previous night's. As five hundred people danced and zoned out to the sounds of Cloud, the house lights came on.

It was a raid. The band petered out as Dapper O'Neil—a loudmouthed, old-school conservative who was on the city's licensing board—came jogging up the stairwell to the second-floor stage, a dozen police officers in tow, certain that he'd find drugs everywhere. Nelson watched them fan out to search the premises. A police detail was already at every show, so the clientele "sort of knew to come to the shows high." The underground press helpfully prescribed such etiquette. "Nobody minds you going zonked," *Broadside of Boston* advised, "but leave the stuff at home. If one person gets busted, the place is closed. Licenses don't grow in fields."

Dapper O'Neil made his way to the balcony and cast his eyes upon a floor littered with empty plastic casings. The Devil's Disciples, a motorcycle gang, liked to watch the action from up here, inhaling amyl nitrate poppers for quick head rushes. But now all that remained was the packaging. He had brought a *Boston Herald Traveler* reporter along for the big drug bust—now what? Dapper stormed back downstairs and grilled Nelson. Did he have a valid license to operate? Nelson produced it. In desperation, Dapper spun around and saw a frightened young woman working the soda pop station.

He walked slowly toward her. "How 'bout the pop?" he barked.

Later that week, Dapper O'Neil hauled Riepen and Nelson into court for the one thing he found amiss at the Boston Tea Party: an expired soft drink license. "Your honor," Riepen explained to the judge, doing his hayseed routine, "we're just trying to keep kids off the streets of Boston, is all. Give 'em something to do!"

Riepen, in one of his signature three-piece suits, was right at home, walking back and forth in front of the judge, putting on a performance of blissful innocence. "Now, if I knew there was a problem with our soft drink license, you know I would've corrected it right away. This is merely an oversight and by no means a sign of managerial ineptitude." Then, with the professional timing of an old vaudeville routine, Riepen and Nelson recounted the overblown raid on the club in vivid detail.

The judge forced a furious Dapper to apologize to Riepen and Nelson, right there in the courtroom. His florid face turned even redder. "SODA POP RAID FIZZLES," blared the next day's *Boston Herald Traveler*.

Dapper kept looking for ways to get the club in trouble, even harassing the Tea Party for plastering the city with flyers that featured the word "psychedelic." But for the most part, Nelson and Riepen made sure there was nothing to complain about. One occasion in late 1968 deserves a note: When Fleetwood Mac played past the city's curfew, policemen walked onstage and unplugged their amps. Two kids in the crowd, Tom Hamilton and Joe Perry—soon to start a band called Aerosmith—watched in horror as the "kick-ass" set was cut short.

JONATHAN RICHMAN GREW UP in the suburb of Natick, but whenever his father wasn't using the family car for his job as a traveling salesman, Richman would flee his neighborhood to soak up the sounds of the city. "When I was sixteen," he said, "I heard the music of the Velvet Underground and everything changed for me." One spring afternoon in 1967, while loitering in Harvard Square, he saw someone walking down the street that he recognized from photographs.

"Excuse me, are you Lou Reed?" Richman asked.

"Yeah," answered Reed, taken aback. Richman looked like he could have been one of the Li'l Rascals. This was not the kind of person Reed would have suspected to be a fan of his decadent art-rock band named after a book about sexual fetishes.

"I heard your record," Richman said, "and I love the sound you get."

"Really?" asked Reed.

"Yeah, for example, the way you use the guitars like they were drums," Richman explained.

"Wait a minute," Reed said. "Are you saying we use rhythm guitar tracks as percussion instruments?" He was beaming. "That's what we do! *You* heard that?"

The next day, as he had done in the past, Richman showed up at the Boston Tea Party at four p.m. with a hand-painted poster commemorating that night's show. He offered to give the poster to the club if he could slip in early and bypass the age restrictions. Inside, members of his favorite band seemed to already know who he was.

"They grasped how seriously I took the music," Richman later explained. "It was life-or-death serious. It still is for me. If music isn't life-or-death serious, I don't wanna do it. I wasn't a musician yet. The Velvet Underground made me a musician."

Today, Richman is a beloved singer-songwriter with a singularly eccentric point of view and disarming delivery. Unlike nonnative sons like Morrison and Reed, he's composed countless odes to Boston and New England, beginning with his masterpiece, "Roadrunner." It's a gleeful, proto-punk classic—the only rock song that Johnny Rotten claimed not to hate. It's also a gloriously goofy reinterpretation of VU's epic "Sister Ray," a song that was released right as the teenage Richman was getting to know the band.*

A few weeks after Richman met Lou Reed, his father returned home from work with an unsold bingo prize for his son: a junky $10 guitar.

SOON AFTER ITS INCEPTION, the Boston Tea Party had to compete with imitators. Over in a factory space in Brighton Center, a student named Ken Keyes launched a venue called the Crosstown Bus with a series of summer concerts culminating with an appearance by the Doors in August 1967. At the time of booking, the band was on the rise; as showtime neared, "Light My Fire" was already a giant radio hit.

Riepen wondered if the Tea Party was doomed to be swallowed up by competitors. He had an idea. If he could persuade Andy Warhol to turn the Tea Party's weekend of Velvet Underground concerts into a movie starring the audience, that would be a bigger splash than Jim Morrison and company headlining at Crosstown Bus. He called Warhol and said, "Listen, you son

---

* In *Vibrations*, a local *Crawdaddy* knockoff, Richman published a rambling love letter to the group titled "New York Art and the Velvet Underground," complete with a hand-drawn graph whose y-axis spans "Death" to "God," and which charts VU's progress against groups like the Rolling Stones and Jimi Hendrix. Only the Beatles beat the Velvets in the upward crest toward godhead.

of a bitch, I'm the guy that's keeping the Velvet Underground alive here, and you've got to do me a favor and play like you're shooting a movie." Curiously, Warhol agreed, though time lines place this weekend *after* the Velvet Underground fired him as manager. Riepen reportedly told the artist he didn't even care if the camera was empty. The *notion* of shooting a movie would suffice.

"You are the star. You are what's happening. Be a part of Boston's first authentic underground movie," read the flyer touting Warhol's name. For plugged-in members of Boston's counterculture, suddenly a very difficult choice had to be made on August 11, 1967. According to Riepen, Crosstown Bus associates drove by the Boston Tea Party to revel in their victory, only to find "a line of women from Dedham in Pucci dresses three blocks long standing in the rain trying to get in Andy Warhol's next movie," as Riepen put it. Shortly after the Doors left town, Crosstown Bus stalled for good.*

OVER THE COURSE OF 1968, the Velvet Underground played the Boston Tea Party fifteen times. They kicked things off in January with the release of their second album, recorded in two days: the raucous, Nico-less, Warhol-free *White Light/White Heat*. On the back cover, in stark black and white, the band poses in front of the Boston Tea Party.

Riepen booked them happily and frequently, though he still thinks they were "a joke." In his memory, every junkie in Boston would show up to their shows because of the song "Heroin," and Reed "would always please

---

* For decades, it seemed that Warhol might have taken Riepen's advice and skipped loading film into the camera, as no movie starring the Velvet Underground and a sold-out Boston Tea Party audience was ever released. Riepen vaguely remembers Warhol intending to use the footage for a larger project called *American Revolution*. Then, in 2009, the Andy Warhol Museum located the film canisters in its archives. The thirty-three-minute, 16mm *The Velvet Underground in Boston* is disjointed, full of illogical cuts and zooms, and the band sounds muffled. Still, it's one of the only two pieces of film of the Velvet Underground during their original run performing live with sync-sound, and the only one in color.

the crowd by singing it." Reed was singing from experience, but the song had no connection to any current fix. According to a 1971 interview, he had tried the drug in his Syracuse University days, contracting hepatitis the very first time he shot up. This certainly didn't mean he stopped using other substances. By the time VU started routinely playing in Boston, amphetamines were the chemical of choice for Reed and one or two others in the band. "In the 20th century, in a technological age living in the city, there are certain drugs you have to take just to keep yourself normal like a caveman, just to bring yourself up or down," Reed would later tell his most perceptive critic, Lester Bangs. "They don't getcha high even, they just getcha normal."

"JONATHAN, CAN YOU MAKE this curve with your ring finger?" VU guitarist Sterling Morrison asked Jonathan Richman.

Richman had brought his bingo-prize guitar to the Tea Party and lingered in a corner of the dressing room until members of the band offered him something in the way of lessons. "They physically taught me how to play," he recounted. "That's where I got *everything*."

The band eventually took to their sixteen-year-old mascot. "Occasionally, I drove them around in my father's car," Richman recalled. "I would go to some of the parties they'd go to. I was part of this crew." Another member of the crew, Robert Somma, reported that at a certain point Richman even talked like Reed. "His friendship with the band was genuine," he says. "But here was this kid from Natick, suddenly speaking with a Long Island accent. I think Lou *barely* tolerated that, but was also kind of flattered." Richman would later pen a mea culpa with his 2010 song "My Affected Accent."

If the Velvets were busy, Richman would wander through Cambridge and sometimes pick up an issue of *Avatar*. ("I wasn't sure I understood all of it but could see they admired this Mel fellow," he says.) Meanwhile, another young Velvet Underground fanatic was also reading *Avatar*, and he felt he understood *everything* it published, especially the Mel-centric pages. Wayne McGuire had been arrested and convicted for selling the paper in November 1967. For his loyalty, Lyman invited him and other salesmen to Fort Hill for a celebratory dinner, and McGuire dedicated himself to turning the population of Boston on to his guru's brilliance. Once the Velvets started frequenting the Tea Party, the band got rolled onto McGuire's hero roster, leading to his *Crawdaddy* essay "The Boston Sound," easily the most intense endorsement of the Velvets to be published during their career. "NOW IS THE TIME FOR DISTORTIONS TO BURN," McGuire screams via typewriter, "with flaming sword in hand I will clear away those ugly growths which parade as insightful musical criticism. . . . This is a review of the Velvet Underground, this is a review of the end of the world."

For all his raving, McGuire audaciously predicted their future fame as one of the "primary myth-makers of our generation," and pinpointed the hard-to-explain dynamics of their trademark drone, in full display on *White Light/White Heat*. The drone, McGuire wrote, "has two levels, high-pitched and low-pitched (corresponding to the drones of the central nervous systems), which are produced by two very heavy nervous systems belonging to Lou Reed and John Cale respectively. The drone is not always heard but rather felt as pure essence and perpetual presence."* In the same breath, McGuire trashed MGM's Boston Sound campaign, and suggested a direct connection between the Velvet Underground and Mel Lyman. They are "merely vessels through which greater forces are working and they listen attentively." In that moment before Reed became a legend and Lyman faded

---

* This jibed with Richman's description of the band's live act. "Your eyes would go from one person to the other and you'd say, 'Who's making that particular sound?'" Richman recalled in a 2013 radio interview. "You'd hear this harmonic tone in the background. No one was betraying it by their facial expression, they were all just blandly playing their instrument. But there's this fifth ghost tone coming from somewhere. All these strange ghost tones."

into obscurity, they revealed to McGuire the two paths open to an artist in Boston 1968.*

McGuire's most groundbreaking insight into the Velvet Underground was that Reed's lyrics were about something more than surface-level depravities. "All this time you probably thought the Velvet Underground was talking about drugs, homosexuality, and sadomasochism," McGuire wrote. "Look a bit closer. 'Sister Ray' is not about shooting meth, fellatio or murder. Rather, it is describing the greatest cosmic upheaval in the history of man and you are living in the midst of it."

ROB NORRIS HAD MOVED TO BOSTON in March 1968, straight out of high school—incredibly, because MGM's Boston Sound campaign had convinced him the city was going to be the next San Francisco. For $80 a month, he split a place on Mission Hill with some roommates. "I didn't really have to work," he says. "I just basically lived at the Tea Party."

Norris met Lou Reed backstage at the Tea Party in 1968. The singer was scooping a sawdust-like substance out of a jar and into his mouth. They were the only two people in the back room. Reed stared at Norris before asking him if he was on amphetamines. Norris said no. Reed explained that the jar was full of wheat germ, which he gulped before shows, then subjected the young fan to an antidrug rant. Norris mentioned that he had been

---

* In 1976, Peter Laughner paired the two together in his *Creem* review of the first Modern Lovers album. "Jonathan Richman is nothing if not a Lou Reed protégé," he wrote. "[A]pparently when the Velvets were sequestered in Boston's student ghetto in late '68, Jonathan found his guru in Lou. At least it wasn't Mel Lyman." It's possible that Reed and Lyman met; according to the Fort Hill Community, the Velvet Underground sometimes spent the night in a Fort Ave. Terrace house after a Tea Party show. On one such occassion, when Nico simply helped herself to someone's bed, the German singer was bluntly instructed to find somewhere else to catch some sleep. Personnel from the band and a Fort Hill Community member had certainly crossed paths at least once before; Faith Gude and VU's whip dancer Gerard Malanga had a brief affair in the early sixties. Malanga even wrote a poem about the unlikely free-speech champion, entitled, simply, "Faith Franckenstein."

in the audience at Summit High School in New Jersey three years prior, witness to the first Velvet Underground concert. Reed smiled, then happily introduced Norris to the rest of the band in the other room: *"He was there!"*

As part of the VU's backstage club, Norris was shocked by how much astrology and the occult dominated the conversation. He recalls the janitor/ de facto backstage manager at the Tea Party, a mystic, statuesque presence named Mitch Blake, as being the resident expert. The campus stud at the University of New Hampshire, Blake underwent a transformation while working on a farm in New Hampshire, "growing vegetables with prayer and working with a nature spirit." "He and Lou became friends because of this interest in mysticism and astrology," Norris says. "Lou was *really* into it. He was talking about kinds of healing that could be done with rays and levitation. He was very into healing, and he was very emphatic that 'White Light/White Heat' could be taken two different ways." Blake concurs that, around this time, one of Reed's chief artistic concerns was that his audience didn't understand his lyrics at all.

This blew Norris's mind. If there was ever an obvious song about the thrills of an amphetamine rush, it was the album's rollicking title track. Yet Reed explained to Norris and Blake one night that, while it definitely painted a scene of drugs and excess, it was also about enlightenment, Christian purity, and the healing power of "white light," which Reed had discovered in a book called *A Treatise on White Magic*. The author, Alice Bailey, was a New Age pioneer who wrote twenty-seven books on esoteric subjects before her death in 1949—or rather, she claimed to transcribe the dictation of a Tibetan spirit, Djwal Khul. Of the many occult ideas found in her writing, Reed gravitated to her theory of the Seven Rays of Energy. Seven forms of an intangible power were beaming down to Earth, Bailey wrote; which ray a human locked on to would determine much about their personality and future. It's not hard to imagine Reed studying Bailey, transforming "Second Ray" to "Sister Ray." Norris theorizes that another song off the second album, "I Heard Her Call My Name," might even be about

Reed's intense attraction to Bailey's work. ("I know that she's long dead and gone . . . I heard her call my name.")

"You will relax your physical body, endeavor to quiet your astral body as far as may be, and to steady the mind," Bailey wrote in *A Treatise on White Magic*. "Call down a stream of pure white light, and, pouring it through your lower vehicles, you will cleanse away all that hinders."

Reed was unusually forthcoming about this side of his interests in a 1969 radio interview:

> When I was in L.A. I saw a reverend who reads your aura and tells you your previous incarnations and removes entities from you. I had an entity that had to be removed. [. . .] I've been involved and interested in what they call *white light* for a long time. A woman named Alice Bailey who has some rather remarkable books out, she was a telepathic secretary. It's kind of an incredible book, *A Treatise on White Magic*. [. . .] It tells you how to go out and do it all.

At the time, Reed was fond of passing along the *Treatise* to people he felt were ready. Recipients include Billy Name (denizen of Warhol's Factory, who designed the blacker-than-black cover of *White Light/White Heat*) and superfan Jonathan Richman. "One of my big mistakes was turning him on to Alice Bailey, that's where that insect song comes from," Reed told *Spin* in 1986. "I said, 'Do you know, Jonathan, that insects are a manifestation of negative ego thoughts? That's on page 114.' So he got that. That's a dangerous set of books."* Richman's consumption of *White Magic* helps explain what a song called "Astral Plane" is doing on his 1976 debut, *The Modern Lovers*. In an album largely about girl troubles and lovingly name-checking

---

* Both Reed and Richman would write about insects from the Bailey perspective, Reed with "Ocean" in late '68 or early '69 ("Insects are evil thoughts, thought of by selfish men / It nearly drives me crazy") and Richman in '76 with "Hey There Little Insect," with the childlike request ("Don't scare me so / Don't land on me, and bite me, no").

Boston locales, "Astral Plane" sticks out. "But I'll prove my knowledge of what's inside," Richman sang, "when I intercept you on the astral plane." As bassist Ernie Brooks told *Vice*:

> Jonathan was a big fan of Van Morrison's album *Astral Weeks*—that's such a beautiful record. I wasn't sure if Jonathan was actually able to do that, enter a girl's dream—but he really believed in it, which is where that song, "Astral Plane," came from—the idea that you can communicate in another dimension with someone who's hard to reach in everyday life.
>
> He'd call me in the middle of the night, saying, about a girl we both knew, "Ernie, I think I entered her dream. Do you think that's right?"
>
> And I'd say, "Well, Jonathan, I guess it's OK, I dunno . . ."

Eventually, Van Morrison *also* found his way to Alice Bailey. Certainly, with an album called *Astral Weeks*, there's a chance that Morrison encountered her writings while in Boston,* but concrete references to Bailey's work didn't show up in Morrison's songs until the 1980s. "I'm a dweller on the threshold . . . Watch the great illusion drown," Morrison sang in 1982, initiating a three-album, three-year stretch in which he explicitly cited Bailey's teachings. *Beautiful Vision* even opens with its own "Ray" song, "Celtic Ray." The liner notes for 1984's *Inarticulate Speech of the Heart* mention Bailey's book *Glamour: A World Problem*. The "illusion" Morrison sings about in "Dweller on the Threshold" is what Bailey referred to as Glamour—a mirage of fear, ignorance, and greed that traps the unenlightened. "I've read *Glamour* four or five times," Morrison explained in 1982, "and I get different things out of it each time."

---

* Morrison would later cryptically remark to a journalist that during his Boston residency he visited an astrologer who passed along information that had stuck with him, even years later.

Morrison biographer Clinton Heylin claims Morrison's early songwriting was, in part, "a determined study of childhood visions." As a boy, Morrison's solitary hours were filled with deep, intense daydreams and even instances he would later classify as astral projection. "Every now and then these experiences happen," he said in 1972. "I'll be lying down on the bed with my eyes closed and all of a sudden I get the feeling that I'm floating near the ceiling looking down." Then, in 1977, "I had some amazing projections when I was a kid . . . you can have some amazing hallucinogenic experiences doing nothing but looking out your window."

Morrison would later reflect that no one had been around to unpack these visions, and that songwriting had become a way to share these moments with others. Musician Clive Culbertson remarked that Morrison was a "walking library" of information about ritual magic, and writer Steve Turner reported that it wasn't unusual for a casual dinner with the singer to open with a question like "What do you think about the blood of Jesus?" By the 1990s, Morrison had pulled out of the mystic, though maybe not by choice. When a friend brought up their old Bailey fixation, Morrison sadly replied, "I haven't got anybody to talk about that stuff anymore. Musicians don't know about that."

There's no account of Reed and Morrison ever being close, or bonding over Alice Bailey, in 1968 or beyond, save for an aside at a shambolic 1996 gig at New York's Supper Club. Morrison wasn't connecting with the crowd; for over half an hour, he staved off requests for old songs, arguing with an audience member over whether he was a genius. Then, according to an *MTV News* story entitled "Van Morrison Guided by Voices?," he mentioned unwanted visitations, and advice from someone who'd been through it as well:

> I said, "Lou, all this stuff is going on . . . all these noises, voices in my head all the time." So he gave me . . . the real rap. . . . He says, "You know what? When you hear the voices, ya just say

that's not me. . . . Just step back and say, 'That's not really me . . .
that's somebody else!'"

The Velvet Underground's debut as a four-piece rock band was a long time
coming. Reed seemed hell-bent on cleaning house, and members' final performances with the band always seemed to happen in Boston. Nico and
John Cale played their final sets with the Velvets at the Tea Party in 1967
and 1968, respectively. Nico knew something was wrong when she showed
up characteristically late and tried to walk onstage near the end of the set;
Reed wouldn't let her. The connection between the Velvets and Andy Warhol, the man who had given the band their initial notoriety, was severed in
the summer of 1967 with the help of lawyers. "I'd never seen Andy angry,
but I did that day," Lou Reed told David Fricke in 1989.

Despite the group's lack of commercial success, several parties vied for
the manager position. In the end, they chose a sketchy young man named
Steve Sesnick, who promised that popularity was just around the bend. Sesnick was from New York, but he was constantly visiting the Tea Party, trying to insert himself into the club's success. (Later he'd falsely claim to be
part owner.) Sesnick so aggressively starved New York from the live VU
experience that their old New York audience started showing up at the Tea
Party. "You could tell," Steve Nelson says. "The Boston crowd would look
all scruffy and messy and then suddenly these hip people wearing furs and
silks would walk in."

Cale was the last to be excised, on September 28, 1968. Sterling Morrison pinned the dismissal on Reed's jealousy; Cale blamed Sesnick's divisive
nature and Reed's longing to push the band toward a more mainstream
sound. (The violist-bassist had recently talked about placing their guitar
amps underwater for the next album.) With previously booked shows only
a few weeks away, the search for a replacement began immediately.

Doug Yule grew up in Great Neck, New York, but came to Massachusetts to attend Boston University in 1965. He began playing in cover bands

soon after arriving, and in 1967 he joined the Grass Menagerie alongside Walter Powers and Willie Alexander, two Lost refugees. Menagerie's manager found him an apartment on River Street in Cambridge, where Velvets Morrison and Reed occasionally crashed after playing the Tea Party. None of the band knew him well, and only Morrison had heard him play guitar before, but upon Sesnick's recommendation, Yule replaced Cale without an audition in the fall of 1968. With so little time before the next set of VU tour dates, there was no room for an exhaustive search.

Just as important, perhaps, Reed was pleased that the astrological balance of his band would be preserved: Yule was a Pisces, as was Cale. In addition to being astrologically compatible, Yule and Reed actually looked quite a bit like each other. Reed messed with audiences by introducing Yule as his brother. He also turned over lead vocal performances to Yule on some new songs, especially on recordings, to overcome the limitations of his own voice and utilize the sweetness of Yule's delivery. For later generations of Velvet Underground fans, it comes as a shock to discover that some of the great songs on the self-titled fourth LP and the swan song *Loaded* feature Yule's voice, not Reed's.

Though primarily a guitarist, Yule agreed to play bass. Less than twenty-four hours after accepting the job, he was in New York staying up all night with Reed, learning thirty VU songs. "I thought it was really interesting that the first song they performed was 'Heroin,'" Steve Nelson said of VU's December 1968 shows, their first post-Cale dates in Boston. "They were sort of saying, 'We're still the Velvet Underground, take this, go fuck yourself.' It was great. Crowd still loved it."

MOST NIGHTS AT THE TEA PARTY ended with a large pile of money on the office desk, but Ray Riepen wasn't taking all that much home after expenses. Desperate to turn an otherwise total success into a profitable business, Riepen hired an ambitious BU student named Don Law to replace

Steve Nelson as manager in the summer of 1968. Law seemed to be full of ideas how to expand the business. "That first night he came in wearing beige chino pants and a powder blue button-down collar shirt," employee Betsy Polatin says, recalling the staff's initial suspicion that Riepen had ruined things by hiring a square. But Law genuinely loved rock 'n' roll, and under his direction, UK acts from Jeff Beck to Led Zeppelin came to play the club. These groups couldn't yet pack stadiums stateside, but the creation of midsize ballrooms in Boston, New York, and San Francisco made it feasible for them to cross the ocean for a visit.

Van Morrison could technically be considered one of these UK imports, save for the fact that he could walk from his apartment to the Tea Party. At the first Van Morrison Controversy show that Law booked there, the building almost burned to the ground.

"I'm on the floor and all of a sudden I look up as Van Morrison is singing, and there are *flames* coming through the fan above his head," Law says. He and Mitch Blake grabbed fire extinguishers and raced up the stairs that led to the roof ladder. Morrison, who clearly noticed the blaze, had the presence of mind to keep singing—a song, no less, about climbing a ladder—and as the two men put out the fire, a cocktail of water, foam, and debris rained down on the band. After the concert, a stoned audience member approached Morrison and Law, making it clear they had mistaken the fire and its extinguishing as part of the light show.

JONATHAN RICHMAN FINALLY found the nerve to perform songs in front of other people later in 1968. "I knew I couldn't play or sing like the other guys," Richman recalled. "I figured I had a feeling and that was enough. I knew I was honest."

Sometimes Richman didn't even have a guitar, according to Willie Alexander, who saw an early performance at one of the free Sunday afternoon concerts on Cambridge Common. "He would just sing on top of him hitting his fuckin' baseball glove for percussion. People thought he was wonderful. I thought he was completely out to lunch. And that was a *good* thing."

Four years later, in 1972, Richman would record an album for Warner Brothers with his band, the Modern Lovers; John Cale produced most of the tracks. The result was a rock touchstone, with Jonathan's peculiar but sincere songs backed by a banging band: future Talking Head Jerry Harrison on keyboards, future Car David Robinson on drums, and future lawyer Ernie Brooks on bass. *The Modern Lovers* wouldn't see release until 1976, and in the intervening years, *something* made Richman swear off electric instruments and his dedication to glorious, droning Velvet-style noise—a dream or vision, à la Van Morrison.

"I don't think it was so much that he was getting tired of the old songs as he was developing this idea that the whole rock-'n'-roll-star-making machinery was corrupt," bandmate Ernie Brooks recalled. "And part of that was the whole system of burning fossil fuels to generate electricity, using a lot of power for amps and sound systems, playing stadiums—you know, feeling that there was something wrong in profiting from all these things—and he started tying it all together in his mind and decided that he didn't want the Modern Lovers to be a conventional rock 'n' roll band."

The combination of Jonathan's complete sincerity and the strange reasons he was doling out to explain the change made it hard to understand exactly what was happening. "The band has to learn volume and to play softer," Richman said in 1973, otherwise "infants wouldn't like us because we hurt their little ears, and I believe that any group that would hurt the ears of infants—and this is no joke—sucks." Even decades later, at a 2016 acoustic show at the Middle East club in Cambridge, Richman stopped the show midway through to inform the sound engineer that he could still hear a slight electric hum in the room, and could anything be done?

The first incarnation of the Modern Lovers did not survive Richman's transformation into a full-blown nature boy. Robinson, who would later co-found the Cars, recalled an "obsessed" Richman wanting to do shows on street corners and rest homes, asking that he "play a rolled-up newspaper by banging it against my fist."

EVEN IN THEIR HOME AWAY FROM HOME, some people simply hated the Velvet Underground. The *Globe* complained about their "headache-making and ear splitting" music, while *Boston After Dark* noted that they performed like "automatons with a fairly lackluster attack and endings that broke off like racing cars hitting a brick wall at full-tilt." Elsewhere, reviewers complained that they dressed sloppily in sweatpants, or expressed disbelief that their drummer was female.* But it wasn't just the overly dramatic Wayne McGuire spreading the gospel of the Velvets in Boston. The height of VU evangelism could be found in *Fusion*, a nationally distributed magazine published out of Boston. Its editor, Robert Somma—formerly of *Crawdaddy*—was one of the band's "pet" writers, and in April 1969 praised their third album as "technically perfect." He even recorded some voiceovers for radio spots promoting that very same record.

Somma socialized with the band whenever they performed in Boston, often joining them afterward at the Cambridge apartment of Ed Hood.† The star of Warhol's 1965 film *My Hustler*, Hood was a balding, intellectual, entertainingly bitchy man who was taking a stab at an English degree at

---

* "An honest-to-goodness chick playing percussion—do you believe it?" MIT's *The Tech* asked incredulously. Conversely, in late 1967, the *Boston Herald Traveler* ran a positive profile of Maureen Tucker with the headline "SHE GAVE UP COMPUTERS TO PLAY DRUMS IN BAND." "A regular 9-to-5 job was too confining," Tucker told reporter Laura White. "I felt mentally as well as physically captured by machines." At one VU Tea Party show in 1968, Tucker opened their set alone with a fifteen-minute drum solo. "She just commanded the stage," commented one witness. "She was really quite an impressive display."

† On the edge of Harvard Square, 4 University Road was a magnet for scenesters. Peter Wolf, *Avatar* writer Charles Giuliano, and *Astral Weeks* flutist John Payne all lived there. After a series of murders at the complex in the sixties—including one of the Boston Strangler deaths—it became known as "The Murder Building." Hood was found dead in the same apartment in 1982; the case was never solved.

Harvard. The gatherings contained the feeling of a transcendental salon—
"séances," Somma calls them. In Jonathan Richman's 1992 song about the
band, he sang, "Wild wild parties when they start to unwind / A close encounter of the thirdest kind." Over Chinese food, Reed would hold court and
rave about theosophist Alice Bailey; Hood would balance a cocktail on his
head and recite the opening of *Paradise Lost*. Doug Yule cryptically al-
luded to spending "a lot of time together in strange places and strange situ-
ations," and Sterling Morrison enjoyed repeating a story about encountering
a dwarf with a gun in Boston who threatened to kill him.

It would all come to an end, sort of, in 1970, when Lou Reed abandoned
the band he'd built, turning his back on the Velvet Underground and, for a
while, on music altogether. He was supposedly displeased with the direction in which Steve Sesnick wanted to take the band, and might have been
developing a new kind of competitive, unhealthy relationship with Yule as
well. After his departure, Reed, twenty-eight, moved back to Long Island
where he worked for his accountant father as a typist for $40 a week. One
night Reed showed up unannounced at Somma's Ipswich apartment to get
high and watch TV. As the stoned pair tuned in the film *Fantastic Voyage*—
a movie about scientists converted into miniatures and injected into a
body—Reed turned to Somma and gravely declared, "This is going to be
very disturbing."

Somma sensed Reed was going through a profoundly difficult time and
made attempts to keep his creative juices flowing. To encourage Reed, he
published some of his poems in *Fusion*. Like Morrison with his poem on the
back of *Astral Weeks*, Reed's direct references to Boston were limited to
verse, never finding their way into any of his VU or solo songs. "And in the
back pornography too / (distilled, that is, to Boston taste)," Reed wrote in a
piece about walking through the shops of Cambridge. In his *Fusion* poems
from 1971, you can track his struggle to keep it together after leaving the
band. In "We Are the People," the magical rules of Alice Bailey's White
Magic seem turned against him: "We are the insects of someone else's

thoughts, a casualty / of daytime, nighttime, space and god." Reed was no longer seeing his own negative thoughts as bugs; now he'd been demoted from god to pawn, a mere bug in some grander entity's vision. It would be two years before Reed took the stage again.

Today, Robert Somma's life couldn't be more distant from the rock journalist profession that brought him close to Lou Reed in the late sixties and early seventies—Somma is currently a bankruptcy attorney at a law firm in Boston; in 2004 President George W. Bush appointed him as a federal judge, a position he held for three years. From the conference room of his office suite, there's an incredible view of Boston, including the Fort Hill tower where he spent a harrowing afternoon in 1971; Somma was once detained and harassed by the Fort Hill Community after *Fusion* published a critical piece about the members' way of life. When the discussion turns to whatever happened to Mel Lyman, I mention that the FHC say he died in 1978. "If it came from them," Somma replies, "I'm not sure I'd believe it."

IN JULY 1969, Riepen and Law relocated the Boston Tea Party from Berkeley Street to a larger space across from Fenway Park on Lansdowne. The lack of PRAISE YE THE LORD above the stage wasn't the only difference; fans and musicians thought that the new locale simply didn't contain the magic atmosphere that made the original room so special. Bigger acts like T. Rex, the Byrds, Led Zeppelin, and the Kinks all performed there. Still, Riepen could see that his financial plan for the club wasn't panning out. In 1968, he had sold $300,000 in public stocks, figuring that Boston's status as the quintessential college town would keep renewing the club's audience. But according to the *Globe*, the 1970 student strike protesting the Vietnam War caused admissions to plunge, with the fiscal year ending in May showing a $40,000 loss. "The only people who made money out of this," one Tea Party stockholder grumbled, "are the rock musicians themselves."

The artists *were* demanding higher guarantees; it was impossible for the

Tea Party to go back to the smaller-scale bands it used to host on Berkeley Street. In its last months of operation, the club hosted everyone from Traffic to Little Richard, who brandished a pistol in the presence of Don Law after an impossibly energetic performance, demanding prompt payment be deposited into a glittering suitcase. On December 29, 1970, Sha Na Na headlined the Boston Tea Party's final show. "They say I was some eccentric lawyer with a seedy midwestern accent, a rube that all of these clever people used to get rich," Riepen says. "But let me tell you, there wasn't anybody that dreamed of any fucking thing like the Tea Party in Boston when I got there."

MANAGER STEVE SESNICK found no cause for the Velvet Underground to split just because Lou Reed was gone, and the rest of the members agreed at first. Then Sterling Morrison quit after a show in Houston, and Yule recruited Walter Powers and Willie Alexander, whom he'd left behind in the Grass Menagerie. Moe Tucker, the sole original Velvet, hung on through the early seventies. At a show in 1971, David Bowie excitedly talked to Doug Yule for fifteen minutes, only later learning it wasn't Lou.

Yule later said that the trouble all started with Sesnick. "I was like a kid thrown into the deep end of a pool and told to swim," he said. The manager took advantage of the fact that the members of VU had a habit of not talking things over among themselves, allowing him to divide and conquer. "I would be told by him that I was better than Lou and that the others were not really my friends," Yule said.

"You can't con someone unless they're greedy," Yule admitted, "and I was real greedy."

Willie Alexander, now in his seventies and living in Gloucester, shows me a "cheat sheet" scribbled with song titles—the total information he received hours before playing his first VU show. A chord progression ends with the directive "Watch Walter." A note at the bottom reads, in Yule's handwriting, "Fuck it/Fake it."

"That was what I had to go on," Alexander says. "Some people thought I was John Cale."

Thus the Velvet Underground transformed from a groundbreaking New York art-rock group into a better-than-average bar band from Boston. Like a ghost ship sailing through the club circuit, they burned off any excitement still attached to their name. Before Lou Reed resurrected the band in 1993, the Velvet Underground's final performance was at a ski lodge in Vermont, featuring no original members. The audience kept asking Yule to turn down the volume.

SIX

Scenes from the Real World

THE FIVE MEN, identically dressed in gray suits, straw Stetsons, and dark glasses, had never met before, but their actions had been planned in advance. In the basement of the Boston Mercantile Bank on Congress Street, two guards were transporting sacks of cash into the vault when the men sprang into action. Two of them stepped off the elevator, guns drawn, forcing customers to sit along the wall while the other three disarmed the guards. A woman in a business suit screamed. As more customers unwittingly stepped off the elevator and into the crime scene, one of the robbers shot a hostage in the ankle as a warning. The cart full of cash was wheeled toward the exit. As the mystery men left, one of them rolled a canister toward the huddled hostages. An enormous cloud of pink smoke filled the hallway.

Outside, a sixth man sat in a station wagon. One by one the five others left the bank, tossing two sacks each into the car, then dispersing. Across the street, on the tenth floor of an office building, the mastermind watched through binoculars. It was the largest heist in Boston since the 1950s Brink's robbery, and it had all gone off without a hitch.

· · ·

SCREENWRITER ALAN TRUSTMAN wasn't surprised. He had been planning it for more than twenty years.

Trustman was born in Brookline in 1930. At fifteen, he got a summer job at the First National Bank in downtown Boston, where he sorted checks all day and imagined pulling off the perfect heist. As an experiment in theft, he had a friend cash a $100 check, which he removed from his alphabetical sorting and shredded. Check cashed, Trustman returned the money and informed his bosses of the security hole. They knew such a scheme was possible, but decided it would cost far more to install preventive measures. They didn't fire him.

After graduating from Harvard Law School, Trustman was hired at Nutter McClennen & Fish, where his father was a partner. From his corner office, Alan could look down at the First National Bank of Boston. His heist fantasies returned with a vengeance. But instead of committing a felony, he turned his idea into a screenplay, pounding out *The Crown Caper* over the course of seven Sundays in 1967.

Without any connection to the movie business, he naively sent the result to Alfred Hitchcock. Amazingly, Hitchcock's assistant read it, liked it, and phoned Trustman. She explained that in order to get his script in front of a reputable director, he needed an agent. Trustman had his firm's best switchboard operator flood the lines at William Morris until an agent agreed to speak with him. The man who took him on, John Flaxman, was a fan of Norman Jewison's recent movie *The Russians Are Coming*. Flaxman met the director at the airport in New York before a trip, handed him Trustman's script, and told him to make a decision within ten minutes of landing in Los Angeles. Somewhere over the Midwest, Jewison knew that his next motion picture would be *The Thomas Crown Affair*.

Soon after, during scouting visits to Boston, Jewison learned just how close the title character was to its author. When Jewison suggested certain details of the heist were unbelievable, Trustman brought him to the actual bank and walked him through each robber's route. "He was incredulous that no one stopped us, asked us anything, or paid any attention to us. I looked like a bank employee, but Norman had a California tan, an expensive camel-hair, non-Boston coat and non-Boston sideburns well below his ears," Trustman says.

Jewison signed up, and Steve McQueen was keen to play the title role. He didn't strike the director as a natural fit: "The character wears suits, Steve." But since Jewison's last picture with the actor, McQueen had become the world's biggest box-office draw. McQueen, who had never worn a suit, even in a film, made an impassioned pitch and got the part.

Trustman balked; how could "this thug, this biker, this dead-end kid" play his Boston Brahmin thief? At Jewison's urging, Trustman screened McQueen's oeuvre, cataloging "everything he liked to do, everything he did not like to do, everything that made him comfortable, and everything where he looked stiff and frozen." He "McQueened" Crown's lines, capping each at six words, and added scenes where the character zoomed around in a dune buggy. McQueen loved it.

Thrilled by the prospect of a Steve McQueen picture being filmed in town, the mayor's office gave Jewison plenty of support. But this didn't guarantee a smooth shoot in public locales, as reported in a 1977 *Boston Magazine* article. For a scene on Beacon Hill, just as Jewison had called "Action!" a patrolman strolled into the shot and told the crew they couldn't film there.

"But we have permission from the mayor's office!" a production assistant insisted.

"You've got to go through district headquarters," the cop said, dumbfounding Jewison and the crew. To lose a day's shoot to get the official permit would set the production back $90,000. You don't have to read too hard between the lines of the story to grasp how things were resolved: "A production assistant and the officer took a stroll around the block. When they returned, production was resumed."

Throughout filming, cameras were concealed during public shoots, to capture more natural performances from the actors and background extras. When it was time to film the movie's climactic robbery, there were very few indicators a shoot was under way. "Our heisters scared a lot of customers and pedestrians who thought they were seeing a real robbery," Jewison told *The Boston Globe*, "but oddly no one tried to interfere. I think they were afraid of getting involved."

McQueen was playing a fictional version of Trustman, and there were times during production when the lines between the two men became blurred, even competitive. "I had recently bought a new suit, which I used to do every five years. It was a very nice suit. And I was wearing this suit on the set." Suddenly, Steve McQueen stormed off—a "tantrum" as Trustman described it—refusing to film his next scene. Norman Jewison quietly pulled Trustman off to the side and told him, "He says your suit is better than his. I think it would be helpful if you left." Trustman was in shock; McQueen didn't even like wearing suits.

After spending months turning Trustman's fantasy into a kind of reality, the production wrapped and the Hollywood filmmakers exited Boston. For the writer, it must have been like waking from a dream. There was no evidence left behind of the events that had just transpired—the heists, the famous endless kiss between McQueen and costar Faye Dunaway. Had any of it really happened? It was a question that arose again and again across 1968, as daydreams and brutal reality alike became fodder for the silver screen.

"BOSTON IS CELEBRATING a big bank robbery this week," the *Globe* reported on June 16. The all-day premiere gala kicked off with the presentation of "the Thomas Crown purse" to the winner of the sixth horse race at Suffolk Downs, followed by a party on a yacht, a cocktail reception at the New England Aquarium, and a parade downtown. McQueen arrived via helicopter. "Think of it," Norman Jewison told an interviewer, "a movie shot in Boston. Nobody ever shoots movies in Boston."

The film drew mixed reviews. Pauline Kael called it a "chic crappy movie." "Possibly the most under-plotted, underwritten, over-photographed film of the year," Roger Ebert declared. "Which is not to say it isn't great to look at." Made for $4.3 million, the film grossed $14 million, and Bostonians were delighted to see their city in a major Hollywood production. During the premiere, the crowd cheered and gasped as much for tense plot points as for cameos by local residents. Of course, many extras were annoyed by their absence from the finished product. "They cut off my face, but you can hear me all right," one insisted.

Trustman scored again with his script for *Bullitt*, also starring McQueen, later that year. But he didn't enjoy the celebrity (Boston papers covered his messy divorce), and keeping his on-screen avatar happy could get tricky; Trustman refused McQueen's order to write him a screenplay in which the main character was a "loser." His output devolved into B-movies. The phone stopped ringing. "Movies are commercially packaged dreams," Trustman would later write in *The Atlantic*, "and as long as people are packaging dreams, other people will pay the price to open the package and see the dream."

SOME DREAMS ARE NIGHTMARES. Another major motion picture emerging from the city that year grew not from a pleasant reverie but from a waking horror.

Between 1962 and 1964, thirteen women in the Greater Boston area were murdered in their homes, without any sign of forced entry. The papers attributed the crimes to the "Sunset Killer," the "Phantom Stranger," and the "Mad Strangler" before the simplest moniker won out: the Boston Strangler. Even after the media warned them never to open their doors to strangers, the murders continued. "HYSTERIA SOLVES NOTHING," one *Boston Herald* headline read, stirring up more hysteria. Landlords installed bigger, better locks. Some women acquired tear gas or guard dogs; others packed up and left town. And in a city where the Watch and Ward Society had primly banned suggestive entertainment for years, the crimes of a sexual deviant must have been particularly unsettling.

The murders were still happening when the first dramatization surfaced in 1964. Victor Bruno starred in *The Strangler*, whose title character *The New York Times* described as "a corpulent young man with a fetish for dolls and fingers that tingle toward the opposite sex." The film stoked the tangible aura of fear in Boston, floating wild guesses as to the type of sicko responsible.

Next up: the true-crime literary version. "My interest was not so much in writing a book about the Boston stranglings as it was to write about what happens to a great city when it is besieged by terror," author Gerold Frank wrote in the preface to 1966's *The Boston Strangler*. While accounts of real-life atrocities have always found readers, it's around this time that a subgenre emerged: the true-crime nonfiction novel, most often credited to Truman Capote's 1965 bestseller *In Cold Blood*. Right on its heels, though, was Frank's book, and its loose ends made for an even more chilling read. "If the reader is left feeling that there is more to be known, that the authorities are not quite satisfied," one review read, "it is only because such is the case."

Frank rooted his story in firsthand accounts and interrogation transcripts. By the second half of his investigation, there was a likely suspect in custody. Shortly after Chelsea, Massachusetts, native Albert DeSalvo confessed to being the one and only Boston Strangler, he signed a release granting Frank exclusive and perpetual rights to publish biographical material about him.

DeSalvo was born in 1931. His father beat everyone in the family and regularly brought home prostitutes, making no attempt to hide them from his children. Albert's early forays into shoplifting and animal torture led to reform school. Afterward, he joined the army, meeting his wife-to-be, Irmgard, in Germany before settling in Malden, Massachusetts. The couple had two children together, and he appeared to be a doting husband and father. But DeSalvo led a disturbing double life.

It started with the Measuring Man incidents. In this ruse, DeSalvo showed up unannounced, claiming to be "Johnson" from "The Black and White Modeling Agency." He complimented the woman who answered the door, took her measurements, and promised her modeling work, before parlaying the moment into sex. The success of this bizarre scheme speaks to DeSalvo's natural charm. Next came the Green Man crimes, in which DeSalvo donned a green workman's jumpsuit and pretended to be a maintenance man, gaining access to women's apartments and raping them. "I'm not good-looking, I'm not educated, but I was able to put something over on high-class people," DeSalvo explained upon his capture in 1961. "They were all college kids and I never had anything in my life and I outsmarted them."

DeSalvo often said strange things to his victims, suggesting a man in agony over his compulsions. Once, running out of a victim's apartment, he yelled, "Don't tell my mother!" Sometimes he would go home and "cry like a baby" as he watched his crimes reported on TV. But it's what happened after his admission to the Green Man crimes that triggered a lifetime of second-guessing.

In October 1964, DeSalvo broke into a Cambridge house and sexually assaulted a newlywed. He was arrested and sent to Bridgewater State Mental Institution for an evaluation. There, DeSalvo began dropping cryptic comments and boasts. One doctor noted he was a manipulative attention grabber with "an extensive need to prove what a big man he was." "I'm known as the Green Man now but soon I'll be known by another name," he told a social worker. The following March, DeSalvo confessed to being the Boston Strangler to an up–and-coming lawyer named F. Lee Bailey. There are three prevailing theories regarding his confession: (1) he was the killer, or one of the killers, and couldn't resist taking credit; (2) he lied about it, for attention; (3) he was encouraged to confess by his ward mate, George Nassar, a criminal with a high IQ, who some believe committed the murders himself.

State Assistant Attorney General John Bottomly, chief of the Boston Police "Strangler Bureau," arrived at Bridgewater to interrogate DeSalvo.

In the opinion of one Bridgewater doctor, DeSalvo had a legitimate photographic memory, and thus had no problem doling out details to Bottomly. Was DeSalvo vividly recounting memories, or just stories he had been told? Adding to the murk was the fact that Bottomly had never conducted a criminal investigation in his life; while getting inside DeSalvo's head, he was also unwittingly providing the man with new information.

Published in late 1966, *The Boston Strangler* was an instant bestseller. It took readers right up to the moment when DeSalvo was judged competent to stand trial for the Green Man crimes. Outside of his confessions, there was no substantial evidence with which to try him for the stranglings. But the Green Man trial would serve as a proxy for Strangler guilt in the public's mind. This is precisely what DeSalvo wanted, it seemed: the notoriety without the electric chair. In his mind, the sale of his life story as the Boston Strangler would support his family forever and make him a star. "If a man was the strangler, the guy who killed all those women," DeSalvo asked, "would it be possible for him to publish his story and make some money with it?"

The Green Man conviction, the exhaustive news coverage, and Frank's bestseller all shaped public perception. What cemented it was *The Boston Strangler*, the 1968 film based on the book. It was, in many ways, far more damning than Frank's scrupulous account, removing all doubt about DeSalvo's guilt. Arriving in the fall of 1968, *The Boston Strangler* would be America's first trial-by-movie.

DIRECTOR RICHARD FLEISCHER initially hired acclaimed British playwright Terence Rattigan to work on the *Strangler* script, but the result was unfilmable, to say the least: Instead of detectives using brain work to collar the killer, a computer generates the name of the suspect: "Darryl Zanuck"—the same name as one of the founders of 20th Century Fox, for some reason. Rattigan also raised eyebrows when he repeatedly asked Gerold Frank about the size of DeSalvo's penis. Rattigan was replaced.

Fleischer went with an unexpected actor for the lead. "What's a nice guy like Tony Curtis doing strangling women, even if it is only a film?" one newspaper joked. Fleischer had a discomfiting take, claiming the star "has the same attractive personality, the same appealing charm that could allow a man to talk his way into any woman's apartment."

Curtis, forty-two, had made his name in both comedy and drama over his career. But the drag blast *Some Like It Hot* became his calling card after its release in 1959, and by the mid-sixties, he wasn't finding parts with gravitas. "I wanted to play DeSalvo so much I would've spent three years in jail as compensation," Curtis said. In lieu of the slammer, Curtis gained fifteen pounds, studied medical records, wore ankle weights to alter his gait, and installed brown contact lenses. He visited crime scenes and devoured all the coverage.

The actor was in the middle of a divorce. A "shy girl from Cambridge" was spending a lot of time at his suite. His accent was passable. The film was already behind schedule. "There's a little bit of the Boston Strangler in everyone," Tony Curtis would later declare.

Fleischer was flummoxed when the police announced their refusal to assist the on-location shoots. Additionally, Boston's finest forbade the use of real police cars and uniforms, and wouldn't let the designers photograph the inside of the police station to make replicas. There were more difficulties afoot, including the fact that no one knew how explicit the movie could be. Fleischer would shoot a scene for maximum gruesomeness, then again in a tamer fashion, in case the censors were looking to snip.

Meanwhile, others hinted that lawsuits might be ahead, depending on how the film turned out. Attorney General Edward Brooke made it clear that if the script did not accurately reflect his association with the case, there might be trouble. 20th Century Fox offered Brooke $50,000 to work on the film, then $100,000, to no avail. Edmund McNamara of the Boston Police Department was less subtle, threatening massive legal trouble if the movie even implied his existence. Attorney General Elliot Richardson said the film might adversely influence a future trial. John Bottomly, one of two actual participants who couldn't resist working on the film, protested this objection, pointing out that no public official in the movie explicitly says that DeSalvo is the Strangler.

Production wrapped in February and the filmmakers traveled back to the West Coast. In the summer of 1968, Albert DeSalvo asked a judge if he could see the movie in advance of its release. The request was part of a preliminary injunction to prevent the film from being screened anywhere in Boston.

When the film opened in October, the city didn't roll out the red carpet the way it had for Trustman and Jewison's caper. Critics were frosty as well. "There have been lots of movies about murders, but very few about real murders, using real names, while they are still a daily memory for the living," Roger Ebert wrote. "The problem here is that real events are being offered as entertainment. A strangler murdered 13 women and now we are asked to take our dates to the Saturday night flick to see why." Unlike Frank's book, the movie version was "a deliberate exploitation of the tragedy of Albert DeSalvo and his victims."

As the camera closes in on Curtis's face one last time, Fleischer shoehorns a call to action: "The film has ended, but the responsibility of society for the early recognition and treatment of the violent among us has yet to begin." Some writers fell for the messaging. "The film is—although I hesitate in using this word—entertaining as an excellent character study," wrote a *Daily Illini* reviewer. "And it surely does serve as a public service— not only for young girls threatened by social deviates, but for understanding the criminally insane."

For Digby Diehl at the *Los Angeles Times*, however, the movie set a shocking precedent for libel-as-entertainment. DeSalvo had *not* been found guilty of any of the actions he's shown carrying out in the film, Diehl wrote, warning that "anyone could stand next before the celluloid jury." Curtis, who so passionately believed the role would revive his career, must have been disappointed, but it went beyond bad reviews for the actor. Shortly after the release of the film, Curtis began to receive anonymous letters in the mail with cryptic messages. "You're not the Boston Strangler, I am."

Albert DeSalvo sued for $2 million in damages after he was unable to prevent the film from screening in Boston. "DeSalvo said the film portrays him as a 'vicious and depraved individual' and that it shows a 'reckless disregard for the truth,'" the *Globe* reported. *Albert H. DeSalvo v. Twentieth Century Fox Film Corporation and the Walter Reade Organization* would be the last time he appeared in a courtroom. It was during this case that certain testimonies called into serious question DeSalvo's identity as the true strangler. Bridgewater State Hospital's Dr. Ames Robey said he didn't believe DeSalvo committed the murders, calling him "a very clever, very smooth compulsive confessor who desperately needs to be recognized."

But James Lynch, 20th Century Fox's lawyer, built a strong case, attempting to show that DeSalvo approved the project and encouraged its creators, even making a leather wallet for director Richard Fleischer. DeSalvo and Detective Phil DiNatale, the only other real-life participant who assisted in the creation of the film, had exchanged many letters, one in which DeSalvo promised the detective complimentary tickets to see the movie. DeSalvo's lawyer insisted that his client be able to view the film, but the judge disagreed. Albert DeSalvo returned to Walpole State Prison to serve out his life sentence.

On November 25, 1973, he placed a call to Dr. Robey, the Bridgewater psychiatrist who doubted Albert was the strangler. DeSalvo now wanted to entrust him with some important information. He would not tell him the specifics over the phone, so the doctor promised to visit him first thing the next morning. "He was going to tell us who the Boston Strangler really was, and what the whole thing was about," Robey later said. The next morning while preparing to head to Walpole, Robey saw the news on TV: Albert DeSalvo had been found murdered in his cell. Among his belongings, investigators found a poem that Albert had written.

Here's the story of the strangler yet untold
The man who claims he murdered 13 women, young and old
Today he sits in a prison cell
Deep inside only a secret he can tell
People everywhere are still in doubt
Is the strangler in prison, or roaming about?

IN FEBRUARY 1967, a month after Fox purchased the rights to Gerold Frank's book, Albert DeSalvo and two other inmates escaped from Bridgewater State Hospital. For twenty-four hours, the city of Boston was once again in the grip of strangler terror. His cohorts were caught drinking in a bar in Waltham. DeSalvo was found wearing a stolen sailor's uniform in a store in nearby Lynn. Upon capture, he told reporters that he had escaped to call attention to the terrible conditions at Bridgewater. "Maybe people will know what it means to be mentally ill," he said, calling out the insufficient rehabilitation tools offered to him at Bridgewater.

While DeSalvo was criticizing the hospital on the nightly news, a few miles away, a former attorney named Frederick Wiseman was editing documentary footage he had shot at the same hospital the previous year. The finished product, *Titicut Follies*, would bolster DeSalvo's argument tenfold. Many of the politicians and doctors involved in the DeSalvo/Strangler case were also major players in the subsequent legal debacle surrounding *Titicut Follies*, and the documentary can seem like a shadowy real-life counterpart to the big-budget feature.

Filmed at Bridgewater while DeSalvo was an inmate awaiting trial for the Green Man crimes, *Titicut Follies* kicked off Wiseman's unparalleled fifty-year career as a documentarian. But for decades, you couldn't see it: In January 1968, the film was permanently banned from being screened in the Commonwealth of Massachusetts by Judge Harry Kalus, who described it as a "nightmare of ghoulish obscenities."

. . .

FREDERICK WISEMAN WAS a Yale-educated Boston University law professor before he dove into filmmaking. Almost thirty and bored with teaching, he began taking his students on field trips to Bridgewater State Hospital in the late fifties to show them how the state treated the criminally insane. It was a place where chaos had ruled for decades. In the 1880s, Bridgewater was a co-ed facility where inmates raised livestock and harvested crops; one historian wrote that "convalescing patients mingled with violent ones, inmates damaged much of the asylum property, the atmosphere was disorderly, and the patients were clearly not under firm control." A *Globe* profile from the early sixties called it a "colony of lost men," noting that one patient had been picked up for vagrancy in 1901 and remained there ever since.

Wiseman's interest in filming at Bridgewater had an antiauthority slant, but since the hospital was in dire need of renovations, Superintendent Charles Gaughan supported the project, hoping it would force his superiors to see the difficulties his staff endured. The film would be "about a prison and the people who are in it and those that administer it," Wiseman petitioned Governor John Volpe, promising that "no people will be photographed who do not have the competency to give a release."

After a year of meetings, Wiseman's three-person crew commenced filming in April 1966. Gaughan was pleased that "the movie men" could capture some of the institution's annual spring talent show, known as "Titicut Follies." ("Titicut" was the Native American name for the land upon which the hospital was built.) Because inmates and staff both participated in the hospital variety show, and everyone is in costume, it's difficult for a viewer of the film to ascertain their real-life roles. This unsettling confusion is how the finished documentary begins.

The guards, in general, welcomed Wiseman, but it was made clear that he was never to come into contact with Albert DeSalvo—who now, as the self-confessed Boston Strangler, was Bridgewater's highest-profile inmate, with a lawyer who complained about hospital conditions to the press on a daily basis. Gaughan's deputy told Wiseman that if the director approached DeSalvo, he would personally "belt him." ("I don't think this constitutes censoring," Gaughan said.)

After shooting eighty thousand feet of film in twenty-nine days, Wiseman began the arduous job of assembling the footage. The final eighty-four-minute black-and-white film is a singularly powerful experience: no formal interviews, title cards, or soundtrack, only a series of stark scenes conveying the terror and confusion of Bridgewater State Hospital. Patients are stripped naked, grilled about their masturbation habits, taunted by guards, and in one instance force-fed through a tube.

In August 1967, *Titicut Follies* was accepted to the New York Film Festival. An early notice in the *Saturday Review* praised it as "a startling example of film truth," while raising an ethical question: "Where does truth stop and common decency begin?" Then came a chain of events that would hound the director for decades. "Some little biddy from Minnesota wrote to [Attorney General Elliot] Richardson, saying she read the review asking how can you allow something like this to happen?" Wiseman grumbled to *Newsweek* that fall.

It's ironic that a filmmaker so lauded for documenting reality over the years started his career with a bitter legal battle in which prosecutors argued that he was distorting the truth. Wiseman claimed that all of the state's postediting restrictions were never discussed; the state disagreed. He initially seemed to prevail. In late September, despite the efforts of the state of Massachusetts, *Titicut Follies* screened at the New York Film Festival and began a commercial run at another New York theater. Wiseman's *Follies* were on the loose. The *Avatar* reviewer had a unique angle: He was a Bridgewater alum. The article, in issue 12, takes the reader through a beautiful New England town, along a wooded path, to a looming structure like a medieval castle. He mixes his own memories of his dark residency at Bridgewater with commentary on the film:

(l to r) Jeff Barry, Bert Berns, Van Morrison, Carmine "Wassel" DeNoia (with cigar), and Janet Planet at a Bang Records promotional party held on a boat on the Hudson River in New York City, 1967.

Berklee student Tom Kielbania on bass at Spring Sing on Boston Common, April 20, 1968. Kielbania was a member of every one of Van Morrison's various lineups while the singer was living in Boston.

TV host David Silver asks Mel Lyman, "Do you think 1968 is a holy year?" Lyman replies in the affirmative. Between them, a star sculpture created by John Kostick.

Cover image of *Avatar* issue 23, April 12, 1968: a protest on Boston Common with the city's skyline in the distance.

Avatar's premier issue placed Ralph Waldo Emerson, who had died eighty-five years prior, on the front cover. Other cover stars included Timothy Leary and a depiction of the Statue of Liberty distributing copies of *Avatar* in the wake of the paper's ban. All illustrations by Eben Given.

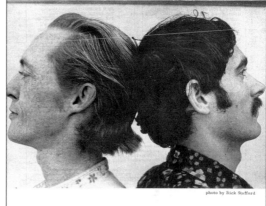

A full-page ad printed in *Avatar* for Murray Lerner's *Festival*—a 1967 documentary about the Newport Folk Festival. Top to bottom: Mel Lyman, Donovan, Bob Dylan, Joan Baez.

"They look like Jim Kweskin and Mel Lyman, and they are. But they are also members of United Illuminating." (l to r) Mel Lyman and Jim Kweskin on the cover of *Broadside of Boston*, August 1966.

"This insistence on perfection and beauty is evident throughout the Fort Hill houses . . . Mel's apartment, particularly, is beautifully appointed." *The Boston Globe* explores and maps the Fort Hill Community, February 1, 1970.

"There was a feeling in the air, you felt you were a part of something. *That* has disappeared. That does not exist anymore." Jessie Benton Lyman as seen in the pages of *Avatar* in 1968, when the feeling was in the air.

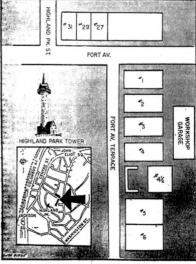

Beacon Street Union. (l to r, back to front)
John Lincoln Wright, Dick Weisberg,
Wayne Ulaky, Bob Rhodes, Paul Tartachny.

"I constantly felt like I was in a dream,"
David Silver remarks about his unlikely
journey from a visiting instructor at Tufts
University to WGBH TV show host.

MGM Records passed along only
a few specific requirements to
designer John Sposato: Make it
"psychedelic," include references
to the Revolutionary War,
and evoke the city of Boston.
This centerfold *Billboard*
advertisement arrived on
January 20, 1968.

"Remember the Boston Sound?" Chevy
Chase once asked a reporter. "Really
heavy on violins." Chamaeleon Church
in their rehearsal loft. (l to r, back to
front) Ted Myers, Tony Schueren,
Chevy Chase, Kyle Garrahan.

Orpheus in 1968. (l to r) Eric Gulliksen,
Jack McKenes, Harry Sandler, Bruce Arnold.
For Arnold, the only downside to the band's late-
sixties fame in New England was the way locals
pronounced the band name: "*Ahhh*-fee us."

Original poster for the Van Morrison Controversy's appearance at the Catacombs, August 9–10, 1968. At this subterranean club, Morrison first performed in the style that would define *Astral Weeks*.

Unlikely movie stars and members of the Fort Hill Community: Mark Frechette and Daria Halprin grace the cover of *Rolling Stone* in March 1970. "The whole movie embarrassed me," Halprin remarked about Michelangelo Antonioni's *Zabriskie Point*.

Spring Sing on Boston Common, April 20, 1968. At left, Emerson College student and Carole King collaborator Rick Philp on guitar. At right, Van Morrison, clad in a striped suit, smiling and confident.

Photographer Michael Dobo was assigned to work with writer David Felton for his *Rolling Stone* story about Mel Lyman and the Fort Hill Community in Roxbury. Dobo snapped this picture of two Community members in front of the Highland Park tower as the sun set.

Part one of David Felton's "Lyman Family's Holy Siege of America" was published as the cover story for *Rolling Stone* issue 98 on December 23, 1971.

"I don't believe in Jesus, I don't believe in the bible, and I don't believe in Mel Lyman." Charles Giuliano on his former roommate's turn toward the messianic.

"We were out on the hilltop in the middle of the night, running around the tower at top speed, flying above the ground, it seemed." Michael Kindman's memoir of his time with the Fort Hill Community is one of the most in-depth accounts of what life was like under the leadership of Mel Lyman in the late sixties.

The Velvet Underground in Cambridge, 1969. (l to r) Doug Yule, Moe Tucker, Lou Reed, Sterling Morrison. The band performed at the Boston Tea Party forty-three times between 1967 and 1970, citing it as their "favorite place to play in the whole country."

Parker Memorial Hall was built in 1870 as a tribute to the Reverend Theodore Parker, who had once predicted that Spiritualism would become "the religion of America." Nearly a century later, this popular spot for Spiritualist lectures and séances housed both the Boston Tea Party and the Fort Hill Community's Film-Makers' Cinematheque.

The Velvet Underground creating what *The Boston Globe* would later describe as their "headache-making and ear splitting" music live at the Unicorn Coffee House at 825 Boylston Street. Lou Reed on guitar, Maureen "Moe" Tucker on drums.

The Boston Planchette: one of the calling cards of the city's nineteenth-century reputation as "the Mecca of the spiritualistic faith." The device was designed to transcribe messages from the afterlife; the Ouija board later came with its own variation of the planchette.

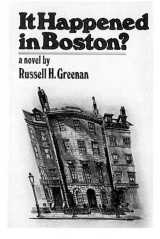

Published in 1968, Russell H. Greenan's debut novel tells the story of a talented painter from Boston who seeks to meet and confront God via an occult ritual.

Peter Wolf and Van Morrison, friends for life, backstage at a May 1972 Morrison concert at the Aquarius Theater in Boston.

(below) The distinctive neon sign for Ace Recording Studios located at 1 Boylston Place. *Astral Weeks* producer Lewis Merenstein had worked at Herbert and Milton Yakus's studio several times prior to auditioning Van Morrison there in 1968.

A young Bostonian runs into the street during the middle of a citywide spontaneous celebration triggered by Lyndon Johnson's March 31, 1968, announcement that he would not seek reelection.

AWOL serviceman Raymond Kroll is forcefully removed from Marsh Chapel at Boston University by FBI agents, October 1, 1968.

The doctor is like nothing I have ever seen before. His suit is a cheap flannel and most of his teeth are missing. What is left of his blond hair is pulled back over his fleshy face. "Have you ever had a Homosexual experience? Sucking and Fucking? Are you addicted to marijuana? Do you hate your mother? Your father?"

"Obviously you are a gentleman, it is too bad I would like to have you as a guest at my house. We should drink wine and listen to Mozart. But unfortunately I am not allowed to do that." I try to impress him with my lucidity.

I never knew for sure how long I was in solitary.

After several days a fellow starts to talk to me. I am thrilled now to have a friend. I ask him questions. Soon however I realize that he is completely out of his mind. He is the Third Eye and sees into the minds of all men. But he is a human being and I am so alone. [. . .]

Titicut Follies was shot entirely in the F ward. This means that they concentrated on the men that are genuinely insane. We are allowed to hear only one man who raises doubts of his insanity. We are not allowed to see E ward where at least half the men are fully rational.

The therapy is Thorazine. At every meal the guards come around and give out the pills. The men try not to take them because they realize that Thorazine means the sleep walking death. Once you are on Thorazine they take you deeper and deeper always more Thorazine until there is no mind at all.

Once every two weeks you take a shower. Once a week you get a glass of milk, once a week an orange, once a week a movie.

"What do you think of your Mental condition?" [Dr.] Robey asks.

"I do not wish to give an opinion as I feel that I am under observation and that my remarks may be construed against me."

They look at each other and nod as if in a show of hands vote. "You are very sick. Prepare yourself for a long stay, but don't worry we will cure you."

The state won a temporary ban on *Titicut Follies* on September 22, 1967, and hearings on the matter began in October. Bridgewater's Gaughan deplored the film's "message of shock." *Commonwealth v. Wiseman*, like *De-Salvo v. 20th Century Fox*, constituted a tug-of-war over the right to show a movie, both questioning whether the participants had the mental awareness to sign a release form. During the testimony of John Marshall, Wiseman's primary camera operator, someone noticed that one person in the room, acting as a member of the press, was actually Timothy Asch—the second camera person for *Titicut*. Asch, it turned out, had been filming the entire proceedings. He was promptly accused of deception, and people theorized that Wiseman and company were making a new film *about* the trial of *Titicut Follies*. All of Asch's footage was going to be edited into a sequel (possibly titled *Beacon Hill Follies*, it was nervously conjectured), or worse, intercut into the existing film to reveal a new layer of bureaucratic hypocrisy. This turn of events did Wiseman no favors. The trial now focused on three principal allegations against Wiseman: that he had breached an oral contract, perpetrated a gross invasion of privacy, and intended to profit from the film.

"The real privacy sought to be protected in this case," Wiseman's lawyer argued in court, "is the privacy of Massachusetts not to be made a laughing stock." A *Globe* op-ed agreed, saying that the film "causes 'rational,' middle class people to confront their own lack of abiding concern for the fate of Bridgewater's unfortunates, and therefore stirs the deepest pangs of guilt. Could it be that this is the central reason why [the movie] has met with such outrage in Massachusetts?"

When asked to explain the intent or effect of certain scenes in the film to the court, Frederick Wiseman time and again gave a five-word answer: "The film speaks for itself."

In January 1968, Judge Harry Kalus ruled that Wiseman had breached an oral contract and invaded privacy rights with the creation of *Titicut Follies*, calling it "80 minutes of brutal sordidness and human degradation" and "a piece of abject commercialism, trafficking on the human misery . . . of these unfortunate humans." It was the first ruling based on the right to privacy made in a Massachusetts courtroom and set a chilling precedent for documentary filmmakers. "On the contract issue, the judge simply believed the state over me," Wiseman told *Vice* magazine in 2007. "He also declared the negative should be burned." The negative was spared, but *Titicut Follies* was permanently banned from being shown in Massachusetts. Later that spring, Judge Kalus extended that ruling to apply anywhere outside of the state as well, essentially sentencing the movie to life in a vault.

A few months after the ruling, a film starring Tony Curtis portraying a supposed mass murderer opened nationwide. *The Boston Strangler* was free to disseminate misinformation for profit, but Wiseman's film—one that could actually trigger positive social change—had been rendered invisible.

Even after a new hospital was built in 1974, Bridgewater superintendent Gaughan maintained his opinion that *Titicut Follies* hurt more than aided the institution. (Wiseman, who later said that he never had political motivations for creating the film, was pleased to learn about the improvements at Bridgewater.) In the ensuing decades, Wiseman made numerous appeals to free his debut film—all failures. But after Wiseman came upon a headline in the mid-eighties that read "TITICUT FOLLIES JUDGE DEAD," he began a fresh, aggressive campaign. In 1990, a judge ruled that *Titicut Follies* was protected by the First Amendment and could be publicly screened. *Titicut Follies* had escaped its life sentence.

TWO MONTHS AFTER the assassination of Martin Luther King Jr., and three days before Robert F. Kennedy was killed, an icon of a different sort was shot dead—at least briefly. Valerie Solanas, a feminist author and schizophrenic, slipped into Andy Warhol's studio and fired her gun three times. The first two shots missed, but the third hit its target. Warhol was on the phone with one of his performers, who mistook the sound of gunfire for a Velvet Underground–era whip being cracked inside the Factory. At 4:51 p.m. doctors declared Andy Warhol dead. A minute and a half later, he came back. "Since I was shot, everything is such a dream to me," Andy Warhol told *The New York Times* in November. "I don't know what anything is about. Like I don't even know whether or not I'm really alive or— whether I died. It's sad."

As Warhol convalesced, Jonas Mekas, the forty-four-year-old Lithuanian-born New Yorker, found himself the de facto spokesman for the experimental film world. Headlines like "UNDERGROUND MOVIES GET PUBLIC ACCEPTANCE" appeared in major periodicals throughout the year, and every story had a quote from Mekas. Over at WGBH, *What's Happening, Mr. Silver?* showed Mekas's *Notes from the Circus*, with a soundtrack by Jim Kweskin's Jug Band, in its entirety. This episode of the show explored the idea of what an experimental film was exactly, which was kind of like defining a word using that word.

Despite the failure of Mel Lyman and George Peper to create a successful Boston Film-Makers' Cinematheque, Mekas was happy to see his friends find popularity and controversy with *Avatar*, to which he occasionally contributed. In one piece, he wrote: "DON'T CRITICIZE. If you think you don't like something—don't write about it. Try to write only about what you like in a movie, write only about those movies which you like, why you like them. . . . Remember, that when you are criticizing, you may be criticizing God. So think twice. See if you can separate man's work from God's work."

Wondering how he might have felt about his old friend Mel actually declaring *himself* God, I visit Jonas Mekas in Brooklyn, where his loft holds a flood of books, films, posters, and ephemera. There seems to be no delineation between his living quarters and his archives.

"In private, when Mel didn't have to sing or play loud, he was very low, you could barely hear him, but it was incredible," the ninety-two-year-old Mekas says, his accent still strong. "Quite incredible. I just cannot compare to anybody."

Mekas gives me a DVD of his film *In Between*, a collection of sequences that didn't find a place in *Walden*, a diary film that's like a who's who of the New York avant-garde of the 1960s. It ends with a long shot of Mel Lyman playing banjo on a Manhattan rooftop as the sun rises. The bewitching music somehow invokes Americana while utilizing a Middle Eastern scale. Between footage of Salvador Dalí and Allen Ginsberg, there's a snippet from the time Lyman lived with Mekas in the mid-sixties. "MEL (GOD) MAKES COFFEE," reads the title card.

"It was one of those long, hot, slow summer days," Mekas recalls. "Mel brought some coffee beans but we had no coffee pot. So he collected all kinds of parts and dishes and Mel put a perfect coffee pot together. We never had better coffee." Around the time of the coffee miracle, in 1966, Mekas watched Mel write an entire book in one sitting, which he modestly titled *Autobiography of a World Saviour*. Mekas decided to publish it. "Mel was a nice guy, so I said *why not?*"*

"The mind is a beautiful instrument when it is played with love, when it is used to REVEAL, to HELP, to bring together that which has been separated," Lyman wrote, introducing his signature all-caps emphasis mode of writing. *Autobiography* is what converted future *Crawdaddy* founder Paul Williams to the Church of Mel, even though Lyman would later describe the book as an elaborate put-on to amuse his Scientologist friends. "I never understood this admiration where everyone was looking at Mel in awe when he said 'I'm God,'" Mekas says. "He always said it with a smile, like a joke, but everyone else took it like a gospel. He did not look at life and universe and God with such seriousness. He thought it was all closer to the laughing

---

* The same year, in an issue of *Film Culture*, there's a listing for a "full evening show [of] . . . light, images, voice, human presence" available to be booked, created by Mel Lyman and Jonas Mekas.

Buddha. You can see from my footage of him, as little as I have. This idea of this Puritanic seriousness—he did not believe in that type of God."

In the spring of 1968, Mekas lectured at Boston College, a gig he used as an excuse to visit his old friend's commune in Roxbury. To him it resembled a "little village," with no strangers or tourists around, and marijuana plants growing right outside the door. He filmed the plants, and the members too. "I got one shot of all of them, the whole family in one room, like a family portrait. It was not that they were afraid of Mel . . . they were obsessed with him." It's then that Mekas confirms a legend about the Fort Hill Community: a basement of one house known as the Vault, where they put members of the community who had misbehaved. "They had their own laws and if someone did something really nasty they had their own prison. Mel showed it to me! He gave me a tour and they had their own prison for punishment. They were in some ways strict with regulations they had to follow. There was something very old-fashioned about them, not very modern. But you felt good being there."

Mekas doesn't find the idea of his friend running a private basement prison completely beyond the pale: "Instead of turning to the police they solved their own problems," he says, adding, "I don't think he was capable of doing wrong. Whatever happened that was wrong must have come from the people around him. They went overboard in whatever they were doing."

MEL HAD A NEW MULTIMEDIA VISION in 1968, something he named "The Magic Theater"—a potential two-story complex with a screening area, recording studio, and film lab—and instructed the community to start building it behind 5 Fort Ave. Terrace. George Peper described the plan's crown jewel: the Cockpit, a small command station just big enough for Mel, where he could "run the films, the music, the lights, everything at once."

Around this time, Don West, an assistant to a vice president at CBS, became enchanted by the Fort Hill Community. He began working on a pilot about the Family, presciently entitled *The Real World*. "I just fell in love with the Hill," he said. "And, I thought, they with me [*sic*] . . . [T]hey thought I was the route to taking over CBS. . . . I suspended most of my critical judgment and just let it happen, if you know what I mean." West worked closely with Peper until he was finally granted an audience with Lyman, who screened for him some of his recent work. One documented all of the community's children waking up in the morning; another captured Jim Kweskin in the middle of an acid trip.*

Despite Lyman's lack of technical training, West was "really affected" by the films. When West asked Lyman if he could follow a script for a possible TV project—a documentary about communes—Lyman declined, dissing him with an astrological slight: "You double Cancer!" Later, when West screened a rough cut of *The Real World* for the community, Family member David Gude pulled out a gun and said, "You talk about *The Real World?* This is the real world." Undeterred, West showed the pilot to CBS, which declined to pick it up. When West returned to the Hill for his equipment, they refused to give it back. It's one of the incidents that the Fort Hill Community claims *Rolling Stone* fabricated, but even today Don West confirms it happened.

The Magic Theater never materialized. Growing impatient, Mel ordered that the unfinished structure be razed. A film studio in Roxbury was not going to be how the Family attained mainstream film or television exposure. Miraculously, it seemed, by the time they leveled the Magic Theater, a new path had appeared: A member of the Lyman Family was on the cover

---

* *Avatar* writer Charles Giuliano, who appears in the *Rolling Stone* piece under the pseudonym Harry Bikes, speaks about a private film screening he attended on Fort Hill one night in 1968. "I can remember one of the movies that I saw there was of a woman that was pregnant. Mel fed her a hallucinogen and filmed her. And I look at this and, I mean, here she is pregnant and she's high and hallucinating. And you can see the expression on her face was anything but comfortable. What gives you the right to inflict that onto a woman in that condition? I mean that is beyond abuse."

of *Look* magazine promoting his debut starring role in Michelangelo Antonioni's hotly anticipated movie *Zabriskie Point*.

THE NATIONWIDE SEARCH for a leading man had dragged on for a solid year before finally hitting Boston in the summer of 1968. The stakes were high: *Zabriskie Point* was going to be Antonioni's first film shot in America. The acclaimed Italian director wanted to tell a story about America's counterculture youth, the very same demographic that was so adept at sniffing out phonies—meaning that the film's authenticity hinged on his choice of the right actor.

Antonioni had been shooting compelling, critically praised art house movies since the fifties, such as the enigmatic *L'Avventura*, but his breakthrough was 1966's *Blow-Up*, a hip mystery that captured mod-filled swinging London. The news that this major auteur's next film would be shot in the United States, released by MGM, and star American actors sent a wave of excitement through the counterculture.

Sally Dennison, nineteen, from Framingham, had an inkling that directing might be her calling, but in a pre-film-school world, she had to figure out her own path. After briefly working for Fred Barzyk on *What's Happening, Mr. Silver?*, she decided to simply seek out her favorite film director. "I'm a pistol," she says. "When I wanted something I went after it." Dennison flew to Rome and asked where the "film people" hung out; a day later she was sitting in the same café as Michelangelo Antonioni. Like Alan Trustman mailing his script to Hitchcock's office and getting a reply, Dennison had taken a blind leap and found a soft landing. She passed along a note saying she'd love to work with him, and he immediately hired her to be part of his American adventure.

A few months later, Dennison was scouring the United States for the angry young man who could manifest the director's dark American vision.

She visited city after city, interviewing hundreds of hopefuls. In Los Angeles, casting director Fred Roos found someone "on the money perfect" for the role: an unknown carpenter named Harrison Ford. Antonioni wasn't impressed by the future *Star Wars* actor, but it wasn't because he was inexperienced. "Like many European directors, Antonioni felt he could get a performance out of anyone," Roos explained. The search continued.

Dennison returned to her home base in June 1968, where she connected with *Avatar* contributor Ed Beardsley, who gave her names of promising locals, including himself. The area scene was enthralled by the project. A reporter for the *Boston Free Press* badgered her for details as she held auditions at Arlington Street Church. "All I can say is that it's a story about American contemporary youth," she offered.

Q: What kind of a lead is it to be?
A: It has to be a young man who's involved with what's going on.

Q: How long do you think it's going to take you to get the movie started?
A: I don't know. We're mystified. We're very mystified. We can't find this boy. We know he must exist.

Cruising through Boston in an MGM limo after another unsuccessful round of auditions, Dennison spotted a situation unfolding at a bus stop. A sailor and his girlfriend were fighting. But it was the guy *watching* them fight who caught Dennison's eye. The tall, good-looking, intense young man was taking it all in, seeming anxious and impatient, when someone in an apartment above the scene, fed up with the bickering, threw a potted plant toward the bus stop. Dennison told the driver to stop as pandemonium ensued. The young man looked up at the plant-launching culprit, shook his fist, and hollered a rage-filled string of obscenities. In his moment of uncontrolled anger, he embodied the same rebel spirit that made James Dean so magnetic. Dennison's colleague, producer Harrison Starr, grabbed him from behind and asked, "How old are you?"

"Twenty," he answered, as he was escorted into the limo. Dennison was amazed: Their missing puzzle piece had fallen into place, as swiftly as a flowerpot tossed from a window. Starr raved over the two clinching attributes of their new find: "He's twenty and he hates!"

Mark Frechette had just been cast as the lead in *Zabriskie Point*.

RAISED IN FAIRFIELD, CONNECTICUT, Frechette started rebelling in his teens, getting booted from over a dozen schools. He was eighteen the first time his name made the papers—in the police blotter, for a "breach of peace" charge. When a *Zabriskie Point* employee somehow got hold of his medical records, they learned he had been placed in mental institutions twice. The psychiatric evaluation detailed a troubled childhood, distorted religious views, and a deep distaste for authority, advising that he be approached with caution. The information was never passed along to Antonioni. "He wasn't equipped to handle the life he came into," Harrison Starr said in hindsight. "I did the best I could to help him. But Mark had his destiny. It couldn't have been changed."

Frechette married at seventeen, had a child, and moved to Roxbury, Massachusetts, in 1966. "I was a self-respecting hippie dropout bum," he told *Rolling Stone*'s David Felton. "Then I started reading the *Avatar* and it changed my life."* He didn't know anyone from the community personally at that point, but had made a practice of walking around the park surrounding the Cochituate Standpipe in the middle of the night when his child couldn't sleep. With his kid strapped to his back, Frechette would think

---

* Faith Gude, one of the most influential women in the Fort Hill Community, had spotted Mark while selling *Avatars*; she was so bowled over by his good looks that she put an issue of the paper into his hands.

about what he'd read in *Avatar*. "Mel really made me see what a fool I'd been. It made me grateful that the Hill was there, that Mel was there."

Frechette had made some unsuccessful attempts to speak with Mel, but after being cast in the film he was granted an audience. Lyman told Frechette that he could be the instrument that brought *Avatar* to Hollywood, and the young actor agreed. A week earlier, Frechette had been panhandling in Harvard Square, in between carpentry jobs; now he had been chosen as uniquely special by *two* controversial artists. In late August 1968, armed with a complete run of *Avatar*s in his suitcase, Mark Frechette set out for California.

ZABRISKIE POINT'S TITULAR LOCALE is a lookout spot in Death Valley National Park, its name an homage to a mining operation once head-quartered nearby. "The feeling of space and time reminds me of the moon," Antonioni told the press. "And the hills look as if no man has ever walked over them."*

Rumors were circulating that the film would feature anti-American themes. *The New York Times* reported that the movie's executive producer "flatly denied . . . that the troupe had filmed scenes in the kitchen of the Ambassador Hotel in Los Angeles" where Robert F. Kennedy had been killed just months before. "We were all followed and tracked by the FBI," Sally Dennison recalls. "Everyone was *sure* we were making a radical film. It made me very paranoid, I must say." The American film crew often re-ferred to Antonioni as a "pinko dago pornographer."

For the film's opening, a faux-documentary glimpse into a meeting of activist students, Antonioni cast Kathleen Cleaver, a high-ranking member of the Black Panthers, to deliver the dialogue. The FBI was actively trying

---

* It later provided the backdrop to some of the Tatooine scenes in *Star Wars* and the cover of U2's *The Joshua Tree*.

to dismantle the Panthers, and her inclusion either initiated or magnified surveillance of the movie. When asked what the film was about, Antonioni would offer something like "America is my true protagonist." *Look* magazine declared, "MGM still claims it doesn't know what *Zabriskie Point* is all about." The real problem was, neither did Antonioni.

The production was about to encounter a series of hurdles, but Antonioni's choice of leading man would become his most reliable headache. That's not to say Antonioni didn't like Frechette; he was by all accounts quite fond of him, even as he resisted the movie he was starring in. "There is something mystical about him," Antonioni mused to *The New York Times*.

The two leads, Daria Halprin and Frechette, met for the first time in August on set in Los Angeles, where Antonioni filmed the opening sequences.* "[Mark was] sitting there in his big armchair, looking like a zombie, not saying a word to anyone, real white and pasty," Halprin recalled, "and he's got these huge Benjamin Franklin glasses on."

"Are you wearing a wig?" Mark flatly asked Daria.

Their chemistry was natural: The two began an affair during production. Still, both leads were shy, inexperienced, and needed prodding. "Turn and grab Mark as if you really wanted him," Antonioni instructed Daria. "Oh Michelangelo," Daria chided, "you Italian pervert!" *Look*, one of many media outlets that dispatched a journalist to the set, reported that Antonioni was drawn to Daria's "bratty, free, earth-child quality" and believed Mark had "the elegance of an aristocrat, though from a poor family."

The *Times*'s coverage bordered on fanatical: reporting on the film at length before and after its release, hailing the inexperienced Frechette as "this year's James Dean." Frechette wasn't impressed or fazed by the press coverage; he was just trying to figure out the best way to promote the Fort Hill Community. Press agent Beverly Walker recalled that Frechette

---

* Halprin had been cast after Antonioni watched Jack O'Connell's *Revolution*, a documentary about Haight-Ashbury. She appears at the end: nude, nineteen, and beautiful.

"brought copies of *Avatar* to the producer, the director, the reactionary Southern crew, and always, to every journalist that visited the set, tirelessly explaining over and over again the importance of non-violence. Everyone indulged him. 'Oh, this is very interesting.' After all, he was the star."

In mid-September 1968, as Antonioni was moving the seventy-person crew from downtown L.A. to Death Valley, Frechette left the set for what would be the first of several unscheduled breaks from making *Zabriskie Point*. "Mel had announced that the Aquarian Age was about to begin, on the date of a particular astrological configuration that most others didn't interpret that way," Lyman follower Michael Kindman recalled. "It was time to 'come home.'" Members of the community returned to Roxbury from all over the country, watching the sun rise on Fort Hill together, certain the New Age had commenced. Frechette, emerging as an important member of Lyman's inner circle, was more excited about the events of his visit home than he had been by any of the moviemaking process. "That was the first time I heard [Mel's] music," Frechette explained. "We stayed up and smoked some of his fantastic weed, and listened to his music. All the music he ever recorded he played for me that weekend." Frechette reluctantly departed for Death Valley with a stack of Mel's tape reels, hopeful that Antonioni might consider it for the soundtrack.

"It's hard to say what he thought of them," Mark told *Rolling Stone*. "I noticed that during one of the more spirited pieces he was twitching in his chair quite a bit." The soundtrack, featuring Pink Floyd and John Fahey, was one of the strongest features of the finished film, but it did not feature the music of Mel Lyman. After this failure, Frechette tried sneaking issues of *Avatar* into shots, setting it up so Lyman's image would be visible in the frame. Each time, an incensed Antonioni spotted the planted image and chucked it.

Meanwhile, Daria Halprin was falling head over heels for Frechette, and she was far more receptive to his stories about his community back home. "After eight or nine months of my ranting and raving [Daria] had a vision," Frechette said. "She saw the face of Melvin. She must have recognized it from the *Avatar* cover since she'd never met him before. A few days later she made her decision for Mel and agreed, once the movie was finished, to live with her costar on Fort Hill." For Mark, scoring a successful conversion revealed how little was being included in Antonioni's portrait of revolutionary America. Frechette's Fort Hill Family believed the revolution was spiritual; here, the Italian director was filming a surface-level political revolution. In protest, the leading man flew back to Boston, refusing to continue working on the film. It was going to be impossible now, Frechette figured, for Antonioni to continue to ignore the Fort Hill Community.

"The whole thing was a big Hollywood lie, it wasn't real," Frechette told Lyman. "So I put a stop to it. I quit." Antonioni's American film debut now held hostage by its own lead, he finally agreed to two of his star's demands: Frechette could rerecord some of the dialogue to tone down the political nature of his character, and after completion of the film, Antonioni would spend ten days at Fort Hill.

Back in California, five months behind schedule, *Zabriskie Point*'s production team was heading toward a literal blowup—a culminating scene in which a house in the desert explodes, sending the residue of American culture into the air. "No one knew how high and wide debris might be flung," recalled Walker. "Local airports were keeping planes away."

In gorgeous slow motion, set against a haunting Pink Floyd track, refrigerators, rotisserie chickens, a cucumber, a box of Special K, onions, apples, beer bottles, a newspaper, and hundreds of books launch into a perfect blue sky, then fall to the ground. The film was finally finished.

With *Zabriskie Point* wrapped, Mark and Daria drove east across the United States, to their new home in Fort Hill. As the *Globe* would put it in 1970:

> No plastic living beside the Hollywood pools for them. Frechette
> and Miss Halprin are members of the community of 100 or so men,
> women, and children on the Roxbury hilltop.

The somewhat utopian group is headed by 31-year-old Mel Lyman and is a completely cooperative community.

Miss Halprin, a West Coast girl, has been at Fort Hill since last April. "Yes, I will make more films if that is what I am expected to do. I will do it for Mel. I'll do anything to serve my purpose of living." Asked what that was she replied, quietly, "Mel, to serve Mel."

THREE DIFFERENT MGM presidents had been involved with *Zabriskie Point* by the time it was released. There was talk that the company was about to go belly up, or be sold off. In February 1970, when the troubled production finally arrived in theaters, a man named James Aubrey headed MGM. To Antonioni's face, Aubrey called *Zabriskie Point* a masterpiece, but privately, he was deeply worried. MGM was in for $7 million—he needed the picture to succeed, and the finished project smelled like disaster. In desperation, he decided that the silent ending, in which Daria drives into the sunset alone after the explosion, was too bleak. What if she rode out to an uplifting song, to convince audiences that they had not just been taken for a pointless, dour ride? He tapped his young protégé, Michael Curb, to write a tune with Roy Orbison and sneak it into the final print without Antonioni's knowledge. Curb, the new president of MGM Records—a role in which he would trash the Bosstown Sound and purge the label's "drug acts"—also wrote the liner notes for the soundtrack. "If seeing is believing, then experiencing is being," he incoherently declares. The finished film has only a slightly clearer message.

Unsurprisingly, almost no one cared for *Zabriskie Point*. Journalists jumped at the chance to explain how a genius director from Italy got America wrong. Vincent Canby in *The New York Times* called it "one of his most ambiguous and least profound films . . . [As] a dramatization of what he sees as a contemporary American state of mind, it is both superficial and overly intellectualized." Richard Goldstein wrote that the film "is far more interesting to me as a failure than *Blow Up* was as a success," imagining the director traveling the country, "[m]eeting real Black people and politely asking where the next race riot was being held." Local music magazine *Broadside* noted its beauty, then lamented, "too bad the medium isn't the message. The director has seriously misread America." Nevertheless, the film made its two plucked-from-obscurity leads semifamous, landing them on the cover of *Rolling Stone*.

The press tour kicked off a month after the film's release. If the couple were not ready to star in a major motion picture, they were spectacularly ill equipped to execute a press tour. In nearly every interview, the leads disparaged the movie and/or its director. The *Rolling Stone* cover story called the movie "seriously flawed" but of "exceptional importance." It was as if this Italian director's failed attempt to capture American youth culture had emboldened that same youth culture with the confidence to say: *Here is what we're not.* It lent credence to the idea that the New Left movement and hippie revolutionary scene were *real*, complex, and easily mischaracterized, even by a sympathetic maestro such as Antonioni.

As they gave interviews, the young couple already knew that most people regarded the film as a flop, and they agreed. "Antonioni didn't represent reality," Frechette told the *Globe*. "It is all surface phenomenon, period piece, part of the prehistoric past." Halprin took it further: "The whole movie embarrassed me." Both claimed that Antonioni barely gave them any direction. On *The Merv Griffin Show*, Mark threw a punch at another guest, Pulitzer Prize–winning author Tony Dolan, who had written critically about *Avatar* in 1968.

Perhaps MGM's PR people were pointedly ignoring their stars' interviews, or maybe they perceived Mark and Daria's trash talk as some weird form of antimarketing. In any case, things reached a new low the following month, when the couple appeared on *The Dick Cavett Show*.

After interviewing film critic Rex Reed and director Mel Brooks, Cavett sets the stage: *They didn't know each other before the film, they now live together in a commune.* The couple walks out, towering and beautiful; the audience applauds. Everything seems pretty standard for a talk show appearance, save for one problem: The actors are barely talking. Cavett prompts Frechette to tell the now infamous bus-stop-casting story, but he refuses: "I was cast at a bus stop. That's about it." When asked about their living situation, Frechette tells Cavett, "It is a community, but the purpose of the community is not communal living. . . . The community is for one purpose, and that's to serve Mel Lyman."

MGM suspended the tour. Mark and Daria resumed their life together in Roxbury. Michelangelo Antonioni never made good on his promise to visit.

WHEN DARIA MOVED to Fort Hill with Mark, they were welcomed as commune royalty. "Mark loved being one of the Hill workers, when he wasn't planning future filmmaking endeavors with Mel or going off to act in a couple of Grade-B movies," community member Michael Kindman later recalled. "Daria had a harder time fitting in, and was really out of her element. Mel and Jessie named their baby after her, but that didn't help."

In September 1970, Mark left to go perform in a movie in Yugoslavia, leaving Daria alone on Fort Hill for the first time. "From fairly reliable, anonymous sources we know that life on Fort Hill gradually became very trying for Daria," David Felton wrote. "She may have been too independent for their tastes, but several people have mentioned violent encounters, some physical, between Daria and the Fort Hill women, particularly Jessie."

A publicist at MGM recalled to Felton that Daria asked for help getting work in commercials around this time. Her *Zabriskie Point* earnings had all been ceded to the Fort Hill Community, she confessed. When the publicist found a job for her, Daria was ordered back to Fort Hill for "retraining." Later, with both Mark and Daria in Los Angeles at the new West Coast Lyman outpost, Daria left the community and asked Mark to do so as well. He did, but days later a few community members showed up with an airline ticket to Boston. Frechette accepted the offer, glad that the decision had been made for him. In the end, he chose the Lyman Family over Daria Halprin.

"People on the Hill have to learn to put Melvin and the community ahead of themselves, and she just couldn't do that," Mark later explained. "I don't know if she'll ever come back." She didn't. Daria appeared in one more film, 1972's *The Jerusalem File*. That year, she met, married, and had a child with Dennis Hopper—the star, writer, and director of a counterculture film that audiences actually had gone out in droves to see, 1969's *Easy Rider*.

THE THREE MEN dressed differently. Mark, now twenty-five and sporting a mustache, wore an olive green suit and carried a suitcase. Terry was casual in short sleeves, and Herc had on dark sunglasses and a shirt resembling a guard's uniform. He stood at the front door with his hand in a paper bag. Inside was a .38-caliber revolver. The three men had walked a mile to rob the New England Merchants National Bank.

This was not something from a new Mark Frechette movie. This was a scene from the real world.

At 4:50 p.m. on Wednesday, August 29, 1973, Mark Frechette approached a woman at a desk outside of the teller station and asked her about a loan. She told him she was assisting some other patrons, but her associate could help. Mark told the second bank employee he needed a $2,500 loan. "I've got a steady job," he nervously told her as he slid a note across the table. It read: *There are three of us, we're going to rob you, don't get alarmed.* She waved a security guard over; Mark revealed his gun and instructed him to place his weapon on the desk. The guard then led Mark and Terry—Fort Hill member Sheldon T. Bernhard—back into the tellers' area. "We don't want anyone to get hurt," Mark told the staff. The employee at the loan desk triggered the silent alarm. Each teller station cleaned out their till into Mark's suitcase. The total take was $10,156.

The third Hill person, Chris Thien—nicknamed Herc—was in the foyer, disguised as a security guard. Two police officers sped to the location within minutes of the alarm. The first officer, patrolman Daniel Fitzgerald, rushed through the front door and tried to disarm Herc, who managed to throw the officer to the ground. As patrolman Maurice Flaherty approached, he spotted his partner on the ground and fired his gun twice, hitting Herc both times. Inside, Mark and Terry watched in horror as their friend fell to the ground. "Put your hands up!" the officers screamed, moving into the main area of the bank. Once Terry and Mark were disarmed, two doctors who had witnessed the robbery wanted to attend to Herc, but the police wouldn't allow it. He was carried on a stretcher to nearby Peter Bent Brigham Hospital and pronounced dead on arrival. "In committing their act," former FHC member Michael Kindman wrote, "they answered a question I had been considering for a long time: who would be the first to die for, or because of, Mel?"

Mark and Terry were held at the Charles Street Jail on bail of $2,500, the same dollar amount as the fake loan they had inquired about, which neither could afford. There was a theory that a fourth member of the Fort Hill Community had been involved with the robbery: A line of fishing wire had been tied around Herc's leg, and the cops assumed it led to a getaway car whose driver could give a tug if he saw police. "It must have gotten tangled on his leg as we walked over," Frechette offered.

Why did they do it? One of the first stories had Frechette telling the police he was "evicted from the commune for non-payment of rent the week before he was arrested on the robbery charge." Frechette is never quoted saying this again, but the reason makes sense: Frechette loved Lyman and the community so much, even choosing it over romantic love with Daria Halprin. If the community had evicted their superstar for missed rent, he would have tried anything to get back in. Two decades later, Beverly Walker told *Film Comment* that "Mark would not cooperate with his own defense because it would've meant turning against Mel Lyman."

Another motive appeared in the *Globe*. "We did it as a revolutionary act of political protest," Frechette claimed. "We had been watching the Watergate hearings on television. . . . We saw the apathy and we felt an intense rage. . . . Because banks are federally insured, robbing that bank was a way of robbing Richard Nixon without hurting anybody. . . . We just reached the point where all that the three of us really wanted to do was hold up a bank. And besides . . . standing there with a gun, cleaning out a teller's cage—that's about as fuckin' honest as you can get, man." The press was primed to jump on this claim; in August 1973, the nation's biggest political scandal was dominating the news. Coconspirator Terry Bernhard still cites this as the motive. "It was a revolutionary act. Money? Yeah, sure, I need some money," he told a documentary filmmaker in 2008. "But I certainly didn't want to rob a bank. . . . I tried to talk them out of it."*

A week after the facts of the case were reported, an in-depth feature on Mark and the incident appeared in just about every newspaper in town. (The *Globe* even mocked Mel Lyman's signature style in the opening: "Mark Frechette has spent the past week in cell 104, Charles Street Jail. He's had time to reflect on what he's been DOING and what he's been NEGLECT-ING.") Additional motives were floated. "The anger was in those boys," Jessie Benton said. "It was real hard for them. We had 16 kids to feed, and we can't buy meat. To me, robbing a bank is like robbing the government. Everybody's money is insured." From inside their cells, Mark and Terry realized that the sixties were long gone. "We haven't changed," Frechette said. "Everybody else is gone. Where did they go?" The Lyman Family just didn't seem cut out to handle the changes that the 1970s had in store for so-ciety. "Much of what Mark was saying . . . seemed oddly out of synch with

---

* A final theory appeared fourteen years later. In a 1987 issue of *Filmkultúra*, director Dezso Magyar recounted that he and Frechette wanted to adapt a part of *Crime and Punishment* "because we felt that America was like a Dostoyevsky-type world." Every other day, the actor would call from Boston, saying he almost had the necessary funds. "One day he called me and said that he would bring the five million dollars the next day. Great! I was watching TV in the evening when it was announced that . . . Mark Frechette attempted to rob a bank at gunpoint . . . and was ar-rested." It's true that Frechette wanted to adapt *Crime and Punishment*, but it's hard to believe that he imagined that much money could be waiting for him inside a small Roxbury bank—not to mention the fact that this was the same branch where the FHC kept its own savings.

the decade," Vin McLellan wrote in the *Phoenix*. "Apparently in the isolation of the Fort Hill community there still lives a few bits of 1966."

For the first time since the negative *Rolling Stone* exposé, local reporters made their way up the hill and into 5 Fort Ave. Terrace. Passing through the "Tolkien Hobbit" wall built around Mel's house, they were greeted by beautiful women in "oddly formal" cocktail dresses. In a room dubbed the Connection—a room built to join two houses on Fort Ave. Terrace—George Peper, Jessie Benton, and Faith Gude were ready to explain how their friends had made an honest, rational decision to rob that bank.

The Real Paper's Joe Klein—the future *Primary Colors* author—went up first.

JOE: "Was the bank robbery a way of standing up for the truth?"

JESSIE: "We haven't changed. But we've watched as the society around us changed—all the hope for this country is going down the drain with assassination, fizzled revolutionaries."

FAITH: "The motivation for the ripoff was a product of where this country is at. We've sat and watched Watergate week after week. And so, in desperation, those boys did up front what the government was doing in secret."

JOE: "But they had guns."

JESSIE: "Yes, and the first chamber in each of the guns was empty. There wouldn't have been any violence if that bank teller hadn't pushed that silent alarm and called the cops. To us, the big question is, what was that teller protecting? Was pushing that button worth Chris' life?"

FAITH: "It was a way of keeping Watergate alive. They weren't simply three thugs."

JOE: "What does it mean for your future? Are you going to start knocking off banks now?"

JESSIE: "We don't know. We're in great darkness and we know a
change is coming."*

Mel was nowhere to be found. He was traveling, they told Klein. They
passed along his only message, the hope that Herc hadn't died in vain. Klein
proceeded down to the Charles Street Jail to check in with Frechette. "Before, when I was out on the street," he said, "there had been something inside me, something that stopped me from stepping in line, getting in
place . . . I kept landing in jail and fucking up."

"But you're back in jail now, aren't you?" Klein asked. "Is it any different now than it was before?" It was as if it was the first time in years that
someone outside of the Lyman Family had finally made a valid point that
Frechette could understand.

"I never asked myself that," he said. "That's a hell of a question."

IN APRIL 1974, Mark Frechette and Sheldon "Terry" Bernhard pleaded
guilty upon recommendation of their lawyer Harvey Silverglate, the same
man who helped the community through the *Avatar* obscenity trials. There
was no defense to be mounted. The two men were sentenced to six to fifteen
years. Inside prison, other bank robbers found it hilarious that Terry and
Mark had no idea they needed to be out of the building within two minutes
to successfully pull off the heist.

Though it might not have been an actual motive, Mark and Terry *were*

---

* In the next issue of *The Real Paper*, Klein published a letter from an ex–community member.
"Non-material?" asked the critical letter. "Why does Mel travel in a Cadillac limousine with
TV, telephone and bar? Why does he own a $15,000 camper and have several wives; not
to mention all the stereo equipment, television, swimming pools, and estates in California?
Money is tight on the Hill—even for food—but that's because of overexpansion and poor
management."

truly obsessed with the Watergate scandal. "They call themselves the 'Stars in Stripes,'" Tom Snyder told the NBC viewing audience in late March 1975. "Fifteen inmates at the prison colony in Norfolk, Massachusetts, who spent the weekend reenacting the Watergate crimes behind bars. The prisoners performed their version of the White House transcripts, complete with an exact replica of the president's Oval Office. The play was directed by Mark Frechette." Terry, wearing a prosthetic nose, was Nixon. "I held up a bank and got five to 16," he told a reporter. "Nixon held up a country, and he got a pardon."

Frechette had hand-selected murderers and thieves from the prison yard to play Watergate figures such as H. R. Haldeman and John Ehrlichman. "I'd love it if Nixon were here tonight," Terry said. "Especially if he were wearing a blue shirt." The opening night audience included Senator Ted Kennedy and Edward Brooke, the former Massachusetts D.A. who was involved in both the *Strangler* and *Titicut* legal cases. "The president [and his collaborators] were portrayed tonight by convicts," one prisoner told reporter Mike Barnicle. "That's gotta shake you. Just a little bit."

Then, six months later, on September 27, 1975, Mark Frechette was found dead in the Norfolk County Prison weight room. A 150-pound barbell was on his neck. He was twenty-seven.

In the weeks leading up to his death, Frechette had lost weight and sunk into a deep depression. "Being in that kind of a place for someone like Mark was absolutely hell," Bernhard recalled. Prison officials had listed him as having "questionable stability" and scheduled him for an October psychiatric appointment. Was his death a freak accident? Suicide? Foul play? The prison officially ruled the death as the first; both Silverglate and Beverly Walker suspected the last. "We were close to getting out. We would've gotten parole in a couple of months," Bernhard sadly noted in 2008.

Mark Frechette's tragic story became a permanent part of *Zabriskie Point*. It all seemed beyond coincidence, as if his own life were a movie that transformed him from an anonymous carpenter, to a famous actor and devotee of Mel Lyman, to a criminal acting in jail. With no experience, he was cast by one of the most famous directors in the world based on his everyday behavior. His character was named Mark; he was wanted for murder. Onscreen and on the streets, he was the confused rebel with a gun.

Terry Bernhard, the remaining survivor of the bank robbery, served his term and returned to the Fort Hill Community. He played piano on Jim Kweskin's 1979 *Side by Side* album. He still resides with his fellow Hill members, sometimes performing with local jazz trios. The prison where he was initially held after the failed holdup is now a luxury hotel called the Liberty, featuring a bar and nightclub named Alibi and Clink, respectively.

"IT WAS A good bank robbery," Frechette had told the press from jail. "Maybe it wasn't a successful one, but it was real, ya know?"

SEVEN

I Saw You Coming from the Cape

IT'S POSSIBLE THAT no one besides Peter Wolf has heard any recording of Van Morrison's various Boston lineups since they toured around New England in the summer of 1968. Even the musicians who made up the Belfast singer's first steady, American live band haven't heard Wolf's bootleg. Wolf himself hasn't listened to his tapes of the Van Morrison Controversy performing at the Catacombs in over a decade, as he explained to me while staring at the boxes containing the reels on his bookshelf.

After I publish a brief account of meeting with Wolf, conjecture about these Boston tapes bubbles up on assorted online message boards and the pages of *Uncut* magazine, but no one brags about hearing them. What did the *Astral Weeks* songs sound like before producer Lewis Merenstein's jazz ringers got hold of them? Was the album's timeless vibe invented on the spot, in the studio, or was the foundation laid down in Boston? And what did the songs sound like before Van had his midsummer night's dream about getting rid of electric instruments?

Online, the bottom of an old Boston Tea Party poster, for a series of 1968 shows, catches my eye: "The Van Morrison Controversy and The

Road Light Show can be seen on WGBH-TV, Wednesday May 29th, 7:30 PM–8 PM." Could audio *and* video of a Boston lineup be moldering in the basements of WGBH? David Atwood, who directed WGBH's *Mixed Bag*—a half-hour show presenting local rock and jazz bands—is the man who would know. A natural archivist, Atwood has a home collection of tapes of his directorial work, and a pocket calendar detailing what he did every day at WGBH. Consulting his notes, he confirms that the show aired that night. My hopes start to soar, even after he tells me that the episode is not in his personal archive, but might be in WGBH's. A few days later, bad news: This episode is nowhere to be found.

In 2016, the rest of Van's Boston players emerge from the woodwork, eager to talk. One of them is drummer Joey Bebo, who multiple sources claimed was deceased. Over a plate of nachos, Bebo jokes that for all this time he thought *they* had all disappeared. Now retired from his job as a computer programmer, he's become a prolific writer of what he calls techno-thrillers. In one, a scientist discovers a powerful telescope, then goes missing. Plot twists ensue. By the time he's rescued, he's invented "a ray to look back into the past."

Bebo arrived from Plattsburgh, New York, to attend the Berklee School of Music in 1966. In the early spring of 1968, one of his classmates, bassist Tom Kielbania, invited him to audition for Morrison. Bebo wasn't thrilled at first, dismissing Them's "Gloria" as "teenybopper stuff." But he was in no position to turn down a paid job: His parents had caught wind of his penchant for pot, and he felt the pressure of supporting himself. "If it wasn't jazz or serious soul, I just wasn't interested," Bebo recalls. "I was about to work with one of the best songwriters and singers of all time and I didn't have a clue."

En route to guitarist John Sheldon's home off Harvard Square, Bebo and Kielbania got stoned out of their skulls. The sideburned Bebo looked like a pirate, in purple shirt and bell-bottoms; Sheldon gave off the vibe of a "preppy vampire" in his red blazer; Kielbania had stringy hair, dark shades, and frumpy clothes. Van sat silently in the corner. When it was time to play, they ripped into "Gloria," Bebo keeping his eyes on Van, looking for tempo and dynamics. Next up in the audition: "Brown Eyed Girl," featuring an aggressive rock guitar line, Bebo says, like "Jimi Hendrix meets Bob Marley." Bebo got the job.

The band learned more than two dozen songs for their summer tour. In the weeks leading up to the first show, there were backyard games of Frisbee and lunches in Harvard Square. But even during breaks, it was difficult to get Morrison talking. The only time you could get definitive opinions out of the singer was by asking him about other performers. Tom Kielbania would mention another band, and Morrison would usually sum them up as "those faggots." The trash talk would flow freely after Morrison had a few drinks. Bebo remembered Van saying that he couldn't smoke dope due to "burning my brain on hash when I was younger." (Janet Planet concurred with this assessment. "He was absolutely drinking back then. Alcohol is definitely his drug of choice. He doesn't need anything to expand his mind any further. . . . He needs the downer—the closer-offer.") Bebo says Morrison drank heavily before taking the stage, every single show.

"I had never been in a group that did everything together like this before," Bebo says. "Most of my career I simply showed up for work with my drums and that was the extent of it. Van's band was different." Another difference was the pay. Bebo got $150 a week for rehearsal and $150 per show, no matter what the end-of-night payout was. (Kielbania recalls it as being $50.) Morrison also employed two roadies for each performance.

For Bebo, who had recently visited Van and Janet's less-than-palatial Cambridge digs, this was a confusingly large sum. Where was it all coming from? Eventually he pieced together that Morrison already had financial backers by the start of summer. According to Janet Planet, a Boston-based music manager named Richard asked Van to move to the city, play some gigs, and be managed by him. "He was not affiliated with a company at all," she says. "It turned out he was not an effective manager, although he certainly got us out of a tight spot in [New York]." But Morrison jettisoned Richard after realizing he was "a complete whacko" who told at least one band member that he was associated with the Cosa Nostra. Kielbania says a man named Frank booked all of Morrison's New England concerts that summer.

Regardless of who was funding the touring, or how much money exactly was behind it, many elements of it remained shoestring. The band crammed into a junky van to drive out of the city for their first show together at the Rainbow Ballroom and Rollerdome in Hyannis Port on Cape Cod. Finally warming up to his new bandmates, Morrison told them stories of touring with Them. At the Rollerdome, Morrison, Bebo, and Kielbania drank beers in the van while Sheldon and the roadies set up. A cop knocked on the window: It was against the law to sit and drink in a parked car. He pulled them out of the van for questioning in front of a line of kids waiting to get in to see them play.

The manager kicked up a fuss, asking if the cop knew that the man in the van was a star; the cop said he didn't care if they were the Beatles. The promoter brought up the fact that the police were getting paid to oversee a concert tonight, and if Van Morrison and his players were going to be arrested, there would be no show. Morrison fumbled through a mea culpa: "We didn't mean disrespect. We do it all the time back home." The police finally dropped the act, and the band rushed to the stage, where a throng of teenage girls had gathered. Bebo thinks Morrison was especially nervous during the incident with the cops because of deportation fears. The anxiety turned electric when the band started playing—"sizzled like cooked bacon," per Bebo. When the band closed with "Brown Eyed Girl," the audience erupted. As the band exited the Rollerdome, one of the cops said, "Not bad."

Packing up, Bebo saw Morrison do something odd. "There were a few girls standing around, all teenyboppers. All young girls. And Van goes up to one of them and he whispers in her ear. And her eyes go wide and she quickly walks away like she's scared."

What did he say? Bebo doesn't know, but says he witnessed it a few times that summer. "I'd see him go up to a young girl, whisper something, and it was always the same reaction, every single time."

EVERYONE IN THE BAND AGREES THAT, along with the *Astral Weeks* songs, both "Moondance" and "Domino"—future Morrison classics—were written and developed that same summer as well. According to guitarist Sheldon, he and Van first stumbled upon "Domino" at the Boston Tea Party, fooling around onstage before the audience was admitted. It was based on Sheldon "playing a lot of treble on the guitar and playing something that sounded like 'Mona,'" the Rolling Stones' version of a Bo Diddley song. Morrison was on drums as Sheldon chimed out the chords. "He swung this mic over and started singing. And the song came from there. As soon as he finished he said, 'That's a real motherfucker.'"

Drummer Bebo confirms that the band performed an extended version of the song that, with young Sheldon's affinity for feedback, came off like a "musical paroxysm." Sheldon also remembers messing around with a Grant Green song called "Lazy Afternoon" at one rehearsal; Morrison requested some alterations, and began singing a melody that would eventually morph into the song "Moondance." Kielbania corroborates this version of events. His favorite moment from 1968 was playing "Moondance" for the first time in Cambridge: "New song. Same bass line ever since."

The band was remarkably busy that summer, playing at rock clubs, roller rinks, high school gyms, amusement parks, and outdoor festivals. One former Wayland High School teacher and some of his former students patch together their memories of the evening: *He threw a temper tantrum onstage about feedback. He was paid $400 for the performance and someone stole his microphone after the show.* Meanwhile, at the Psychedelic Supermarket, the Tea Party's dumpy competitor, Morrison tried to quit before playing the final set. Less than ten people were in the audience, but owner George

Papadopoulos demanded that they finish.* Morrison countered that Papadopoulos had promised at least a hundred people, a fact the club owner denied. "Van exploded, packing as many f-words as he could into the next few short sentences," Bebo recalled. "I had never heard such an outburst at that point in my life."

Bebo explains what happened next: Van, "in a foul mood, with his back to the small audience that had finally started to arrive, turned it into a stressful rehearsal, stopping us in the middle of the songs and changing the tempos halfway through the choruses." A young musician from Salem named Ed Morneau remembered this specific show, its sour atmosphere still shading his opinion of the singer to this day: "He performed a few tunes, then walked off. People were pissed. I immediately disliked him and still do." John Sheldon's overall memory of the entire summer is something akin to that night at the Psychedelic Supermarket. "It was just on the edge of madness," he says. "It's a miracle we played anywhere, it's a miracle we got to any gigs at all."

The summer was littered with moments like these; for Morrison, a musician who had already thoroughly paid his dues, it must have been painfully humbling. After one club date, a mean-spirited audience member walked up to him and said, "You wrote that song, 'Brown Eyed Girl'?" Morrison nodded. "When I first heard it on the radio," the guy told him, "I thought, *man, the Rolling Stones have really gone downhill.*"

Back to the Cape, this time at a churchlike venue with atrocious acoustics. "John was playing particularly loud and raucous, with a lot of out-of-tune chords and feedback," Bebo says. Sheldon started smashing Bebo's cymbals with the head of his guitar, apparently inspired by Pete Townshend's onstage theatrics. After the first set, Morrison disappeared into the dressing room and his Southern Comfort, while Bebo confronted Sheldon

---

* Don Law recalled that when a long line started to form for a show at the Psychedelic Supermarket, Papadopoulos would actually take a ladder outside the venue, climb up to the marquee, and raise the posted price of admission to the audible groans of the gathered audience.

about his cymbal attack. Sheldon admitted he got carried away. But at the top of the second set, Sheldon started to once again hit Bebo's drums so aggressively that a cymbal stand crashed to the stage. Morrison whipped around, screaming, "It's too fucking loud!"

Bebo stormed off the stage to yell at the guitarist, but couldn't find him. At last, opening a closet door, Bebo saw Sheldon inside, cutting his arm with a penknife. Bebo asked if he was crazy. Sheldon told him he was.

"Okay, John," Bebo said, unsure how to proceed. "Your crazy act worked."

But it wasn't an act. Though Sheldon doesn't recall this specific incident, laughing as I recount Bebo's tale, he doesn't doubt it happened. As a fifteen-year-old, John Sheldon had been committed to McLean Hospital, a psychiatric institution in Belmont, formerly known as Asylum for the Insane. "I was *submitted* in the spring of 1966," he says. "I got out in the fall of 1967. And I met Van a few months later."

Years passed before Sheldon accessed his McLean files. He learned that the official diagnosis had been "adolescent turmoil," and that the doctors' main goal had been to get him through his awkward years without hurting himself. Unlike the horror show of Bridgewater State Hospital, McLean was beautiful, with spacious grounds designed by Frederick Law Olmsted, who became a patient there twenty-five years later. "Everyone makes the same comment," Alex Beam writes in *Gracefully Insane*, his book about McLean. "It doesn't look like a mental hospital." The idea was simple: a calm, pastoral setting might help in easing a disturbed mind. Artists like Sylvia Plath, Ray Charles, and James Taylor—the songwriter who had taught Sheldon guitar basics as a kid—had all gone there.

Sheldon learned to smoke pot at McLean. "You could hide anything, you could get anything, somebody was always going into town and coming back with something," the guitarist told Alex Beam. In a strange coincidence, after Sheldon stopped playing with Morrison, the man who stepped into his place—flute player John Payne—also happened to be a McLean alum. Payne's time at the hospital happened to overlap with that of his first cousin, once removed, who was none other than the poet Robert Lowell. According to Payne's sister Sarah, the two relatives recognized each other on the grounds, but barely spoke in their medicated haze. "He was incredibly high and incredibly drugged," Payne reported to Sarah, "and even though he was talking to you, he was a million miles away."

At the end of the eventful, traumatic Cape Cod show at the churchlike venue, Morrison's band ambled back into the van to get back to Boston. On this particular night, their transportation had been arranged by Sheldon, not for the first time. ("When your seventeen-year-old guitar player that's living at home has to go arrange transportation, you probably aren't crossing all your T's," he jokes.) Driving home, Sheldon smashed the rental into the back of a truck on the Southeast Expressway. No one was injured, but the van now had a gaping hole in the hood. The accident might help illuminate the opaque poem on the *Astral Weeks* sleeve. Not only is it the album's only mention of time spent in Massachusetts, but it specifically names Hyannis Port, the Cape Cod town where, by all available evidence, Van traveled to only twice, the second time being the show described above. The eleven-line verse takes us from Hyannis Port to Cambridgeport, where he and Janet lived. Is the *Astral Weeks* poem about returning home to Janet after a particularly bad show down the Cape? Could the phrase "bumper to bumper" refer to the car accident?

Morrison would loathe this kind of connect-the-dots. In 1985 he trashed the whole genre of lyrical analysis: "People are saying, 'Well, this means this about that, and he was going through that when he wrote this.' . . . So you get to the point where you're afraid to write anything, because you know somebody's gonna make something [out] of it. . . . I'm very unanalytical about what I do." And yet, Morrison himself has often recontextualized his own stories and lyrics over the years. (Biographer Clinton Heylin called him "the master revisionist.")

Safely back in Boston, Van Morrison and the Controversy next opened for California soft-rock band the Association at Frank Connelly's Carousel Theatre in Framingham. Backstage, members of the Association excitedly talked to Morrison—they were in the know. When Morrison recognized a moment to be gregarious as advantageous to his career, he could turn it on without a problem. "Much like when the DJs came backstage to talk to him," Joey Bebo recalled, "Van was holding court." An hour later, about to go onstage, Bebo and Kielbania commented on how nice the Association guys were; Morrison declared them to all be "faggots." They opened with the long, electric version of "Domino." The crowd was polite; the subsequent *Boston Globe* review noted that the group "never really communicated." Even if it had been glowing, Morrison probably would've found fault with the assessment. Bebo once watched Morrison read a largely positive write-up, crumple up the paper, and call the writer an asshole.

The gigs kept coming: the Cambridge Electric Ballroom, Hampton Beach Casino, an in-studio performance at Ray Riepen's new station, WBCN, the Comic Strip in Worcester. Morrison was in Boston to work and the itinerary proves it. In August, the band played Rocky Point Amusement Park in Rhode Island. Bebo recalled "thousands of people . . . all there to see Van." The band tried to make their basement rehearsal gear work for the gigantic outdoor venue, to little effect. What's worse, Bebo busted the head of his snare drum on the first song. As it happened, none of that mattered: Van's voice alone could carry a show, and the crowd was in a frenzy. Bebo had caught wind that Morrison was promised a percentage of the admission fee for this concert, and forgetting all the nights Van had paid him $150 when he himself was barely paid, the drummer tried to lead an insurrection demanding a larger piece of the take. "They all came to see me," Morrison calmly explained before walking away. "It was a lesson I never forgot," Bebo wrote in his memoir, "and from that moment on I understood my place."

Most of Van Morrison's Boston electric band agree on what happened at the beginning and middle of the summer, but memories diverge about the end. Did the electric band record anything together? There are certainly no live bootlegs even whispered about for this lineup; Peter Wolf's tape is of the acoustic, post-anti-electric-dream trio, and the WGBH performance is Van backed by saxophone and Kielbania on bass. According to Sheldon, someone from Bang Records came to Boston at the behest of Ilene Berns to induce Van to cut some new demos, a representative "sporting an out-of-date Beatle haircut and talking a lot about trendy, bubblegum pop songs." He was "sort of like an operator who wanted to get a little ditty out of us."

It's true that Ilene Berns eventually forced Morrison to record his contractually obligated songs for Bang. The result was the infamous "nonsense" or "revenge" recordings (sample titles: "Ringworm," "Want a Danish"), recorded in New York the following year. As absurd as the lyrics are, they seem to confirm Sheldon's memory of someone from Bang Records visiting Boston. "This here's the story about dumb, dumb George / Who came up to Boston one sunny afternoon," he sings in "Dum Dum George." In the track, Morrison wails about a record producer who brags about making lots of money and number one hits. Because many of these contractually obligated songs seem to specifically delight in making fun of Bert Berns and his old label, it's reasonable to assume that the "dumb" record producer who visited Boston was most likely working for Bang.

In this session, regardless of who or what prompted it, they laid down the dirty, "rocking, really good" version of "Domino" and other new songs, though Sheldon has never heard them since. Bebo confirms that the band made some demos at Ace Recording Studios, but he recalls it being on Van's own dime, with the goal of wooing a new label. Along with "Domino" they laid down a tune called "Lorna." "This wasn't like the gigs where everything was so loud and chaotic that he was just a thread in a wild tapestry of sounds barely audible through my own playing," Bebo wrote. "It was the moment that I truly became aware of how good he really was."

Bebo says that the Ace producer didn't think he was "rock" enough, and brought in another local percussionist: "You know Victor, the one-armed drummer?"

This was Victor "Moulty" Moulton, of a garage band called the Barbarians. Moulty had lost his left arm in an explosion at fourteen, and clutched his drumstick with a prosthetic claw. The Barbarians found minor fame with their two-minute exploration of androgyny, "Are You a Boy or Are You a Girl?" Their second-biggest hit was "Moulty," in which the drummer talk-sang, in a rich Boston accent, his personal story of overcoming teenage tragedy, on top of chords that sound a whole lot like "Hang On Sloopy."* "[Van] needed a heavy drummer," Moulty says, "and I was definitely heavy duty." In Moulty's memory, he declined Morrison's offer to join the band after this recording session. But according to Bebo, Morrison didn't care for Moulty's bashing, and requested that Bebo be brought back.

Herbert Yakus, half of the sibling team that ran Ace, says that a Van Morrison session, with or without Moulty, would have been just another day's work compared with their usual clientele. Because of the eventual fight with his brother Milton over the royalties to "Old Cape Cod"—a hit for Patti Page in 1957 that originated at Ace—Yakus is at first reluctant to stir up the past ("That song *made* Cape Cod!" he yells at me). "There were weird bookies paying for women to make records all the time," he recalls. "I had a priest who fell in love with a woman singer. He took the church's money and paid me to cut a record with this woman. The problem was, when these songs went nowhere, they'd threaten me like it was my fault." Another time, a woman came in with a stack of records and told Yakus, "When I die, I want you to play these records in this order as they prepare my body for burying at the morgue." (He did.) At one point, the studio even offered to install secret recording equipment in the rooms and cars of spouses who were suspected of cheating. Ace went belly up in 1971, and save for a few recordings that Herbert decided to take home, like a

---

* While "Moulty" was released by the Barbarians and landed the group back on the *Billboard* charts, it turned out Victor's backing band for the recording was the Band—as in *The Band*, who were smack dab in the middle of their turn backing Bob Dylan. The rest of the Barbarians were embarrassed by the single and the band broke up the next year.

Louis Armstrong session, all of it went in the trash or to other studios to be taped over.

How and why did the band shift from what Bebo calls a "strictly electric" sound to an acoustic approach in the weeks leading up to the September recording of *Astral Weeks*? Bebo contends that it was all because Kielbania's instrument broke at one of the band's first Catacombs shows. The bass was sending nothing but electrical noise to his amplifier, as an impatient Morrison watched from a nearby table. With no hope of fixing it, Kielbania ran out of the club and into his nearby alma mater, Berklee, to borrow an acoustic bass. Bebo claims they reworked some of the newer songs "almost as if it was rehearsal. We played soft and jazzy behind Van's wailing vocals."

What about John Sheldon's memory of Van's dream—the dream instructing him to stop using electric instruments?

Bebo shakes his head. "I have no idea where John's coming from, but I know he was this crazy kid. And he may have seen things a little differently, but nothing like that." Kielbania remembers his bass crapping out on him, but doesn't recall this as being the accidental turning of the tide. He doesn't remember Morrison's dream, but he doesn't find it all that unlikely either. After all, later that fall in New York, Morrison would wake Kielbania in the middle of the night to jam on a new song that had just come to him, in a dream about an "electric radio."

Sheldon doesn't waver. He recalls "rehearsing without Joey and with just Tom and me on the acoustic guitar. It was very clear that Van didn't want any electric instruments." He admits that his memory of Van Morrison's dream sounds strange, but thinks it outrageous that he could have made it all up. "I remember very clearly that he said that and then next thing I know we were rehearsing acoustically."* All the while, Van

---

* Another key figure disputes one of Sheldon's vivid memories. Producer Lewis Merenstein denies ever calling Van Morrison a genius, at the Ace audition or elsewhere. Sheldon insists he heard it, but is there a chance it actually came from the mouth of Richard, the manager, or the Bang Records emissary?

Morrison was writing and refining the songs that would end up on his 1968 masterpiece. "[Van] was doing the tracks that were to become *Astral Weeks*," recalled Mick Cox, a guitarist who was recording in New York with his band Eire Apparent. "I stayed up for two or three days [in Cambridge] and recorded some stuff with him—just fantastic music."

By the end of the summer, the Van Morrison Controversy was fraying, Sheldon says. The original manager—Richard or Frank—was no longer there by August; the money was running out. Janet Planet does recall that the Boston manager wanted to charge Van an arm and a leg for every little thing he did. Soon after, Lewis Merenstein came to Ace for the audition, and the guitarist understood he'd been politely removed from the band.

Joey Bebo, of course, has a different memory. After the Ace demo sessions, the whole band sat in a semicircle as Van asked who would be staying on after the summer ended. Bebo had the "distinct impression that something had happened over the week of cutting demo tapes": a record contract. John Sheldon told Van that he couldn't do it, as high school would be resuming, and Kielbania immediately said yes. Bebo was the only one who asked to sleep on it.

The first member of his family to attend college, Bebo agonized over the decision on a night walk through Boston. "There was the Prudential, towering over the peaks of dozens of apartment buildings," he recalled. "Suddenly I felt small . . . I felt like I lived a charmed life. I didn't know who to thank, so I thanked God." He burst into tears. The next morning he told Van Morrison he would return to school in September.

Hearing the music today, Bebo says he would have "given it all up—all my education—to play with Van again. I just want to get back there."

Unlike Joey Bebo, John Sheldon remained in the music world long after that summer. Immediately after the Morrison gig ended, Sheldon joined the local band Bead Game, which surfaced in a lot of the Bosstown Sound coverage, though their first album didn't appear until after the scene's heyday. He went on to write songs that would be recorded by his old friend James

Taylor. "September Grass" and "Bittersweet" both appeared on albums that went platinum for the singer-songwriter. Sheldon most recently has performed a piece called *The Red Guitar*, a reference to the Fender he bought off Taylor in the early sixties. I ask Sheldon if, looking back, he wishes he had some kind of writing credit for "Domino" or "Moondance." If he could have anything, he says, it wouldn't be royalties, but the long-lost recording of "Domino."

"The rest of the band didn't like it," he says. "But that's the one that we wrote together, that's the one that rocked. The version we made together *was* rock and roll . . . it was awesome. I just wish that *I had it*."

Tom Kielbania, now retired and living happily with his wife in Chicopee, has similar feelings. "In my whole life, this is all I got to offer," he tells me in his backyard, referring to his time playing bass for Morrison. "This is it!" he says, banging the picnic table for emphasis. Would hearing the recording of the Catacombs show be meaningful?

"Yeah," he says. *"I. Would. Freak. Out."*

With all the discrepancies between the memories of Morrison's Boston players, the tape would surely offer some clues as to whose version of events of the summer of 1968 is most accurate, as well as documenting the local contributions to the songs that would comprise *Astral Weeks*. But after our evening together, Peter Wolf has become unreachable, and the likelihood of my hearing his tapes has vanished.

EIGHT

A Little More Light into the Darkness of Man

HALF A CENTURY of work has paid off: The houses on Fort Ave. Terrace, once dilapidated, are now gorgeous and homey. Inside #5, each room has its signature artisan flair, such as ornate woodworking around a door frame. Two Family members, one of whom has lived here since the late sixties, are my guides. We walk through the Connection and approach a long dining room table, where fifty Family members might be seated at Thanksgiving dinner. A framed picture of Mel Lyman hangs in many of the rooms. A page of his writing, mounted and displayed, decorates a narrow staircase in the back.

On this day, residents are doing dishes, enjoying coffee, watching television. Meeting the older members, I rewind their faces by fifty years to figure out if they were once featured in an *Avatar* photo spread. Some people get introductions, others remain nameless. At one point, someone resembling a piano player and would-be bank robber Terry Bernhard waves hello from the kitchen. In the living room of another house, Mel Lyman's banjo rests in a chair by the window, as if enjoying the view of Highland Park and the tower.

As we pass into the backyard, one of my hosts, a college professor named Randy Foote, plucks a grape off a vine on the trellis and pops it into his mouth. I do the same. With no fences to separate the lawns of the Family's houses, Fort Ave. Terrace's backyard seems to go on forever. I realize that this place is a paradise for about a dozen baby boomers. The view is lovely and the grapes are free. Is this what the endgame of a successful sixties commune looks like?

If this is a happy ending, it's a hard-earned one. In their early years, the Fort Hill Community harassed and frightened scores of people who crossed their path. Ex-members have taken the Family to court, trying to claim their share of the communal wealth. That's to say nothing of Mel Lyman augmenting his natural charisma with LSD, wielding the drug to foster devotion. Michael Bowen, cofounder of San Francisco underground newspaper *The Oracle*, recognized this when he met Lyman out on the West Coast. Upon seeing footage of Lyman's "psychedelic sessions," Bowen got a bad vibe. "He was using LSD to turn these people into zombies, reprogramming them," Bowen said. "We wanted none of that."

In the late fifties and early sixties, Boston and Cambridge served as ground zero for both the folk music revival and the origin of the American hallucinogenic revolution. From Harvard Square, chemicals and chord progressions leaked into the ether, drifting westward through America, altering the culture along the way. The histories of both movements converge in Mel Lyman. While rock's psychedelically inclined songwriters receive most of the credit for diving into the alternate worlds opened by LSD, Lyman's saga is a reminder that the folk revivalists, nurtured by Professor Timothy Leary's hallucinogenic rebellion at Harvard, first took that leap into the unknown.

Leary's explorations were often considered well intentioned if reckless; by contrast, Lyman's had an ulterior motive. Paula Press, all of seventeen when she arrived at Fort Hill in 1968, recalled her LSD journey as arranged by Mel. "He gives really strong doses, and I hallucinated and everything," she told *Rolling Stone.* "He was growing horns, they were growing all over the room, and he was changing from various kinds of animals." Similarly, novelist Kay Boyle, who lived on the Hill to be near her two children, was aghast when she listened to a tape of her daughter, Faith Gude, in the middle of an acid trip. "I love you, I love you, this is so marvelous," Gude said hysterically. "Oh Mel, you are the most beautiful man."

In his published writings about LSD, Lyman sounded more like Leary than a scary man sprouting horns. "There is no reason to fear it, we created it because we NEED it, like the electric light," he wrote, in a dense 1967 essay. "Everybody wants to know about it and that is proof enough of its importance. LSD does what alcohol did when IT was new and what EVERY new creation does, it lets a little more light into the darkness of man."

IT'S NO COINCIDENCE that Lyman's acid evangelism took root in Boston, the true birthplace of American hallucinogenic culture. The year was 1949, the location was the Boston Psychopathic Hospital on Fenwood Street, a mile and a half from Fort Hill. Dr. Otto Kauders, head of neurology and psychiatry at the University of Vienna, lectured on a new drug that mimicked mental psychosis. In the audience, Dr. Milton Greenblatt and Dr. Max Rinkel listened in awe as he described how a small dose had driven its inventor temporarily crazy. "We were very interested in anything that could make someone schizophrenic," Greenblatt recalled. If doctors could cause temporary insanity with a medicine dropper, they might better understand how to treat their patients. Perhaps LSD-25 could even help cure schizophrenia. Rinkel arranged an order of LSD-25 to be shipped from Sandoz Laboratories in Switzerland to Boston.

Neither Greenblatt nor Rinkel took the first dose of LSD in North America—for that, they turned to their boss, Dr. Robert Hyde. Rinkel gave Hyde a glass of water with 100 micrograms of LSD, less than half of inventor Albert Hofmann's initial, accidental dose. Feeling no effect, Hyde insisted he be permitted to make his rounds. Rinkel trailed him, later reporting that he "berated us and said the company had cheated us, given us plain water. That was not Dr. Hyde's normal behavior; he is a very pleasant man." Hyde and Rinkel soon ran larger LSD-25 tests on student volunteers at Boston Psychopathic.

The CIA caught wind of the study's unusual results and was eager to fund the operation. For them, a drug like this was valuable for far more than studying mental illness. They might develop a truth serum or find a way to reprogram minds. In 1953, Rinkel and Hyde began receiving grants from one of the CIA's fronts, the Society for the Investigation of Human Ecology. Soon, hundreds of students from Harvard, Emerson, and MIT were unwittingly assisting the agency's research into the possibility of mind control.

The subjects knew they were receiving something called LSD, and that reactions would range from "pleasant" to "unpleasant," but nothing prepared them for how otherworldly, surreal, or ego-crushing the experience might be. "We lost a couple," Philip Slater, one of Rinkel's assistants, told author Don Lattin. "One had to be hospitalized. Another went out in the street to see if cars were real." None of those involved in the experiments had the proper training or understanding to guide participants through what could be a positive, life-changing moment. In 1994, Dr. Robert Reid told the *Globe* that he was aware of at least one death associated with the program. "They gave this patient LSD one morning and when I came back from lunch that day, I was told she had hung herself in the downstairs bathroom."*

Intelligence agency director Allen Dulles described the CIA's efforts as

---

* It wasn't all a horror show. One of the earliest subjects was Latvian-born painter Hyman Bloom, an important artist in the Boston Expressionism movement. Bloom may have been the first artist anywhere to experiment with LSD's effect on creativity, and undoubtedly the first to do so in the United States. He was asked to draw two portraits of Rinkel, one at the beginning of the trip and another at the peak of the experience. The result was beautifully abstract. "[He] lost himself making dots and dashes," Rinkel told the *Globe*, which reproduced the drawings in the paper in 1965.

a "battle for men's minds." It was rumored that the Soviets were working day and night on "brain perversion techniques," so to compete, Dulles authorized a secret operation called MK-ULTRA. The objective was mind control, and LSD was just one of the possible keys, along with isolation, verbal abuse, and hypnosis.

Once again, the agency turned to Boston for assistance, in the form of Henry A. Murray, a Harvard professor who researched psychological screening tests and brainwashing techniques. Subjects submitted a short essay explaining their personal philosophy. Upon arriving the next day, they would be escorted into a harshly lit room, where a young lawyer tore their belief system apart. Murray designed the entire experience to be surprising and brutalizing.*

As Murray's tests continued in 1959, a dazzling new lecturer arrived on campus. Timothy Leary, a thirty-nine-year-old Massachusetts native, was a wunderkind in the field of psychology, author of a 1957 book, *The Interpersonal Diagnosis of Personality*. Relatively "straight" when he first arrived at Harvard, Leary was permanently altered in the summer of 1960 after consuming "seven of the Sacred Mushrooms of Mexico" during a trip to Cuernavaca. By the end of the night, Leary was reborn. "It was the classic visionary voyage," he wrote in 1968. "You are never the same after you've had that one flash glimpse down the cellular time tunnel. You are never the same after you've had the veil drawn."

Back at Harvard, Leary wrote Sandoz, requesting hallucinogens for academic research. "We expected to receive a long form back that had to be filled out and signed by various people," Leary's assistant George Litwin

---

* One test subject, Theodore Kaczynski, later became infamous as the Unabomber, sending a series of deadly bombs over a period of seventeen years. The FBI forensic psychiatrist who examined Kaczynski reported that the young student began having nightmares and concocting revenge fantasies around the time of Murray's experiment, and even worried about the possibility of mind control. (Despite rumors that Murray gave his subjects LSD, there is no evidence of this, and Kaczynski denied it.)

recalled. "Instead, what came in the mail was a large bottle of psilocybin pills with a little note that said, 'Good luck in your research. Let us know your findings.'"

Murray was interested in hallucinogenics, but hearing about Leary's recent experiences with magic mushrooms convinced him to experiment himself. It even seemed like a professional advantage: Leary declared that he learned more about psychology in his five-hour Mexican mushroom trip than in his preceding fifteen years of research. With Murray and others swayed by Leary's enthusiasm, the school approved the Harvard Psilocybin Project; he was now sanctioned to administer doses to students. The trips differed from those at Boston Psychopathic by emphasizing a supportive environment: Not only did you take LSD, but LSD also took *you*. If you were in a paranoid state under hospital lights, the trip would likely be horrific. If the tripper took the time to adjust her set (current mental state) and setting (physical location) before swallowing the pill, the chances for a positive experience grew exponentially.

RICHARD ALPERT FIRST spotted his colleague Timothy Leary working in a tiny office he had built himself in what had formerly been a closet. They became drinking buddies, and soon taught a course together called "Existential Transactional Behavior Change." Leary invited Alpert, ten years his junior, to be part of the Harvard Psilocybin Project. During his first trip, Alpert saw the versions of himself that he had groomed over the years. Then these social constructs peeled away, leaving only "a place where 'I' existed independent of social and physical identity." Alpert wanted everyone to feel this same sense of pure being. "We gave [psilocybin] to jazz musicians and physicists and philosophers and ministers and junkies and graduate students and social scientists," he later wrote. Only 3 percent "transcended all form and saw just pure energy . . . a homogeneous field. It has been called the White Light."

As the son of a prominent Boston attorney, Alpert had always been on the fast track to professional success; he had already been a visiting professor at Berkeley before arriving at Harvard, impressive for a man not yet thirty. "Before I got involved with Tim, I was leading a shady life," he later said. "I was a professor and I was cruising parks and men's rooms." In Cambridge, he hosted dinner parties in his antique-filled apartment. He drove a Mercedes-Benz and flew a Cessna. "I was living the way a successful bachelor professor is supposed to live in the American world." Psilocybin made him realize something was wrong: "It was a hustle."

Despite Alpert's upstanding reputation, Harvard still fretted over the project. The study courted controversy, which reached a fever pitch in 1962, as papers ran headlines like: "HARVARD EATS THE HOLY MUSHROOM, RELIGIOUS VISIONS PRODUCED BY DANGEROUS BRAIN DRUGS." The chairman of the psychology department announced that any participating students would be dropped from the PhD program.

The details of how Harvard fired Richard Alpert, thus shuttering the Harvard Psilocybin Project, are not flattering to any of the parties involved. Leary and Alpert had promised the administration that they would not give any undergraduates the hallucinogenic pill, but Alpert made an exception for an attractive student named Ronnie Winston. Winston's friend and former roommate, Andrew Weil, was also desperate to try psilocybin, but Leary and Alpert turned him down. Weil pressured Ronnie Winston for details about the experience, then published an exposé in *The Harvard Crimson*. The school fired Alpert in May 1963.

YES—*THAT* ANDREW WEIL. Dr. Andrew Weil has one of the most recognizable faces in wellness; you've definitely seen him and his signature bushy white beard, whether on his PBS series, the covers of bestsellers like *Spontaneous Healing*, or as a guest on *Oprah*. Before he got famous, his writing led to the firing of Alpert and Leary; then, in 1968, he found himself in their shoes.

Shortly before arriving at Harvard, where he would study ethnobotany and become a *Crimson* editor, Weil read an article about a college student who died of a mescaline overdose while in search of inspiration for a creative writing class. A phrase in the piece—"galaxies of exploding colors"— captured Weil's imagination. "I resolved to devote my ingenuity to getting and trying mescaline," he wrote. At Harvard, Weil and Winston lobbied Leary for a dose; Leary declined but gave tantalizing descriptions of what these chemicals offered. "It is exhilarating. It shows us that the human brain possesses infinite possibilities. It can operate in space-time dimensions that we never dreamed even existed."

Writing on Harvard stationery, Weil found a company willing to ship him mescaline directly, and soon started blasting off his classmates. He required everyone to write up a report of their experience, like a miniature version of the school's sanctioned psychedelics project. As Weil was playing Leary Junior in his dorm, Richard Alpert broke his promise to the university and gave Ronnie Winston psilocybin. When Weil found out, he not only glimpsed Alpert's hypocrisy, but felt personally rejected. Soon he was working with both the *Crimson* and the administration to expose the Psilocybin Project, even as his own mescaline experiments continued. Weil's betrayal had a silver lining for Alpert and Leary: Both men became instant heroes of the counterculture.

Weil enrolled at Harvard Medical School, where he wanted to conduct a legitimate, properly controlled study of marijuana and bust the myths surrounding it. Studying the medical literature about any drug with any scandalous associations, he discovered only "a vast collection of rumor, anecdote, and secondhand accounts."

It wasn't until his final year of medical school, in 1968, that this became possible—just barely. Joe Oteri, Boston's so-called pot lawyer and one of *Avatar*'s defenders, bet Weil that he would never receive approval for the experiment. Harvard was especially strict because of the psilocybin project's demise, which Weil himself had brought about five years earlier; the threat of drug-related lawsuits loomed large. But in another irony, Weil's role in the Leary-Alpert debacle helped push the experiment through. "I got some minutes of the debate of the Harvard Medical School group that had to approve it, and there were actually statements that I was the one blowing the whistle on Alpert and Leary," he says. "That was one of the reasons that they agreed to let it go forward." In a twist that Philip K. Dick would savor, the pot study was green-lit, in part, because Weil had been a narc.

Harvard didn't make it easy, telling Weil he couldn't give the drug to people who had never tried it before. Weil balked. His entire experiment *required* marijuana-naive subjects. "It was the only way to standardize set," Weil notes. He began looking for pot virgins in his circle of friends, and failing that, took out ads in the local papers. "It took two months of interviewing prospective volunteers to come up with nine men from the student population of Boston who had never tried marijuana."

Throughout, Harvard badgered Weil, threatening to deny him academic credit if he strayed from their guidelines. "They wouldn't let it be done on their premises or any affiliated institutions, and they wouldn't let their students be used as subjects," Weil says. He felt so attacked he even reached out to his old nemesis.

"I'm in the same situation you were in," Weil told Richard Alpert over the phone.

Science published Weil's marijuana study in December 1968. "It made the front page of *The New York Times*, so I think people were impressed," he recalls. The findings were simple, elucidating things anyone who has ever smoked a joint would recognize, but that wasn't the point. The experiences offered by marijuana and more potent drugs were nearly impossible to quantify scientifically, but many of their supposed dangers found their way into print. Weil's work was a response to antidrug propaganda that appeared in newspapers regularly, with headlines like "BABY'S DEFORMITY BLAMED ON LSD."*

RICHARD ALPERT WOULDN'T become a spiritual leader until 1968, but by 1963 he had a following.

After his firing from Harvard, his research was now limited to 23 Kenwood Avenue in Newton. Richard Alpert looked around at all the people suddenly living in and visiting his house—artists, socialites, madmen, and even Leary's children—and mindfully noted that a cult was forming. "We were a cult turned inward," he would later say. The core group comprised Alpert, Ralph Metzner, Tim's children Susan and Jack Leary, and heiress Peggy Hitchcock, supplemented with an impressive roster of visitors, including Allen Ginsberg, Charles Mingus, and William Burroughs.

Alpert's Newton neighbors had never seen anything like it: cars coming and going at all hours, rock music blasting from open windows. The city council heard complaints; the *Boston Herald* announced, "BIG 'FAMILY' STIRS PROTEST: MEN DO THE DISHES IN NEWTON COMMUNE." The entire operation picked up stakes and moved to a mansion owned by Peggy Hitchcock's family, a vast estate in Millbrook, New York, which Ralph Metzner

---

* The *Science* publication launched Weil's writing career, but it seems he may have been publishing in other publications at the same time—under a pseudonym. According to editor Wayne Hansen, a short-lived *Avatar* column, "The Illuminated Pharmacologist," was Weil's work under an assumed name. Sure enough, consulting the issues in question, there are two lengthy pieces written by one "William Andrews," with a tone and content nearly identical to Weil's other writing at the time; the bio even describes him as a "fourth-year medical student in psychopharmacology living in Boston."

Weil remembers *Avatar* and the Fort Hill Community, but "does not recall" writing for the underground paper. Instead, he says, he wrote a critical piece on the community for *The Harvard Crimson*. Attempts to locate that particular article were unsuccessful, but Weil described it as such: "I was over there a couple times and talked to people. But, you know, I was very peripherally involved and I saw a little bit. It really was a cult around Mel Lyman. I'm not sure I knew quite what to make of it."

later described as "an ever-changing scene of magic and creativity." But internal disputes would eventually rip apart the community, and Alpert ditched the scene, more confused than ever.

Disillusioned with Leary, Millbrook, and, to an extent, hallucinogens too, he decided to seek answers outside the culture he was raised in. Alpert wanted to find out if Eastern holy men could tell him what LSD actually was. He spent three months wandering the Middle East with a bottle of the drug before landing in Nepal with full-blown depression. His attempts to have spiritual masters decode LSD had failed. He kept trying to explain his interesting backstory to his guide, Bhagwan Das, who would respond: "Don't think about the past. Just be here now." Bhagwan Das led Alpert to a valley in the shadow of the Himalayas, where they found a small man in his sixties, wrapped in a blanket, surrounded by a small group of followers. Bhagwan Dass fell at the feet of Neem Karoli Baba. Alpert expected to be disappointed. Then the guru told him that he, Alpert, had been thinking of his mother, who had died from a bloated stomach, the night before. It was true. Spellbound, the ex–Harvard professor burst into tears.

"Maharaji indicated he wanted to try LSD," Alpert said. "I didn't know if that was wise because he was old. One pill would have been enough for a person like me. He took all the pills at once. Nothing happened. He didn't have any reaction. He was saying, 'It's in you.'" For Alpert, this was the first time he witnessed someone take acid and emerge believing that godliness remained inherently inside the self—no drug necessary. Maharaji christened him Ram Dass, servant of God. Months passed, his beard grew. "You make many people laugh in America?" Maharaji asked him one day. It was time to go home.

When he stepped off the plane at Logan Airport in late 1968, he didn't resemble the man who had departed for India the year before. Barefoot and bearded and wearing a robe, he didn't even have the same name. Home at last, Ram Dass just wanted to "sort of be by myself in a cabin on my father's farm and just live like I lived in India." But driving his father's Cadillac to pick up some groceries in a small New Hampshire town, he ran into some kids trying to score acid.

Ram Dass asked why they were asking. "Well, we see a Cadillac from Massachusetts and a guy that looks like you and we assumed. We were waiting for a connection to come into town—we assumed you're it."

"I'm not that kind of connection anymore," Ram Dass told the kids.

"Well," one of them said, confused, "what kind of connection are you?" They listened, rapt, as he described his experiences in India. "They came to the house and then they brought their friends and then they brought their parents and the ministers and the whole thing developed until pretty soon 200 to 300 people were coming every weekend just to hang out and talk about spirit and stuff like that," Ram Dass said.

"The family felt that to some extent it was an invasion of our privacy," William Alpert, his brother, admitted, in the documentary *Ram Dass: Fierce Grace*. "On the other hand we realized that Richard was doing a very good thing here. I know my mother-in-law, for example, was absolutely in love with him. She said, 'Whenever you have him over the house, please let me be there. I just find it so peaceful to be with him.'"

The press delighted in the story of the notorious Harvard drug prof turned guru. Reporter Robert Taylor followed Ram Dass around for a *Globe* profile, initially planning to unveil a fraud. Instead he found one of "the most engaging, lucid, and extraordinary persons I ever encountered and I am still deeply stirred by his splendid human qualities."

"At Harvard I was a Good Guy. Then a Bad Guy. Then a Bad Good Guy," Ram Dass told him. "Now I'm almost back to being a Good Guy again."

AS LSD USAGE skyrocketed in the United States, fewer users kept tabs on set and setting. Many didn't know the dosage of what they were ingesting, or if it was even LSD in the first place. The backlash over psychedelics grew, until 1966, when Senator Thomas J. Dodd called for a Senate sub-committee to look into regulating the drug. Leary was brought in as an expert witness. Massachusetts senator Ted Kennedy went on the attack, asking him to detail the drug's harmful effects. "Sir, the motor car is dangerous if used improperly," Leary told the subcommittee. "Human stu-pidity and ignorance is the only danger human beings face in this world." *The New York Times* headline made it sound like Leary was against his own cause: "LEARY SEES CRISIS IN USE OF LSD."

"The key to your work is advertising," media critic Marshall McLuhan advised him over lunch, after hearing his less-than-stellar testimony. "You're promoting a product. The new and improved accelerated brain. You must use the most current tactics for arousing consumer interest. Associate LSD with all the good things that the brain can produce." From now on, he *always* had to smile when in public: "Wave reassuringly. Radiate courage. Never complain or appear angry . . . you must be known for your smile." It worked: The image of a smiling Leary, even when handcuffed, is what most people remember to this day. All he needed now was a slogan, which he landed on a few days later while taking a shower: "Turn on, tune in, drop out."

Leary's campaign for expanded consciousness brought him back to Cambridge in 1967. He agreed to debate MIT professor Jerome Lettvin and have the whole event filmed for WGBH, airing with the title *LSD—Lettvin vs. Leary*. Lettvin, a frequent guest on *What's Happening, Mr. Silver?*, was a boisterous, opinionated crowd-pleaser. At first, the two agreed that ban-ning drugs outright would create a black market and increase demand. But tension mounted, culminating in Lettvin's literally calling bullshit (the word aired, unedited) on some of Leary's claims.

He hit a low point in 1968. "A year ago LSD was almost as big as Tim Leary," wrote the *Democrat and Chronicle*. "Today they are both terribly vieux chapeau." Even media institutions once on Leary's side were now taking potshots at him. Reviewing his latest book, *High Priest*, *The New Republic* declared that "his rhetoric has a patina of phoniness." The *Globe* hit even harder: "Leary is a pathetic pioneer, involved in a crusade that must finally destroy him, not because of the degenerative dangers in LSD, but because of the kookie manner in which he has thrown his challenge at society." Even *Mad* magazine jumped in, giving his six-word mantra a dark twist: TURN ON, TUNE IN, DROP DEAD.

The Staggers-Dodd Bill passed in October, making LSD illegal in the United States. A few months later, Leary was arrested for marijuana possession in Laguna Beach, for which he would receive a ten-year sentence.

BACK IN CAMBRIDGE in 1964, Leary and Alpert had left a woman named Lisa Bieberman in charge of the boring details as they spent more time at the Millbrook commune. As a Radcliffe math and philosophy student, Bieberman had been by the pair's side since the beginning. "I'd always wanted to have a mystical experience," she told the *Crimson*. "I began to hang around Leary's office after classes, licking envelopes, typing letters, and running errands. And I faithfully read all the papers they put out." When Leary and Alpert founded the International Federation for Internal Freedom, to continue their work without Harvard's assistance, they made Bieberman their office manager. Bieberman stayed the course while everyone else moved into more decadent territory. She wanted to provide sensible resources for potential trippers. "Bieberman was the ultimate responsible entheogen user," Joyce Milton recalled. "A highly spiritual person, she took drugs only as an aid to meditation. The Millbrook crowd considered her boring." Andrew Weil remembers her differently. "She was a wild woman, a staunch supporter of Leary and IFIF, often caricatured by Leary's critics," he says. "Very outspoken."

While Leary, Alpert, and Metzner were writing a manuscript based on the *Tibetan Book of the Dead*, Bieberman took a more practical approach to helping people. In 1963, she opened the Psychedelic Information Center in Harvard Square, publishing the *Psychedelic Information Center Bulletin*—the

PIC Bulletin for short. Prior to Bieberman's bulletin, the only local source of drug-related information available was a woozy, anonymous newsletter titled *Leaves of Grass*.

PIC's services, it turned out, were high in demand. Her phone would ring at two a.m., the callers wanting to know "When does this stuff wear off?" or what to do when the cops pick up your girlfriend with 40 kilos of pot. These cries for help inspired Bieberman's Psychedelic Telephone Directory, a simple list of friendly people you could call if you got into trouble. "There should be someone more appropriate to phone than your mother, your ex-girl, your psychiatrist, or the President," she said. For fifty cents, you could purchase a large list of names and numbers that were willing to pick up your call and talk you down from a terrifying trip.

Bieberman's no-nonsense approach now seems ripe for parody. She made an educational film titled *LSD: You Are Not a Bird*, and published a chart that asked "How High Are You?" As Leary and Alpert coated all of their statements with Eastern mysticism, Bieberman made sure her writing wouldn't be out of place in a high school nurse's office. In her definitive publication, *Session Games People Play: A Manual for the Use of LSD*, she laid out the possible traps one might encounter in the middle of a trip—and a guide to escaping them. "I wanted to make the drug available to people who had never taken it," she wrote.

Her quest to bestow the miracle chemical on the uninitiated ended abruptly in 1966 when Bieberman was busted for sending LSD through the mail. The *Crimson* reported that it was the first trial in New England on such charges. Bieberman was found guilty on all four counts, the penalty for which could include a four-year prison sentence, but when it came time for her sentencing, the judge was lenient: "If I were you I would disassociate myself from Dr. Leary's group and think for myself," he said. She was given a year's suspended jail sentence.

Bieberman already sensed how corrupt the movement had become. "Flower power is no substitute for integrity," she wrote, describing the

204 · RYAN H. WALSH

vacant dropouts who loitered outside the Psychedelic Information Center. Eulogizing a friend in the pages of the *PIC Bulletin*, she noted, "Jim belonged to a time when we thought the world could be enlightened just by flooding it with acid."

By 1968, she was ready for a do-over. She wrote a long feature for the *Globe* on the "betrayal and promise" of the psychedelic experience, exposing what Leary and his followers had become. "People have left Millbrook because their marriages broke up, because they were falsely accused by Leary of being heroin addicts, because they 'freaked out' on LSD, because they sensed that the neuroses they went there to cure were getting worse instead of better, or because Leary just got tired of them." In her estimation, the psychedelic establishment "brainwashed" kids into thinking they were part of a revolution, and she no longer wanted any part of it. (Leary shot back in his book *The Politics of Ecstasy*, calling Bieberman "a pure-essence eccentric paranoid in the grand tradition of bullheaded, nutty women.")

She published one more article on psychedelics, in late 1968, which reads like a Dear John to the substance that changed her life. In her piece, Bieberman makes the unlikely argument that the LSD experience is actually simple. "It is not bizarre, but clear," she wrote. The experience did nothing more than let the user be certain of several specific truths, which she outlined beautifully and succinctly, starting with:

> The world is real;
> The God who created it is alive, and will stay that way;

THE GOD WHO CREATED IT IS ALIVE, *and will stay that way*. But what happens when users start believing they're the creator?

Ram Dass recounted a visit to a mental asylum. "I met a patient there who told me he was God. I said to him, 'So am I.' He was quite upset because he wanted to be the only one.

"You see, we all want to be God. But the fact is we are *all* God."

It seems fitting that Mel Lyman first got the idea that he might be God at the former Richard Alpert's Newton home in the summer of 1963.

Charles Giuliano remembers those sojourns to 23 Kenwood clearly. "Mel always had that kind of messianic side to him even before Kenwood," he says. "He had climbed the mountain and had the tablets." Lyman, Giuliano, and John Kostick were all living in a house together in Waltham when Mel began to talk about the place he had been visiting in Newton to acquire morning glory seeds. The two roommates followed Lyman, stunned that they could simply walk through the front door. Alpert and Leary's Harvard scandal had been all over the papers that spring—they were infamous. Giuliano recalls staring awestruck at a telegram from Leary in Mexico affixed to the fridge, instructing Richard Alpert to send "the best cats to Mexico."

Giuliano recalls one man living there who would trip and take on the persona of Tarzan the Ape Man, climbing up trees in the backyard. Richard Alpert was there too, of course, but it was Bruce Conner, a powerhouse renaissance artist working in collage, film, and painting, who made the deepest impression. "Very trippy, very pranky, very complicated," Giuliano says. "I remember him being in the basement of Kenwood editing movies and some of those movies becoming some of the most important films of that time." Years later, on the occasion of his 2016 MOMA retrospective, *The New York Times* would concur, calling him "one of the great outliers of American art." His 1962 film *Cosmic Ray* was an underground hit, and some see him as the father of MTV, for his video work with artists like Devo.

Winding up in Massachusetts after time spent in Mexico, Conner got close to Lyman and his folk music circle. Unable to find like-minded visual artists in the area, he performed with Jim Kweskin and Geoff Muldaur at Club 47, sometimes "flailing about" on harmonica, or using his own conceptual scores.

Conner recalled his first encounter with Lyman. "[He] was there three or four nights a week at the coffee grinder, grinding up [morning glory] seeds from this 500-pound bag we had in the kitchen," he told *Rolling Stone*. "And everybody was getting fucked up. Mel just had them swallow the seeds, not soak them and everything the way it said in *Anthropological Review*, and all these people were falling down on their faces and hemorrhaging and falling down in the bathroom and talking about how great it was afterwards." Eventually, Lyman and Conner got around to discussing God and cosmic consciousness. From the *Rolling Stone* exposé:

> "And I told Mel one of my private theories. I said that mostly what people do when they talk about God is a projection of what they think God is, and it always comes down to a projection from a person. So the best way to find out what God is is to say you're God yourself. And maybe the first way to do this was if somebody was on the phone and they said, 'Oh my God!' and then you say, 'Yes? What is it?' And you could just go on from there.
>
> "I didn't think about it after that," said Conner. "It was just an idea—I wasn't gonna use it myself. But in retrospect, I figure Mel must have used it."*

"IT WAS THE ERA OF THE BODHISATTVAS," Giuliano says. "Everyone at that time had dropped acid, and seen God, and thought they were the godhead. EVERY SINGLE PERSON you encountered was, to some extent, a deity." Even a member of Van Morrison's Boston band experienced this phenomenon—without acid. During the manic episode that led flutist John Payne to end up at McLean Hospital, the Harvard student had the idea

---

* Conner also erroneously announced his own death on two occasions as a conceptual art prank—bringing to mind Felton's conjecture that Lyman might have later faked his own death, to live out his days anonymously abroad.

that he might in fact be God.* "Johnny turned on the radio by his bed and instructed it to go faster or slower, and he found the radio would go faster or slower at his command, and he became frightened by the power," Payne's sister Sarah recalled in her memoir.

"Don't crucify me!" he shouted. "I came here searching for truth, *veritas*, and Harvard doesn't know what *veritas* is!"

Meanwhile, in the letters section of *Avatar*, readers interrogated Lyman on the truth of his continued declarations of deityhood. One reader described a recent acid-induced religious experience wherein Mel Lyman appeared inside a Copley Square church as the face of God. "WHAT GIVES?" the reader demanded. "Either you've got me believing your egotistical ideas or maybe you really are him?!?!"

"I really am him," Lyman replied. "Shouldn't be so hard to take, imagine how it makes ME feel."

VAN MORRISON WASN'T trying to trigger spiritual conversions with his new songs. But for producer Lewis Merenstein, something about the title track of *Astral Weeks* almost did.

"It was Van, alone with a guitar, and he played 'Astral Weeks' the song for me right then and there," Merenstein says. "I got the distinct feeling that he was *going back in time*, going back *to be born again*, and it moved me, spiritually, quite a bit." What he sang for Merenstein was closer to something you'd hear at Club 47 than on a psychedelic Bosstown Sound record, but on another level, the deceptively simple song seemed like something entirely original. *Astral Weeks* minted its own genre.

"It's all coded spirituality," Merenstein insists. "The whole album.

---

* Around the time that Payne and his relative Robert Lowell overlapped at McLean, the famous poet himself had a God-tinged revelation; Timothy Leary had turned Lowell on to acid a few years earlier. "Now I know what Blake and St. John of the Cross were talking about," Lowell told Leary. "This experience is what I was seeking when I became a Catholic."

That's why people are so mystified by it. Who is born again? *Who is Madame George?** The mystery grows because it's all a spiritual quest that is essentially unknowable. The radio won't play songs about Jesus or spirituality, you know." Merenstein explains that had he traveled to Boston six months earlier or later, the mystery and power of the song might have been lost on him. He might have shrugged and asked, "What does that even mean?" He tells me, "It hit me right where I was in that period of my life."

The 2015 re-release of *Astral Weeks* speaks to Merenstein's interpretation. The original album fades out with "Slim Slow Slider" at around the three-minute mark, but on the extended version, the chaotic riffing gives way to just Morrison and Payne, a hymn for voice and flute. A song that once documented the loss of a lover, possibly to heroin, now ends in a vision of the divine, as Morrison sings "Glory be to Him" over and over.

THE VIBRANT FOLK SCENE WAS DYING. The 1967 opening of the Boston Tea Party had, almost overnight, rendered Club 47 in Cambridge old-fashioned. In 1968, inspired by Mel Lyman's intense appearance on *What's Happening, Mr. Silver?*, his old bandmate Jim Kweskin exhibited increasingly strange behavior onstage. "The last few months were the dumbest," said mandolin player Geoff Muldaur. Someone in the audience would request a song, and Kweskin would try to have a conversation instead of just

---

* Fifty years on, listeners still parse the identity of Madame George. It seems straightforward enough: We see her "in the corner, playing dominoes in drag," and most fans consider the titular figure of *Astral Weeks'* centerpiece to be a drag queen. "[W]ith the promises of the forbidden, of drink and cigarettes, drugs and music, sex and fantasy," Greil Marcus writes, the titular character "gathers young boys around herself to stave off a killing burden of loneliness." Lester Bangs puts Morrison in the picture, saying that his depiction of "a lovelorn drag queen" is sung "with such intense empathy that when the singer hurts him, we do too." (Incredibly, Morrison himself denies that the character is a drag queen.) What does it mean that "George" is Van's actual first name? Or that it often sounds like he's singing "Madame Joy"—which was the song's original title? Perhaps the best way to contemplate all this is with a Ram Dass saying in mind: "Treat everyone you meet like God in drag."

performing. "The disbanding of Jim Kweskin's Jug Band was the most obvious sign that the Cambridge/Boston musical community was breaking up," wrote Eric Von Schmidt in his memoir of the era.

The Fort Hill Community, of which Kweskin was now a part, wanted to keep Club 47 alive. They threw a benefit concert on March 24, 1968, but instead of music, they played tapes of Lyman talking. The audience felt tricked. When *Avatar* editor John Wilton showed up, he saw that "total insanity had erupted, beginning with Eben [Given] breaking up furniture and ending with a free for all on stage." A huge brawl ensued. People sobbed uncontrollably. It was Mel Lyman's birthday.

It should come as no surprise that this benefit concert did not save Club 47, which closed a month later. Kweskin released a solo album that year titled *What Ever Happened to Those Good Old Days at Club 47? Broadside*, once the folkie's bible, now covered the Bosstown Sound. LSD was illegal, and the folk scene had given up the ghost.

What kind of God would allow these things to happen?

NINE

The Noises That Roar in the
Space Between the Worlds

"THE DETAILS ARE GRISLY, the people are lunatic, but the results are magnetic," *The New York Times* wrote about one of the strangest novels to appear in 1968—or any year. The book was Russell H. Greenan's *It Happened in Boston?*, the very punctuation a provocation. The lucid but deeply unhinged narrator is a painter of genius, working in the meticulous style of Da Vinci and other Renaissance masters. Outraged by the death of his friend Littleboy, and the destruction of his canvases—not to mention the cruelly transient nature of all things—Alfred Omega (as he's sometimes called) demands some face-to-face time with his Creator. But how to summon the Almighty? "I haunted the public library and the book shops on Huntington Avenue, ever in quest of new fodder," he explains. "How I hunted! Sundays found me in churches, and Saturdays in mosques and temples. I joined societies, attended lectures, subscribed to periodicals." Omega studies horoscopes, tarot, and Ouija boards before finally locating the instructions he's seeking in a bookstore on Columbus Avenue: a tome containing "various formulas for communicating with the other world." First, he merely summons an angel. Then, slipping cyanide into sugar bowls at diners, he murders seven Bostonians. As the book draws to a close, Omega's human sacrifices seem to lead to his desired meeting with God—or is it all a fever dream?

Eleven novels followed *It Happened in Boston?*, but Greenan, who is in his nineties and living in Providence, admits that his debut had "a kind of psychometaphysical aura" that set it apart from the rest. Greenan lived in Boston off and on for a number of years, beginning in 1950; he ran two antique shops, and loved the European charm of its cobblestone streets. But despite his taste for the past and proclivity for the arcane, he had no idea that the city had been a hotbed of occultism in the previous century. Indeed, it's uncanny that no one who was writing about or working with occult practices in Boston in the late sixties—neither Greenan, nor Lou Reed, nor the Fort Hill Community, nor Jonathan Richman—realized Boston once used to be *the* place from which to reach the astral plane.

AMERICAN SPIRITUALISM—the belief that the living could communicate with the dead—can be traced to the central New York town of Hydesville, where in 1848, the two young Fox sisters heard—and somehow produced—knocking sounds, which they said came from souls in the afterlife. Spiritualism grew into a quasi religion that was embraced in cities like New York and Chicago, but none did so as fervently as Boston. Starting in 1857, at the corner of Province and Boswell streets, the movement opened the offices of its most popular newspaper, *Banner of Light*, just as Beacon Hill became home to a number of well-known mediums like Fanny Conant and the Berry Sisters. "That city is really the Mecca of the spiritualistic faith," the *Fort Wayne Weekly Gazette* said of Boston in 1895. "In no other city are there so many mediums, such a multiplication of circles and congregations."

The first great Spiritualist church in America—dubbed "the Great Spook Temple" by the press—opened in 1884 at the corner of Exeter and

Newbury streets. A half mile away at 53 Berkeley Street stood Parker Memorial Hall, opened fourteen years earlier as a tribute to Reverend Theodore Parker, who predicted that Spiritualism would become "the religion of America." Nearly a century later, this popular spot for Spiritualist lectures and séances housed both the Boston Tea Party and the Fort Hill Community's Film-Makers' Cinematheque.

For those who required visual proof, Boston was also the origin of Spirit Photography, which appeared to capture the specter of the deceased, looming behind a living person. Engraver William Mumler, who claimed to stumble upon the phenomenon in 1861, eventually converted his Washington Street engraving workshop into a full-time "Spirit Photography" studio. A few years later, local entrepreneur G. W. Cottrell began mass-producing his "Boston Planchettes," selling them for a dollar a pop out of a stationery store on Cornhill Street. Carved from black walnut with three caster wheels, these tools were the first such devices in the country, designed to fill a blank piece of paper with messages from the beyond. (Later, Ouija boards came with their own variation.)

The city being such a magnet for Spiritualism, it was only a matter of time before one of the accidental founders of the movement showed up. In 1872, Margaret Fox set up a séance studio on Washington Street, where, shockingly, one of her first visitors was Mary Todd Lincoln, the assassinated president's widow. For ten days, she made frequent visits to Fox's parlor, attempting to contact her husband on the other side via group séances. According to coverage of the rituals in *The New York Times*, "the spirit of her lamented husband appeared and, by unmistakeable manifestations, revealed to all present the identity of Mrs. Lincoln."

Trying to make sense of all this was the American Society for Psychical Research, headquartered in the cozy alley known as Boylston Place, a few doors down from the studio where Van Morrison would audition "Astral Weeks" some eighty years later. Inside, like a real-life *X-Files* department, respected psychologists including Harvard's William James explored the validity of the claims of Spiritualism and such phenomena as hypnosis and precognition.

It happened in Boston? Indeed.

BY 1968, all but the most dedicated historians of the occult had largely forgotten Boston's strange spirit history. But T. Mitchell Hastings, owner of a classical music radio station on Newbury Street, still took careful stock of such matters.

Hastings, a 1933 Harvard graduate, was an unusually close friend of the "Sleeping Prophet" Edgar Cayce, who made predictions and detailed subjects' past lives while in a trance state. The Sleeping Prophet's celebrity is hard to imagine today: Irving Berlin, George Gershwin, and Woodrow Wilson all sought his counsel. As Mitch Horowitz notes in *Occult America*, words like *reincarnation*, *meditation*, *past lives*, and *psychic* became household terms through Cayce's influence. Hastings's parents were wealthy Spiritualist Manhattanites, who had introduced their son to Cayce during sessions held at their home in the early 1930s. Cayce predicted their son would find success in a field dependent on "electrical energy."

In February 1934, Hastings took Cayce for a ride in his Pontiac, all the way to Arizona, where, in the presence of a certain crystal formation, they experienced a revelation that supposedly heightened their powers of clairvoyance. Already worried about what people thought of him, Hastings kept this mystic vacation a closely guarded secret. But after his 1954 invention of an FM transistor that could function inside a moving car, he didn't care who knew of his eccentricities. (One Cayce biographer claims that Hastings's FM invention was a direct by-product of the Sleeping Prophet's "trance counsel.")

In the late 1950s, Hastings formed the General Broadcasting Network as a "Golden Chain" of East Coast FM stations all dedicated to classical music: WNCN New York City, WHCN Hartford, WXCN Providence, WRCN

Long Island, and WBCN Boston. "[Hastings] lived in another world; he could have been an extraterrestrial," program director Ron Della Chiesa recalled. "But he also believed in the power of classical music to awaken the spirit and mind." Poor business decisions had broken apart Hastings's "Golden Chain"; by the late sixties only WBCN remained in his collection of FM radio stations. In 1968, when his radio empire seemed to be just about finished, Hastings met a man who would turn everything around: Ray Riepen, Kansas City lawyer and owner of the Boston Tea Party. Riepen was interested in playing some weird music on WBCN very late at night.

RAY RIEPEN'S DAILY drives from his rock club to his apartment might as well have been victory laps. Almost by accident, he had turned the Boston Tea Party into a resounding success, both with the music fans who bought tickets and with the journalists covering the scene, including Riepen's every move. The logical next step? A radio station that would play the same acts that performed at the Tea Party. Riepen pulled station earnings reports for the area, looked at the bottom of the list, and walked right over to WBCN. T. Mitchell Hastings had already filed for bankruptcy once, and was on the brink of filing again. Before his death in 1945, Edgar Cayce had predicted that the lost city of Atlantis would rise again in 1968. Cayce had also convinced Hastings that he'd been an Atlantean scientist in a previous life, which is all to say: The station owner had planned for a weird twelve months. So when Riepen asked to commandeer the airwaves between midnight and six for rock 'n' roll ("Your audience goes to bed at 8:30, so what's the harm?"), Hastings said yes.

For the second time, Riepen's entry into a new Boston business venture was facilitated by someone with mystical beliefs. Between Hastings and the Fort Hill Community, everywhere he turned in Boston, it seemed that if there wasn't some kind of corruption or miles of red tape to wade through, there was an astrology chart or a story about a psychic encounter.

For his new venture, Riepen embarked on a fact-finding mission at Boston area college radio stations. He wanted amateurs. At Tufts' WTBS, he startled Joe Rogers, a local kid who broadcasted at night under the moniker Mississippi Harold Wilson. "I went over while he was on the air," Riepen says. "There weren't any locks on the door or anything, so I let myself in." Rogers was spooked by "a guy in a three-piece suit and very severe-looking glasses just standing in the doorway."

Like the team-building montage in a heist movie, Riepen stomped all over town, rounding up amateur DJs. Peter Wolf received a similar visit, though Riepen first hit him up for money, to see if he'd invest in the station.

"Ten thousand dollars?" Wolf was aghast. "Ray, I don't have *ten* dollars."

"Well, listen, you've got ten thousand records!" Riepen countered. So why not be a DJ?

Joe Rogers didn't expect anything to come out of his late-night encounter, but six weeks later, on March 15, 1968, he was summoned to appear at 171 Newbury Street at ten p.m. to start work—the very first broadcast of WBCN's new late-night format. Rogers hiked up four flights into a claustrophobic cluster of rooms. He could barely speak that first night on air—thanks, in a roundabout way, to Mel Lyman. Muriel, a friend of the DJ's, had recently gone to Fort Hill, interested in contributing art to *Avatar*. Lyman gave her a private LSD session and proceeded to pantomime his own crucifixion for her. "It flipped her out," Rogers said, and she spent some time at McLean Hospital to recover. The day of Rogers's first shift, Muriel noted how tense he looked and offered him one of the downers that she had been given at McLean to process the residual stress from her run-in with Mel. The DJ took it, then dropped to the floor, barely able to stay awake. He walked glacially toward the turntable and placed a Frank Zappa LP down. His nerves and the meds sparked a comically odd demeanor. "Go do your goddamned radio show!" Riepen yelled from the other room. "Don't fuck it up!"

Leading with "Nasal Retentive Calliope Music"—two minutes of col-laged sound effects, percussion crashes, high-pitched laughter, and record-skipping noises—must have made it sound like demons were tearing apart the station, even to people who had tuned in specifically to hear something differ-ent. Cream's "I Feel Free" returned things to the realm of melody. Riepen knew a good hook when he saw one, so he followed the spirit of the Tea Party's successful name and dreamed up WBCN's slogan: The American Revolution. "Ugly Radio Is Dead," the ads read, and the desired audience knew *exactly* what that meant: loud DJs, obnoxious cadences, insipid jingles, the same bubblegum pop played every hour. "Once people hear the music we play," Riepen told the *Globe*, "they'll find it difficult to go back to the Top Forty."

For two hours that first night, Joe Rogers made odd bedfellows on the air—spinning Jim Kweskin's Jug Band after Canned Heat, say—but he barely spoke between songs. When he did, the words came out slowly. Rog-ers somehow stayed awake, then tossed to Peter Wolf. The Hallucinations front man had walked from his place in Cambridge carrying a crate of vi-nyl; his knowledge of musical history would be unmatched among the orig-inal WBCN DJs. His cohost gave his wild on-air persona the name Woofa Goofa. Wolf was one of the few Boston "freaks" that Riepen actually devel-oped a friendship with. "Because of my relationship with Ray, I was given carte blanche," Wolf explained. This freedom included playing obscure blues musicians and a band from Belfast called Them.

It must have seemed like a sign from above when hard-on-his-luck Van Morrison, recently transplanted to Cambridge, started hearing himself on WBCN. When the mysterious DJ started asking for mail, Morrison knew what to do. In the spring of 1968—after Peter Wolf and Van Morrison fi-nally met in person at the Boston Tea Party—Morrison began hanging out with Wolf during his overnight shifts at WBCN.

Over the years, many Morrison songs invest radios with an almost reli-gious power. In "Brown Eyed Girl," his lone solo hit at the time, the singer ventures into the unknown—an "old mine"—armed only with a transistor radio. Later, in songs like "Wavelength" (1978) and "In the Days Before Rock 'n' Roll" (1990), the radio's a conduit for the sublime or divine. On the rave-up "Caravan," the singer constantly turns the volume dial to be able to access "the soul" of the song. In the concert film *The Last Waltz*, he's in convulsions as he directs the Band to "turn it up," as though playing the musicians like the radio in the song.*

That summer in Boston, Morrison occasionally performed his harrowing song "T.B. Sheets." Bassist Tom Kielbania got the backstory straight from the man himself. In high school, the singer knew a girl who was dying of tuberculosis. "He went to see her because he felt really bad, but he got upset because all she wanted to do was listen to music on the radio." On the 1966 recording, the singer offers to turn on the radio for her, if she wants to hear some tunes. Three decades later, Morrison would dismiss any autobiographical content as "absolutely absurd." The song, he said, was "complete and utter fiction." But Kielbania disagrees. He thinks he's located Van's Rosebud. "It's *why* he sings about radios a lot." It has to do with *this* girl and her obsession with the radio.

Van's awe at the power of radio calls to mind some of the earliest public reactions to the invention. Early listeners thought it worked via telepathy, or could be used to contact the dead. One reporter put it this way: "You are fascinated, though a trifle awestruck to realize that you are listening to sounds that, surely, were never intended to be heard by a human being." In 1922 *The New York Times* declared that it "brought to the ears of us Earth dwellers the noises that roar in the space between the worlds." For some, it

---

* One of the more cryptic lines in "Astral Weeks" has the singer "talkin' to Huddie Ledbetter / Showin' pictures on the wall." In the late sixties, Morrison kept a framed portrait of his musical hero Leadbelly, né Huddie Ledbetter. Sometime after *Astral Weeks* came out, feeling burdened by the image, he was about to throw it out. "At that moment I was fiddling around with the radio—I wanted to hear some music—and I tuned in this station and 'Rock Island Line' by Leadbelly came on," he said in a 1978 interview. "So I just turned around, man, and very quietly put the picture back on the wall."

did seem awfully close to the promises of spiritualism: Through use of a device, whether it be a Ouija board or a radio, messages from elsewhere seemed to drift in through the window.

In later years, Morrison would even describe his songwriting process as akin to tuning in a specific frequency on the radio, as if making music were about searching for the right melody and lyrics already existing in the ether. Sometimes the songs would come to Van while zoning out in front of a rolling tape recorder, but sometimes they even arrived in his sleep. While briefly living with the singer in New York in the fall of 1968, Tom Kielbania was woken up at three a.m. An idea had taken Van out of his sleep, and he wanted to capture it. He ordered the bleary-eyed Kielbania to grab his bass. "He starts singing this song about an electric radio," Kielbania says. "He dreamt it that night and we played it a couple of times so he could get it in his head."

He was almost certain this was a first draft of "Caravan." Electricity was flowing once again.

RAY RIEPEN'S HIPPIE SALESMEN found it easy to sell $5 broadcast ads to every head shop and thrift store on Mass Ave. Even Mel Lyman tried to associate himself with the coolest thing in town: *American Avatar* No. 3 sports a picture of him bugging his eyes out, trying to look even weirder than usual, under the words "LISTEN TO WBCN 104.1 BOSTON." "Previously, radio was just these terrible little AM stations," Tea Party manager Don Law recalls. "It didn't allow for much exposure for music, and FM completely blew the doors open for that. It was a huge shift." With an extended microphone cord, a WBCN DJ could climb onto the roof of 171 Newbury Street and speak to the entire city while the sun rose over Back Bay. "It was like looking over the rooftops of Paris," DJ Jim Parry wistfully remembered.

Soon a remote broadcast station was installed in the Boston Tea Party, where Fort Hill's Moon in Leo shop had recently closed. The merger was a brilliant move. "It didn't hurt us if we could talk to people like the Who, Led Zeppelin, Jeff Beck, or Rod Stewart between sets," Rogers says. It was a perfect loop: WBCN drove people to the Tea Party, and seeing bands at the Tea Party made people want to hear more at WBCN. If a DJ was broadcasting during a concert, they had to cover themselves and the microphone under a heavy blanket for soundproofing. This lo-fi trick worked, but made it look like ghosts had taken over.

In some ways, WBCN turned its hip marketing slogan—"The American Revolution"—into reality. Not only did the station's free-form nature trigger changes in the music industry, but it let DJs fearlessly wade into politics and protests even as the station's FCC license hung in the balance. Riepen obtained subscriptions to foreign news services to get the most accurate information about the developments in Vietnam, insisting his DJs refer to the other side as the "National Liberation Front" instead of the Americanized term "Vietcong." "It was important to let people know where they could get advice on what to do about the draft and the war," Joe Rogers explained. "The station insisted that [listeners] become informed on the subject." Riepen may not have sported a shaggy hairstyle, but his beliefs were legitimately aligned with the culture he was commercializing.

The Kansas City lawyer had proven the experts wrong; clearly, the youth market in Boston was "hipper than the assholes running broadcasting in America," as he put it. He had proven his point to T. Mitchell Hastings too, who turned over twenty-four-hour control of the station to the freaks in May—just two months after their debut.

Though the station's makeover was a success, all of Hastings's original hires—from the front desk girl on up—*hated* the weirdos who saved WBCN from bankruptcy. Ray Riepen recalls that Hastings fought the new programming every step of the way. "[He] was such a classical music lover and saw FM as the salvation for that music," Don Law noted. Which made it even more shocking to Hastings when he learned that the listeners embraced WBCN's rock offerings more than its classical programming. This was nothing like what his old friend Edgar Cayce had predicted. *Where was the lost city of Atlantis? And who the hell was Frank Zappa?*

The board of directors sold Ray a majority holding of the station's shares, making him the president and breaking Hastings's heart. Hastings tried to bring him down. Even the on-air personalities of WBCN grew to resent Riepen. Despite fostering the kind of environment that allowed them to do such a thing in the first place, they began to trash their boss live on the air as a loudmouthed big shot. By the time they unionized in 1971, Riepen had had enough. He sold his shares back to T. Mitchell Hastings for $220,000.

NONE OF THE STATION'S DEVOTED New England audience was aware of this behind-the-scenes strife; for WBCN fans, it was a nonstop miracle they could dial in at home or, thanks to T. Mitchell Hastings's earlier invention, in their automobile. "Driving alone at night, in the darkened car, reassured by the nightlight of the dashboard, tuned to a disembodied voice or music, evokes a spiritual, almost telepathic contact across space and time, a reassurance that we aren't alone in the void: we have kindred spirits," Susan J. Douglas wrote in *Listening In*, her history of the medium of radio.

If you changed a few words of that description and set them against a two-chord backdrop, you'd essentially have "Roadrunner," Jonathan Richman's classic Modern Lovers anthem about driving at night with the radio on. Bandmate John Felice described the song's inspiration: "We used to get in the car and we would just drive up and down Route 128 and the turnpike. We'd come up over a hill and he'd see the radio towers, the beacons flashing, and he would get almost teary-eyed. . . . He'd see all this beauty in things where other people just wouldn't see it. We'd drive past an electric plant, a big power plant, with all kinds of electric wire and generators, and he'd get all choked up, he'd almost start crying."

"Roadrunner" ends with the Modern Lovers chanting "Radio On!" as Richman maniacally lists the signs of the modern world unfurling all around him: factories, auto signs, a 50,000-watt radio signal, all of it an ode to "the power of Massachusetts." In 1966, when late-night drives were inspiring Richman, he was listening to an AM station, as he warbles in the song. But just two years later, a teenager borrowing her parents' car would have locked onto 104.1 on the other band. FM *was* a revolution—thanks to both Hastings's invention and Riepen's idea to play deep-cut album rock. In Boston legend, you could travel from one end of the city to the other with no radio in your car and always be in earshot of someone blasting WBCN.

T. MITCHELL HASTINGS was disturbed by the type of music that had saved his radio station, but he probably approved of the counterculture's sudden embrace of all things occult. On February 11, 1968, under the headline "WHAT A DECK!," *The Boston Globe* summarized the mystical moment to area readers: "An ancient fortune-telling card game called Tarot has become a favorite pastime for young Americans . . . it's the newest manifestation of the recent upsurge in interest in games of the occult." Ouija boards and ESP once again became all the rage in Boston. It was also the year the *Globe* started running the kind of daily astrology horoscopes that even church-loving readers enjoyed checking. If you wanted to know how your day might unfold, Jeane Dixon's star-crossed predictions were waiting for you on page 18.

"Newspapers were specifically looking for ways to stay current, and astrology columns provided a means," author Mitch Horowitz explains. "The counterculture was interested in all things mystical, provided they seemed to break with the religious culture of the 1950s." But why? Cultural critic Camille Paglia put forth an interesting theory in 2003. "The baby-boom generation was the first to grow up in the shadow of nuclear war," she wrote. "The sixties generation, in other words, had been injected with a mystical sense of awe and doom about the sky. This is one possible reason for the sudden popularity and ubiquity of astrology, which for most of the twentieth century had been a fringe practice." It was like 1868 all over again.

Of course, the Fort Hill Community and *Avatar* had jumped on the astrology train early; in 1967, the underground newspaper listed everyone's star sign in the masthead, and a "Using Astrology" column ran in every issue. This practice functioned almost like a "second tongue" for the FHC, closely guiding the group's decisions, as the *Los Angeles Times* would later note.* The January 5, 1968, issue of *Avatar* featured this unsigned poem:

> *I met a man today, like many, who didn't like astrology*
> *It is mysterious and such . . . he felt.*
> *Yes it is, I now reply, Astrology is the study of US*
> *and we are indeed a mystery; and funny that myself comes right*
> *before mystery in the Thesaurus*

PUBLISHED BY RANDOM HOUSE, *It Happened in Boston?* arrived in late 1968 with a pitch-perfect marketing campaign, summed up by the tagline: "It is impossible. It is real. And it happened in Boston." The Watch and Ward Society didn't lift a finger to ban it; indeed, the weird new novel seemed of a piece with the burgeoning New Age climate.

In the closing chapters, Alfred Omega's terrible murders are revealed— yet no God appears as promised. So the narrator dons a disguise and begins a desperate escape out of Boston via Commonwealth Avenue, with police in pursuit. As he proceeds through the city, the idea of suicide becomes

---

* Up on Fort Hill, there could be a chicken-or-egg quality to the assessment of someone's actual personality and the one suggested by their astrological sign. When Faith Gude caught wind that new Family member Daria Halprin wished she could change her sign, the *Zabriskie Point* star was needled about it in a recorded conversation, finally replying, "Because I won't have to work at anything . . . because I could just be a fantastic person." During *Astral Weeks* flute player John Payne's one visit to the Fort Hill Community in 1969, an initial misreading of his sign triggered a temporary royal treatment. "It felt great. I was enthusiastic, going 'yeah, Capricorn!' Then someone rushed over and said that December 16 wasn't a Capricorn, it was a Sagittarius." The room totally deflated and the excitement brewing around Payne vanished instantly.

palatable, and he heads toward Cottage Farm Bridge to "tidy up my life by concluding it."

His escape is interrupted on the Boston University campus, where two men recognize him. Just as it seems that there's no way out, the tormented painter suddenly gets his wish: a meet and greet with God. Before his eyes, the city transforms into "parallelepiped houses of colored crystal rose," while the sky becomes "a bronze bowl encrusted with a pair of blood-red suns." The stage is set; God approaches.

While Greenan doesn't cite it by name, the description—"three arched entrances set at the top of a flight of broad granite steps" near some "buildings of Boston University"—suggests that the church in question is Marsh Chapel at 735 Commonwealth Avenue. Greenan confirms to me that this is indeed the place he had in mind.

The information isn't trivial, but a sort of accidental skeleton key to the book—because the most famous real-life event to take place at Marsh Chapel was *also* an attempt to access God through unorthodox, even scandalous, means: the Good Friday Experiment of 1962, aka the Marsh Chapel Miracle, in which Walter N. Pahnke and Tim Leary brought twenty divinity students into the basement of the chapel and fed half of them psilocybin pills.

Greenan was blissfully unaware of the experiment while writing the book. "I chose the chapel by chance," he tells me. "When I first came to Boston, I lived and worked in the Kenmore Square area, and often walked by the chapel. It does seem an odd coincidence. Why in heaven's name did they hold the trial in a church?"

Like Greenan's narrator Alfred Omega, they wanted to know if there was a shortcut to meeting God.

Pahnke and Leary are deceased, but Dr. Gunther Weil, who was a facilitator at the Marsh Chapel Miracle, is still alive. Weil (no relation to Andrew Weil) was pursuing his doctorate at Harvard in the early sixties when, like Lisa Bieberman, he began to work closely with Leary and Richard Alpert. He also assisted Leary during his Concord Prison Experiment with psilocybin.

Later, Weil would open the Intermedia Recording Corporation on Newbury Street, working with a fledgling local band named Aerosmith through the demo-cutting process for their song "Dream On."* But in the early sixties, before the Beatles had ever stepped down upon U.S. soil, Weil's focus was on exploring inner worlds. "We were the experimenters," Weil says. "[The Good Friday Experiment] was [Pahnke's] idea, and we ended up buying into it."

On the morning of April 20, 1962, Pahnke, Leary, and Weil brought twenty divinity students into the basement of Marsh Chapel and gave half of them 30 milligrams of psilocybin, and the other half a placebo. Most of the facilitators, of course, also took psilocybin. The Good Friday worship service being conducted upstairs in the main chapel was piped into the smaller basement chapel's speaker system. Reverend Howard Thurman, the chaplain of the church and a major influence on BU graduate Martin Luther King Jr., was aware of (and supported) the experiment that was happening beneath his feet, but his congregation had no idea. "It was probably the greatest Good Friday in two thousand years—or it was for half the subjects," Leary drolly noted.

It quickly became apparent who had received which dose. As Reverend Thurman patiently explained the virtues of being born again to the sober congregation sitting in the pews, a more vivid religious experience was unfolding downstairs. "Everything in the world just seemed to grow inwardly with life. And I don't mean just living things, even inanimate things. They

---

* "Aerosmith was a kind of ragamuffin Boston street-kid group who was managed by an alcoholic Irish manager," Weil says. "They came in and did a demo. I liked it a lot. They didn't have the money to do a deal and they didn't really know what they were doing. I offered them a deal: I would arrange for them to have a producer and I would give them the studio time in exchange for a percentage of the album." Weil brought in Adrian Barber, a "madman English rock-and-roller psychedelic character" who had produced *Loaded* with the Velvet Underground three years prior. Though Aerosmith's 1973 self-titled debut was initially a flop, the single "Dream On" hit #6 upon its 1976 reissue. Unlike Lou Reed, Steven Tyler didn't have much use for Alice Bailey, but he was fond of another occultist, Aleister Crowley. "I've practiced Crowley Magick so I know it works," Tyler wrote in his memoir. "I'm not saying that every girl I slept with came at the same time or that I asked her to pray for the same thing I was praying for; namely that Aerosmith would become the greatest American band."

just *lived*," experiment participant Randall Laakko reflected later. Another subject, known as K.B. in Pahnke's notes, recalled that "it left me with a completely unquestioned certainty that there is an environment bigger than the one I'm conscious of." Huston Smith, the future author of the bestselling *The World's Religions*, was also in the basement that Good Friday. While Smith had previously experimented with psilocybin, he considered the Marsh Chapel Experiment his first direct personal encounter with God—"the most powerful cosmic homecoming I have ever experienced."

One subject who received the psilocybin got up to deliver his own sermon, but only gibberish emerged from his mouth. Another became convinced that God had selected him to deliver the message that a Messianic Age was about to dawn, and a thousand years of global peace were just around the corner. The subject raced down the chapel steps to Commonwealth Avenue, grabbed a letter from a postman, and "crumpled it up," according to author Don Lattin's reconstruction of the day. Whatever the letter contained, the subject surmised, was nothing compared to the message he had just received from God.

"The original Good Friday experiment is one of the preeminent psychedelic experiments in the scientific literature," Rick Doblin wrote in his 1991 follow-up study. Its "fascinating and provocative conclusions strongly support the hypothesis that psychedelic drugs can help facilitate mystical experiences when used by religiously inclined people in a religious setting." In 1966, even *Time* raved about the trial's results: "All students who had taken the drug experienced a mystical consciousness that resembled those described by saints and ascetics."

"Psychedelics can definitely bring about religious experiences," Gunther Weil tells me. "They can stimulate a profound experience of spirituality. In this particular instance, these were divinity students, so the imagery and ritual [in the chapel] conveyed the Christian metaphor.

"Having said that," he adds, "I wouldn't go so far to say that it creates a permanent shift in consciousness. It opens the window to a possibility. You get a kind of preview of coming attractions."

We get a preview of Alfred Omega's coming attractions in the final paragraphs of *It Happened in Boston?* What they actually represent isn't entirely clear. But think about it: There are hundreds of churches in Boston, and by some unconscious decision, Greenan concluded his novel about a tangible encounter with God in the exact location where scientists and drug-swallowing subjects attempted a startlingly similar feat.

It happened in Boston.

TEN
Something in the Bricks

ON SEPTEMBER 11, 1964, Martin Luther King Jr. and the president of Boston University posed on the stone stairs of the school's Marsh Chapel for a photograph.

King was at the peak of fame. A year earlier, he had delivered his "I Have a Dream" speech at the March on Washington; he would win the Nobel Peace Prize in December. As his star rose, threats of violence mounted, and King wanted his papers kept safe for posterity. His choice of institution: Boston University, where he had received his doctorate in theology in 1955. "I had the privilege of studying here for three years," King told a reporter, "and it was this university that meant so much to me in terms of the formulation of my thinking and the ideas that have guided my life." Boston was a second home to the Atlanta native. It was the city where he met his future wife—over lunch at Sharaf's on Mass. Ave.—and found a mentor in Howard Thurman, who conveyed to him Gandhi's belief in nonviolence as a force "more positive than electricity."

On April 5, 1968, thousands thronged outside that same church to mourn King, assassinated the day before in Memphis. The crowd spilled onto the sidewalk underneath a low, gray sky. "A few years ago, a young man walked up these steps and used our classrooms and read our books," Dean Robert Hamill pronounced. "Today he walks no more on this plaza or walks the streets of America. The world asks, 'What is happening in our land?'"

THROUGH THE EARLY PART of the twentieth century, Boston had a reputation as a racially progressive city, though contradictions were rife. The Puritans claimed to find slavery repugnant, but Massachusetts still played a vital role in the slave trade. The first colony to adopt slavery, Massachusetts was also the first state in the union to abolish it. The Beacon Hill brownstone of escaped Kentucky slave Lewis Hayden became an important stop on the Underground Railroad, and it was in Boston that William Lloyd Garrison founded the New England Anti-Slavery Society, working alongside Frederick Douglass.

After the Civil War, tensions developed between the growing number of Cotton Belt migrants and the small but influential group of "Black Brahmins" on Beacon Hill. Disputes rose about everything from where to hang your laundry to the acceptability of throwing dice in the streets. "To Boston-born blacks, the lesson was clear," J. Anthony Lukas wrote in *Common Ground*, his Pulitzer Prize–winning book about race relations in Boston. The newcomers were "dragging them under, destroying their 'special relationship' with whites."

In the coming decades, the number of African Americans arriving in the Commonwealth continued to grow, soon far outnumbering the Black Brahmins, moving into the brownstones of the South End and Roxbury. In the century between the end of the Civil War and 1968, the black population of Boston grew from 2 percent to 15 percent; most of the increase was between 1940 and 1960, as whites moved to the suburbs. While the black population grew, opportunities did not. "The only Black people I saw were people who had mops, or were driving the elevator up and down," according to John

Curtis Jones, who grew up in Roxbury in the 1940s. "They were doormen, cab drivers, factory workers, and maybe working in the garage."

By the spring of 1963, even those actively ignoring politics recognized that the civil rights movement had arrived in Boston. On the Common, ten thousand people marched to support the battle for equality unfolding in Birmingham, Alabama, led by King. Later that summer, the black population of Boston engaged in a one-day boycott of work, commerce, and public transportation to highlight discrimination. Since 1815, Boston had funded separate public schools for black and white students; work to undo this segregation had begun in the mid-nineteenth century, but now the movement had a new urgency. In September, Tom Atkins, Harvard graduate student and newly appointed Boston NAACP director, led protesters into the school department building on Beacon Street, where they demanded action. Louise Day Hicks and other Boston school committee members went about their day, pretending not to notice the protest even as they had to physically step over African Americans in the hallways.

Martin Luther King Jr. led a 22,000-person "March on Boston" in April 1965 to call attention to the civil rights work that the city desperately needed. Before the march, King toured Roxbury (routinely referred to as a "slum" by *The Boston Globe*), where the surge in black residents was inversely related to the property values and quality of city services. King told the crowd at Boston Common that the conditions in Roxbury were deplorable, but that he had come "not to condemn, but, instead, to encourage this great city." "The vision of the New Boston must extend into the heart of Roxbury," King said.

School committee member Louise Day Hicks emerged as Kevin White's opponent in the 1967 mayoral election, running on the slogan "You Know Where I Stand"—a dog whistle to racists and pro-segregation citizens. White defeated Hicks by a mere twelve thousand votes. In his inaugural speech on New Year's Day 1968, White echoed King in calling for a "New Boston," but the voting results were clear: A large part of the city was fine with the old one.

MAYOR KEVIN WHITE was taking in a screening of 1939's *Gone with the Wind* when he got the news: Martin Luther King had been shot in Memphis. At City Hall, aide Barney Frank drafted an official statement. In 1968, the future congressman was a young, cigar-chomping, quick-witted political savant. The day of King's death, the *Globe* had profiled Frank as someone who had "his finger in every pie." It was Barney Frank who reminded White that his predecessor's decision to send a sizable police force into Grove Hall the year before had been a disaster.* Instead, it was suggested, black community leaders should have a chance to visit troubled areas to encourage cooler heads to prevail. Some critics had nicknamed White "Mayor Black" for his focus on African-American issues, while others in the black community felt he had given them only the "illusion of inclusion."

Over at the Boston Tea Party, a milestone evening had become something else. Building on the success of its weekend shows, the club started booking Thursdays. The first night, April 4, was to be christened by Muddy Waters, with Peter Wolf's Hallucinations opening. "I never heard anything like it," manager Steve Nelson recalls. "This was like being at a wake in Muddy Waters' apartment or something, and everybody was crying."

After an all-nighter at City Hall, Mayor White's mind raced with ideas to prevent the assassination from igniting violence. Looking over the day's list of concerts and theatrical offerings was the furthest thing from his sleep-deprived mind. But newly elected Boston councilman Tom Atkins—the first African American to hold that post in Boston in seventeen years—had

---

* In June 1967, a Mothers for Adequate Welfare demonstration turned into a weekend of riots and violent clashes with the police, injuring dozens. Forty-four people were arrested, including Tom Atkins.

his eye on one show in particular: James Brown was scheduled to perform at the Boston Garden that evening. James Byrd, a DJ at Boston soul radio station WILD 1090 AM, had tipped Atkins off to the potential for trouble. "It's too late to cancel it; the word won't get around in time," Byrd said. "There'll be thousands of black teenagers down at the Garden this evening, and when they find those gates are locked they're going to be pretty pissed off."

Atkins explained the precarious situation to White and Frank. *James who?* Neither had heard of him. But riots linked to concerts—that was something they were familiar with. History suggested that whether Brown's show was canceled or not, there might be trouble.

IT STARTED IN THE SPRING OF 1956. At a "rock 'n' roll dance" at MIT, a student was badly injured, leading police to shut down a similar event the next week in Roxbury. When Chuck Berry and Jerry Lee Lewis hit Boston in May 1958, chaos erupted in the streets after the show when a group of twenty-five boys in identical satin jackets got rowdy. Papers claimed that the law-abiding youths suddenly became "bedeviled into gangsterism" and "ran berserk." A sailor was stabbed, dozens of others were beaten. The district attorney indicted show promoter Alan Freed under antianarchy laws, declaring he had unleashed a "form of rock 'n' roll paganism" in Boston. Freed was eventually released, but Mayor John Hynes had seen enough, grumbling, "These so-called musical programs are a disgrace and must be stopped. As far as I'm concerned, Boston has seen the last of them."

After Hynes left office in 1960, the total ban on rock shows lifted, save for some at the Boston Arena and the Boston Garden. City censor Richard J. Sinnott was in charge of figuring out if an act was rock 'n' roll or not, and in turn, whether they could book a concert at those venues. The Beatles were allowed at the Garden, for instance, because "they are not really R-'n'-R." As for the Beach Boys, Sinnott vacillated. "Some people have claimed that they're folk singers," he said.

Whoever decided that James Brown was not rock 'n' roll in 1968 had been woefully misinformed.

WHAT IF THE *Brown concert was broadcast live on television?* It was an audacious, nick-of-time proposal. (No one remembers who came up with the idea, but some accounts point to Barney Frank.) Each home viewer would be another person not on the street. WGBH was an obvious choice: The station had filmed Timothy Leary's '67 debate at MIT with a few hours' advance notice. David Atwood, who had manned the controls for *What's Happening, Mr. Silver?*, jumped at the chance to direct the show. Everyone was happy with the plan, except James Brown.

The morning of April 5, the singer was in New York working on a TV special titled *Man to Man*. The show's contract dictated that Brown was not to participate in any other East Coast television appearances until after it aired a few months later. When Brown's New England representative, James Byrd, told Councilman Atkins the singer would *likely* be fine with this decision, he had no idea about the *Man to Man* clause. Greg Moses, Brown's manager, was livid when he found out about the telecast. Contract aside, Moses thought the live broadcast would kill the size of the Garden crowd—a blow to the performer's pocketbook and pride.

Atkins told Mayor White that the city would need to cover the lost earnings from concert tickets. Which seemed absurd—but what could he do? With each passing hour, the city's immediate fate seemed to hinge upon the details of James Brown's live show. It was Friday; a wrong move that night would trigger a weekend of unrest. At last White agreed, but demanded circumspection. "If word ever gets out we underwrote a goddamn rock star with city money, we'll both be dead politically," he said to Atkins. Meanwhile, White assured the citizens of Boston that the situation was under control. He appeared on a WGBH program hosted by Louis Lyons, "a salty old New Englander" who had nearly broken down on air speaking about

King's death the night before. White said that the city was working closely with the "negro leadership" of Roxbury and that there was "reason for apprehension but not alarm." That evening's "memorial" event, White said, would allow people to let off some steam. "I hope we're going to weather this," he solemnly remarked.

Impromptu vigils popped up on Boston Common, Post Office Square, and in front of Marsh Chapel. National Guard units went on standby. Inside the Boston Garden, Atwood and his WGBH crew set up three cameras—two in the balcony, one from behind the stage, so that they could cut to Brown's perspective. Outside, a young concertgoer approached a policeman and asked whether the show was still on. "Yeah," the cop replied, "but if I were you I wouldn't come. . . . It could be a little edgy in there. You can get a refund."

There was a certain irony in pinning the hopes of civic peace on a performer as notoriously hot-tempered as Brown, who had once showed up at a Georgia nightclub to fire shotgun rounds at a musical rival who had mocked his signature cape routine onstage. Still, many in the black community did look up to him as a role model and a civil rights spokesperson. To Brown, Black Power meant "black pride and black people owning businesses and having a voice in politics," as he wrote in his 1986 autobiography. "I wanted to see people free, but I didn't see any reason for us to kill each other."

Atkins and Brown discussed possible solutions on the drive from Logan Airport, while inside the Garden musicians and the WGBH team both got ready. If the city of Boston would cover his financial losses, Atkins finally suggested, then perhaps Brown could alter the clause in his *Man to Man* contract? The singer had done some calculations: He was poised to lose $60,000 that night. Atkins had persuaded the mayor to cover the difference, but no one had imagined a figure so substantial. With this promise in place, Brown gave WGBH the okay to air his concert live. The singer even talked to fans before curtain, telling them it didn't make sense to turn their rage over Dr. King's death into a riot at a concert. The mayor arrived at six and finally met Brown. Later, White would describe the encounter as a collision between two arrogant people. In the one photo of White, Brown, and Atkins backstage at the Garden, the mayor appears to lecture the other two men.

"I'll get you your money," White promised the singer. "But I want you to get up on that stage and put on a performance. I don't mean a musical one, either."

What Mayor White definitely did not tell James Brown backstage was that the city simply did not have the money to pay him $60,000. He'd worry about that later. Right now, all that mattered was that the show work some kind of miracle.

"LADIES AND GENTLEMEN, apologies, we're still waiting for the audio connection to the Boston Garden for the memorial concert this evening featuring negro singer Jimmy Brown and his group," WGBH announcer Bill Pierce explained to those tuning in. "Cohosting the concert will be Mayor Kevin White. That's coming up next on this station. The time: 8:30." As rioting in D.C. came within a few blocks of the White House, James Brown took the stage in front of approximately 1,500 souls and launched into "If I Ruled the World," a vision of a better life for everyone.

Then Atkins addressed the crowd in the Garden and at home. "He's been doing some things around the country where, if other people were to join with him, would make a big difference," the councilman said, as Brown stood behind him with his arms behind his back. When Atkins suggested people send in donations to the Martin Luther King Trust Fund to City Hall, Brown applauded, and so did the audience. As the councilman reverently introduced Kevin White, Brown realized that the tone was all wrong: This was a concert, not a campaign stop. As Brown grabbed the microphone from Atkins, the surprised councilman exclaimed "Wait a minute!" But Brown knew what he was doing. "I had the pleasure of meeting him," Brown said, in a tone his fans could relate to, "and this is a swingin' cat.

Mayor Kevin White. Give him a big round of applause, ladies and gentle-men, he's a swingin' cat." White, who had mistakenly referred to the singer as James Washington all afternoon, allegedly asked an aide to remind him of the actual name just before walking out onstage.

White reminded the audience that they were at the Garden to listen to "a great talent: James Brown." James Brown laughed as the audience cheered. "But we're also here to pay tribute to one of the greatest Americans: Dr. Martin Luther King," White continued. "Twenty-four hours ago, Dr. King died . . . for *all* of us. Black and white." Now he directly petitioned his city not to riot, without using that word. "Stay with me as your mayor, to make Dr. King's dreams a reality in Boston." The audience was slower to clap at this, so Brown got it going for them, maybe the only time in his career where he played onstage hype man for a white person.

"He's a young man, ya dig?" Brown told his fans as the mayor left the stage. "So he's thinking together."

With the night's all-important business concluded, Brown proceeded to do what he did best: Deliver one of the best live shows anywhere on the planet, anywhere in time. "It's getting late in the evening," he sang, teasing out the intro to "That's Life," a 1963 song made famous by Frank Sinatra. With its eerily off-by-a-month lyrics ("You're riding high in April/shot down in May"), it was a potentially chilling opener, but the crowd was too happy to notice, gasping as Brown did his first 360-degree spin of the night. Even though upbeat numbers dominated the set, you could hear something mournful in Brown's cathartic wailings. ("He was a man who knew how to express the utterances and the screams and the feelings of a whole people," Al Sharpton would later comment about the show.) In the wings, Marva Whitney, a featured vocalist who was also Brown's girlfriend, prayed for everyone's safety as she waited her turn.

Reports started rolling in from police officers all around the city: Boston was a ghost town. "This concert was like magic," Tom Atkins recalled. "The city was quieter than it would've been on an ordinary Friday night." This was true even at 53 Berkeley Street, where the Amboy Dukes, a Detroit band led by guitarist Ted Nugent, played for a near empty house at the Tea Party.

Marva Whitney performed four songs while Brown changed outfits backstage. Then saxophonist Maceo Parker announced that the city was very quiet and calm. "The reports also say that everyone is home watching the TV program," he said, hailing the show and its broadcast as a "big success."

Brown reappeared, clad in a blazer, and ripped into "Get It Together." Had the mission already succeeded? Was it too early to declare victory? The band blasted through its second set with urgency. That Friday night, a repertoire of songs consisting of two-chord vamps and only a handful of repeated lyrics vibrated with an extra hypnotic quality. Brown's inspired, electric fits of dance between verses took the place of guitar solos, and at times he appeared to float across the stage. His musicians, trained not to take their eyes off Soul Brother #1, accentuated Brown's dramatic movements with an extra snare hit or burst of saxophone. To get the band to cut the heat, the singer would suddenly freeze, hands in the air in a motion of surrender.

He would typically close his shows draped in a sequined cape, escorted slowly to the wings by a handler, as though against his will. It signaled that the performer would give it his all, would just keep going if it were up to him. *The only reason I stay alive is because my team knows when to get the cape and drag me offstage.*

On April 5, the cape routine was especially magnetic, drawing young fans to clamber onto the stage. One of Brown's entourage managed to push the first kid off, but suddenly a contingent of Boston police officers, nearly all white, swarmed the stage and forced back the surge. Inside WGBH's mobile broadcast unit, David Atwood was getting worried. At some point in the proceedings, the station had decided to re-air the concert immediately upon conclusion. But now that things were deteriorating, Atwood questioned the plan. "That was really tense," Atwood recalls. "Is this going to turn into a major riot? I held back visually, trying to walk this fine line between showing what was going on and not trying to over-show what was going on." If a riot was about to go down, should WGBH keep airing the concert?

Brown whispered to the man with the cape, who folded it up and briskly left. The band segued into the closing song, "I Can't Stand Myself (When You Touch Me)." After another interaction with a stage jumper and a Boston cop, Brown called off the band mid-riff. "Wait a minute!" he shouted. "I'll be all right. I'll be fine." As Brown asked the police to clear the stage, the crowd cheered wildly. One kid, then two, then six now surrounded the singer. As police reemerged, Brown insisted, "Wait a minute! They're all right, it's all right!" The phrases sounded like signature Brown lyrics, now shouted without any music behind them. Amid the chaos, the house lights came up.

"Let me finish the show for everyone else," Brown said. "We gotta show we're young men and young ladies. Wait a minute, *wait a minute*!"

Atwood cut to the rearview shot as Brown, who sounded angry for the first time all evening, yells, "Now, *We. Are. Black.* Can't you all go back down and let's do the show together? We're black, don't make us all look bad. Lemme finish doing the show." Another fist-pumping audience member, unaware that the time for games had long passed, approached Brown.

"You make me look very bad, 'cause I asked the police to step back and you wouldn't go down. No, that's wrong. It's wrong. You're not being fair to me, yourself, or your race. Now I asked the police to step back because I thought I could get some respect from my own people. Don't make sense. Now are we together, or we ain't?" The crowd cheered in the affirmative. Suddenly the stage was clear again. An agitated Brown turned back to drummer Clyde Stubblefield and ordered, "Hit the thing, man." The house lights went back down.

"Good God," Brown howled in the spotlight. "Can't stand your love."

Strobes, bows, handshakes. Then it was done.

· · ·

"IN JUST A MOMENT we're going to do something rather wild for television," WGBH's Bill Pierce announced. "If you have any friends who would've enjoyed tonight's concert at the Boston Garden, won't you tell them that we're going to repeat the show right now?"

As the band rolled out of town on the tour bus, they couldn't believe what just happened. The musicians had assumed that the show would end in a "ball of fire." That night, major rioting hit more than one hundred American cities, with places like Detroit, Chicago, Baltimore, and D.C. bearing the brunt. Dozens died, twenty thousand arrests were made, and damage estimates reached $45 million. In Boston, by contrast, the disturbances were surprisingly minor, especially for a city with so much racial tension. Marva Whitney would later say that Brown's performance that night did not come without a cost. "I know [James] went through something mentally. He knew whether it went down wrong, bad, or indifferent, whatever, he knew that he would get blamed for it. To tell you the truth, I was glad when we got out of there."

On Monday morning, recovering from a 103-degree fever, Tom Atkins heard that the city might be wriggling out of its promised payout to Brown. The councilman threatened to publicize the news if Mayor White didn't make good on his word. But White wasn't exaggerating; the city didn't have the funds to write out a simple treasury check. The mayor approached the so-called Vault—a group of powerful, old-Boston moneymen who, behind the scenes, had been fixing potential catastrophes since the late 1950s, when the city was on the verge of bankruptcy. They balked upon hearing White's unusual request for a payout to Brown.

"Well, the city is at stake here," he told them flatly, "so whatever you think you can do."

By the time he walked back to City Hall, a sum of money had been extended to deal with the issue. Some reports say far less than sixty grand was earmarked for the singer; according to J. Anthony Lukas, the city had pressured the Garden to waive its share of the receipts that night, which reduced the city's bill to Brown to $15,000. A close Brown associate, Charles Bobbit, claims they were never paid more than $10,000. In Bobbit's telling, when he told Brown about the missing money, the singer shrugged his shoulders and said, "Well, we're doing a good thing." Mayor White, in a 2008 documentary, repeats the old figure: "It was worth the 60K."

THAT SPRING AND SUMMER, people came together en masse: in a stadium in Roxbury, on the Common, by Arlington Street Church and Marsh Chapel. Faced with the rising body count in Vietnam and assassinations at home, the public assembled to grieve, meditate, connect. On the evening of April 4, Robert F. Kennedy had memorialized King to an Indianapolis crowd while on the campaign trail; two months later, he too was gone. As political scientist Ross Baker later noted, "the two killings seemed to make a compelling argument to many that the peaceful path was a dead end and that the resort to violence was now acceptable." Eerie headlines ("DID KING EARLIER HAVE PREMONITION OF DEATH?") pumped up the terror. On *The Tonight Show*, Truman Capote told Johnny Carson that the turmoil was part of an occult plan to overthrow the American government.

For over a year, students had regularly gathered in Boston Common to protest the war and support the civil rights movement, but that summer something strange happened: A large contingent of young people simply started living there. "In Hippievilles around the country," the *Globe* reported in June, "the word is out: 'See You in Boss-Town This Summer.'" The article predicted that dropouts would be migrating from all over the country to grab a piece of public lawn—an accurate forecast.* "As the hot

---

* The only dip in the Common's population growth that summer was due to a rampant rumor that an asteroid named Icarus was going to destroy the Earth's population mid-June and only two locations would be spared: Tibet and Colorado. No one knows how the rumor started, but American hippies flocked to Colorado en masse. At an observatory in Cambridge, employees

weather sets in, they frolic in the Frog Pond or listen to rock concerts by such groups as the Ultimate Spinach," *Time* reported. In June the hippies declared they wanted to clean up the Common and its surroundings, so the Parks Department issued rakes, shovels, and a nearby lot where they could grow vegetables. They grew marijuana instead.

For Mayor White and his trusted aide Barney Frank, the hippies on the Common were fairly low on their list of priorities, but soon, phone calls from freaked-out parents captured their attention. The flip side of the story developing on the Common was a rash of young runaways from the suburbs. In the summer of 1968, if a teenager ran away in the Boston area, they were likely to end up at the Common or up on Fort Hill. "There was a cult issue [up on Fort Hill], with children disappearing," Frank says, but he was wise enough to recognize that direct police intervention there would only galvanize a group like that (it certainly worked out that way in regard to the *Avatar* obscenity trials). Instead, Frank addressed that trouble spot by having a private meeting with Fort Hill Community member Lewis Crampton, encouraging him to consider turning young runaways away from the Family.*

As the Common's full-time residents grew, the mayor instituted a midnight curfew, which took effect on June 28. "The hippies," White said, "are no longer a novelty." Barney Frank hired a kind of "hippie whisperer," Dr. Stanley Klein, to be a full-time presence on the Common, both to try to understand the community's way of life and to offer help to those who needed it. After a June 29 protest of the curfew erupted into violence, Judge

---

fielded frantic calls about Icarus. "The space kooks really came out of the wood work," a spokesman for the observatory told the *Globe*. Some MIT students dreamed up a contingency plan involving "nine nuclear-tipped Saturn rockets, borrowed from the U.S. Moon program." Icarus missed Earth by four million miles.

* This talk didn't seem to make much difference; to wit, the eighteen-year-old daughter of a Harvard Law School professor arrived with some friends on Fort Hill a year later, in 1969. That daughter, Eve Chayes, would become pregnant by Mel Lyman shortly after moving there, subsequently taking on his last name, though their marriage ceremony at the time was not of the legal sort.

Elijah Adlow—fresh off sparring over the artistic merits of the *Avatar* newspaper—began sentencing squatters, explaining that he would not allow the Common to become a flophouse. "You've made a disaster area out of what used to be the most beautiful part of Boston," he told a courtroom full of longhairs. These kids were merely "looking for something," the defense insisted; Adlow told them they weren't going to find it at the corner of Charles and Beacon.

The media latched on to the Summer of the Hippie as a lighter alternative to the coverage of the other major youth story unfolding at that time: protesting the Vietnam War. Since 1964, the draft had come to resemble a lottery of death, plucking young men out of their communities, dropping them into danger a world away. More than eleven thousand U.S. servicemen had died in 1967, a tally that '68 was set to top. The brutal imagery of the Tet Offensive, piped into American homes early that year, gave even the staunchest hawks pause. Belief in the illegality and immorality of the war moved from the fringes toward the mainstream. "For it seems now more certain than ever that the bloody experience of Vietnam is to end in a stalemate," CBS anchor Walter Cronkite told his viewers. "To say that we are closer to victory today is to believe in the face of the evidence, the optimists who have been wrong in the past."

Those under twenty-six hoping to dodge the draft could do it legally, by hiring lawyers to find loopholes, or illegally, by faking an undesirable condition or simply not showing up. Fort Hill's Michael Kindman put together a strategy based on stories of community members who had done it before. "I woke up and took a small dose of LSD to make sure I would be a little disorientated and uninhibited," he wrote. "I volunteered that I was both gay and a communist, and was unresponsive to the psychological interviewer. He made it clear I was not the kind of person they were looking for." For musician Ted Myers, of the band Chamaeleon Church, staying awake on speed for a solid week before his Selective Service physical did the trick. He told the examiner he wanted a gun to kill some people. "They called me weirdo and faggot," he says. "The docs didn't even make me drop my pants."

Boston became an epicenter for Vietnam War resistance, perhaps because of its role as the birthplace of the American Revolution, or its proximity to Concord, where Henry David Thoreau had written on civil disobedience a century earlier. "You could just *feel* it," one activist remarked. "There was something in the bricks." At a protest on the Common, an older attendee declared what marketers at MGM Records, DJs on WBCN, and the prognosticators on Fort Hill had been claiming all year: "Boston and New England will once again be the beginning point and inspiration for a second and badly needed American Revolution."

Among the most passionate antiwar activists were area professors, including MIT's Noam Chomsky and Howard Zinn at Boston University. "I don't believe we owe loyalty to a government that lies to us," Zinn, a World War II veteran, told a crowd at the Common. "I do believe we owe loyalty to our fellow Americans who are in danger of being killed by the incompetence of this government."

Ray Mungo was one of many BU students under the sway of Zinn. "While other teachers might sign a petition, Howard would join the sit-in," Mungo says. "He put his body on the line." Zinn was a close mentor to the group of BU resisters, who often had breakfast at his house. Short and bespectacled, Mungo seemed wise beyond his years, and made vivid, moving appearances on *What's Happening, Mr. Silver?* He deluged *Avatar* with letters until they finally put the dynamic demonstrator on the cover.* His editorial direction at *BU News* was so inflammatory that the university threatened to

---

* Though Mungo got along with Mel Lyman, he resisted attempts to get him to join Fort Hill. Meanwhile, issues of *Avatar* were finding their way to servicemen in Vietnam, some of whom sent letters back. "There are a lot of people who don't want to be here," one such letter explains. "But what should we do? Drop out? Then every little pissy-ass country going will want to test this country and its ideals which allow people like you and me to say what we want, when we want."

withdraw its financial support for the troublemaking paper—"the nation's only college paper with its own reportorial staff in Vietnam," Mungo noted. With his friend Marshall Bloom, he founded the Liberation News Service in 1967—a kind of antiwar AP wire service, one that could "reach millions of readers without having any power and very little money," Mungo says. "We made *everyone* a media."

By the summer of 1968, the Liberation News Service became enough of a federal annoyance to warrant an infiltration by members of the FBI. The undercover agents divided and conquered the organization by writing and distributing a finger-pointing manifesto full of insider information entitled "And Who Got the Cookie Jar?" In fact, many underground and student newspapers in Boston received visits from the FBI in the late sixties, including *Avatar*. When feds visited the office at 37 Rutland Street, *Avatar* editor Wayne Hansen let them search the location freely and they left soon afterward. Outside, Hansen found the agents trying to get into their own car with a coat hanger, their keys locked inside. He walked over to the scene with his camera, but the agents begged him not to take pictures, which he obliged. By the time the FBI arrived at *BU News*, word had gotten out. Alex Jack, an editor at the paper, had prepared some materials in preparation for their visit. "Thank you for coming. I just have a few questions," Jack told the agents, and handed them a three-page questionnaire. As they left in a huff, other students followed them to their car, pretending to take notes on their every move and muttering, "Ah, yes, very interesting."

It was a brutal summer for the resistance. In May, four of the Boston Five—local men who had been charged with aiding draft resisters—were found guilty of conspiracy, in a trial that the prosecuting attorney described as "more exciting than sky-diving"; now it appeared that the most trusted adviser of early parenthood, Dr. Benjamin Spock, was headed to prison. In early June, a "weird and dirty-looking" young couple walked into Boston's Selective Service office and poured black paint into file cabinets, making portions of the database unreadable. They were charged and found guilty in October. In July, the stabbing of two servicemen on the Common went down late one Tuesday night, marking a turning point in what was previously considered a fairly lighthearted phenomenon. When chanting hippies disrupted Vice President Hubert Humphrey's downtown presidential rally in late September, Mayor White's patience finally ran out. The media claimed he ordered a "police war" on the protesters; arrests piled up, and the Common's grass was conveniently scheduled to be torn up for "routine maintenance." The Summer of the Hippie was coming to an end. By the time the Common curfew was found to be illegal in Suffolk Superior Court in December 1968, the cold weather had made the issue moot.

James Brown's Boston Garden show certainly prevented an immediate wave of violence from sweeping over the city, but it was not as if racial tension simply evaporated. Mayor White's sigh of relief lasted approximately a day. On Sunday, April 7, the United Front, a coalition of nearly every black organization in the city, was organized and ratified. On Monday, five thousand people convened at White Stadium in Roxbury—no whites allowed. United Front representatives read aloud twenty-one demands—most strikingly, a call for immediate black ownership and black leadership at all businesses and schools in their communities, as well as renaming schools and other institutions after heroes of the movement.

The language was startling: "As of 12:00 A.M. Monday April 8 1968 all white owned and white controlled businesses will be closed until further notice, while the transfer of the ownership of these businesses to the Black community is being negotiated through the United Front." Lastly, the UF stated that the mayor needed to make $100 million available to the black community.

The demands incensed Mayor White. He voiced his support for the NAACP's recommendations for Boston, which had been crafted and delivered after the NAACP and UF separated their efforts in the wake of King's death. Councilman Tom Atkins was upset by Mayor White's swift rejection of the United Front, adding, "Neither this mayor nor any other mayor can decide what part of the black community he is going to deal with, and for the mayor to say that he will receive suggestions from one group and not from another is the epitome of stupidity." Less than a week ago they had been applauding each other onstage at the Boston Garden; now they were trading barbs in the press. The *Globe*, reporting on why the UF felt justified in their gigantic ask, noted that "some black intellectuals compare Roxbury to a colony, where the economy is controlled from without by a colonial government."

Over in Franklin Park, whose greenery covered parts of Dorchester, Jamaica Plain, and Roxbury, "the American flag was lowered and the Black Nationalist flag was raised," Skip Ascheim reported in *Avatar*. "Keep your eyes open," *Avatar* announced. "The first phase in the liberation of Roxbury has begun."

UP ON THE HILL, the Mel Lyman Family braced for what might happen in Roxbury after the assassination of Martin Luther King Jr. Even as *Avatar* ran stories blasting institutionalized racism, there was friction between the Fort Hill Community and residents of the predominantly black neighborhood, where Lyman had put down stakes in 1966. For over a year before King's death, the Family posted armed guards to send a message that they weren't going anywhere. "The Hill was locked down that April," a neighbor, Alison Burke, recalls. "The police basically left our part of Roxbury to vigilante control."

In the early summer of 1968, the group of black men who patrolled parts of Roxbury, often running into Lyman's Fort Hill patrol, suddenly had an official name: the Black Panthers. Founded two years earlier in Oakland, California, the Black Panther Party focused on monitoring and challenging police brutality. Soon FBI chief J. Edgar Hoover would call Huey P. Newton and Bobby Seale's volunteer army of young black men in leather jackets and berets "the greatest threat to the internal security of the country." The party's fifth chapter opened in Boston.

Delano Farrar, a Northeastern University student, opened two Panther headquarters in Roxbury. The group plastered the South End and Roxbury with posters, gave *Avatar* street hawkers a run for their money with its own newspaper, started a breakfast program for kids, and opened a free health clinic. "The Panthers call their breakfast program 'socialism,'" the *Globe* wrote. "Others consider it charity. Still others consider it indoctrination." "We are twenty-four-hour revolutionaries dedicated to the needs of black people," Farrar declared in response. Their health clinic—a trailer stationed on Tremont Street in the South End—was soon riddled with bullets—shot by local cops, the Panthers claimed.

At some point Boston's Black Panthers became interested in all the white people living on Fort Ave. Terrace, acting like Highland Park was their private property. From the Panther perspective, these folk-music-loving weirdos ought to move to a different part of the city and return the neighborhood to the black community. Jessie Benton recalled the community receiving a message that the Panthers were planning to set fire to their houses to clear them out of Fort Hill. Benton would sit inside and "make sure they could see the glint off the rifle on the window."* Lyman sent out word that he'd rather negotiate, but on the appointed day he sent his wife in his place. "It was a political move, of course, that Mel sent a woman and didn't come himself," Jessie Benton recalls. "There were several of the men with me

---

* "I certainly don't pretend all races are the same," Lyman told *Rolling Stone*. "Ever since I was a kid I've had trouble with Jews. But I also believe a man of any nationality can rise above that nationality, can put that nationality to use . . . I like to talk in topical languages 'cause people can get into it. Like I might say something like, 'all niggers are stupid,' you know? Just to wake people up, get them involved." When pressed on any of his controversial statements—including similar homophobic remarks—Lyman would dodge the charge by claiming that their ability to shake people into the present moment justified the slurs as a means to an end.

who were all packing." Nevertheless, a truce was forged, and tensions between the two groups subsided.

AS A KIND OF INDIRECT RESPONSE to the United Front's twenty-one demands, Mayor White earmarked $56 million to aid Boston's black community in May 1968. The UF promptly blasted the measure as an insult to the black community, planned with zero input from the people it meant to help. The full effects of White's May '68 decisions would take years to play out, but each remaining month of that turbulent year would contain its own set of racial confrontations, many of them unexpected victories for the civil rights movement. In late April, black students at Boston University seized an administration building to call attention to the fourteen urgent demands they had for the school. After a twelve-hour standoff, the administration conceded to all of them—most based around the promise of more black students and scholarships at BU—except for the request to rename a building after Martin Luther King.

And in the wake of airing the James Brown concert, WGBH replaced *What's Happening, Mr. Silver?* with *Say Brother.* "Included will be news from the ghetto, interviews with black people," the WGBH press release read, "and a forum for all shades of Negro opinion." The tone-deaf description belied the show's outspoken content, such as the roundtable in which a local artist said, "There is great talent in the black community—we know this because white people are constantly stealing everything we have and packaging it and calling it whiteness."

Say Brother was hosted by James Spruill, a Brandeis graduate and actor who had lived with Mel Lyman, Charles Giuliano, and John Kostick in Waltham in the early sixties. Spruill would also found a theater company for black artists in the fall of that year. "There must be a black theater for the black community, our own voices in our own playwrights, and the more black rage the better," he told an interviewer. "Black people refuse to go around not being recognized anymore."

Thinking along similar lines, Charles M. Holley and John Curtis Jones started Black Music Inc. in late '68, with the intent of passing out shares to ordinary citizens in Roxbury. Instead of one black performer becoming extremely wealthy—and instead of allowing whites to rip off black artists—the setup would let the black community become invested in the production of their music. Black Music soon blossomed into more than a record company. After Riepen and Don Law moved the Boston Tea Party, Holley and Curtis snatched up the lease and opened a private club, the Common Ground, in September 1969. For $15 a year, anyone could hang out and make music at 53 Berkeley Street, five days a week.

Black Music Inc. not only grabbed the lease on the FHC's former Film-Makers' Cinematheque locale, they were also poised to move into the middle of their commune. Around this time period, the owner of 4 Fort Ave. Terrace wanted to remove the Lyman residents and sell the building to Holley and Jones. But because the Fort Hill Community had taken a crumbling house and turned it into a well-constructed, vital part of their commune, the idea of the original owner profiting off their hard work—and of someone outside the Family living in the center of their commune—drove members so crazy that they began dismantling the building from the inside during the middle of the night. When the owner was about to sell to Black Music Inc., she discovered that where plumbing, walls, and floors had existed the week before, now there was just an empty shell.

A former member of the community explained to *Rolling Stone* what happened next: "Naturally the neighborhood became enraged. There was a meeting between Black Music Inc. and Fort Hill, sort of as a prevention of war. A bunch of our guys went down there, and I remember at one point we said, 'OK, if you want a war, we'll give it to you!' And as I say, we were ready, we had guns and everything." When the frustrated owner of 4 Fort Ave. Terrace finally sold the house at a bargain price to the Fort Hill

Community, the first thing they did was raze the property to the ground. Bewildered, *Rolling Stone*'s David Felton asked why.

An anonymous source replied, "The point is, you see, we live for the moment."*

One Family member, Ed Fox, said in 1968, "Black power is beautiful, man, and it's good for Negroes to do their thing. But we're into our own scene. They're parallel movements." It sounded supportive, but it also sounded a lot like the same old call for segregation cloaked in hippie garb. This brand of casual racism would pale in comparison to the overt racism that awaited the city; the legal battle over school busing in the mid-1970s would turn South Boston into a hate-filled war zone, branding the city with a reputation for embracing bigots that resonates with some observers even to this day.

THE ACTION RETURNED to Marsh Chapel on October 1, 1968.

The long, hot summer had drawn to a close, with leaves starting to dot the plaza outside of the church. Inside, approximately one hundred students gathered around Raymond Kroll and Thomas Pratt. Both had recently gone AWOL from their military duties; the idea was to protect them in a way that would double as a visible act of protest. The idea of offering sanctuary to AWOL soldiers was a new maneuver for the Vietnam resistance movement, a tactic pioneered in May at Arlington Street Church. Few believed it would hold any legal weight, but the symbolic power of the gesture would equal that of dozens of protests.

Kroll and Pratt's arrival marked the first time Marsh Chapel was used as such a sanctuary. At the end of the first night, something strange happened:

---

* Michael Kindman recalled the saga of #4 going like so: "During the negotiation process, Mel had a dream one night about fighting with Lena, the landlady. In the dream he was hitting Lena on the head; awake the next day, he interpreted this as an instruction to damage the roof of the house, so it would lose its value and she would be more ready to sell."

Private Pratt donned a disguise and escaped via the chapel's rear door, claiming he'd been manipulated. Kroll remained, telling reporters, "The Resistance and the School of Theology are not using me in any way for anybody's gain except mine." Was it all a complex stunt to make the resistance look bad? Would Kroll follow Pratt? Over the next few days, more students arrived. A cafeteria and medical station materialized, while rock bands played in the same basement where Leary and his crew tried to attain the divine via chemicals. By Wednesday, a thousand people were protecting Kroll at Marsh Chapel. From the pulpit, Howard Zinn expressed his support for the "ongoing free-speech exercise," wondering if the chapel's role as a safe haven might become permanent.

As cop cars repeatedly cruised down Commonwealth Avenue to keep an eye on the situation, Kroll's lawyer announced inside that his client wanted to be "taken out physically as a symbolic act." Early Sunday morning, FBI agents entered Marsh Chapel to find young people sleeping in the pews. "This is the FBI," an agent barked, as others swarmed the church looking for Kroll. "We will give you fifteen seconds to clear the aisle."

Kroll, a scrawny eighteen-year-old, went limp, but the agents grabbed hold of him as if he were a wild bull. Outside, a Liberation News Service photographer snapped a stunning shot of Kroll, his face in agony, his shirt ripped to shreds. The agents on the left and right of Kroll looked away, but the one up front, an older man in a black Stetson, smiled as he wrenched Kroll's hand. By the following week, the photo was etched into the heads of resisters nationwide.

The incident broke activist Alex Jack's patience and perhaps his sanity. "The Sanctuary at Marsh Chapel has shown, simply, that there can be no sanctuary . . . from oppression, from racism, from militarism," he wrote in the *BU News*. "No place is sacred." Forget about incremental progress; for Jack, it was time for a revolution, the birth of a new society where "exploitation is structurally impossible, where power is returned and exercised by the people, where there is no distinction between religion, politics, or art, where in short there are no sanctuaries because no one is oppressed."

From Timothy Leary's Good Friday Experiment to the celebration and mourning of Martin Luther King, from the fantastic visions of Russell H. Greenan to the broken sanctuary for two deserters, Marsh Chapel is one of those landmarks that seem to act as a lightning rod during this wrenching time in the nation's life.

Sometimes advocates for peace are killed. Sometimes it seems like you can communicate directly with God—or that maybe you *are* God. Sometimes you refuse to fight, but the war comes to you anyway.

"Rise up," Alex Jack wrote in the wake of Raymond Kroll's capture, "and utterly destroy this universe."

ELEVEN

We Have All Been Astrals Many Times

A WEEK BEFORE members of the Fort Hill Community and *Avatar* staff turned a Club 47 benefit show into a chair-smashing, face-punching disaster, the underground newspaper suddenly announced that Mel Lyman would no longer write for the newspaper. In the previous issue, the "Letters to Mel" section was half praise, half questioning his claim to being God—business as usual. The issue even ended with an uncharacteristically sweet Lyman poem about hope for the future. So it came as a shock to readers when they opened issue 22 to see the news, along with Lyman's last "To All Who Would Know" piece, below the spookiest photo of him yet:

I am going to burn down the world
I am going to tear down everything that cannot stand alone
I am going to turn ideals to shit
I am going to shove hope up your ass

I am going to reduce everything that stands to rubble
and then I am going to burn the rubble

and then I am going to scatter the ashes

and then maybe SOMEONE will be able to see SOMETHING

as it really is

WATCHOUT

On the same page as the announcement was the self-referential declaration: "BUT MEL LYMAN IS THE AVATAR."

It was a perplexing move. Why would the Fort Hill Community sabotage its one reliable, popular form of communication? The FHC still boasted about what they were going to produce—one follower stated that their company, United Illuminating, would one day "be the only company in the entire world, building model cities for a new world and making the stars shine at night." But outside of *Avatar*, they had little to show for their grand ambitions. Lyman kept referencing films he was about to make and release, but the public never saw them. When it came to music—one of the group's undeniable talents—they pursued concerts and recordings in an odd manner as well. When audiences showed up to hear the Lyman Family's music, they could instead be subjected to a "dialogue with the audience until [Kweskin and Lyman] felt confident that the audience was really present, really open-hearted and ready for whatever was to happen," as Kindman wrote in his memoir. "The music thus became a reward for the audience for making the musicians feel welcomed and understood spiritually." Unsurprisingly, fights broke out at these shows.

People from all over the world had been showing up on Fort Hill to check out the scene. But as Mel's fame grew, protective measures became necessary. He was never in the *Avatar* office; as editor Charles Giuliano put it, Lyman's contributions were done by "remote control." Not all of *Avatar*'s writers cared for this setup. "One day in the late spring of 1968," according to a *Fusion* piece about the FHC, "a powerfully built black man, who wrote under the name of Pebbles, made his way to the top of Fort Hill and demanded to see Mel. No one could stop him, and he went right to Mel's house and knocked on the door." (Everyone I asked about Pebbles's full name had no clue: "He was just Pebbles.") Jessie Benton answered, and the two argued. The *Avatar* contributor told Jessie Benton that *he* was God, more powerful than Mel Lyman.

This incident upset Jessie and Mel.* Some believed that what happened next was due to a dream their leader had, but it was most certainly a reaction to Pebbles's visit: Mel ordered the Fort Hill Community to cease all other activities—including work on *Avatar*—and construct a wall around his house.† "The people outside of Fort Hill were thrown into turmoil," Paul Mills wrote in *Fusion*. "They had obligations to advertisers, they had articles and news to publish, but the Fort Hill editors had abandoned *Avatar*." The wall stands to this day.

When *Avatar* No. 24 arrived in late April, there was no news section, just the inner magazine that included all of the FHC's content, which for this issue comprised page after page of photos of Alison Peper on LSD. Kindman, one of the few community members with actual experience publishing an underground newspaper, recalled it being a "declaration of spiritual war by Mel."

On the cover, under a photo of fourteen men proudly standing by their work-in-progress, was an ominous note.

---

* Some attributed Lyman's messianic turn to his relationship with Jessie, who took on a similar role her mother had played in protecting her husband Thomas Hart Benton's time and talents. Ex–Jug Band member Maria Muldaur summed it up: "Mel had many old ladies in his life, but it was when she was with him that it really started being the 'inner circle' and the 'outer peons,' and you couldn't get in to see Mel, and things got more and more mysterious. . . ."

† "Mike Bloomfield visited the hill while they were building the wall," I'm told during my tour of the Fort Ave. Terrace houses, "and he pitched in and helped them out." Staring at the symbolic and functional construction, it boggles the mind to think that the guitarist from Bob Dylan's infamous Newport concert, the man who appears on the recording of "Like a Rolling Stone," helped lay the bricks.

You know

what we've been doing

up here on Fort Hill?

We've been building a wall around Mel's house

out of

heavy, heavy stone.

The issue represented Mel and the FHC "thumbing their noses at the other members of the Avatar alliance, challenging them to get with the Hill's program or split," Kindman wrote. Tensions between the Hill and Valley people—non–Family members who worked on *Avatar*—had been building for months.* Pebbles and the stone wall brought things to a head.

A meeting was called on the Hill. Around a large table at 4 Fort Ave. Terrace, the two parties gathered to discuss the goal of the newspaper. Charles Giuliano represented the Valley contingent, and Mel Lyman, of course, spoke for the Hill people. Here were two old friends—who had gone on road trips together, once shared the same girlfriend, and reached astronomical levels of intoxication together at 23 Kenwood—now facing each other as bitter opponents. The entire meeting was being recorded. "I was struck by the intensity of the conversation and the emotions being exchanged," Kindman recalled, "and by the seeming contempt in which the non-Hill people were being held. There seemed to be no room for compromise."

There was no compromise, but there was a capitulation. The Valley writers could continue publishing a newspaper, but they couldn't call it *Avatar*. That was fine with Giuliano, who went immediately to work on non-*Avatar*. Issue 25 ended up containing all the best elements of the news section of *Avatar*: an article on Boston's controversial urban development plan, a

---

* Even outside of the controversial, expanding Lyman coverage in *Avatar*, Charles Giuliano noted how difficult it was to keep their readers happy. "The Resistance wants us to be a radical paper, the artists want us to be lewd and lascivious, the musicians want us to put down the Boston Sound, while others think we should talk more about drugs."

think piece titled "What Is the Underground?," news about Roxbury and Somerville, as well as an article by "William Andrews," wherein he dispelled common myths about drugs. The cover had no logo or title, but Ed Beardsley decided to place a reversed *Avatar* logo on the inside cover. Readers who held the paper up to the light would see it seep through, winking that the publication was still, secretly, the one and only *Avatar.*

"Mel was furious," Michael Kindman recalled. "In retaliation, he ordered his 'boys' to take action." This was war. Up on the Hill, David Gude had a plan: The FHC should seize the unauthorized *Avatar*s before they hit the streets.

The heist kicked off at 4:30 a.m. on May 11. A run of 45,000 issues had just arrived at 37 Rutland Street, "the bundles still warm from the presses," according to Family member Brian Keating. Inside, the only staff present was Pebbles, who was either working late or living at the office. Pebbles stalled the Fort Hill mob, but eventually they loaded the papers into their cars. Charles Giuliano notified the police, who laughed when they heard what had happened to his precious underground newspaper. The fleet of Fort Hill cars zoomed back to Highland Park, where every faux-*Avatar* was locked up inside the Cochituate Standpipe.

Giuliano was devastated. "For the better part of a week there were negotiations, threats, scenes," Giuliano told *Rolling Stone.* "Fort Hill invited us all up for a big steak dinner at [Jim] Kweskin's house, and we tried to iron it all out." But the outcome of this meeting had already been determined by Mel Lyman. As the two parties argued, Kindman and some other FHC members removed issue 25 from the tower and sold it for scrap paper, converting an expensive print into thirty-five bucks. At the end of dinner, the downtown editors were informed about what had just happened to issue 25. The message was clear: If the Lyman Family wasn't going be part of *Avatar*, there would be no *Avatar.*

After consulting the paper's original charter, the Valley team's lawyer saw a clear path to victory. "We called a board meeting," Dave Wilson says, "and simply voted the entire staff out." The Fort Hill contingent didn't object, and begged Wilson not to subpoena Mel, as it would constitute a parole violation. Wilson and Giuliano were legally allowed to continue to publish a paper called *Avatar* without input from Fort Hill.

After slaving over the first issue of the new paper for weeks, Ed Beardsley, livid that he had been passed over for the lead role in *Zabriskie Point* in favor of Mark Frechette,* destroyed the entire ready-to-print newspaper overnight. Just how much of his action was fueled by anger about *Zabriskie*'s casting and how much might have been secret revenge instructions from Mel Lyman cannot be determined ("Beardsley was the perfect double agent for Mel; he didn't know who he was from day to day," Giuliano comments). Giuliano and Wilson laboriously removed the crumpled layout from the trash and slowly re-created it. "It was not a great artistic triumph, but we did it," Giuliano told *Rolling Stone*. "We did it. We did the fucking paper."

Some referred to it as *Avatar II* or *The Boston Avatar*, and if you didn't know any better, you might have thought it was business as usual, judging from the front cover during its six-issue run that summer. Inside, however, was all news, no Mel. Wilson thought they were the best issues they ever did, serving the community at large.

Dave Wilson quit *Avatar II* in the early summer of 1968 to refocus on

---

* Ed Beardsley would have to settle for the role he did finally land: In 1971 he was cast in a made-for-public-television movie starring David Silver and directed by Fred Barzyk entitled *America Inc. America Inc.* is an odd, ahead-of-its-time meta-movie that combines scripted scenarios and documentary footage and, perhaps most surprisingly, is constructed as a way to show what happened to popular Boston TV host David Silver after *What's Happening, Mr. Silver?* was canceled. Even director Fred Barzyk appears on camera early on, shocked to see just how "dropped out" Silver has become since their collaboration on the show together. Silver leaves his wife, Karen, and embarks on a road trip with Ed Beardsley to find himself and discover the country. The soundtrack is provided by, you guessed it, Mel Lyman; a new song, "River," has since emerged on a bootleg release entitled *Birth*. Over the end credits, as if the music selection had been made last minute, or an argument had arisen over it, you hear Fred Barzyk overdub an announcement: "Theme music courtesy of the Lyman Family."

Broadside of Boston, the long-running music publication that was a model for Paul Williams's *Crawdaddy*. Wilson never fell in line with the worship of Mel Lyman like *Crawdaddy*'s Williams did, but he holds no grudges. "I think of Mel rather fondly," Wilson says, laughing, "but I didn't agree with 99 percent of what he was up to." When Wilson left *Avatar II*, he sent Lyman a letter explaining that the struggle was over and wishing him good luck. Days later, two of Lyman's foot soldiers appeared at Wilson's door with a crystal decanter of marijuana as a peace offering. "Mel said that was the most spiritual letter he's ever received," one of the men told Wilson. "I heard the rumors," Wilson says, "that maybe Mel didn't actually die. I really don't know. He was always a really gaunt, ascetic-looking person. I'd guess he died, perhaps from diabetic causes." With Wilson gone, Giuliano couldn't keep *Avatar II* afloat much longer. He agrees with Wilson's guess that their former friend died of complications from diabetes. "I could be wrong," Giuliano says. "But Mel was into total self-indulgence. If there's something that's taboo, do it to the max. His idea of a really good time was to sit there and eat a pound of fudge. Mel could eat a pound of fudge. And so at some point he lost all his teeth. And so I think he probably abused his body in a way that caught up with him."

Starting in October 1968, a new, glossy magazine from the FHC arrived. *American Avatar* made no pretense of covering local politics, but did run a fair amount of national political content, filtered through what Family members called Hill Philosophy. "Today the great people are the musicians, the actors, the filmmakers, the COMMUNICATORS!" Lyman declared in the first issue. "The spirit that begat this country is playing a new instrument . . . Let the Nixons and Humphreys and Wallaces keep house for us, we have a lot of work to do."

The Fort Hill Community tried to expand their audience beyond Boston, passing the magazine out to festivalgoers at Woodstock. But *American Avatar* folded after four issues. Without a print outlet, things got weirder on the Hill.* Increasingly, Lyman dictated his followers' sleeping, bathing, and sexual schedules. One day all the Tauruses would be asked to leave the Hill; the next, a prohibition on having children would be announced. "Mel was making plans to accelerate the rate of change on the Hill, to intensify the internal struggle each of us was going through," Kindman wrote. "We found clues everywhere." When the Beatles' *White Album* arrived later that year, Kindman and his friends swore they heard a message buried in the garbled collage of "Revolution 9": "Here's to Mel, king of the world."

W ITH *AMERICAN AVATAR* BEHIND THEM, the Lyman Family returned to music. They attempted to record something to set the new band apart from the Jug Band legacy. In late July 1969, Lyman and Kweskin asked their old bandmates Maria and Geoff Muldaur to put down some vocals at Petrucci & Atwell Studios on Newbury Street, not far from WBCN's headquarters. They recorded a transcendent version of Curtis Mayfield's "People Get Ready," with the Muldaurs' vocals bringing tears to Mel's eyes. The rekindling of this creative collaboration was short-lived, as Maria and Geoff were given the hard sell to join the FHC later that same night. "Hey, I love Mel because he's a great guy, not because he's God," Geoff explained. The room went deathly silent; the Muldaurs were not invited back.

The other acts working at Petrucci & Atwell knew to keep their distance from the Fort Hill Community singers. According to musician David Palmer, the Lyman crowd took over the studio while he was working on

---

* Around this time, the Lyman Family made its first appearance in a book, though the names were all changed. Henry Gross's 1968 *The Flower People* took readers on a tour of hippie/commune America. For the Fort Hill section, Mel Lyman is renamed . . . David Lynch. "It is a paramountly happy tribe, with David Lynch its godlike guiding chief, smaller family subdivisions within it, and single individuals in unaffiliated abundance." Seven years later, the mother of FHC's Faith Gude, Kay Boyle, published *The Underground Woman* (1975), a novel in which Lyman Family members also appear under new names. The leader is "Pete the Redeemer," who "would be acknowledged the greatest folk singer since Woody Guthrie, and his albums would outsell even Dylan's."

material there with his old friend Rick Philp, who was briefly Van Morrison's first Boston guitarist in 1968. Women from the FHC began hanging around, charming the entire staff, Palmer says of the Lymans. "They wanted nothing but *their* music recorded there."

Freaked out, Palmer and Philp went elsewhere, but things would soon get far worse for Philp. On May 24, 1969, a few weeks after performing with Van Morrison at the Ark club, Rick Philp went to a house on Beacon Street to retrieve a few of his guitars that had gone missing. He was never seen alive again.

PHILP AND PALMER had known each other since their high school days in Warren, New Jersey, where they started a group called the Myddle Class. If the name sounds familiar, it's because they were the headlining band at the 1965 concert that would mark the Velvet Underground's first show ever: an eight p.m. engagement at a school gym in Summit, New Jersey. (Ticket price: $2.50.)

The unlikely pairing was facilitated by Al Aronowitz, who managed both bands. He was new to the job, but not to the music world. A longtime *New York Post* music critic, Aronowitz introduced Bob Dylan to the Beatles, and was present at the Basement Tapes sessions. As for the Myddle Class, Aronowitz's babysitter had told him about them.

A few months before the Summit High show, Aronowitz introduced the young band to husband-and-wife songwriting team Carole King and Gerry Goffin, and together they started cutting tracks. "Their music had an edgy sense of urgency," King wrote in her memoir, *A Natural Woman*, raving about Philp's "inventive guitar parts" and the band's "raw but unmistakable" talent. On the first single, "Free as the Wind," King and Goffin shared writing credits with young Philp and Palmer. "New label, new group and new Goffin-King material has smash hit possibilities," *Billboard* raved. "Folk rocker is a powerhouse!"

Aronowitz sent the Myddle Class out on the road when he could, which tightened up an already powerful live band. But for all its talent, the Myddle Class kept missing their big break. "The band was just not going to work, and we could feel it," Palmer said in 2015. "Carole and Gerry were having problems in their relationship. . . . It was just bad, bad timing for everybody concerned." Philp enrolled at Emerson College in Boston, and Palmer followed in the summer of 1968.

Handsome, polite, and thoughtful, Rick Philp hadn't let his band's flirtation with fame go to his head. Because of his father's pressure to pursue a business career, his wardrobe consisted mostly of suits. Beneath the bourgeois trappings was a phenomenal guitarist. "The deep love for writing and playing music that possessed him was impenetrable," his girlfriend, Kathy West, later wrote.

No one involved recalls how Rick Philp was introduced to the ex-singer of Them. But by March 1968, he was rehearsing with a short-lived Boston combo—the first of three—that Van Morrison fronted during his Bay State exile. Bassist Tom Kielbania remembers being impressed that Philp had recorded demos for the Monkees, and felt he was a good fit.* For this lineup, Morrison used a rehearsal room at the National Express Recording Studio in the South End. June Benson, who lived above the studio, remembers hearing Morrison before she saw him. "The music was daily. 'Brown Eyed Girl' played almost endlessly that summer," she says. "We would try and talk over it, clean the house with it blaring, eat with it blasting. It was just *never ending* when Van was there."

This first Boston band—Philp, Kielbania, and a forgotten drummer—played one confirmed show: Morrison's first live appearance in Boston,

---

* A memory from Philp's Emerson College girlfriend, Elayne Kesller, suggests that, although their collaboration was brief, Philp and Morrison had struck up some kind of friendly rapport; for instance, the night Martin Luther King was assassinated, she remembers being at Van Morrison's Green Street apartment with Rick and watching TV coverage of the riots while they all sat on Morrison's bed in shock.

Spring Sing, in front of what would be one of his largest audiences for the entire year. It was also the first show in which Morrison used the enigmatic moniker the Van Morrison Controversy. In Dick Iacovello's pictures of the band, a long-haired Morrison, resplendent in a multicolored striped suit and tie, commands the stage; at times, he even smiles. Rob Norris, a Myddle Class fan and future member of a Lou Reed–less VU, was bowled over by the show, comparing the sound to Van's *Blowin' Your Mind!*

After the semester ended, Rick Philp chose working with Carole King over Van Morrison; he and his roommate, Harvey "Dog" Alter, made the long drive to Los Angeles together. King had rented a house in Laurel Canyon for Philp, Alter, and Kathy. During this summer in L.A., it became increasingly clear to Kathy that Harvey was growing a little too possessive of Rick. After the first night, Harvey scolded the reunited couple for keeping their door closed. Later, Harvey told Rick and Kathy a disturbing story from his summer restaurant job, in which he witnessed a meat slicer blade decapitate the operator. He smiled as he recounted the incident, the truth of which they couldn't determine.

Back in Boston, in late 1968, there were two mysterious fires in Rick and Harvey's apartment; trying to stay positive, Rick noted to Kathy that the guitars were undamaged. The arson squad found evidence that the fires were purposely set. The following spring, the guitarist moved to Brighton to distance himself from Harvey Alter. Philp's letters to Kathy depict someone trying to keep his head above water; even good news was immediately followed by a sense of sinking hope. "I'm playing with Van Morrison May 1," he wrote, noting in the same letter that his father had told him to get a real job—to stop being so "dirty and disgusting."* Kathy recalls the most

---

* The date refers to Van Morrison's three-night stand at the Ark, a new club on Lansdowne Street meant to compete with the Boston Tea Party. Fort Hill Community member John Kostick had created a gigantic version of one of his Buckminster Fuller–inspired metal star sculptures to hang from the ceiling inside the Ark. (Smaller versions were churned out in Kostick's Roxbury workshop and sold by FHC members; decades later, a Kostick star appeared on an

heartbreaking line: "That crap about people are basically honest and really want some kind of meaningful relationships with other people is just bullshit." Shortly after the letter was mailed, Rick's guitars were mysteriously stolen. Fed up with Boston, he made plans to get to L.A. as soon as the semester ended.

Sometime during the week of May 19, Philp received a phone call from Alter. Harvey said he'd found Rick's guitars, and if he came by their old basement apartment at 233 Beacon Street, he could take them back. Within a few days, some of Philp's classmates and professors noticed he was missing.

Rick had mentioned to a friend that he was going to Harvey's apartment to retrieve his guitars; this information was passed along to detectives. Five days after that attempt to retrieve his instruments, police entered Alter's apartment to find Rick's decomposing corpse under some blankets on Alter's bed.

"He's dead," Harvey Alter told the officers. "I killed Rick." He was twenty-two years old.

The medical examiner called it a "complex homicide," involving multiple blows to the head, a broken chair leg, and a length of rope. Rick's history professor, John Coffee, recalls the story that eventually emerged: Harvey Alter had had a crush on Rick, who wasn't gay. Yet so long as Harvey didn't come on to him, Rick didn't see a problem. "But he started coming on to Rick. So Rick moved . . . and Harvey said, you know, 'If I can't have him, nobody can.'"

His lawyer devised an elaborate defense, proposing that the two young

---

MIT professor's desk in the film *Good Will Hunting*.) In May 1969, underneath a giant, spinning Kostick star, Van Morrison performed *Astral Weeks* in its entirety during one if not all three of these concerts, something he wouldn't do again until 2008 at the Hollywood Bowl. Kielbania was still on bass at this point, with John Platania on guitar, Bob Mason on drums, and flutist/saxophonist Graham Blackburn; Philp and *Astral Weeks* alum John Payne appeared as special guests. Confirmed audience members include Jonathan Richman and Peter Wolf. Soon after this show, most of the *Astral Weeks* songs would be excised from Morrison's set list, rarely or never to be performed for another forty years.

men had taken drugs and engaged in consensual sex. Things had gotten out of hand, the lawyer said, as the drugs (it's never clear which ones) kicked in. Kathy and others close to Rick saw this as pure fabrication: Rick was only an occasional marijuana user, and had never displayed any bisexual tendencies. After two weeks of testimony, the judge accepted a plea of the lesser charge of manslaughter on Alter's behalf, citing the drug use as a major factor in his decision. "It is unfortunate, that so many of our young people who have a chance to gain an education spill it down the drain by the use of illegal drugs," the judge declared, adding in a bizarre aside that he wished more college students would attend murder trials to witness "real tragedies" instead of going to see the musical *Hair*.

IN VAN MORRISON'S EVOLVING BOSTON LINEUP, the teenage John Sheldon replaced Rick Philp sometime in May 1968. I ask Sheldon if, in a way, it makes sense that Morrison rejected the frenetic, electric version of the songs that Sheldon was pushing that summer in an attempt to create shelter in his otherwise turbulent situation. Sheldon says, "He was looking for something in the music—he was searching for *something*—and he wasn't getting it with the rock and roll thing."

Producer Lewis Merenstein heard this searching, this quest, in September 1968, when Van's audition of "Astral Weeks" at Ace Studios stunned him to the core. He tells me this repeatedly over the phone, then even more emphatically when we meet outside a coffee shop near his home in Manhattan. In aviator glasses and black baseball cap, the eighty-year-old Merenstein seems tall even though he never gets up from his motorized scooter. His voice is frail, and I lean forward to catch his words.

In the live room at Ace studio, Merenstein wasn't even certain that Morrison *understood* what he was singing about; it was like hearing something being poured out of the man's subconscious. Merenstein said to his partner, Bob Schwaid, "Bob, what are we wasting time for? Let's go make a record."

The three drove to New York City that same night, he says. En route, Merenstein tried to tell Morrison about some of the bands and albums he had worked with previously. "He wasn't impressed. So I stopped talking." They deposited the singer at a hotel, and the three arranged to meet at Schwaid and Merenstein's Midtown office in the morning.

This would be the first time Morrison had returned to New York since fleeing earlier in 1968. "I won't go into details but I think it's sufficient to say Bert Berns & Bang was a Fucked Up Bad Scene," Morrison once wrote to a musician friend. Was he nervous that Carmine "Wassel" DeNoia might come around? When he arrived at the office the next day, he needed a drink. "There's never *a* drink with Van," Merenstein says. "I don't know how long we were there, but he finally got talking about his music." They discussed who would play on the album; Morrison suggested his Boston musicians, but Merenstein opposed the idea. "We had a fight over it," he says. "But I had more conviction about why it should be my way."

A compromise was reached: Merenstein would choose the musicians, but Morrison could bring Tom Kielbania and John Payne from Boston to New York. They wouldn't play on the record, but Warner Brothers would pay them to attend the sessions—out of courtesy, and in case something about their arrangements needed clarification. The next day, Morrison came to Merenstein's office and played him all the potential songs for the record.

Was Merenstein surprised that it was so different from "Brown Eyed Girl"? "Everything he *did* surprised me," he says. "It was just him and a guitar. It was so awesome I can't even tell you how moved I felt by his ability to communicate."

Upon first hearing the song "Moondance," Merenstein briefly considered including it on the album. But it was "too warm, too lovey" for *Astral Weeks*. Merenstein contacted jazz bass player Richard Davis to book him for the project and to explain to him the other musicians he wanted present at the sessions—some by name, some just by referencing the instrument and feel he wanted. Merenstein and Davis became close friends in the ensuing decades, but when the producer speaks about Davis's musicianship, he still sounds worshipful. "Davis's playing is the foundation that the Earth is floating on!"

The first session was booked for September 25, 1968, at Century Sound Studios on 135 West Fifty-second Street.

BEFORE THE FIRST NOTE was committed to tape, Payne and Kielbania knew they wouldn't be on the record. "I'm sorry, Tom, I really am," Morrison said, in an unusual show of emotion. Kielbania was upset by the news, but there was some consolation in learning that his replacement was Richard Davis. "I idolized him at that time," the former Berklee music student says. "I was a freaking jazz musician, after all!" If the two Bostonians had a loose plan to talk their way onto the record, Tom's chances were dashed the moment Davis walked in the door. For John, there was still hope.

The studio filled up with Merenstein's chosen team: Davis on bass, Jay Berliner on guitar, Connie Kay on drums, and Warren Smith Jr. on vibraphone—all respected jazz musicians. (A New York flute player who appears on two tracks goes unnamed in the liner notes, and none of the musicians can recall who it was.) In the control room, Brooks Arthur, the engineer and owner of Century Sound Studios, manned the boards, while Merenstein stood behind him. Payne and Kielbania sat on the couch, watching. It was dusk as they tuned up their instruments; most of them had already worked a session or two earlier that day. Consulting his work diary from that year, guitarist Jay Berliner notes he had just recorded jingles for both Noxzema and Pringles potato chips before showing up to start working on one of the most celebrated albums of all time. There was no project title yet; Berliner's gig diary merely says "Van Morrison."* None of the musicians had heard of him before.

---

* Precisely one week before the first *Astral Weeks* session, Jay Berliner recorded guitar for a band called the Astral Projection who were cutting an album titled *The Astral Scene*. Surprisingly, the record is not psychedelic in any musical sense, but rather a brand of blandly sunny

Berliner remembers the unusual way the band was introduced—or *not* introduced—to the star of the project. "This little guy walks in, past everybody, disappears into the vocal booth, and almost never comes out," he said. "Even on the playbacks, he stayed in there." The other musicians confirm this. Davis, now retired and living in Wisconsin, focuses on what he found important about the sessions. "Well, I was with three of my favorite fellas to play with, so that's what made it beautiful. We were not concerned with Van at *all*, he *never* spoke to us."

Van's default mode of noninteraction was familiar to his Boston bandmates, but this level of shyness was extreme. "He seemed spaced out," Payne told biographer Clinton Heylin, "as though he was in a lot of personal pain." Perhaps, in the presence of players who were part of the Modern Jazz Quartet or Charles Mingus collaborators, Morrison simply became overwhelmed by nerves. His old producer Bert Berns had always had too many ideas; now, in the company of a producer who just wanted to let things happen naturally, the freedom could have been disorienting. Berliner swears the singer's isolation booth was full of some kind of smoke (Berliner claims Morrison called it "vegetable weed"), but no one else has this exact recollection.

"I don't know what he was doing in there!" Davis says. "He's a strange fella!"

Perched on a stool, Morrison clutched his guitar, opened the binder of his new songs that Janet Planet had collated for him, and waited for Brooks Arthur to hit record. For the session musicians, this was just another gig, but for Morrison, it must have felt like the last chance to breathe life into his faltering career—to be born again, as the title track proclaims. It is a point of contention whether lead sheets or chord charts were provided, but Davis believes

---

pop, with titles and lyrics that occasionally evoke New Age beliefs. The singer concludes the final track by singing, "Was it just a dream? The Astral Scene!" Between this forgettable *Astral* record and *Astral Weeks*, the industrious Berliner also recorded jingles for Eastern Airlines and a few songs with Dionne Warwick.

Morrison just strummed the song and sang it from the booth once or twice, with the musicians improvising their parts on top of his composition minutes later. Tom Kielbania claims he demonstrated some bass lines he had developed back in Boston for Davis; Davis denies this, but Payne confirms it.

That a group of players who had been knee-deep in ad-jingle-land hours before then pivoted to create the singularly beautiful music found on *Astral Weeks* seems incredible, but by all accounts this was actually the case. Guitarist Jay Berliner's schedule was so flanked by commercial work, in fact, he joked that he could have mistaken the session for another advertising job. "*Astral Weeks*, I mean, what a *long* jingle," he says, laughing. "And what *are* we selling here, exactly?"

Jingles are thirty seconds; pop songs, about three minutes. But Morrison's new compositions called for takes that could stretch beyond nine minutes. Kielbania recalls that what ended up on the album was often an edit of a much longer jam. Jay Berliner finds this plausible, and recalls Lewis Merenstein at the control booth window smiling, rolling his hand in a "keep going!" motion. That first night, they laid down "Beside You," "Cyprus Avenue," and the epic "Madame George," which hit the five-, seven-, and nine-minute mark in their final versions. Everyone was so pleased with the results that they started to talk about trying one more before calling it quits.

When John Payne heard it was going to be "Astral Weeks," a song he had been playing with Van live back in Boston, he began to loudly campaign for permission to perform. "John was basically crying when I told him he wouldn't be on the album," Lewis Merenstein recalls. "I said, 'It's not anything to do with your playing, it's just not the concept I had.'" Payne begged the hired flutist to let him borrow his instrument, as he had left his own at the Chelsea Hotel.

"Oh man, I just wanna go home," the unknown musician replied, yawning.

"Please," Payne said, with all the intensity of a young man recognizing the special opportunity before him. "*Please* let me play on this song."

Merenstein and the weary flutist finally gave in, and John Payne took a seat inside the live room. The twenty-two-year-old Harvard dropout and second cousin to poet Robert Lowell had just talked his way into a session with some of New York's best jazz musicians. "I was a cocky kid I guess," Payne says. "I thought I was hot stuff. I was a little nervous, but mostly I was just excited because I had been playing with him and I *knew* I could do it." By all accounts, the song that appears on the album is the very first take. "The interaction between Jay Berliner and me playing off each other and the whole way Van was just there listening to it was just amazing," Payne says. "I still think it's the best thing in the record. The first track." The unknown flutist—name lost to history—was not called back for the subsequent sessions.

Six days passed between this first session and the next. Somewhere on Ninth Avenue, Warner Brothers' Joe Smith made the successful bagful-of-twenty-grand drop-off to the sketchy associates of Bang Records. Also during this week, on the label's payroll and with nothing better to do, John Payne and Tom Kielbania took a personality test. Before they knew it, the two Bostonians found themselves taking a Scientology class. "A new, and quite apparently phony 'religion' called Scientology is beginning to emerge from the lower depths," *Women's Wear Daily* reported a month before. "In the United States, it is still basically unknown except to cultists and a few curios-ity seekers. But in recent days, subway posters have appeared in New York urging everyone: 'Step into the world of the totally free.'" Kielbania remem-bers doing "all the stuff where you stare into people's eyes for two hours straight and try to change their emotions." Kielbania thought there might be something to it, but at $1,500 for a six-week course, the price was too steep.

Van Morrison wouldn't dabble in Scientology until the eighties (he thanked founder L. Ron Hubbard in the liner notes to 1983's *Inarticulate Speech of the Heart*), but already had a deep interest in occult writing. "Van had a friend in high school who was a librarian in Belfast," Kielbania says. "This guy had *all* the occult books. This guy used to read them all, and he went insane! So Van was always kinda interested in that." That fall in New

York, Morrison and Kielbania hit every occult bookstore, hunting for a particular title Van wanted: *Secret of the Andes*, "about flying saucers and people coming to visit this planet." Once they found it, they dove in.

Written by George Hunt Williamson under the pseudonym Brother
Philip, this 1961 text reads like a welcome packet for visitors to our planet,
its contents largely transmitted to Williamson via Ouija board. "The Earth
is a classroom for gods, but a strange classroom indeed! Some of the people
of the more magnificent worlds are actually envious . . . because they know
that on Earth, if you can combat such negativity you have to be a powerful
spirit." As in Lou Reed's preferred occult book, Alice Bailey's *A Treatise on
White Magic* (1934), the Seven Rays are also discussed here. Even more curiously, Brother Philip describes visitors to Earth he calls "astrals":

> The astral forces are helping too. There are many great beings
> who are assisting both space men and yourselves. They are acting
> as emissaries, doing what work they can. Some of them perform
> fine services on the battlefields, on the streets, and in the offices,
> each acting as mentors and guides to the people of the world. After
> all, we have all been astrals many times. We have been astrals as
> many times as we have been mortals in that sense.

Morrison had definitely written "Astral Weeks" by the time he and Kielbania got hold of this book, and the phrase itself had come to him even
earlier—back in Belfast, where it popped into his head while staring at a
painting by his friend Cecil McCarthy. The words suggest a time and a
place; they roll off the tongue like an incantation, some long-lost relative of
abracadabra or *hocus pocus*, slowly forgotten over centuries.

"There were several paintings in the studio at the time," McCarthy explained. "Van looked at the painting and it suggested astral traveling to
him." The painting was new, but for Morrison, the concept of an astral plane
was not. In the seventies, he told interviewers about strange incidents he

experienced as a child—lying in bed with "the feeling that I'm floating near the ceiling looking down," and other "amazing projections." His out-of-body experiences as a boy help explain the obsession with youth that runs through *Astral Weeks*. In these songs, the singer longs to return to an age when the world functioned like magic. "And I will never grow so old again," he sings on the triumphant, Yeatsian "Sweet Thing." In "Beside You" we meet Little Jimmy and a "barefoot virgin child"; in the epic "Cyprus Avenue," the longing for youth takes on a more troubling form—what seems to be an adult yearning for a fourteen-year-old girl. The whole dreamlike plot of "Madame George" is filtered through "a childlike vision leaping into view."

Is it unusual for someone in his early twenties to already be so nostalgic for, and obsessed with, his youth? Around this time, Van Morrison gave Tom Kielbania a kind of clue: He was an only child. "That bothered him," Kielbania says. "We were in some hotel room, just talking, and he said, 'You know, people shouldn't be allowed to just have one kid, because you miss out on a whole bunch of stuff.'" Kielbania, also without siblings, could relate. "He thought that it was a terrible thing that happened to him."

But writing *Astral Weeks*'s lyrics wasn't necessarily so deliberate—indeed, it might have been the opposite. Fast-forward to 1986's *No Guru, No Method, No Teacher*, in which Morrison surprisingly echoed some of the imagery and phrasing from his breakthrough LP from 1968. The "childlike vision" returns, as does the "garden wet with rain" of "Sweet Thing."* When Morrison was asked how he wrote the newer song ("In the Garden"), he answered, "Oh yeah, I didn't write that. I was sitting in my flat one night and this voice said to me, 'Write this down,' and I pulled out the paper and I just wrote down what he told me, and that was the song."

Whether you find any validity in this kind of claim, what *is* certain is

---

* On the *No Guru* song "Tir Na Nog"—a reference to an Irish myth about a land that delivers everlasting youth—Morrison again sings about someone kissing his eyes, as he does on "Astral Weeks": "Could you find me? Would you kiss-a my eyes?" The words suggest some kind of previously arranged secret code, a way for two lovers to recognize each other in the next life.

that Morrison himself believes some of his songs arrived fully formed, via a kind of automatic writing. Janet Planet insists that Van's writing style, circa 1968, involved a stream-of-consciousness transmission that he would record and edit down after playback. Had Morrison arrived in Boston eighty years earlier, his new songs might have been studied by William James and the American Society for Psychical Research rather than reviewed in *Rolling Stone*. As he told writer Ritchie Yorke in 1979, "I didn't know what some of the stuff on *Astral Weeks* was about until years later. . . . If the spirit comes through in a 'Madame George' type of song, that's what the spirit says. You have very little to do with it. You're like an instrument for what's coming through."

THE NEXT RECORDING SESSION, early on the morning of October 1, went poorly. No one was feeling it, and after three hours of an undefinable tension, Merenstein sent everyone home. Timing is everything—not only in the scheduling of a session, but in the building-block sense: Music is made up of countless choices of timing. This becomes readily apparent when listening to the alternate takes on 2015's expanded *Astral Weeks* release. In take 4 of "Madame George" and take 1 of "Beside You," Morrison makes subtle changes in phrasing and lyrics, and chooses different words to repeat over and over like a mantra, drastically altering the feel of the songs. After being so intimately familiar with the takes that make up the iconic 1968 release, hearing these recordings evokes an alternate reality, in which these classics have yet to be set in stone. It's as if Morrison is in the same boat as the musicians who had just heard the songs moments before Merenstein hit record.

Two weeks passed before the third and final recording session on October 15. Not only did the musicians have to nail the remaining songs, but in Merenstein's quest to find something appropriate to place at the end of the record, the group ran through "Royalty" and "Going Around with Jesse James," two stray numbers pulled from Janet's binder. No one liked them,

so Morrison kept flipping through, finally landing on an austere set of lyrics, for a song that wasn't even familiar to the Boston musicians. "I used
'Slim Slow Slider' to make it work," Merenstein says, about the album's
haunting last chapter. "Make it fade into the mystic."

The whole band played the first take. Then Merenstein called everyone
into the control room, leaving Van, Davis, and Payne, now on soprano sax,
to try a sparser version. After Morrison sings the lyrics about a dying
ex-lover, an abstract jazz jam ensues. Merenstein later cuts the sprawl, so
that the whole album seems to end on a note of helplessness, even terror: "I
just don't know what to do."*

After the take, Payne and Davis walked back into the control room to
find everyone completely silent. Up until this point, Merenstein had praised
each take right after it was done. Now there was total silence. Morrison remained in the vocal booth. "Maybe everyone was just tired," Payne says,
"or maybe they were moved by it." Merenstein's choice to end the record
with lyrics about dying was inspired: After the last notes fade, a flip of the
platter results in being "born again." *Astral Weeks* contains a built-in mech-
anism for reincarnation.

At the subsequent overdub sessions, Payne and Kielbania again tagged
along, making them witnesses to the entire process of creating the record.
Arranger Larry Fallon, fresh off adding a lush orchestral sound to Nico's
Chelsea Girls, directed the horns on "The Way Young Lovers Do," the
harpsichord on "Cyprus Avenue," and strings throughout. "Everything
else was written out, but Larry wanted the guy to improvise on violin for
'Madame George,'" Payne recalls. "The guy said he couldn't do it. He
wasn't an improviser. So Fallon called up someone and said, 'Get me some

---

* When I played the extended mix of the song for John Payne, he sat with his head in his hands
for twenty seconds, before solemnly telling me, "That's not what happened." It was the first
time he had heard the cut section since recording it in 1968. In Payne's memory, there were four
or five *additional* minutes of "Slim Slow Slider," working up into an abstract jazz freestyle.
"This is very disappointing," he said. "Maybe it doesn't exist."

damn improvisers.' So, this other guy came in and he smoked it." Payne and Kielbania recall watching the violinist from the control booth and jumping out of their seats with enthusiasm. "He was unbelievable," Payne says. "No one told him what to do. Tom and I were flipping out, it was so good." Morrison, who seemed just as enthused as his Boston bandmates during the creation of these finishing touches, would feel differently about the end product before it even hit record stores. Just weeks after completion, according to Payne, Merenstein quickly put the finished product on the office turntable so that when Morrison walked in, they'd all be enjoying his incredible new LP. The singer waved away the praise and told him to turn it off. "They ruined it," Morrison later insisted. "They added the strings. I didn't want the strings. And they sent it to me, it was all changed. That's not *Astral Weeks*."

Due to the Bang contract, there would be no stand-alone single from the album, but in December 1968, someone at Warner Brothers wondered if a separate nonalbum track could be released in tandem as a workaround to the contract. Berliner and Warren Smith Jr. from the *Astral Weeks* sessions joined Morrison, Kielbania, and drummer Buddy Saltzman at Century Sound to record a track called "The Sky Is Full of Pipers." The idea of an *Astral Weeks*–esque pop single, especially with that Pink Floydian title, taunts the imagination, but the song was never released—and seems to have disappeared completely.

"Van seemed quite happy with the album at the time, he truly did," Merenstein tells me, sadly reflecting on the singer's rejection of his contributions in the ensuing years. "In fact, *everyone* did, at the moment it was completed."

Morrison would spend the next four decades changing his mind about the album, and trying to figure out a way he could reclaim it as his achievement alone. His insistence that he had conceived the album as an opera seems especially suspect, since "Beside You" and "Madame George" were contractually required to appear on the record in the terms of the Bang settlement—not exactly the kind of thing that usually factors into the creation of an opera.

He turned in the text that appears on the back of the record—that mysterious eleven-line poem that name-drops several Massachusetts locales—to Warner Brothers for printing, but did not provide a lyric sheet. Merenstein sequenced the album and titled each side, respectively, "In the Beginning" and "Afterwards."

"He was raw. He was being reborn, he was a child again," Lewis Merenstein told Clinton Heylin. "He never achieved that again. He searched all over the world of poetry for various ways of expressing himself, but the rawness, the nerve endings weren't there—because he's not *there* anymore."

"The reason Van gets so embittered when people ask him about it is because he cannot share anything," Merenstein explains near the end of our conversation. "Everything has to be him, him, him. The fact that he wasn't in charge of *Astral Weeks* drives him crazy. But it shouldn't! He's a beautiful poet. He should be a kind person with love in his heart." It's highly curious that a man who had insisted that these songs came *through him*, rather than writing them himself, would be so stubborn about sharing credit with a man that Clinton Heylin describes as one of his few "genuine collaborators." Seven months after our interview, Lewis Merenstein passed away at age eighty-one from complications related to pneumonia.

In December 1968, Van Morrison sent for Janet Planet in Cambridge. Now that Warner Brothers had extricated him from Bang Records, what did Boston have to offer him? The music scene was dominated by psychedelic Bosstown rock now, not the folksingers who originally attracted Morrison. Richard, the Boston manager who initially seemed so helpful, had turned out to be too expensive, too eccentric. And Tom Kielbania notwithstanding, most of his bandmates had not made his music a priority: One quit to continue school, one to work with Carole King, while another tried to convert the band into something like Them at their most hyper. He had been in a frightening car accident on the way home from a gig, and harassed by police; the local underground and mainstream press had barely covered him. Sure, he'd miss his new friend Peter Wolf, but he would see him whenever his tours stopped in Boston. The Van Morrison Controversy was over.

Afterwards

WHILE A RECORD PLANT PRESSED *Astral Weeks* to vinyl, Richard Nixon was elected president of the United States.

In November, the same month the Beatles dropped a double album to confound the world, *Astral Weeks* arrived with little fanfare. The cover's circle-in-a-square design gave it a "mystical feel," according to producer Lewis Merenstein. Inside the circle inside the square, Morrison looks down, his hair meshing with branches and leaves. This is not the sweaty, high-as-a-kite singer that Bert Berns tried to sell on the sleeve of *Blowin' Your Mind!* This is Morrison in double exposure, opening himself up to the world, about to be born again.

"I used to sit in front of my set and play the album and think, 'Is this going to disappear into space?'" Merenstein grumbles. He and Morrison's manager, Bob Schwaid, would call Warner Brothers weekly and ask, "What are you waiting for—everyone to forget who he is?" The sparse marketing was deaf to the music's charms. One print ad placed a black bar over the singer's eyes, announcing, "Last night, this man scored," then threw in a baseball comparison for good measure ("Eight home runs: Astral Weeks"). Bassist Tom Kielbania recalls walking into every record store in Manhattan looking for the album, without luck; according to Warner Brothers' Joe Smith, "Nobody wanted to buy it." The label released no single, perhaps because Ilene Berns, now in charge of Bang Records, would have contractually received a cut—or simply because no song was suitable: Over half of them unfurled past the five-minute mark.

After plans for a European tour fizzled, Morrison, Kielbania, and John Payne's replacement left for a promotional tour in February 1969. Afterward, Morrison decided to relocate from New York City to the Catskills town of Woodstock. Merenstein had plans for the next record, and it sounded a lot like a sequel. In the summer of 1969, the producer began tracking *Moondance* with nearly the same lineup that had recorded *Astral Weeks*: Richard Davis, Warren Smith Jr., and Jay Berliner all returned. The idea of the masterfully melodic songwriting found on *Moondance* paired with the feel of *Astral Weeks* sounds irresistible, but at the time, Morrison was rebelling against Merenstein. He had his own vision, and rejected the producer's input. Besides, as far as anyone knew, *Astral Weeks* was a flop, destined for perpetual obscurity.

Add to this Mary Martin, Albert Grossman's former secretary, who was gunning to become Van's new manager. Merenstein found her aggressive and manipulative; he watched his hard work crumble. Merenstein calls the *Moondance* experience "a horror." All of the *Astral Weeks* personnel got the boot, and their takes on these songs have never been heard. While Merenstein would receive an executive producer credit, his contributions did not affect the final recordings, so much so that one of the young engineers on the project—Shelly Yakus, son of Ace Recording Studio's Milton Yakus—doesn't remember *anyone* producing *Moondance*, really. "[Schwaid and I] always felt so much pain whenever we'd talk about this," Merenstein says of their ousting. "We never knew whether the beauty was more or the pain was more." As the legend of *Astral Weeks* grew, people often wanted insight about the title's meaning. "I'll give you his number," Merenstein would sigh. "You can ask him yourself."

Tom Kielbania's decision to leave Van Morrison was a difficult one, but the signs were everywhere. "Do you know what it was like living in Wood-stock then?" Kielbania asks. "Memorial Day weekend: The New York City chapter of the Hell's Angels rolls in. One of these guys tried to get me to go with him someplace. And I knew if I went with him, I wasn't gonna come back." Kielbania raises his eyebrows and says, "Lotta black magic and stuff." During this Woodstock residency, Kielbania's partner, Claudette, watched someone castrate himself and then jump out a window at a party. Additionally, the couple had recently married, and now Claudette was pregnant. When Kielbania told Morrison the news, the singer replied, "I figured that was gonna happen after you got married."

WHEN VAN MORRISON replaced the jazz musicians who made *Astral Weeks* so special, he chose a lineup consisting almost entirely of musicians involved with the Bosstown Sound: Jef Labes of the Apple Pie Motherhood Band on keys, Third World Raspberry bassist John Klingberg, and the horn section from the Colwell-Winfield Blues Band. For decades to come, Morrison would continually rely on Boston musicians for his bands; Labes appears on eight albums, including *Veedon Fleece*, and Rick Shlosser, drum-mer for the Butter, a Bosstown-era Cream knockoff, appears on *Tupelo Honey*, *Saint Dominic's Preview*, and *Hard Nose the Highway*.

Though Bay Stater Jon Landau was attuned to Morrison's Boston con-nection (shouting it out in his 1971 *Rolling Stone* assessment of *His Band and the Street Choir*), that link quickly turned obscure; in 1973, *The Boston Globe* no less wondered why Morrison's live show would "strangely" lean so heav-ily on *Astral Weeks* material. Over the years, an inverse relationship devel-oped between the album's legend and its Boston roots. As the album ascended to masterpiece stature, his Massachusetts stint became less well known. Jonathan Richman tried to keep the story alive in 1993: "Van Mor-rison, his *Astral Weeks* album, a lot of those songs were written in Cam-bridge, Massachusetts. He's from Belfast. I listen to that record a lot and I think Boston, Cambridge again. I went to Cyprus Avenue in Belfast. I found it. I went there."

Richman found the spiritual link between Morrison's native city and the place the singer fled to in 1968. "[Boston's] got a kind of sad beauty to it," Richman told *Q* magazine. "You know what it reminds me of? Belfast." Morrison himself obliquely connected the two cities in "Hard Nose the Highway"—his sole published lyrical reference to his 1968 stomping grounds. But did the lyrics on *Astral Weeks* contain any clues to his turbulent time there? I was resigned to leaving the puzzle unsolved.

While talking with the producer of the 2015 *Astral Weeks* expanded edition, I learned about an outtake still in the Vault—a song that would never see the light of day. The alternate versions that appear on the LP's reissue—including the revelatory "Slim Slow Slider"—could legally be released without additional permission from Morrison, because they'd already been published. But "Train" would require an okay from Morrison, which the label could not secure. In *Astral Weeks* lore, rumors abound that "Train" was an hour long.

Last winter, I got to hear it. There's no question why the song was left off the album. It's a slow-burning blues that simmers for fourteen minutes but never boils; in fact, halfway through you can hear Warren Smith Jr. get bored and change his vibraphone part from the repeated riff to a wandering arpeggio that brings to mind flashback music on an old TV show. But there's also something remarkable, tucked in around the halfway point. Out of nowhere, Morrison intones Massachusetts place-names. The lyrics flow from the poem that appears on the album's back cover—or is the poem a version of the lyrics?

Inside of "Train," you can hear the echt Irish songwriter belt out the town names of Cambridgeport and Hyannis Port as if they were fabled secret villages. It's a surreal discovery. If "Train" had made it onto *Astral Weeks*, the album would have explicitly bridged Belfast and Boston, the home he hailed from and the home he had found. Think of laying a translucent map of one atop the other, the scrambled new geography revealing "some hidden wisdom," as he puts it elsewhere in the song. There are only two songs that reference trains here, this outtake and *Astral Weeks'* nine-minute climax. "Say goodbye, goodbye," Van implores, at the end of "Madame George." "Get on the train / this is the train." George Ivan Morrison bids Madame George farewell, as he boards the Belfast–Boston Express, to the place where his future awaits.

MOONDANCE DID ALL the things that *Astral Weeks* did not. The marketing was stronger and the reception was significantly warmer. "Unlike Van's masterful *Astral Weeks*, this one will be immensely popular," *Rolling Stone* predicted. "Van's picture already fills the windows of record stores and his new music is getting more airplay on FM stations than anything in recent memory." Despite their significant differences, these two albums are forever linked—by Lewis Merenstein's involvement, by their celestial titles, and by a foundation of great songs forged in Boston. "Think of it," Lewis Merenstein later mused. *"Astral Weeks* and *Moondance* and never again. Tons of albums, nothing equal to those albums."

The lionization of *Astral Weeks* was decades in the making. *Rolling Stone*'s assessment of the best music of 1968 didn't even mention it. But sales were steady in the years to come. "We know what's going down with this album now," Joe Smith told Morrison in 1971. "We're going to be selling it for another six years." That was an understatement. Bruce Springsteen's obsession with the record led him to tap Richard Davis to play bass on his 1973 debut and on *Born to Run* in 1975. "It made me trust in beauty, it gave me a sense of the divine," Springsteen said of *Astral Weeks*, forty years later. "It was the same chord progression over and over again. But it showed how expansive something with very basic underpinning could be." Critical pieces also widened the cult, none as important as Lester Bangs's paean to the album. Simply titled "Astral Weeks," the essay first appeared in 1978's

Stranded, a "desert island discs" anthology edited by Greil Marcus, then kicked off Bangs's first collection, *Psychotic Reactions and Carburetor Dung*, published in 1987, five years after his death. "It was particularly important to me because the fall of 1968 was such a terrible time," Bangs admitted up front, and what followed was a glorious, confessional look at pain and redemption that has itself become a classic.

Engineer Brooks Arthur recalls the moment he realized that *Astral Weeks* wasn't going away; it was sometime in the nineties when he was earning a living by producing Adam Sandler's comedy albums. "I was in the bathroom reading an issue of *Rolling Stone*," Arthur says. "It said it was one of the most seminal records ever made. I couldn't believe it."

The lavish praise seemed only to annoy Van Morrison; hundreds of songs later, he was still being asked about *Astral Weeks*. Even its classification bugged him. "Of all the records I have ever made that one is definitely not rock," he griped. "Why they keep calling it one I have no idea." In 2008, he did something that seemed to engage with the constant praise. If people were going to prattle on about *Astral Weeks*, he'd do the entire thing live at the Hollywood Bowl, even bringing back some of the original players, and release the new recording himself in an attempt to claim some of the profits he felt he deserved. When original bass player Richard Davis showed up to rehearsal, he was shocked to see that every note he had improvised in 1968 had been transferred to sheet music. Strict adherence was expected. "Do you know how crazy that is?" Merenstein says, incredulous. "For that kind of playing? After two rehearsal dates Richard was fired. He got paid and went home."

Arthur reports a similar story. As someone who had gone forty years without a proper engineer credit on *Astral Weeks*, he was ecstatic when asked to man the boards at the Hollywood Bowl show. "I told Van I would love to, but that I wasn't as quick as I had been forty years ago," Arthur says. "I told him I'd need an assistant engineer by my side." He never heard back; the gig went to someone else. Besides Morrison, the only member from the original team to make it to the performance was Jay Berliner. His improvised guitar parts had been notated as well, but he wisely just pretended to follow along. Joe Smith watched from the audience. "It wasn't a spectacular show."

Morrison is known as one of the world's best living vocalists. His gruffness and unpredictability are the other side of that calling card. Aimee Mann, leader of Boston band 'Til Tuesday, once shared a meal with Peter Wolf and Morrison where she watched another dinner guest try to make small talk with the singer, asking about a former saxophone player in his band. Morrison blew a fuse. "He went, 'Questions! Questions! Questions!' got up, and stormed out," Mann said. After Jef Labes became part of Morrison's live act, he witnessed the singer sabotage his concerts, including a 1969 Symphony Hall date in Boston that he performed while lying down. At a show in Canada, Labes says, Van humped the piano, telling the crowd, "*This* is what you really wanna see!"

"He's a genius," Labes says, "but he's too crazy for me."

In the mid-seventies, Morrison stormed into the Warner Brothers offices on Christmas Eve with a set of demands for Joe Smith. When Morrison slammed down some papers on Smith's desk, breaking his Cross pen set, Smith got so upset he grabbed Van by the tie, yanked his head to the desk, and told the singer that he never wanted to see him again. Even in calmer times, things could get peculiar. When Smith was putting together his 1988 book *Off the Record: An Oral History of Popular Music*, Morrison agreed to an interview at a hotel, on the condition that he be addressed as "Mr. Johnson." Smith spotted him in the lobby wearing an upturned overcoat and tried to say hello, but Morrison didn't acknowledge Smith whatsoever until he reluctantly called him by his secret handle.

In the early eighties, Morrison and Warner Brothers parted ways. "I remember we almost came to blows because he kept insisting that I guarantee him a No. 1 single," explained label president Mo Ostin. Ex-wife Janet Planet agrees that "[Van] offends people regularly. Then as now, in ways too numerous to mention, he's his own worst enemy." But there's clearly something about his contrarian personality and short fuse that has led to artistic triumphs. "If he had not said no to Bert Berns, if he had continued to be forced into that Top 40 mold at which Bert was so proudly proficient," Planet says, "there would be no *Astral Weeks*."

VAN MORRISON PLAYED Boston's Wang Theatre in the spring of 2016. I went, hoping to catch some astral magic. My hopes faded as he marched through a set of lesser-known songs and blues covers, with a pair of fan favorites tacked to the end. Walking to the train station, I ran into Peter Wolf's friend, the one who'd advised me to bring pastries at the start of my *Astral Weeks* quest a year before. Wolf, he said, had been at the show, but split early. There would be no late-night cruise down Green Street during this visit. But something harkening back to 1968 did happen backstage that night: Bassist Tom Kielbania met with his old bandmate. They shared a brief, pleasant conversation.

"I have the recording of us at the Catacombs," Morrison said. "It's very good!" He told his assistant to make sure Kielbania got a copy. Wolf had intimated to me that his live bootleg was never digitized, but apparently it had been. Maybe he'd forgotten, or didn't want me to know.

Kielbania (who told me about their encounter much later) never received a copy; digitized or prebaked, the recording remained elusive. Then out of the blue, a year after the perfunctory concert, someone got in touch with me. There was a copy of the Catacombs gig that I could listen to. (The source said only a few people had heard it, passed along by someone who used to work for Morrison.) In the course of an afternoon, I went from wondering about the secret history of *Astral Weeks* to listening, jaw on floor, to a show in which Van Morrison became Van Morrison.

The recording from August 1968 clocks in at fifty-four minutes. The fidelity is astonishing: Kielbania's upright bass, John Payne's flute, and

Morrison's acoustic guitar all sound perfectly mixed, with Van's majestic twenty-two-year-old voice soaring over it all. The energy in the room is palpable, and the trio sounds as if it's been playing together for years. Every song has its revelations. They open with a new song, "Cyprus Avenue," not yet immortalized but magisterial and intimate right out of the box. Van fine-tunes the lyrics, while Kielbania's line is nearly identical to what Richard Davis would play on the album the following month—making it extremely likely that Kielbania *did* show the jazz musician some parts he had written back in Boston, despite Davis's insistence to the contrary. Elsewhere, we hear what John Payne might have played had he been the album's sole flutist; on the bootleg, Payne improvises parts for "Beside You" and "Madame George," two *Astral Weeks* songs that he wouldn't play on in New York. The crowd listens intently to each extended outro, waits a second after it's over before erupting into applause. Of the eight songs, three will make it onto *Astral Weeks*, four if you count "Train" (here identified as "Stop That Train"). The rest includes tunes from his Bang tenure and Them's "One Two Brown Eyes" for good measure. All of it comes alive underground, the loose arrangements erasing the clutter of the earlier recorded versions.

Kielbania and Payne haven't heard the music from the Catacombs since performing it fifty years ago, so I pay them each a visit. Payne marvels at how confident his playing is for someone who had heard the repertoire for the first time three nights earlier. During a few numbers, Morrison leaves wide-open spaces for him to solo, and on "T.B. Sheets," he sounds like a Coltrane fanatic crashing a hootenanny. For Kielbania, who didn't play a single note on *Astral Weeks*, this tape is precious proof of his work with Van Morrison. The version of "Brown Eyed Girl," at once pared down and richer, might be the real revelation—the missing link between Van's pop song past and what would unfold on *Astral Weeks*. As we listen to the Catacombs version, Kielbania grins. "This is the way the song should have always been!"

Kielbania takes in the sublime blueprint of "Madame George," noting that although only a few months elapsed between his first meeting with Van and the time the album was recorded, "this is how *Astral Weeks* started." Over the song's three chords, Morrison repeats a phrase that won't make it to the album: "in your own magic way."

In its own magic way, the bootleg brings me back to a time before I was born, plunges me fully into a dream of Boston that I'd immersed myself in through interviews and ephemera, fifty years after the fact. Every note feels familiar but fresh, so that in places the legend of the album—*Astral Weeks*— falls away. I'm Eric Kraft or Peter Wolf or Janet Planet, listening in a state of pure awe. The Catacombs are alive.

Then the music begins to warble, the telltale sign of a reel running out of tape. Before I realize I won't be hearing the rest of this transcendent version of "Madame George," the end comes violently, the music ripped away with a heartbreaking *zzzzzp*. I won't be hearing the end of this plotline. Back to reality.

IN MARCH 1978, Mel Lyman gave his first interviews to reporters since 1971—with a telepathic twist. "In came a young woman with long brown hair, held back from her face by a gold headband," the *Boston Herald American* reported. "Her blue dress was gossamer and a star was at her throat. She knelt on the carpet before a rainbow colored ouija board which rested on a white pedestal. The ouija board was to be my hotline to Mel Lyman, and the gossamer-gowned lady in blue was to be my interpreter." The sentences could have appeared nearly verbatim in the Boston spiritualist paper *Banner of Light* a century earlier. As the medium channeled Lyman into the room, Jessie Benton whispered a suggestion in the reporter's ear: "These answers you should probably write down." The medium opened her eyes and said, "Melvin is here." Why, the reporter asked, after spending so long promising to change the world and expanding his community, had Mel vanished? The planchette glided across the board: "I have found—that I can actually—have a greater—effect—on this planet from—an anonymous position."

Mel Lyman himself was nowhere to be found.

Since 1968, the Fort Hill Community had weathered a lot. In the wake of the *Avatar* obscenity trial, curiosity about the Fort Hill Community grew; word began to escape out of the Commonwealth and into distant underground newspapers and magazines like *Time* and *National Review*. "'Avatar is Mel' but is Boston hell?" the *Berkeley Barb* wondered. *Esquire* dispatched Diane Arbus to Roxbury; her photograph of Lyman, for a story entitled "God Is Back—He Says So Himself," shows an androgynous man with a piercing gaze: Mel as Egon Schiele portrait.

Lyman and Jim Kweskin led a group down to the '69 Newport Folk Festival, ready to unleash their "argue with the audience" routine. As Kweskin determined whether the crowd really deserved to hear Lyman perform, the guru waited in the wings for his cue. "The audience didn't go for this and started loudly demanding entertainment, especially some of the familiar Kweskin Jug Band songs," Michael Kindman recalled. "As the mood got worse and worse, into the breach unexpectedly came Joan Baez, no fan of Mel Lyman, suddenly assuming the role of peacemaker by singing an a capella version of 'Amazing Grace' to calm the audience down and give them some of what they wanted." It strangely mirrored the festival of four years prior, when Lyman had consoled listeners after Dylan's earsplitting set—electricity now replaced by confrontation. Kweskin and the others stormed off, climbed into their cars, and returned to Fort Hill. Later that night at Newport, Van Morrison performed a duo set that included "Madame George."

A month later, actress Sharon Tate and four others were murdered in director Roman Polanski's home in Los Angeles. The horrific crime was part of a series of gruesome murders that would turn out to be perpetrated by a different LSD-ingesting cult, this one led by a struggling songwriter named Charles Manson. Don West, the CBS employee who tried to turn the Lyman commune into *The Real World* television show, was with Family member George Peper when news of the killings broke. According to West, Peper said that his Fort Hill comrades considered Manson to be the Antichrist—which was proof that Lyman was indeed God. The stage was now set: God and the Devil were on Earth, and the grand battle between good and evil could commence.

But there was an element of recognition as well. Faith Gude's mother, novelist Kay Boyle, reported that photos of Manson began to appear on the walls of various houses on Fort Hill; Faith explained to her that the Mansons had made "a gesture against all the things we do not believe in." *The New York Times* quoted one FHC member as saying, "This cat might go out and kill people and Melvin does good, but it's the same spirit." Incredibly, Manson sent Mel Lyman a letter from prison, promising his allegiance and requesting that they break him free. The messiah of Roxbury later called the letter "sad." But one of Manson's followers claimed that there *was* a plan set in place involving landing a helicopter on the roof of the courthouse during the trial. ("They're well organized," she told Paul Krassner, editor of *The Realist*.)

As though putting Exodus 20:3 into action ("You shall have no other gods before me"), the Fort Hill Community kicked off a secret war against other communes led by gurulike figures in 1971. When the leader of the Kerista commune (whose decisions were arrived at daily via Ouija board) wrote Lyman telling him *he* was the messiah, a Fort Hill member showed up and threw his typewriter out a window. Next, the Family targeted Brotherhood of the Spirit, a western Massachusetts commune and rock 'n' roll band led by Michael Metelica, a twenty-one-year-old with a Confederate flag fetish. (Hunter S. Thompson refers to him as "What's His Name" in *Fear and Loathing in Las Vegas*.) "I didn't see any spirit in flesh there today," Mel's new wife Eve told *The New Yorker*. "I saw a bunch of dirty hippies having a love-in." Meanwhile, Faith Gude went to California to observe the inner workings of Victor Baranco's Lafayette Morehouse "sex cult." (Motto: "Fun is the Goal, Love is the Way.") George Peper trailed Gude with a message from Mel, delivered during one of Baranco's "Advanced Hexing" courses, to little effect. Attempts were even made to flip one of Manson's closest followers, Squeaky Fromme, who claimed she was beaten up when she refused to follow Lyman instead of Manson.

IN THE SPIRIT of the 1970 Manson story he cowrote for *Rolling Stone*, David Felton set out to cover what he thought might be its East Coast counterpart. The investigation would take him from Roxbury to Martha's Vineyard, culminating with his long-delayed in-person interview with Lyman at their house in the Hollywood Hills. By then, Lyman had replaced all of his rotting teeth. As the journalist soon realized, he had developed an alter ego named Richard Herbruck with a different personality; Lyman only became Herbruck when he wore dentures.* Upon meeting the frail, toothless man, Felton wondered, "Was this Mel Lyman or some terminal junkie they had bailed out of the deformity ward at County General?"

Since the L.A. contingent of the Fort Hill Community had been placed on a "night schedule," the interview took place at dawn after a long dinner comprising bean curd, mushrooms, noodles, and "stringy green stuff." Lyman recounted his life story. He blamed "those fucking bastards" at 23 Kenwood in Newton—an outpost of Leary and Alpert's International Federation for Internal Freedom—for giving acid to his former sweetheart, Judy Silver, which drove her straight to "the nuthouse." He showed a photo from his funny encounter on TV with Johnny Carson, and described how Family members sometimes spent entire evenings at the L.A. mansion

---

* Richard Herbruck is an actual person, whose name is still listed on the Fort Ave. Terrace mailbox. After arriving at the commune from Ohio in the late sixties, the real Herbruck was given an astrological name, and Lyman began borrowing his legal name to book airline flights and, for some reason, to produce Jim Kweskin's 1971 album *America* for Reprise. Herbruck resembled Lyman, apparently, as did several other FHC members. Lyman used these look-alikes to keep visitors guessing whether they'd met the real man or not.

talking in "different accents." He remarked how well John Kostick's star sculptures were selling lately. "Boston is sort of like a boot camp," he said, explaining how each outpost of his community served an overarching goal. "This is a whole new culture. We're really starting a new country."

Felton finally asked, point-blank: "Are you God?"

No, Lyman answered. He was using the concept as a metaphor. "But I can tell you I know God better than anybody in the world." Felton pushed him for more of an explanation. "All I can tell you is I'm His best instrument on earth." Lyman slipped into the house's swimming pool and remained there as Felton let himself out. Soon, the frail harmonica player floating in the water would be on the cover of *Rolling Stone*. Outside of Ouija boards, he'd never talk to another journalist again.

"What this Mel Lyman guy needs is a good punch in the mouth," someone wrote in. A more eloquent reader predicted that fascist communities like Fort Hill would spread "as long as people continue searching their fears, on acid or straight, and no one else is there to talk them straight and direct and sympathetically about it." The Fort Hill Community felt betrayed by the piece. In the eighties, Felton would occasionally hear from a coworker about running into a Lyman Family member somewhere in New York. "Felton's the devil!" the person would rail. "He *ruined* the family."

As early as 1972, it was rumored that Lyman was rarely—or never—seen by his followers. One writer dubbed him the "Howard Hughes of the Underground." In 1975, the *Globe* tracked down some significant Boston personalities of the late sixties. None could say what happened to the guru of Fort Hill. The question wouldn't go away. "Is Mel Lyman still around?" director John Waters quipped at a Boston appearance in 2004. "I love those sorts of notorious characters." Nobody knew.

THE REASON BEHIND the '78 Ouija board interviews wouldn't make a lick of sense until 1985, when *Los Angeles Times* reporter David Cay Johnston wrote, "His Family says that he died in April 1978, after a lingering illness. He would have been 39." The community's first collective output since *1969*—the short-lived *U & I Magazine*—had coaxed them out of hiding, and their news of Lyman's death seven years earlier was disquieting. If this information was to be believed, then surely his final interviews were those conducted via Ouija board the month before his purported passing. But if he was alive in March 1978, why not just do those interviews in person? Perhaps he was too ill to be physically present. When a reporter asked about the strange interview format, the Family said that it was easier this way, as their leader now orbited the planet in a spaceship. Even stranger, "Members of the community hint at an involvement with the movie *Close Encounters of the Third Kind*," Steven Spielberg's 1977 hit.

The Family let Johnston know that Mel had died by showing him their "holy records," the Pulitzer Prize–winning journalist says, referring to a private manuscript written by Lyman's widow, Eve. (Johnston recently made headlines by appearing on *The Rachel Maddow Show* with one of President Trump's tax records.) They didn't reveal Mel's final resting place, but Johnston suspects either the Boston compound or the Kansas farm. The Family refused to discuss the absence of a death certificate or funeral. Such secrecy even extended to some of their own Family members. "They deny rumors that he fled the Family and lives in Europe," Johnston wrote in 1985.

Since Felton's article, the Lyman Family had grown deeply insular— and financially successful. Their contracting business, Fort Hill Construc- tion, was thriving, catering to Hollywood's A-list, with customers like Spielberg and Dustin Hoffman. Jim Kweskin reminisces about closing a construction deal with music-industry mogul David Geffen, who didn't let on that he had once worked for Kweskin in another life until after the papers were signed. "Do you remember when you were managed by Albert Gross- man?" Geffen asked. "I was the kid over in the corner on the telephone, booking your gigs." *M*A*S*H* cocreator Larry Gelbart raved about the group's artistry, but worried about their place in the modern world. "Once we were talking about what a great man Abraham Lincoln was when one of them looked up at the sky and said, 'Did you see that fleet of spaceships go by?'"

JESSIE BENTON NOW spends winters in Mexico and summers in Martha's Vineyard, where she can easily make the occasional visit to Fort Hill. Sharp and self-aware at seventy-eight, she's a natural storyteller. (She still refers to her father, Thomas Hart Benton, as "Daddy.") There's little hint here of the woman who brooded over Ouija boards or told a reporter that her husband *did* manipulate his Family, but not "for evil." In fact, everyone I speak to from the FHC today is patient and thoughtful—folks you'd assume were part of mainstream society. Did they grow out of their odd beliefs and eccentric behaviors? Was it all just a show they grew tired of putting on? Or maybe this is another show.

The only thing curious about my call with Benton is the unidentified man in the room with her, who sometimes feeds her answers to my questions or provides her with additional details. I ask Benton what parts of the *Rolling Stone* article weren't true, and she says she simply objected to the general portrayal of the Family as "creepy." But some of those scenes, quotes, and incidents are without a doubt creepy, and dozens of other reporters and visitors had also documented similar things emanating from Fort Hill. (And isn't the guy offstage, unseen but heard, also a bit creepy?) She talks about a vital energy that was once present in the world: "There was a feeling in the air, you felt you were a part of something. *That* has disappeared. That does not exist anymore."

Why were you secretive about Mel's death? I ask.

"We were?" She considers for a long time, then finally says, "Perhaps it was just too painful."

. . .

ANIMETRICS, THE COMPANY that makes the algorithms for facial recognition software, analyzes the photograph I found of a man who looks like an older Mel Lyman. Their results are inconclusive. The report tells me that "marionette and nasolabial creases appear similar" and "appearance of long neck and Adam's apple are consistent," but in the end, making the call utilizing just one photograph is impossible. Maybe it's not Mel after all. With all the pseudonyms and look-alikes that litter the Lyman story, I wonder if I've been chasing a false lead this entire time.

I pull real estate filings from the Massachusetts Registry of Deeds related to Fort Ave. Terrace and United Illuminating, Inc., from around the time of Lyman's purported death, and find something startling. On a document dated September 1978, five months after the date of death given to the *Los Angeles Times*, there's a notarized signature provided by one Melvin Lyman. It would have been difficult, but not impossible, to hoodwink a notary and have someone else stand in for Lyman during a signing of a legal document. Again, Mel's "clones" come to mind here. But no matter the explanation, it's an unusual find: a supposedly dead man signing documents months after his reported passing.

There is no death certificate for Mel Lyman. Even close Family member Wayne Hansen—his is one of seven signatures on the realty trust documents—was kept in the dark. "I was told that Melvin died and I believe that," he told the *Los Angeles Times* in 1985. "I have to take on faith that he died." Death certificates are required by law for myriad reasons, but I don't believe the failure to register his passing was done for the usual ulterior motives, such as social security fraud. Rather, it was an act of myth building, a way of keeping him alive. After all, what kind of bible lets you know precisely how God dies? Everyone I spoke to, whether they loved or hated Mel, had a theory about what happened to the musician turned guru.

Lyman's non-ending recasts him as a kind of ghost floating through Boston's counterculture history, impossible to pin down.

But what if this story *had* a definitive ending? I kept searching.

Michael Kindman—the Fort Hill Community member who never entered the inner circle, who felt manipulated by skewed astrology charts, and who finally left the group in 1973—spent much of his post-FHC life trying to break the grip that Lyman had on him. He reconstructed Lyman's astrology chart with an expert, revealing that Mel was not so much an "avatar and cultural leader," but more of a "needy person with a very low sense of self-worth." Kindman's exchange of letters with Lyman in 1977, published later in Kindman's memoir, are some of Mel's last known writings. "Why didn't you use your influence in the community to clear away the bullshit that separated us from each other?" Kindman asked him. Lyman's response, mailed from Martha's Vineyard, begins, "My son, your criticism was well taken," before confessing, "I may have been labeled as some kind of guru or spiritual teacher, in my own secret recesses I never felt this way . . . I only issued orders upon request."

Kindman's rebuttal is incandescent with righteous anger; it's too bad he never mailed it.

> Let's begin by getting something straight; I'm not your son, and never have been. . . . You're about as innocent of wrongdoing as Richard Nixon was, and about as naïve. Maybe take a couple of your favorite wives and kids and helpers and go back to the woods and start over. Remember how you used to threaten to do just that, every year or so? We ingrates just weren't worthy of your presence, and it was too hard to create with all these panderers around, and so forth? You never managed to make the break then; evidently you were as addicted to being followed as we were to following. I'm not sure where you are now in relation to all that, but

in your letter you sure sound stuck. And, man, you sure could make music before.

Kindman learned of Lyman's death the way most people did: a 1985 newspaper piece on the Fort Hill Community. "I imagined Mel killing himself, or becoming depressed and dying of some mysterious disease. Who could know?" he writes. Studying one of the article's accompanying photos, Kindman couldn't be sure that one of the men pictured was actually *not* Mel Lyman. "I believed they were capable of telling the media anything, regardless of the truth."

In 1991, shortly after completing his memoir, Michael Kindman died of AIDS. Poignantly, the final words in his story quote the man he used to follow: "Getting to write about all of it has been a tremendously healing, and confrontational, experience for me," Kindman reflects. "After all, as Mel Lyman used to say, 'Recapitulation is the only real learning.'"

MELVIN JAMES LYMAN was born in Eureka, California, on March 24, 1938, to James and Jessie Mae Lyman, arriving while James was out on the road giving guitar and violin lessons. "I'm afraid Mel was not very pretty when he was born," his father later said of the jaundiced infant. "But his mother was very proud of him." James served in the navy in 1941 and divorced Jessie Mae eight years later; he would subsequently have little interaction with his son. Little Mel loved cats and sitting by himself, daydreaming. At primary school, he provided the drumroll as they raised the flag and was wary of bullies.

In 1955, at age seventeen, Mel studied computer programming at a night school in San Francisco, which some would later cite as evidence that his rambling hillbilly aesthetic was fraudulent. ("I shot dope and ran IBM machines," he wrote in his journal, the sole mention of his computer skills.)

Despite marriage to a woman named Sophie and multiple children, Lyman took off on cross-country rambles, visiting the musicians he worshipped.* One such hero was Woody Guthrie, at the time living at Brooklyn State Hospital in the middle of a long, cruel decline from Huntington's disease. (Bob Dylan was another visiting acolyte.) "I can't ever forget the time he struggled up from his chair and said he was going to hop a freight train and go to the west coast again," Lyman wrote in 1961, "and I knew he'd never seen the west coast . . . I still dream over and over that Woody is well again and raising hell and it's just too damn sad."

By the time Lyman arrived in Asheville, North Carolina, in the early sixties to commune with banjo player Obray Ramsey, his main source of income was selling marijuana. "I have to write my own bible in order to know how to live," he decided. In 1963, several changes appear in his journals: He starts hanging out in New York City and experimenting with psychedelic drugs. "Hallooneysations, hassooleenations," runs one entry. Immersing himself in the New York art scene that Jonas Mekas and Andy Warhol belonged to, Lyman was pulled away from that world by Judy Silver. Deeply in love, he followed her back to Brandeis University, in Waltham, Massachusetts. Around this time, he and Judy both seemed habitually ill. Lyman chalked up his own problems to "infectious hepatitis from shooting heroin with a dirty needle."

"We may study ESP if we live," he wrote. "We probably won't live."

They did. Lyman hit her ("Last night I struck my love and my insides came out"), took acid with her at Richard Alpert's Newton home, and dedicated his second book, *Mirror at the End of the Road*, "To Judy, who made me live with a broken heart." "I don't think Mel ever got over that," says Charles Giuliano, a good friend of the couple at the time, calling it "*the* devastating

---

* Sophie would eventually move to her husband's new community. In 2006, their son, Obray, mentioned on a message board that she had been married to Jim Kweskin for twenty years. In 1985, Sophie told the *Boston Herald* that Mel "never just 'took off.' He made sure we were taken care of, he wrote and called, and when he could, he sent money. We weren't abandoned."

setback of his life." After a police bust during a trip to Florida to check on his marijuana crop, Lyman narrowly escaped jail time by promising to find a job.

The job, of course, was playing with the Jim Kweskin Jug Band. Here, Lyman's life becomes unmistakably rooted in Massachusetts; you can tell from the references that begin to appear in his journals. "I walked into Dunkin Donuts . . . and the waitress talked to me about poetry." (Dunkin' Donuts!) There in Lyman's diary from 1963 is the first inkling of things to come: "I am indeed a supreme being and deserve to be in the company of gods like myself."* *Broadside of Boston* noted his arrival in September 1963, welcoming him as a devoted follower of Guthrie. By then, Lyman was living in Kweskin's attic in Cambridge, working steadily with the band, picking up solo gigs all over Boston, and trying to shake that lovelorn feeling. He noted in a 1965 journal entry that loneliness was his "sole motivation."

It wouldn't be long before Mel Lyman took the darkened Newport stage alone, harmonica in hand. Later, in *Sing Out* magazine, Irwin Silber called Lyman's Dylan-chasing performance "the most optimistic note of the evening."

Which brings the story to where it began—a mournful "Rock of Ages" performed on harmonica, a "tiny hole for all that spirit to go through, that little tiny reed." And now it can end—with mourning for Mel.

MEL LYMAN WORKED hard to become a public figure. He was known for his music, and notorious for his leadership of the Fort Hill Community. It's baffling that the 1985 announcement of his 1978 death sparked no apparent investigation into what happened. Faking your own death—in the eyes of either the public, government, or your family—is extraordinarily difficult, requiring a permanently private life with no contact with the outside world.

---

* In another journal entry, from 1966, he curiously writes, "I'm soon lost in a sea of color and all that astral jazz."

There is no doubt that Lyman was in poor health for most of the seventies. "The dozens of framed photographs of Lyman that hang in the Family's houses depict a man growing progressively ill," David Cay Johnston reported in 1985. "His private writings . . . speak intimately of approaching death." It seems likely that, on some level, his family was telling the truth that he died, even if the dates they provided seemed mysteriously off.

I follow several false leads, including a Cambridge folksinger who tells me he attended Lyman's funeral just fifteen years ago, in the early aughts. The bombshell is defused before the end of the call, as the conversation suggests he's experiencing some form of dementia. Then, one day, someone with a connection to the community—a reliable source—agrees to talk.

Why the secrecy surrounding Mel's death?

"Because it's illegal, what happened."

What happened?

"He committed suicide."

In California, where the act took place, suicide is not illegal. But advising or assisting a suicide is. It's unclear if the Family assisted in any way, but Lyman informed Fort Hill's inner circle that it was going to happen. After fighting a long illness, Mel had decided to stop battling his own body. "It was a weird way to do it, but it was *his* way," the person says. The rampant rumors were entirely false; Lyman did not take on a new identity and head to Europe. According to the source, he purposefully overdosed on drugs in Los Angeles, California, sometime in 1978. What was done with his remains is unclear. His final writings, shown to David Cay Johnston in 1985, can be taken at face value:

> "I know I'm done and I'll stop keeping that body alive. . . . It really is a lot of dead weight and I don't feel it's got much more use, do you know what I'm saying, I was Emerson, I was Lincoln, I was Woody Guthrie and many more but only for short periods of time and I used those instruments because they were ready for me

and I used Mel Lyman in the same way and I am nobody, I just am. Don't be sad, I'll be Mel Lyman as long as I can and in fact I may bring him back with a bang and light him up like a neon bulb and if I don't it's because it wasn't and if I do we will have a real Melvin Christ on our hands. . . ."

Because only certain information about what happened was distributed to various tiers of the Family's members and children, and due to the passing of a man who had spiritually united them—or controlled them—for over a decade, it was a deeply traumatic event for the Fort Hill Community. Several members simply could not accept that he was gone.

"That's when Jessie took over," one tells me.

I think back to Jessie Benton's childhood daydream, the one where she's secretly Persephone, the beautiful queen of the underworld. The last time Ray Riepen saw Benton, in a Kansas City bar, over a decade ago, their conversation was abruptly curtailed by several men behaving unusually territorially; "thugs," he describes them. Riepen then wonders aloud about how much of Benton's leadership style might have been gleaned from her late husband.

THE FORT HILL COMMUNITY thrived on conflict. There was nothing holier than those moments when members "got real," confronting one another with difficult truths. Sometimes this resulted in fistfights on the stage of Club 47, or the destruction of a magic theater they had spent years building, or holding someone in solitary confinement inside the Vault. "Their unspoken law is that you must struggle with the other person," a psychologist friend of the community once said. Among ex-members, this is the reason most often cited for leaving. "Their lifestyle forces them to constantly examine and reveal themselves, and it is not easy to live when you are constantly personally exposed," Wayne Hansen explained after his departure.

It all sounds unimaginably intense and exhausting. Yet they remain, for

the most part, together. There are few examples of communal living societies founded in the sixties that still exist to this day, and certainly none that
were so notorious during their heyday. In their own strange way, the Fort
Hill Community *are* survivors. As Jim Kweskin tells me, "We were and still
are a beautiful family."

From the outside, though, it seems that what they have survived is
themselves.

In 1975, for reasons unknown, the Fort Hill Community reset their calendar year to oo. Up on Fort Ave. Terrace today, in the year 43, the imposing
wall, the houses in the shadow of the tower, the archive of *Avatar*s in the basement, and the Family inside all remain, still, unlikely as it may be, together.

ON CHRISTMAS EVE 1968, three astronauts inside Apollo 8 became the
first human beings to orbit the moon, glimpse its mysterious dark side with
their own eyes, and view Earth as a whole planet. Right before snapping the
famous photograph that would become known as "Earthrise," backup Command Module pilot William Anders exclaimed, "Oh my God! Look at that
picture over there! There's the Earth coming up. Wow, is that pretty." NASA
informed the crew that its television broadcast on December 24 would gar-
ner "the largest audience that had ever listened to a human voice." They received no guidance on what their message should contain, so the astronauts
chose a passage from the book of Genesis. "In the beginning God created
the heavens and the earth," William Anders read. "And God said, Let there
be light: and there was light." On Christmas Day, upon successfully exiting
their lunar orbit, Command Module pilot Jim Lovell told mission control,
"Please be informed there is a Santa Claus." The spacecraft reentered the
Earth's atmosphere on December 27, safely landing in the Pacific Ocean.

The mission had lasted six days, three hours, and forty-eight minutes.
Call it an astral week.

ACKNOWLEDGMENTS

Marissa Nadler—my wife—who put on *Astral Weeks* at the end of our first date and, later, told me I should get a nice writing desk. She deserves all the love that loves to love coming her way.

Thank you to Carly Carioli, who listened to my pitch for a story about *Astral Weeks*'s Boston connections at a party on Beacon Street, greenlighting the piece for *Boston Magazine* shortly thereafter. Thank you to S.I. Rosenbaum, who edited the original story and informed me that it was merely an update of *Raiders of the Lost Ark*. Thank you to David Bieber and the David Bieber Archives for the resources, the guidance, and the astute suggestion that I bring pastries for one interview in particular.

Thank you to Ed Park, my editor at Penguin Press, who reached out after reading the original article with an idea for how it could expand into a full-length book. Without his curiosity, patience, expertise, and enthusiasm, this book could not exist.

My sincere gratitude to PJ Mark, whose assistance throughout was invaluable.

Thank you to everyone at Penguin Press, especially Annie Badman, Karen Mayer, Emily Cunningham, Colleen Boyle, Matt Boyd, Caitlin O'Shaughnessy, Ben Denzer, Scott Moyers, and Ann Godoff.

Thank you to my family for their lifetime of support: Mark and Ramona Walsh, my parents; Gig, Stacy, and Willy Walsh, my siblings. Thank you to Rich, Pam, and Stuart Nadler and Shamis Beckley for your persistent encouragement.

Thank you to my oldest friends, who have always encouraged my creative endeavors and helped in countless personal ways during this entire process: Shannon Kelly Rogers, Brendan Bragg, Andrew Pierce, Jeffrey Prohaska, Julia Papps, John Benda, and Anthony Puopolo.

My dear friend and first reader, Neal Block, whose truthful feedback has kept me creatively honest since 1999.

Hallelujah The Hills, my American rock band, who patiently helped me balance priorities during this process and continually reminded me why stories about the creation of music are so worthwhile: Ryan Connelly, Joseph Marrett, Brian Rutlege, and Nicholas Giadone Ward. Thank you to the band's biographer, M. Jonathan Lee, for traveling across the Atlantic Ocean with a hall of mirrors in tow just as the process of writing this book began.

Thank you to Joyce Linehan at the mayor of Boston's office for the access and connections made possible during research.

Thank you to all my colleagues at ArtsEmerson, whose patience and support was so touching and meaningful. A big shout-out to my student employees, who helped me with research and interview transcriptions, especially Alicia Bettano. Also thank you to Kelly Downes, Katelyn Guerin, Camila Cornejo, and Francine Mroczek.

Thanks to Jesse Jarnow and Sean Maloney for all of the highly specific research assistance and brainstorming.

Thank you:

The Allan MacDougall Popular Culture Archive at UMass, Boston, Selene Angier, Jami Attenberg, Alex Beam, Peter Bebergal, Ami Bennitt, David Berman, Gary Burns, Elizabeth Butters, Jacqueline Castel, William Corbett, Marta Crilly at the City of Boston Archives, John Darnielle, Tyler Derryberry, Andre Diehl, Dave Drago, Christen Dute, Matt Dwyer, Perry Eaton, Craig Finn, Ryan Foley, Josh Frank, Simon Gee, Fred Goodman, The Howard Gotlieb Archival Research Center, Althea Greenan, Joe

Hagan, Courtney Brooke Hall, Peter Higgins and everyone at WGBH, Mitch Horowitz, Rob Johanson, Gary Lambert, Jon Langmead, Ivan Lipton, Paul Lovell and his website punkblowfish.com, Colleen Matthews, Jonathan Miller, Rob Orchard, Matt Parish, Aaron Perrino, James Reed, Rachel Rubin, Leeore Schnairsohn, Christopher Schwaber, Evan Sicuranza, Kendall Smith, Paul Solman, Patrick Stickles, Happy Traum, Steve Trussel and his website http://www.trussel.com/f_mel.htm, Richie Unterberger, Pamela Vadakan, Chris Vogel, Tyler Wilcox.

INTERVIEWS

Willie "Loco" Alexander, Bruce Arnold, Paul Arnoldi, Brooks Arthur, David Atwood, Fred Barzyk, Joseph W. Bebo, June Benson, Jessie Benton, Jay Berliner, David Bieber, Mitch Blake, Scott Bradner, Paul Brinkley-Rogers, Karyl Lee Britt, Ken Brown, Alison Burke, Steve Cataldo, Dick Cluster, Lawrence Cohn, William Corbett, Richard Davis, Sally Dennison, Carmine "Wassel" DeNoia, Michael Dobo, Walter Romanus Donati, Dennis Dreher, Boyd Estus, David Felton, John Flaxman, Barney Frank, Kyle Garrahan, Charles Giuliano, Michael Goldman, Richard Goldstein, Russell H. Greenan, Fred Griffeth, Eric Gulliksen, Wayne Hansen, Aram Heller, Priscilla Hendrick, Jim Horn, Dick Iacovello, David Jenks, Myles David Jewell, Norman Jewison, David Cay Johnston, Peter Kaye, Brian Kelly, Susan Kelly, Tim Kelly, Elayne Kessler, Tom Kielbania, David Kinsman, Sydney D. Kirkpatrick, Dr. Stanley Klein, Jesse Kornbluth, Eric Kraft, Wayne Kramer, Jim Kweskin, Jef Labes, Jon Landau, Don Law, Erik Lindgren, David Linksy, Ivan Lipton, Greil Marcus, Jonas Mekas, Lewis Merenstein, Ralph Metzner, Paul Mills, Phil Milstein, Ed Morneau, Victor "Moulty" Moulton, Ray Mungo, Ted Myers, Holly Nadler, Buell Neidlinger, Steve Nelson, Rob Norris, Bob Olive, David Palmer, Ray Paret, John Payne, George Peper, Stephen G. Philp, John Platania, Betsy Polatin, Verandah Porche, Walter Powers, Paula Press, Arnie Reisman,

Jonathan Richman, Ray Riepen, Joe Rogers, Fred Roos, Robert Rosenblatt, Peter Rowan, Dick Russell, Harry Sandler, Joel Selvin, John Sheldon, Rick Shlosser, David Silver, Harvey Silverglate, Peter Simon, Joe Smith, Warren Smith Jr., Robert Somma, John Sposato, Dick Summer, Barry Tashian, Karen Thorne, Collin Tilton, Alan Trustman, Chuck Turner, Beverly Walker, Peter Walker, Jackie Washington, Dr. Andrew Weil, Dr. Gunther Weil, Dick Weisberg, Kathy West, Dave Wilson, Peter Wolf, Steve Woolard, Herbert Yakus, Shelly Yakus, Bob Zachary, Karen Lee Ziner.

NOTES

PROLOGUE: IN THE BEGINNING

All quotes from author interviews with John Sheldon, Tom Kielbania, Carmine De-Noia, Janet Planet, John Payne, Eric Kraft, and Joe Smith except as follows:

1 **"If I had an axe"**: *No Direction Home.*

1 **"I wanted to save the world"**: Felton, "The Lyman Family's Holy Siege of America."

2 **"the most beautiful music"**: Levey, "Friendly Fifty on Fort Hill—Better Way for People?"

3 **"before I knew what poetry was"**: Cott, "Van Morrison: The Poet."

3 **"That's art, man"**: Heylin, *Can You Feel the Silence?*, 156.

3 **"I looked at him"**: Ibid., 127.

4 **"Pall Malls"**: Selvin, *Here Comes the Night*, 250.

4 **"rock and roll version"**: Ibid., 343.

4 **"I showed up for the session"**: Smith, *Off the Record*, 271.

4 **"He was just torn apart"**: Heylin, *Can You Feel the Silence?*, 153.

7 **"Boston: a famous place"**: Powell, "Pixies: Catalog Album Review."

8 **"That year itself"**: French, *The Women's Room*, 5.

1: AGAINST ELECTRICITY

All quotes from author interviews with John Sheldon, Tom Kielbania, Carmine De-Noia, Janet Planet, John Payne, Eric Kraft, and Joe Smith except as follows:

11 **"my whole being"**: Shteamer, "In Full: Lewis Merenstein, Producer of *Astral Weeks.*"

12 **"the quality of a beacon"**: Bangs, "Astral Weeks," 20.

12 **"just channeled. They just came through"**: Heylin, *Can You Feel the Silence?*, 163.

13 **"Bert loved and identified"**: Ibid., 153.

13 **"So here's this disc jockey"**: Tosches, *Vanity Fair*.

17 **"winces and strains"**: Kraft, *Boston After Dark*.

20 **"We were finally really LIVING"**: Mills, *Hymns to the Silence: Inside the Words and Music of Van Morrison*, 45.

21 **"Too samey . . . It's not about me"**: Gleason, NPR.

2: GOD'S UNDERGROUND NEWSPAPER

All quotes from author interviews with Jim Kweskin, David Felton, Harvey Silverglate, Charles Giuliano, and Dick Russell except as follows:

27 **"It's not like we were Elvis"**: Reed, "The Jim Kweskin Jug Band Celebrates Its 50th Anniversary."

29 **"Sometimes you have to create"**: Felton, "The Lyman Family's Holy Siege of America."

30 **"He worshipped Judy"**: Ibid.

31 **bringing "hate" to everything**: Earle, *Broadside of Boston*.

31 **"Every year, they build on the ruins"**: Ibid.

33 **"The Manson Family preached peace and love"**: Felton, "The Lyman Family's Holy Siege of America."

34 **"He does manipulate us"**: Ibid.

34 **"The only rules"**: Ibid.

35 **"Once the basic requirements"**: Ibid.

36 **"Why don't you just try"**: Lyman, *Avatar* #13, November 12, 1967.

37 **"The great unwashed"**: Reed, *Harvard Crimson*.

38 **"The editors were warned"**: Uncredited, "Incident in Harvard Square."

39 **"I'll rent a goddamn airplane"**: Lyman, *Avatar* #13, November 12, 1967.

39 **"I was a typical Boston College grad"**: Barton, *The Heights*.

40 **"You're falling back on a technicality"**: Reed, "Judge Convicts Two in Avatar Trial: 'What Justifies Words Like These?'"

42 **"Things have never been better for *Avatar*"**: Lyman, *Avatar* #14, November 24, 1967.

46 **"enemy of modernism"**: Nicholson, *Apollo Magazine*.

48 **"promise him" a #1 single**: Hilburn and Philips, "Quotations from Chairman Mo."

49 **"even in the ephemeral state"**: Uncredited, "Cult Leader's Early Years Were Spent on the Move."

3: THE SILVER AGE OF TELEVISION

All quotes from author interviews with David Silver, Fred Barzyk, Karen Thorne, Peter Simon, and David Atwood except as follows:

52 **"I was only able to view the half"**: Lyman, *Avatar* #23, April 12, 1968.

54 **"It makes me angry"**: Silver, *New England Scene.*

57 **"Would you call yourself a director?"**: *WHMS?* Episode: "Underground Films."

58 **"By the end"**: Mcdonald, "The Happening in Studio A."

59 **"Hey kids, your eyes see"**: *WHMS?* Episode: "McLuhan's Children."

61 **"Would you like an *Avatar?*"**: *WHMS?* Episode: "Mel Lyman and the Avatar."

63 **"We are a big funny family"**: Lyman, *Avatar* #17, January 19, February 1, 1968.

64 **"When you've said you're God"**: Silver, "Transcript of an Interview Between Mel Lyman and Dave Silver."

67 **"Good evening . . . The reason you saw"**: *WHMS?* Episode: "Magazine Show."

69 *"What's Happening, Mr. Silver?* **has been seen at this time"**: *WHMS?* Episode: "Reaction to Magazine Show."

71 **"Channel 2 closed in"**: Ascheim, *Avatar* #19, February 16, February 29, 1968.

72 **"masterpiece of camp"**: Mcdonald, "A Cheer for Channel Two."

4: PAUL REVERE IS SHAMED

All quotes from author interviews with Bruce Arnold, Harry Sandler, Dick Weisberg, Robert Rosenblatt, David Jenks, Ray Paret, Karyl Lee Britt, Ted Myers, Kyle Garrahan, Fred Griffeth, Peter Rowan, and Jon Landau except as follows:

76 **"They did so much acid"**: Gerlach, "Joe Smith Interview."

77 **"Liverpool of America"**: Gleason, *San Francisco Chronicle.*

79 **"I started looking at myself"**: Breznikar, "Ultimate Spinach Interview with Ian Bruce-Douglas."

83 **"a fine album . . . the magic that separates"**: Uncredited, *Broadside of Boston.*

83 **"He never was interested"**: Burns, "An Interview with Ian Bruce Douglas."

83 **"The scene is right from San Francisco"**: *Newsweek*, "The Bosstown Sound."

84 **"the word is out"**: Goldstein, "The New Boston Sound and the Rock Scholars."

87 **"G-rated psychedelic bubblegum"**: Burns, "An Interview with Ian Bruce Douglas."

89 **"The country is now looking toward the East Coast"**: Faltz, "Boston . . . The Next San Francisco?"

90 **"the first magazine to take rock and roll seriously"**: Vitellomarch, "Father of Rock Criticism Is Dead at 64."

90 **"I was overcome with the vibrations"**: Landau, *It's Too Late to Stop Now: A Rock and Roll Journal*, 16.

90 **"San Francisco shit corrupted the purity"**: Landau, "Growing Young with Rock and Roll."

91 **"The very real problem that Boston faces"**: Landau, "The Sound of Boston: 'Kerplop.'"

92 **"We would break up every two or three months"**: Myers, *Making It: Music, Sex & Drugs in the Golden Age of Rock*.

93 **"Remember the Boston Sound?"**: Sheehan, "Chevy Chase Is Fletching, Kvetching."

93 **"Chevy's had a Nehru collar"**: Myers, *Making It: Music, Sex & Drugs in the Golden Age of Rock*.

93 **"They wore faggy little suits"**: Simels, Unpublished Chevy Chase Profile for *Rolling Stone*.

94 **"You're not Orpheus!"**: Sheehan, "Chevy Chase Is Fletching, Kvetching."

94–95 **"MGM sells each Ultimate Spinach album"**: Penn, "Selling a New Sound."

95 **"Ian [Bruce-Douglas] has a conception in his mind"**: Ibid.

95 **"These articles and others were enough to overboil"**: Lorber, "Something Called the 'Boston Sound'—by Its Creator."

95 **"Just look at Boston"**: Emerson, "Boston Sound: Eden's Children."

96 **"Spinach must now abandon its eclecticism"**: Murray, *Broadside of Boston*.

96 **"I fired myself"**: Burns, "An Interview with Ian Bruce Douglas."

96 **"But, in their infinite wisdom"**: Myers, *Making It: Music, Sex & Drugs in the Golden Age of Rock*.

97 **"Lisa loved Melvin"**: Felton, "The Lyman Family's Holy Siege of America."

100 **"abuse the people in your organization"**: Somma, "The Boston Sound Revisited."

102 **"hip kind of soul music"**: Landau, "The Sound of Boston: 'Kerplop.'"

102 **"ought to do a lot to wipe out"**: J.K., "Bagatelle Review."

5: THE WHITE LIGHT UNDERGROUND

All quotes from author interviews with Jonathan Richman, Rob Norris, Ray Riepen, Steve Nelson, Jessie Benton, George Peper, Peter Wolf, Dennis Dreher, Betsy Polatin, Fred Griffeth, Scott Bradner, Jim Horn, Mitch Blake, Don Law, Jonas Mekas, Walter Powers, Willie "Loco" Alexander, Peter Simon, and Robert Somma, except as follows:

105 **"My other big record"**: Bangs, "Astral Weeks."

105 **"It is irrelevant that the Velvet Underground"**: McGuire, "The Boston Sound/The Velvet Underground & Mel Lyman."

106 **"This is our favorite place to play"**: Norris, "I Was a Velveteen"

106 **"I stayed in love with Marlon Brando"**: *Ken Burns' America: Thomas Hart Benton*.

107 **"This was our world"**: Theroux, "The Story Behind Thomas Hart Benton's Incredible Masterwork."

107 **"We engaged Jessie to sit"**: Ginzberg, *Children and Other Strangers*, 85.

107 **"She was a natural aristocrat"**: Coyote, *Sleeping Where I Fall: A Chronicle*, 3.

108 **"Riepen would say 'hello'"**: Cobb, "Ray Riepen Rides Off into the Sunset to a New Future."

109 **"20 or more adults"**: Enzer, "In Boston, It's a Tea Party."

113 **"The wedding of the Cinemateque"**: Ibid.

115 **"We'd been doing 'Gloria' for some time"**: Kent, "The J. Geils Band: Hard Drivin' Sweet Soundin' Rock and Roll."

116 **"Nobody minds you going zonked"**: Rotman, "Gripe Time, People."

117 **"When I was sixteen . . . I heard the music of the Velvet Underground"**: Richman, Radio Valencia.

117 **"Excuse me, are you Lou Reed?"**: Ibid.

119 **"You are the star"**: Unterberger, *White Light/White Heat: The Velvet Underground Day by Day*, 158.

120 **"In the 20th century, in a technological age"**: Bangs, *Main Lines, Blood Feasts, and Bad Taste: A Lester Bangs Reader*, 196.

121 **"NOW IS THE TIME FOR DISTORTIONS TO BURN"**: McGuire, "The Boston Sound/The Velvet Underground & Mel Lyman."

122 **"Jonathan Richman is nothing"**: Laughner, "The Modern Lovers."

124 **"You will relax your physical body"**: Bailey, *A Treatise on White Magic*.

124 **"When I was in L.A. I saw a reverend"**: "Interview with Lou Reed," KVAN.

124 **"One of my big mistakes"**: Cohen, "Funny How Love Is."

125 **"Jonathan was a big fan of Van Morrison's"**: Brooks, "Jonathan Richman: In Love with the Modern World."

125 **"I've read *Glamour* four or five times"**: Heylin, *Can You Feel the Silence?*, 370.

126 **"a determined study of childhood visions"**: Ibid., 352.

126 **"Every now and then these experiences"**: Ibid., 6.

126 **"I had some amazing projections"**: Ibid., 7.

126 **"What do you think about the blood of Jesus?"**: Ibid., 353.

126 **"I said, 'Lou, all this stuff is going on'"**: MTV News Staff, "Van Morrison Guided by Voices?"

127 **"I'd never seen Andy angry"**: Fricke, "Lou Reed: The *Rolling Stone* Interview."

130 **"I don't think it was so much"**: Brooks, "Jonathan Richman: In Love with the Modern World."

130 **"The band has to learn volume"**: Cohen, "Funny How Love Is."

131 **"play a rolled-up newspaper"**: Ibid.

131 **"headache-making and ear splitting"**: McKinnon, "Boom, Boom, Boom Bores."

131 **"automatons with a fairly lackluster attack"**: DeTurk, *Boston After Dark*.

131 **"An honest-to-goodness chick"**: Grant, "Talking Rock."

131 **"A regular 9-to-5 job was too confining"**: White, "She Gave Up Computers to Play Drums in Band."

131 **their third album as "technically perfect"**: Somma, "Eponymous Album Review."

132 **"a lot of time together in strange places"**: Mercuri, "Head Held High: The Velvet Underground Featuring Doug Yule."

132 **"We are the insects of someone else's thoughts"**: Reed, "We Are the People."

133 **"The only people who made money"**: Cobb, "Tea Party's Demise in Five Acts."

134 **"I was like a kid thrown into the deep end"**: Mercuri, "Head Held High: The Velvet Underground Featuring Doug Yule."

6: SCENES FROM THE REAL WORLD

All quotes from author interviews with Alan Trustman, Norman Jewison, Beverly Walker, Sally Dennison, Fred Roos, and Harvey Silverglate except as follows:

139 **"The character wears suits, Steve"**: Jewison, *This Terrible Business Has Been Good to Me: An Autobiography*, 161.

139 **"this thug, this biker, this dead-end kid"**: Trustman, *Stories, Some of Which Are True.*

139 **"But we have permission from the mayor's office!"**: Blowen and Grossman, "Making Movies in the Hub Is a Nightmare."

140 **"Our heisters scared a lot of customers"**: Uncredited, "Boston-Filmed 'Crown Affair' Premieres in June 19 Benefit."

140 **"Boston is celebrating a big bank robbery this week"**: Adams, "Gala Premiere Here Wednesday for Boston-Filmed 'Thomas Crown Affair.'"

141 **"Think of it, . . . a movie shot in Boston"**: Ebert, "Interview with Norman Jewison."

141 **Kael called it a "chic crappy movie"**: Kael, "Trash, Art, and the Movies."

141 **"Possibly the most under-plotted, underwritten"**: Ebert, "Thomas Crown Affair."

141 **"They cut off my face"**: Sherman, "Fleeting Glimpses of Selves on Screen Satisfied Bostonian."

141 **"Movies are commercially packaged dreams"**: Trustman, "Who Killed Hollywood?"

142 **"a corpulent young man"**: Archer, "Tony Curtis Comedy."

142 **"My interest was not so much"**: Frank, *The Boston Strangler.*

142 **"If the reader is left feeling"**: Ebersola, "Review: *The Boston Strangler*."

143 **"I'm not good-looking, I'm not educated"**: Vronsky, *Serial Killers: The Method and Madness of Monsters.*

143 **"an extensive need to prove":** "Albert Henry DeSalvo Trial: 1967—Sanity Hearing."

143 **"I'm known as the Green Man now":** Frank, *The Boston Strangler.*

144 **"If a man was the strangler":** Kelly, *The Boston Stranglers.*

145 **"What's a nice guy like Tony Curtis":** Goldstein, "Determination of 'New' Tony Curtis Won Film Role of Boston Strangler."

145 **"has the same attractive personality":** Adams, "Director Searches City for Authentic Locations."

145 **"I wanted to play DeSalvo so much":** Malone, *The Defiant One: A Biography of Tony Curtis,* 137.

145 **"shy girl from Cambridge":** Adams, "No Make-Up for Curtis as 'Strangler.'"

145 **"There's a little bit of the Boston Strangler":** Malone, *The Defiant One: A Biography of Tony Curtis,* 136.

146 **"There have been lots of movies about murders":** Ebert, "The Boston Strangler."

146 **"The film has ended":** *The Boston Strangler,* directed by Richard Fleischer.

146 **"The film is—although I hesitate":** Helford, "New Angle in 'Strangler.'"

146 **"anyone could stand next before the celluloid jury":** Diehl, "'Boston Strangler' Raises Disturbing Questions."

147 **"You're not the Boston Strangler":** Malone, *The Defiant One: A Biography of Tony Curtis,* 141.

147 **"DeSalvo said the film portrays him":** Uncredited, "DeSalvo Seeks $2-Million in 'Boston Strangler' Suit."

147 **"a very clever, very smooth":** Sanchez, "Ames Robey; Psychiatrist Argued DeSalvo Was Innocent."

147 **"He was going to tell us":** Uncredited, "He's Not the Boston Strangler: He Didn't Kill My Aunt."

148 *"Here's the story of the strangler yet untold":* Ibid.

148 **"Maybe people will know what it means":** Junger, *A Death in Belmont,* 217.

148 **"nightmare of ghoulish obscenities":** Pearson, "The Follies of Documentary Filmmaking."

149 **"convalescing patients mingled with violent ones":** Rothman, *The Discovery of the Asylum: Social Order and Disorder in the New Republic.*

149 **"colony of lost men":** Micciche, "Bridgewater Holds Colony of Lost Men."

149 **"about a prison and the people":** Anderson and Benson, *Documentary Dilemmas: Frederick Wiseman's Titicut Follies.*

150 **"I don't think this constitutes censoring":** Goodrich, "Titicut Follies."

150 **"a startling example of film truth":** Anderson and Benson, *Documentary Dilemmas: Frederick Wiseman's Titicut Follies.*

150 "Some little biddy from Minnesota": Brinkley-Rogers, "Titicut Follies."

151 "The doctor is like nothing": *Avatar* staff.

152 "message of shock": Goodrich, "Titicut Follies."

152 "The real privacy sought": Harvey, "'Titicut' Trial Nears Finish."

152 "causes 'rational,' middle class people": Uncredited, "The Two Sides of Titicut."

152 "The film speaks for itself": Anderson and Benson, *Documentary Dilemmas: Frederick Wiseman's Titicut Follies.*

153 "80 minutes of brutal sordidness": Ibid.

153 "On the contract issue, the judge": Pearson, "The Follies of Documentary Filmmaking."

154 "Since I was shot, everything": Leonard, "The Return of Andy Warhol."

154 "DON'T CRITICIZE. If you think": Mekas, "Films."

155 "The mind is a beautiful instrument": Lyman, *Autobiography of a World Saviour.*

157 "I just fell in love with the Hill": Felton, "The Lyman Family's Holy Siege of America."

157 "You double Cancer!": Ibid.

157 "'You talk about *The Real World*?": Ibid.

159 "All I can say is that it's a story": Koefod, "Antonioni Flick: Sally Dennison Interview."

160 "He wasn't equipped to handle": *Death Valley Superstar*, directed by Michael Yaroshovsky.

160 "I was a self-respecting hippie dropout bum": Felton, "The Lyman Family's Holy Siege of America."

161 "Mel really made me see": Ibid.

161 "flatly denied . . . that the troupe": Canby, "Antonioni Makes His First U.S. Film in Death Valley."

162 "America is my true protagonist": Walker, "Michelangelo and the Leviathan: The Making of *Zabriskie Point.*"

162 "MGM still claims it doesn't know": Hamilton, "Antonioni's America."

162 "There is something mystical about him": Ibid.

162 "[Mark was] sitting there in his big armchair": Halprin, "Daria."

162 "Turn and grab Mark as if you really wanted": Canby, "Antonioni Makes His First U.S. Film in Death Valley."

162 "bratty, free, earth-child quality": Hamilton, "Antonioni's America."

162 "this year's James Dean": Bensky, "Antonioni Comes to the Point."

163 "Mel had announced that": Kindman, "My Odyssey Through the Underground Press."

163 "That was the first time I heard [Mel's] music": Felton, "The Lyman Family's Holy Siege of America."

163 "It's hard to say what he thought of them": Ibid.

163 "After eight or nine months of my ranting": Ibid.

164 "The whole thing was a big Hollywood lie": Ibid.

164 "No one knew how high and wide": Walker, "Michelangelo and the Leviathan: The Making of *Zabriskie Point*."

164 "No plastic living beside the Hollywood pools": McKinnon, "'Zabriskie Point' Stars Rap Movie."

165 "one of his most ambiguous": Canby, "No Life in Antonioni's Death Valley."

165 "is far more interesting to me as a failure": Goldstein, "Did Antonioni Miss the 'Point'?"

166 "too bad the medium isn't the message": Uncredited, *Broadside of Boston*.

166 "Antonioni didn't represent reality": McKinnon, "'Zabriskie Point' Stars Rap Movie."

167 "I was cast at a bus stop": *The Dick Cavett Show*.

167 "Mark loved being one of the Hill workers": Kindman, "My Odyssey Through the Underground Press."

167 "From fairly reliable, anonymous sources": Felton, "The Lyman Family's Holy Siege of America."

168 "People on the Hill have to learn": Ibid.

168 "I've got a steady job": "New England Merchants Bank Robbery."

169 "In committing their act": Kindman, "My Odyssey Through the Underground Press."

169 "It must have gotten tangled on his leg": "New England Merchants Bank Robbery."

169 "evicted from the commune for non-payment": UPI Staff, "'Zabriskie Point' Star Is Held for Bank Robbery."

169 "Mark would not cooperate": Walker, "Michelangelo and the Leviathan: The Making of *Zabriskie Point*."

170 "It was a revolutionary act": *Death Valley Superstar*, directed by Michael Yaroshevsky.

170 "Mark Frechette has spent the past week": Sales, "Where Are the Listeners? A Journey from Fort Hill to Zabriskie to Cell 104."

170 "The anger was in those boys": Ibid.

170 "We haven't changed": Ibid.

170 "Much of what Mark was saying": McLellan, "Mark Frechette's 'Personal Act of Revolution.'"

171 "oddly formal" cocktail dresses: Ibid.

171 **"Was the bank robbery a way"**: Klein, "Frechette of Fort Hill: Robbing the Bank for Mel."

172 **"Before, when I was out on the street"**: Ibid.

173 **"They call themselves the 'Stars in Stripes'"**: Snyder, "Norfolk, Massachusetts, Inmates/White House Transcripts."

173 **"I'd love it if Nixon were here tonight"**: Barnicle, "'All the President's Men' . . . in Jail."

173 **"The president [and his collaborators] were portrayed"**: Ibid.

173 **"Being in that kind of a place for someone like Mark"**: *Death Valley Superstar*, directed by Michael Yaroshevsky.

173 **"We were close to getting out"**: Ibid.

174 **"It was a good bank robbery"**: McLellan, "Mark Frechette's 'Personal Act of Revolution.'"

7: I SAW YOU COMING FROM THE CAPE

All quotes from author interviews with Joey Bebo, John Sheldon, Tom Kielbania, John Payne, Janet Planet, Victor Moulton, June Benson, Herbert Yakus, Ed Morneau, David Atwood, and Ivan Lipton, except as follows:

176 **"I was about to work with one of"**: Bebo, *In the Back of the Van*, 8.

181 **"Everyone makes the same comment"**: Beam, *Gracefully Insane*, 1.

181 **"You could hide anything"**: Ibid., 205.

181 **"He was incredibly high"**: Stuart, *My First Cousin Once Removed*, 176.

182 **"People are saying, 'Well, this means'"**: Heylin, *Can You Feel the Silence?*, 259.

187 **"[Van] was doing the tracks"**: Ibid., 176.

187 **"There was the Prudential, towering over"**: Bebo, *In the Back of the Van*, 110.

8: A LITTLE MORE LIGHT INTO THE DARKNESS OF MAN

All quotes from author interviews with Charles Giuliano, Ralph Metzner, Dr. Andrew Weil, Joe Rogers, and Lewis Merenstein except as follows:

190 **"He was using LSD to turn"**: Lundborg, *Psychedelia: An Ancient Culture, a Modern Way of Life*, 279.

190 **"He gives really strong doses"**: Felton, "The Lyman Family's Holy Siege of America."

191 **"He was growing horns"**: Ibid.

191 **"I love you, I love you"**: Ibid.

191 **"There is no reason to fear it"**: Lyman, "To All Those Who Would Know."

191 **"We were very interested in anything"**: Roberts, *Albion Dreaming: A Popular History of LSD in Britain*, 20.

192 **"berated us and said the company"**: Friedman, *The Secret Histories: Hidden Truths That Challenged the Past and Changed the World*, 127.

192 "We lost a couple": Lattin, *The Harvard Psychedelic Club*, 213.

192 "They gave this patient LSD": Bass, "Mentally Ill Patient in LSD Study Is Said to Have Killed Self."

193 "It was the classic visionary voyage": Greenfield, *Timothy Leary: A Biography*, 113.

193 "We expected to receive": Dass and Metzner, *Birth of a Psychedelic Culture*, 14.

194 "a place where 'I' existed": Dass, *Be Here Now*.

194 "We gave [psilocybin] to jazz musicians": Ibid.

194 "transcended all form and saw": Ibid.

195 "Before I got involved with Tim": Dass and Metzner, *Birth of a Psychedelic Culture*, 14.

195 "I was a professor and I was": Dass, *Be Here Now*.

195 "HARVARD EATS THE HOLY MUSHROOM": Leary, *High Priest*, 158.

196 "I resolved to devote my ingenuity": Weil, *The Natural Mind*, 21.

196 "It is exhilarating. It shows us": Lattin, *The Harvard Psychedelic Club*, 57.

196 "a vast collection of rumor": Weil, *The Natural Mind*, 64.

197 "I'm in the same situation you were in": Dass and Metzner, *Birth of a Psychedelic Culture*, 88.

198 "BABY'S DEFORMITY BLAMED ON LSD": Black, "Baby's Deformity Blamed on LSD."

198 "We were a cult turned inward": Dass and Metzner, *Birth of a Psychedelic Culture*, 81.

198 "BIG 'FAMILY' STIRS PROTEST": Castello, "Timothy Leary's Dead, but Before That, He Lived in Newton."

199 "an ever-changing scene of magic": Dass and Metzner, *Birth of a Psychedelic Culture*, 14.

199 "Don't think about the past": Dass, *Be Here Now*.

199 "Maharaji indicated he wanted to try LSD": Ibid.

199 "I didn't know if that was": Ibid.

199 "You make many people laugh": Ibid.

199 "sort of be by myself in a cabin": Parker, "Breakfast with Ram Dass—Interview with Dr. Richard Alpert."

200 "Well, we see a Cadillac": Ibid.

200 "The family felt that to some": *Ram Dass, Fierce Grace*, directed by Mickey Lemle.

200 "the most engaging, lucid": Taylor, "Baba Ram Dass (the Former Richard Alpert, PHD) Shares His Experiences."

200 "At Harvard I was a Good Guy": Ibid.

201 "Sir, the motor car is dangerous": Leary, *Changing My Mind, Among Others: Lifetime Writings, Selected and Introduced by the Author*, 143.

201 "The key to your work is advertising": Greenfield, *Timothy Leary: A Biography*, 282.

201 "Wave reassuringly. Radiate courage": Ibid., 283.

201 "A year ago LSD was almost": McCabe, "Remember Dr. Tim Leary?"

201 "his rhetoric has a patina": Mansnerus, "Timothy Leary, Pied Piper of Psychedelic 60's, Dies at 75."

202 "Leary is a pathetic pioneer": Kenny, "Turned-On, Turned-Off High Priest."

202 "I'd always wanted to have": Conrad, "Local LSD PR-Girl Tells How to Make (and Take) Those Little Sugar Cubes."

202 "I began to hang around": Ibid.

202 "Bieberman was the ultimate": Hanna, "Lisa Bieberman: Extended Biography."

203 "When does this stuff wear off?": Bieberman, *Session Games People Play: A Manual for the Use of LSD*.

203 "There should be someone more": Ibid.

203 "I wanted to make the drug available": Conrad, "Local LSD PR-Girl Tells How to Make (and Take) Those Little Sugar Cubes."

203 "If I were you I would": Uncredited, "Bieberman Sentenced for Shipment of LSD."

203 "Flower power is no substitute": Bieberman, *Two Years in the Psychedelic Movement, 1965–1967: The First Twelve Issues of the Psychedelic Information Center Bulletin*.

204 "Jim belonged to a time": Ibid.

204 "betrayal and promise": Bieberman, "The Psychedelic Experience."

204 "People have left Millbrook": Ibid.

204 "a pure-essence eccentric": Leary, *The Politics of Ecstasy*.

204 "It is not bizarre, but clear": Bieberman, *Phanerothyme: A Western Approach to the Religious Use of Psychochemicals*.

204 "I met a patient there who": McCarthy, "Ram Dass Reemerges."

205 "one of the great outliers": Smith, "Bruce Conner's Darkness That Defies Authority."

205 "[He] was there three or four": Felton, "The Lyman Family's Holy Siege of America."

206 "And everybody was getting fucked up": Ibid.

207 "Johnny turned on the radio": Stuart, *My First Cousin Once Removed*, 168.

208 "The last few months": Von Schmidt and Rooney, *Baby, Let Me Follow You Down*, 291.

209 "The disbanding of Jim Kweskin's Jug Band": Ibid., 301.

209 "total insanity had erupted": Wilton, "Last Week."

9: THE NOISES THAT ROAR IN THE SPACE BETWEEN THE WORLDS

All quotes from author interviews with Russell H. Greenan, Ray Riepen, Joe Rogers, Peter Wolf, Jonathan Richman, Don Law, Mitch Horowitz, and Gunther Weil except as follows:

211 **"The details are grisly"**: Lask, "Crazy Palette."

211 **"I haunted the public library"**: Greenan, *It Happened in Boston?*, 147.

212 **"That city is really the Mecca"**: Uncredited, "The Great Spook Temple Boston Town."

213 **"the religion of America"**: Weiss, *Life and Correspondence of Theodore Parker*, 428.

213 **"the spirit of her lamented husband"**: Uncredited, "A Curious Story About Mrs. Lincoln Reiterated."

214 **field dependent on "electrical energy"**: Kirkpatrick, "Edgar Cayce: MIA."

215 **"[Hastings] lived in another world"**: Alan, *Radio Free Boston*, 16.

215 **"But he also believed in the power"**: Ibid.

216 **"Ten thousand dollars?"**: Goodman, *The Mansion on the Hill: Dylan, Young, Geffen, Springsteen, and the Head-on Collision of Rock and Commerce*, 38.

217 **"Because of my relationship with Ray"**: Alan, *Radio Free Boston*, 25.

218 **dismiss any autobiographical content as "absolutely absurd"**: Heylin, *Can You Feel the Silence?*, 141.

218 **"You are fascinated, though a trifle"**: Douglas, *Listening In: Radio and the American Imagination*, 48.

218 **"brought to the ears of us"**: Ibid., 52.

219 **"It was like looking over"**: Alan, *Radio Free Boston*, 34.

219 **"It didn't hurt us if"**: Ibid., 27.

220 **"It was important to let people"**: Ibid., 48.

220 **"hipper than the assholes running"**: Ibid., 9.

220 **"[He] was such a classical music"**: Ibid., 19.

221 **"Driving alone at night"**: Douglas, *Listening In: Radio and the American Imagination*, 40.

221 **"We used to get in the car"**: Barton, "The Car, the Radio, the Night—and Rock's Most Thrilling Song."

222 **"An ancient fortune-telling card"**: Chapman, "What a Deck!"

222 **"The baby-boom generation was the first"**: Paglia, "Cults and Cosmic Consciousness: Religious Vision in the American 1960s."

224 **"tidy up my life"**: Greenan, *It Happened in Boston?*, 224.

224 **"parallelepiped houses of colored crystal rose"**: Ibid., 228.

224 **"three arched entrances set"**: Ibid., 227.

225 **"It was probably the greatest"**: Lattin, *The Harvard Psychedelic Club*, 74.

225 **"Everything in the world just seemed"**: Cassie, "The Existential Medicine."

226 **"it left me with a completely"**: Doblin, "Pahnke's 'Good Friday Experiment': A Long-term Follow-up and Methodological Critique."

226 **"the most powerful cosmic homecoming"**: Smith, *Cleansing the Doors of Perception: The Religious Significance of Entheogenic Plants and Chemicals*, 101.

226 **"crumpled it up"**: Lattin, *The Harvard Psychedelic Club*, 76.

226 **"The original Good Friday experiment"**: Doblin, "Pahnke's 'Good Friday Experiment': A Long-term Follow-up and Methodological Critique."

226 **"fascinating and provocative conclusions"**: Ibid.

226 **"All students who had taken the drug"**: Lattin, *The Harvard Psychedelic Club*, 79.

10: SOMETHING IN THE BRICKS

All quotes from author interviews with Ray Mungo, Chuck White, Barney Frank, Jesse Kornbluth, Steve Nelson, David Atwood, Ted Myers, Alison Burke, Fred Griffeth, and Jessie Benton except as follows:

229 **"I had the privilege of studying"**: UPI Staff, "Martin Luther King's Widow Responds to Suit."

229 **"A few years ago, a young man"**: Forsythe, "BU Honors 'Fallen Knight.'"

230 **"To Boston-born blacks, the lesson"**: Lukas, *Common Ground*, 59.

230 **"The only Black people I saw"**: Jones, "John Curtis Jones Interviewed by Ivan Richiez, Chris Watson, & Erys Valdez."

231 **"The vision of the New Boston"**: Abraham, "It's Time to Finally Honor Martin Luther King's Ties to Boston."

232 **"his finger in every pie"**: Friedman, "Shoeless Barney Frank: Mayor White's Dynamo."

233 **"It's too late to cancel it"**: Lukas, *Common Ground*, 32.

233 **"bedeviled into gangsterism"**: Uncredited, "After the Brawl Was Over."

233 **"form of rock 'n' roll paganism"**: Uncredited, "Alan Freed's Rock 'n' Roll Show Today Stood Up in Court."

233 **"These so-called musical programs"**: Uncredited, "Rock 'n Roll Banned in Boston After Riot That Probably Never Happened."

233 **"they are not really R-'n'-R"**: Cotler, "Boston Bars Rock and Roll Dance: Police Say Music Leads to Trouble."

234 **"If word ever gets out"**: Lukas, *Common Ground*, 33.

234 **"a salty old New Englander"**: Sloss, "'What's Going On Here?': Louis Lyons and the News."

235 **"negro leadership" of Roxbury**: "Interview with Mayor Kevin White."

235 **"Yeah . . . but if I were you"**: *The Night James Brown Saved Boston*, directed by David Leaf.

235 **"black pride and black people"**: Harris, "The Social Activist Side of James Brown You Won't See in *Get On Up*."

235 **"I wanted to see people free"**: Ibid.

236 **"I'll get you your money"**: *The Night James Brown Saved Boston*, directed by David Leaf.

236 **"Ladies and gentlemen, apologies"**: *James Brown at the Boston Garden*, directed by David Atwood.

236 **"He's been doing some things"**: Ibid.

236 **"I had the pleasure of meeting him"**: Ibid.

237 **"He was a man who knew"**: *The Night James Brown Saved Boston*, directed by David Leaf.

237 **"This concert was like magic"**: Ibid.

238 **"The reports also say that"**: *James Brown at the Boston Garden*, directed by David Atwood.

239 **"Wait a minute!"**: Ibid.

240 **"In just a moment we're going"**: Ibid.

240 **"I know [James] went through something"**: *The Night James Brown Saved Boston*, directed by David Leaf.

240 **"Well, the city is at stake"**: Lukas, *Common Ground*, 36.

241 **"Well, we're doing a good thing"**: *The Night James Brown Saved Boston*, directed by David Leaf.

241 **"It was worth the 60K"**: Ibid.

241 **"the two killings seemed to"**: Walsh, "How Robert F. Kennedy's Death Shattered the Nation."

241 **"In Hippievilles around the country"**: Davis, "U.S. Hippies Flocking to Boston Common."

241–42 **"As the hot weather sets in"**: Uncredited, "Nation: Love-in in BossTown."

242 **That daughter, Eve Chayes**: Johnston, "Mel Lyman: Special Place in Family; Man They Worshiped as God Is Nowhere to Be Found."

242 **"The hippies . . . are no longer a novelty"**: UPI Staff, "Boston Curfew Plan Considered."

243 **"You've made a disaster area"**: AP Staff, "Boston Common 'Disaster Area,' Judge Charges."

243 **"For it seems now more certain"**: Bates, *Reporting Vietnam: Part One: American Journalism 1959–1969*.

243 **"I woke up and took a small"**: Kindman, "My Odyssey Through the Underground Press."

244 **"You could just *feel* it"**: Foley, *Confronting the War Machine: Draft Resistance During the Vietnam War*, 15.

244 **"I don't believe we owe loyalty"**: Ibid., 99.

245 **"Thank you for coming"**: Ibid., 202.

246 **"Neither this mayor nor any"**: Friedman, "Atkins Criticizes Mayor for 'Hasty Statement.'"

247 **"some black intellectuals compare"**: Riddell, "Negroes Call It 'Colonialism.'"

247 **"the American flag was lowered"**: Ascheim, *Avatar* #23, April 12, 1968.

248 **"the greatest threat to the internal security"**: Farley, "Preventing the Rise of a 'Messiah.'"

248 **"The Panthers call their breakfast"**: Davidson, "Panther Image: Ghetto Defense."

248 **"We are twenty-four-hour revolutionaries"**: Googins, "When Panthers Roamed Boston: The Boston Chapter of the Black Panther Party."

249 **"There must be a black theater"**: Marquard, "James Spruill, 73; Actor and Founder of Influential Black Theater Company."

250 **"Naturally the neighborhood became enraged"**: Felton, "The Lyman Family's Holy Siege of America."

251 **"Black power is beautiful, man"**: Davis, "White Revolutionaries Settle in Roxbury."

252 **"The Resistance and the School of Theology"**: Foley, *Confronting the War Machine: Draft Resistance During the Vietnam War*, 314.

252 **"ongoing free-speech exercise"**: Ibid., 315.

252 **"taken out physically"**: Fripp, "1000 Await Police at B.U. Sanctuary."

252 **"This is the FBI"**: Foley, *Confronting the War Machine: Draft Resistance During the Vietnam War*, 315.

252 **"The Sanctuary at Marsh Chapel"**: Ibid., 316.

11: WE HAVE ALL BEEN ASTRALS MANY TIMES

All quotes from author interviews with Charles Giuliano, Dave Wilson, John Payne, Tom Kielbania, Wayne Hansen, Jessie Benton, Lewis Merenstein, Brooks Arthur, David Palmer, Kathy West, Jay Berliner, Richard Davis, and Warren Smith Jr. except as follows:

256 **"BUT MEL LYMAN IS THE AVATAR"**: *Avatar*, March 1968.

256 **"be the only company in the entire world"**: Slung, "Non-Psychedelic Reflections of Fort Hill."

256 **"dialogue with the audience"**: Kindman, "My Odyssey Through the Underground Press."

256 **"The music thus became a reward"**: Ibid.

256 **"One day in the late spring"**: Mills, "An American Avatar: Mel Lyman."

257 **"The people outside of Fort Hill"**: Ibid.

257 **"declaration of spiritual war by Mel"**: Kindman, "My Odyssey Through the Underground Press."

259 **"the bundles still warm from the presses"**: Kelly, "Avatar Job Nets 45000."

259 **"For the better part of a week"**: Felton, "The Lyman Family's Holy Siege of America."

261 **"Today the great people are the musicians"**: Lyman, "Some Enlightening News," 19.

262 **"Mel was making plans to accelerate"**: Kindman, "My Odyssey Through the Underground Press."

262 **"Hey, I love Mel because"**: Von Schmidt and Rooney, *Baby, Let Me Follow You Down*, 296.

263 **"Their music had an edgy sense of urgency"**: King, *A Natural Woman: A Memoir*, 135.

263 **"Folk rocker is a powerhouse!"**: Uncredited, "Myddle Class Review."

264 **"The band was just not going"**: Beaudoin, "Not Everything's Been Said—Remembering the City Featuring Carole King."

264 **"The deep love for writing"**: West, *A Song for You: The Quest of the Myddle Class*, 18.

265 **"I'm playing with Van Morrison"**: Ibid., 240.

266 **"He's dead," Harvey Alter told the officers**: Ibid., 264.

266 **"But he started coming on to Rick"**: Ibid., 257.

267 **"It is unfortunate, that so many"**: Tarbi, "Drugs Cited in Student Sentence."

268 **"I won't go into details but I think"**: Cox, "Mick Cox: A Group of Letters from Van Morrison and Other Correspondence."

270 **"This little guy walks in, past everybody"**: Heylin, *Can You Feel the Silence?*, 192.

270 **"He seemed spaced out"**: Ibid., 193.

272 **"A new, and quite apparently"**: Sheahan, "Scientology . . . Lend-lease Racket."

273 **"The Earth is a classroom"**: Brother Philip, *Secret of the Andes*.

274 **"There were several paintings"**: McDonald, "My Peace Offering to Van Morrison."

274 **"the feeling that I'm floating"**: Grissim Jr., "Van Morrison."

274 **"Oh yeah, I didn't write that"**: Heylin, *Can You Feel the Silence?*, 394.

275 **"I didn't know what some of"**: Yorke, *Van Morrison: Into the Music: A Biography*.

277 **"They ruined it"**: Heylin, *Can You Feel the Silence?*, 198.

EPILOGUE: AFTERWARDS

All quotes from author interviews with John Payne, Tom Kielbania, Lewis Merenstein, Janet Planet, Brooks Arthur, Jay Berliner, Richard Davis, Warren Smith Jr., Peter Wolf, Shelly Yakus, Joe Smith, Jef Labes, John Platania, Rick Shlosser, Jessie Benton, David Cay Johnston, and Jim Kweskin except as follows:

283 **"Van Morrison, his *Astral Weeks* album"**: Hibbert, "Jonathan Richman: The Man Who Hates Sitting Down."

284 **"[Boston's] got a kind of sad beauty"**: Ibid.

285 **"Unlike Van's masterful *Astral Weeks*"**: Uncredited, "*Moondance* Review."

285 **"*Astral Weeks* and *Moondance* and never again"**: Shteamer, "In Full: Lewis Merenstein, Producer of *Astral Weeks*."

285 **"We know what's going down"**: Traum, "Van Morrison: In Conversation."

285 **"It made me trust in beauty"**: Kreps, "Bruce Springsteen Reveals Eight 'Desert Island' Songs."

286 **"It was particularly important to me"**: Bangs, "Astral Weeks," 20.

286 **"Of all the records I have ever"**: Smith, *Off the Record*, 272.

287 **"He went 'Questions! Questions!'"**: Scharpling and Mann, "Interview with Aimee Mann."

287 **"I remember we almost came to"**: Hilburn and Philips, "Quotations from Chairman Mo."

290 **"In came a young woman"**: Moore, "Spaceship Interview Given via Ouija Board."

291 **"The audience didn't go for"**: Kindman, "My Odyssey Through the Underground Press."

292 **"a gesture against all the things"**: Felton, "The Lyman Family's Holy Siege of America."

292 **"This cat might go out"**: Uncredited, "Many Religious Communes of Young People Are Under the Sway of Compelling Leaders."

292 **"They're well organized"**: Krassner, "My Acid Trip with Squeaky Fromme."

292 **"I didn't see any spirit"**: Hertzberg, "Vibes."

293 **"Was this Mel Lyman"**: Felton, "The Lyman Family's Holy Siege of America."

293 **"those fucking bastards"**: Ibid.

294 **"Boston is sort of like"**: Ibid.

294 **"This is a whole new culture"**: Ibid.

294 **"What this Mel Lyman guy"**: Mauer, "Letter to the Editor."

294 **"as long as people continue"**: Williams, "Letter to the Editor."

294 **"Howard Hughes of the Underground"**: Acton, Le Mond, and Hodges, *Mug Shots*.

294 **"Is Mel Lyman still around?"**: Beggy and Shanahan, "Jokes Flow from Waters: Leno Dogs Affleck."

295 **"His Family says that he died"**: Johnston, "Mel Lyman: Special Place in Family; Man They Worshiped as God Is Nowhere to Be Found."

296 **"Once we were talking about"**: Johnston, "Once-Notorious '60s Commune Evolves into Respectability; After 19 Years the Lyman Family Prospers as Craftsmen and Farmers."

297 **"I was told that Melvin died"**: Johnston, "Mel Lyman: Special Place in Family; Man They Worshiped as God Is Nowhere to Be Found."

298 **"avatar and cultural leader"**: Kindman, "My Odyssey Through the Underground Press."

299 **"I'm afraid Mel was not very pretty"**: Felton, "The Lyman Family's Holy Siege of America."

299 **"I shot dope and ran IBM machines"**: Lyman, *Mirror at the End of the Road*.

300 **"I can't ever forget the time"**: Ibid.

300 **"I have to write my own"**: Ibid.

300 **"Hallooneysations, hassooleenations," runs one entry**: Ibid.

300 **"infectious hepatitis from shooting heroin"**: Ibid.

300 **"We may study ESP if we live"**: Ibid.

300 **"Last night I struck my love"**: Ibid.

300 **"To Judy, who made me live"**: Ibid.

301 **"I walked into Dunkin Donuts"**: Ibid.

301 **"I am indeed a supreme being"**: Ibid.

301 **"the most optimistic note of the evening"**: Silber, "What's Happening."

302 **"The dozens of framed photographs"**: Johnston, "Once-Notorious '60s Commune Evolves into Respectability; After 19 Years the Lyman Family Prospers as Craftsmen and Farmers."

303 **"Their lifestyle forces them to constantly"**: Ibid.

304 **"Oh my God! Look at that picture"**: Neuman, "On Anniversary of Apollo 8, How the 'Earthrise' Photo Was Made."

304 **"the largest audience that had ever"**: Uncredited, "Apollo 8: Christmas at the Moon."

304 **"Please be informed there is a Santa Claus"**: Ibid.

BIBLIOGRAPHY

Abraham, Yvonne. "It's Time to Finally Honor Martin Luther King's Ties to Boston." *Boston Globe*. January 14, 2017.

Acton, Jay, Alan Le Mond, and Parker Hodges. *Mug Shots*. New York: World Publishing, 1972.

Adams, Marjory. "Director Searches City for Authentic Locations." *Boston Globe*. November 5, 1967.

———. "Gala Premiere Here Wednesday for Boston-Filmed 'Thomas Crown Affair.'" *Boston Globe*. June 16, 1969.

———. "No Make-up for Curtis as 'Strangler.'" *Boston Globe*. February 11, 1968.

Alan, Carter. *Radio Free Boston*. Boston: Northeastern University Press, 2013.

"Albert Henry DeSalvo Trial: 1967—Sanity Hearing." Transcript.

Anderson, Carolyn, and Thomas W. Benson. *Documentary Dilemmas: Frederick Wiseman's Titicut Follies*. Carbondale: Southern Illinois University Press, 1991.

AP Staff. "Boston Common 'Disaster Area,' Judge Charges." Associated Press. July 23, 1968.

Archer, Eugene. "Tony Curtis Comedy." *New York Times*. June 11, 1964.

Avatar Staff. "Titicut Follies." *Avatar*. November 1967.

Bailey, Alice. *A Treatise on White Magic*. New York: Lucis Publishing Company, 1934.

Bangs, Lester. "Astral Weeks." In *Psychotic Reactions and Carburetor Dung*. New York: Anchor Books, 1987.

———. *Main Lines, Blood Feasts, and Bad Taste: A Lester Bangs Reader*. New York: Anchor Books, 2008.

Barnicle, Mike. "'All the President's Men' . . . in Jail." *Boston Globe*. March 23, 1975.

Barton, Laura. "The Car, the Radio, the Night—and Rock's Most Thrilling Song." *The Guardian*. July 20, 2007.

Barton, Michael. "The Lawyer." *The Heights.* October 6, 1967.

Bass, Alison. "Mentally Ill Patient in LSD Study Is Said to Have Killed Self." *Boston Globe.* January 5, 1994.

Bates, Milton J. *Reporting Vietnam: Part One: American Journalism 1959–1969.* New York: Library of America, 1998.

Beam, Alex. *Gracefully Insane.* New York: Public Affairs, 2009.

Beaudoin, Jedd. "Not Everything's Been Said—Remembering the City Featuring Carole King." popmatters.com. November 11, 2015.

Bebo, Joseph W. *In the Back of the Van.* Topsham, ME: JWB Book Publishing, 2016.

Beggy, Carol, and Mark Shanahan. "Jokes Flow from Waters: Leno Dogs Affleck." *Boston Globe.* May 3, 2004.

Bensky, Lawrence. "Antonioni Comes to the Point." *New York Times.* December 15, 1968.

Berns, Bert. Liner notes. *Blowin' Your Mind!* Van Morrison. Bang Records, 1967.

———. *Phanerothyme: A Western Approach to the Religious Use of Psychochemicals.* Cambridge, MA: Psychedelic Information Center, 1968.

Bieberman, Lisa. "The Psychedelic Experience." *Boston Globe.* January 21, 1968.

———. "The Psychedelic Experience." *The New Republic.* August 1967.

———. *Session Games People Play: A Manual for the Use of LSD.* Cambridge, MA: Psychedelic Information Center, 1967.

———. *Two Years in the Psychedelic Movement, 1965–1967: The First Twelve Issues of the Psychedelic Information Center Bulletin.* Cambridge, MA: Psychedelic Information Center, 1970.

Black, Herbert. "Baby's Deformity Blamed on LSD." *Boston Globe.* November 23, 1967.

Blake, Andrew. "He's Not Quite Emperor of a Boston Empire." *Boston Globe.* January 21, 1971.

Blowen, Michael, and Gary Grossman. "Making Movies in the Hub Is a Nightmare." *Boston Magazine.* February 1977.

Blum, Deborah. *Ghost Hunters.* New York: Penguin Books, 2007.

Blumenthal, Ralph. "Some Retired Runyon Guys Are Still Handing Out Dolls." *New York Times*, December 18, 2000.

Bockris, Victor, and Gerard Malanga. *Up-tight: The Velvet Underground Story.* New York: Cooper Square Press, 2003.

Boyle, Kay. *The Underground Woman.* Garden City, NY: Doubleday, 1975.

Breznikar, Klemen. "Ultimate Spinach Interview with Ian Bruce-Douglas." *It's Psychedelic Baby Magazine.* September 2011.

Brinkley-Rogers, Paul. "Titicut Follies." *Newsweek* (unpublished first draft). November 17, 1967.

Brooks, Ernie, as told to Legs McNeil. "Jonathan Richman: In Love with the Modern World." *Vice*. June 6, 2014.

Brother Philip. *Secret of the Andes*. California: Leaves of Grass Press, 1961.

Burks, John. "Cinema: Fourteen Points to 'Zabriskie.'" *Rolling Stone*. March 7, 1970.

Burns, Gary. "An Interview with Ian Bruce Douglas." *The Terrascope*. 2001.

Canby, Vincent. "Antonioni Makes His First U.S. Film in Death Valley." *New York Times*. November 6, 1968.

———. "No Life in Antonioni's Death Valley." *New York Times*. February 15, 1970.

Cardoso, William. "Tea Party, Boston's Rock Core, Closes Doors from Lack of Funds." *Boston Globe*. January 5, 1971.

Carroll, Matt. "Mel Lyman: A Mind-Control Guru or a Leader Deserving Respect and Love?" *Boston Herald*. November 24, 1985.

———. "The Fort Hill 'Gang' 20 Years Later: Controversial Hub Commune of the '60s Survives and Prospers." *Boston Herald*. November 24, 1985.

Carson, Kit. "GOD IS BACK, He Says So Himself." *Esquire*. February 1968.

Cassie, Rob. "The Existential Medicine." *Baltimore Magazine*. November 2016.

Castello, Caitlin. "Timothy Leary's Dead, but Before That, He Lived in Newton." *Boston Globe*. March 11, 2010.

Chapman, Patricia. "What a Deck!" *Boston Globe*. February 11, 1968.

Chase, Alston. "Harvard and the Making of the Unabomber." *The Atlantic*. June 2000.

Cobb, Nathan. "Boston's Rock and Roll Establishment." *Boston Globe*. December 5, 1971.

———. "Ray Riepen Rides Off into the Sunset to a New Future." *Boston Globe*. September 12, 1971.

———. "Tea Party's Demise in Five Acts." *Boston Globe*. January 17, 1971.

Cohen, Scott. "Funny How Love Is." *SPIN*. June 1986.

Conrad, Allison B. "Local LSD PR-Girl Tells How to Make (and Take) Those Little Sugar Cubes." *Harvard Crimson*. April 29, 1966.

Cotler, Stephen L. "Boston Bars Rock and Roll Dance; Police Say Music Leads to Trouble." *Harvard Crimson*. May 11, 1965.

Cott, Jonathan. "Van Morrison: The Poet." *Rolling Stone*. November 30, 1978.

Cox, Mick. "Mick Cox: A Group of Letters from Van Morrison and Other Correspondence." *Bonhams*. December 18, 2013.

Coyote, Peter. *Sleeping Where I Fall: A Chronicle*. Washington, D.C.: Counterpoint, 2009.

Crowley, Peter. "Velvet Underground: Despair Still Reigns." *The Heights*. March 1969.

Dass, Ram. *Be Here Now*. San Cristobal, NM: Lama Foundation, 1978.

———, and Ralph Metzner. *Birth of a Psychedelic Culture*. Santa Fe, NM: Synergetic Press, 2010.

———, with Stephen Levine. *Grist for the Mill*. New York: HarperCollins, 2014.

Davidson, Sara. "Panther Image: Ghetto Defense." *Boston Globe*. September 8, 1968.

Davis, Susan E. "Avatar Forces the Issue." *Bay State Banner*. February 15, 1968.

———. "White Revolutionaries Settle in Roxbury." *Bay State Banner*. February 15, 1968.

Davis, William A. "U.S. Hippies Flocking to Boston Common." *Boston Globe*. June 19, 1968.

Death Valley Superstar. Directed by Michael Yaroshevsky. 2008.

DeRogatis, Jim. *Let it Blurt*. New York: Broadway Books, 2000.

———, and Bill Bentley. *The Velvet Underground*. St. Paul, MN: Voyageur, 2009.

DeTurk, David. "Velvet Underground Live Review." *Boston After Dark*. September 1967.

DeWitt, Howard A. *Van Morrison: The Mystic's Music*. Horizon Books, 1983.

Diehl, Digby. "'Boston Strangler' Raises Disturbing Questions." *Los Angeles Times*. January 17, 1969.

Doblin, Rick. "Pahnke's 'Good Friday Experiment': A Long-term Follow-up and Methodological Critique." *Journal of Transpersonal Psychology*. 1991.

Douglas, Susan J. *Listening In: Radio and the American Imagination*. New York: Times Books, 1999.

Dylan, Bob. "Carnegie Chapter Hall Program." November 4, 1961.

Earle, Ralph. "United Illuminating." *Broadside of Boston*. August 17, 1966.

Ebersola, Phil. "Review: *The Boston Strangler*." *The Daily Mail*. September 2, 1967.

———. "The Boston Strangler." *Chicago Sun-Times*. October 22, 1968.

Ebert, Roger. "Interview with Norman Jewison." *Chicago Sun-Times*. June 23, 1968.

———. "Thomas Crown Affair." *Chicago Sun-Times*. August 27, 1968.

Emerson, Ken. "Boston Sound: Eden's Children." *Avatar*. March 29, 1968.

Enzer, Eli. "In Boston, It's a Tea Party." *Boston Globe*. May 14, 1967.

Faltz, Batya. "Boston . . . The Next San Francisco?" *New England Teen Scene*. December 1967.

Farley, Jonathan David. "Preventing the Rise of a 'Messiah.'" *The Guardian*. April 4, 2008.

Felton, David. "The Lyman Family's Holy Siege of America, Part I." *Rolling Stone*. December 23, 1971.

———. "The Lyman Family's Holy Siege of America, Part II." *Rolling Stone*. January 6, 1972.

Festival. Directed by Murray Lerner. Patchke Productions, 1968.

Fleischer, Richard. *Just Tell Me When to Cry: A Memoir*. New York: Carroll & Graf, 1993.

Foley, Michael S. *Confronting the War Machine: Draft Resistance During the Vietnam War*. Chapel Hill: University of North Carolina Press, 2003.

Foley, Ryan. "Paragraphs from the Unrealized Tome on Astral Weeks; or, 2,000 Words of Pretentious Hooey." *Throwing Pennies at the Bridges Down Below* (an Astral Weeks blog). 2014.

Forsythe, George. "BU Honors 'Fallen Knight.'" *Boston Herald Traveler*. April 6, 1968.

Frank, Gerold. *The Boston Strangler*. New York: New American Library, 1966.

Frank, Josh, with Charlie Buckholtz. *In Heaven Everything Is Fine*. Berkeley, CA: Soft Skull Press, 2010.

Frechette, Mark, Daria Halprin, and Jessie Benton. "Antonioni's Newest Superstars." *American Avatar*. Summer 1969.

French, Marilyn. *The Women's Room*. New York: Summit Books, 1977.

Fricke, David. "Lou Reed: The *Rolling Stone* Interview." *Rolling Stone*. May 4, 1989.

Friedman, Elliot. "Shoeless Barney Frank; Mayor White's Dynamo." *Boston Globe*. April 4, 1968.

———. "Atkins Criticizes Mayor for 'Hasty Statement.'" *Boston Globe*. April 11, 1968.

Friedman, John S. *The Secret Histories: Hidden Truths That Challenged the Past and Changed the World*. New York: Picador, 2005.

Fripp, William J. "1000 Await Police at B.U. Sanctuary." *Boston Globe*. October 4, 1968.

Gerlach, David. "Joe Smith Interview." *Blank on Blank*. N.d.

Ginzberg, Ruth Szold. *Children and Other Strangers*. Piscataway, NJ: Transaction Publishers, 1992.

Gitlin, Todd. *The Sixties: Years of Hope, Days of Rage*. New York: Bantam, 1987.

Gleason, Josh. "Van Morrison: 'Astral Weeks' Revisited." NPR, February 28, 2009.

Gleason, Ralph. "Dead Like Live Thunder." *San Francisco Chronicle*. March 19, 1967.

Goldstein, Norman. "Determination of 'New' Tony Curtis Won Film Role of Boston Strangler." *Standard Speaker*. January 13, 1969.

Goldstein, Richard. "Did Antonioni Miss the 'Point'?" *New York Times*. February 22, 1970.

———. "The New Boston Sound and the Rock Scholars." *Vogue*. February 1, 1968.

Goodman, Fred. *The Mansion on the Hill: Dylan, Young, Geffen, Springsteen, and the Head-on Collision of Rock and Commerce*. New York: Times Books, 1997.

Goodrich, Roger. "Titicut Follies." WHDH. October 18, 1967.

Googins, Nick Fuller. "When Panthers Roamed Boston: The Boston Chapter of the Black Panther Party." *What's Up Magazine*. 2006.

Grant, Steve. "Talking Rock." *The Tech*. October 1, 1968.

Green, Jennie. "The Unlikely Sisterhood." *Boston Globe Magazine*. December 1, 2002.

Green, Robin. "Beyond Shazam at Guru Gulch." *Rolling Stone*. August 3, 1972.

Greenan, Russell H. *It Happened in Boston?* New York: Random House, 1968.

Greenfield, Robert. *Timothy Leary: A Biography*. Boston: Mariner Books, 2006.

Grissim, John Jr. "Van Morrison." *Rolling Stone*. June 22, 1972.

Gross, Henry. *The Flower People*. New York: Ballantine Books, 1968.

Hajdu, D. *Positively 4th Street*. New York: Picador, 2011.

Halprin, Daria interview, conducted by Joey Goldfarb, Daria Halprin, Mark Frechette, Faith Gude, David Gude, Eben Given. "Daria." *Pluto Magazine*. 1970.

Hamilton, Jack. "Antonioni's America." *Look*. November 18, 1969.

Handlin, Oscar. *Boston's Immigrants, 1790–1880: A Study in Acculturation*. Cambridge, MA: Belknap Press of Harvard University Press, 1979.

Hanna, Jon. "Lisa Bieberman: Extended Biography." erowid.org. March 28, 2012.

Hansen, Wayne. "How Escalation Brought the Chief to the Bargaining Table." *Avatar* #19. February 16, 1968.

Harriman, Jane. "Avatar Descends on Boston: The Underground Press Speaks Up." *Boston Globe*. October 8, 1967.

Harris, Aisha. "The Social Activist Side of James Brown You Won't See in *Get On Up*." *Slate*. August 8, 2014.

Harvey, Joseph. "'Titicut' Trial Nears Finish." *Boston Globe*. December 15, 1967.

Heath, Todd W. "Family Sings Blues Over '50s Song." The Associated Press. September 25, 1983.

Helford, Paul. "New Angle in 'Strangler.'" *Daily Illini*. November 20, 1968.

Hertzberg, Hendrik. "Vibes." *The New Yorker*. August 7, 1971.

Heylin, Clinton. *All Yesterdays' Parties: The Velvet Underground in Print, 1966–1971*. Cambridge, MA: Da Capo Press, 2006.

———. *Bob Dylan*. New York: Harper Entertainment, 2003.

————. *Can You Feel the Silence?* Chicago: Chicago Review Press, 2004.

Hibbert, Tom. "Jonathan Richman: The Man Who Hates Sitting Down." *Q Magazine*. May 1993.

Hilburn, Robert, and Chuck Philips. "Quotations from Chairman Mo." *Los Angeles Times*. December 11, 1994.

Horowitz, Mitch. *Occult America*. New York: Bantam Books Trade Paperbacks, 2010.

Hoskyns, Barney. "The Eden Project." *Mojo*. December 2001.

————. *Small Town Talk: Bob Dylan, The Band, Van Morrison, Janis Joplin, Jimi Hendrix and Friends in the Wild Years of Woodstock*. Cambridge, MA: Da Capo Press, 2016.

Hutchinson, Sean. *Crying Out Loud*. Santa Barbara, CA: John Daniel, 1988.

"Interview with Lou Reed." KVAN, Portland, OR. November 21, 1969.

"Interview with Mayor Kevin White." *Louis Lyons and the News*. WGBH. April 5, 1968.

James Brown at the Boston Garden. Directed by David Atwood. WGBH. April 4, 1968.

Jarnow, Jesse. *Heads*. Cambridge, MA: Da Capo Press, 2016.

Jewison, Norman. *This Terrible Business Has Been Good to Me: An Autobiography*. New York: Thomas Dunne Books, 2005.

J.K. "Bagatelle Review." *Fusion*. September 1968.

Johnston, David Cay. "Mel Lyman: Special Place in Family; Man They Worshiped as God Is Nowhere to Be Found." *Los Angeles Times*. August 4, 1985.

————. "Once-Notorious '6os Commune Evolves into Respectability; After 19 Years the Lyman Family Prospers as Craftsmen and Farmers." *Los Angeles Times*. August 4, 1985.

Jones, John Curtis. "John Curtis Jones Interviewed by Ivan Richiez, Chris Watson, & Erys Valdez." Cooperative Artists Institute. www.tribal-rhythms.org. 2010.

Junger, Sebastian. *A Death in Belmont*. New York: W. W. Norton & Company, 2009.

Kael, Pauline. "Trash, Art, and the Movies." *Harpers*. February 1969.

Kaiser, Charles. *1968 in America*. New York: Grove Press, 2002.

————. "Avatar Heist." *Boston Free Press*. June 1968.

Kelly, Brian. "Avatar Job Nets 45000." *Boston Free Press*. May 1968.

Kelly, Susan. *The Boston Stranglers*. New York: Pinnacle Books, 1995.

Ken Burns' America: Thomas Hart Benton. Directed by Ken Burns. PBS Home Video. 1988.

Kennedy, Bob, Mel Lyman, Wayne Hansen, and Eben Given. "Interview Transcript." *Avatar*. August 18, 1967.

Kenny, Herbert. "Turned-on, Turned-off High Priest." *Boston Globe*. September 29, 1968.

Kent, Nick. "The J. Geils Band: Hard Drivin' Sweet Soundin' Rock and Roll." *New Musical Express*. January 20, 1973.

Kindman, Michael. "My Odyssey Through the Underground Press." In *Voices from the Underground: Insider Histories of the Vietnam Era Underground Press, Vol. 1.* Edited by Ken Wachsberger. Tempe, AZ: Mica Press, 1993.

King, Carole. *A Natural Woman: A Memoir*. New York: Grand Central Publishing. 2012.

Kirkpatrick, Rob. *1969*. New York: Skyhorse, 2009.

Kirkpatrick, Sidney. "Edgar Cayce: MIA." *Venture Inward Magazine*. April–June 2012.

Klein, Joe. "Frechette of Fort Hill: Robbing the Bank for Mel." *The Real Paper*. September 12, 1973.

Kneeland, Paul F. "Association Says Little but the Sound Is Good." *Boston Globe*. August 6, 1968.

Koefod, Rowland. "Antonioni Flick: Sally Dennison Interview." *Boston Free Press*. June 1968.

Kornbluth, Jesse. *Notes from the New Underground*. New York: Ace Publishing Corporation, 1968.

Kraft, Eric. "Poetic Pop Guitarist Van Morrison Begins Career Anew at Catacombs." *Boston After Dark*. August 1968.

Krassner, Paul. "My Acid Trip with Squeaky Fromme." *Huffington Post*. September 6, 2009.

Kreps, Daniel. "Bruce Springsteen Reveals Eight 'Desert Island' Songs." *Rolling Stone*. December 18, 2016.

Kruskall, Stephen I. "Lisa Bieberman Held on Charge of Mailing LSD." *Harvard Crimson*. June 1, 1966.

Landau, Jon. "Growing Young with Rock and Roll." *The Real Paper*. May 22, 1974.

———. *It's Too Late to Stop Now: A Rock and Roll Journal*. San Francisco: Straight Arrow Books, 1972.

———. "The Sound of Boston: 'Kerplop.'" *Rolling Stone*. April 6, 1968.

Lask, Thomas. "Crazy Palette." *New York Times*. February 5, 1969.

Lattin, Don. *The Harvard Psychedelic Club*. New York: HarperCollins, 2010.

Laughner, Peter. "The Modern Lovers." *Creem*. August 1976.

Leary, Timothy. *Changing My Mind, Among Others: Lifetime Writings, Selected and Introduced by the Author*. Englewood Cliffs, NJ: Prentice Hall, 1982.

———. *High Priest*. Berkeley, CA: Ronin, 1995.

————. *The Politics of Ecstasy*. Berkeley, CA: Ronin, 1968.

Lee, Martin A., and Bruce Shlain. *Acid Dreams: The Complete Social History of LSD; The CIA, the Sixties, and Beyond*. New York: Grove Press, 1985.

Leonard, John. "The Return of Andy Warhol." *New York Times*. November 10, 1968.

Levey, Robert L. "Avatar Closes Its Mel." *Boston Globe*. March 26, 1968.

————. "Fort Hill: Re-inventing Life on a Hilltop in Roxbury." *Boston Globe*. February 1, 1970.

————. "Friendly Fifty on Fort Hill—Better Way for People?" *Boston Globe*. December 12, 1967.

Levin, G. Roy. *Documentary Explorations*. New York: Anchor Press, 1971.

Lorber, Alan. "Something Called the 'Boston Sound'—by Its Creator." *Goldmine Magazine*. April 1992.

Lovell, Paul. "The Boston Sound—Rock in Boston 1967–69." punkblowfish.com. December 18, 2010.

Lukas, J. Anthony. *Common Ground*. New York: Vintage Books, 1986.

Lundborg, Patrick. *Psychedelia: An Ancient Culture, a Modern Way of Life*. Stockholm, Lhasa, Mojave: Lysergia, 2012.

Lyman, Mel. *Autobiography of a World Saviour*. New York: Jonas Press, 1966.

————. "Mel Lyman on Music." *New England Scene*. October 1968.

————. *Mirror at the End of the Road*. An American Avatar Publication. New York: Ballantine Books, 1971.

————. "Some Enlightening News." *American Avatar*. October 1968.

————. "To All Those Who Would Know." *Avatar*. March 29, 1968.

Malone, Aubrey. *The Defiant One: A Biography of Tony Curtis*. Jefferson, NC: McFarland, 2013.

Manseau, Peter. *Vows: The Story of a Priest, a Nun, and Their Son*. New York: Free Press, 2005.

Mansnerus, Laura. "Timothy Leary, Pied Piper of Psychedelic 60's, Dies at 75." *New York Times*. June 1, 1996.

Marcus, Greil. *When That Rough God Goes Riding: Listening to Van Morrison*. New York: Public Affairs, 2010.

Marks, John D. *The Search for the "Manchurian Candidate": The CIA and Mind Control: The Secret History of the Behavioral Sciences*. New York: W. W. Norton & Company, 1979.

Marquard, Bryan. "James Spruill, 73; Actor and Founder of Influential Black Theater Company." *Boston Globe*. February 11, 2011.

Matza, Michael. "We Still Are Family—The Lymans of Fort Hill Then and Now." *Boston Phoenix*. July 16, 1985.

Mauer. Joe. "Letter to the Editor." *Rolling Stone* #100. January 1968.

McCabe, Charles. "Remember Dr. Tim Leary?" *Democrat and Chronicle*. August 8, 1968.

McCarthy, Michael. "Ram Dass Reemerges." *Pacific Sun*. January 15, 2001.

Mcdonald, Gregory. "'The Ark,' 'Boston Tea Party' Merge." *Boston Globe*. July 10, 1969

———. "A Cheer for Channel Two." *Boston Globe*. November 17, 1967.

———. "The Happening in Studio A." *Boston Globe*. December 31, 1967.

McDonald, Henry. "My Peace Offering to Van Morrison." *The Guardian*. February 11, 2006.

McGuire, Wayne. "The Boston Sound/The Velvet Underground & Mel Lyman." *Crawdaddy*. August 1968.

McKinnon, George. "Boom, Boom, Boom Bores." *Boston Globe*. September 22, 1967.

———. "'Zabriskie Point' Stars Rap Movie." *Boston Globe*. March 10, 1970.

McLellan, Vin. "Mark Frechette: Making of a Bank Robber?" *Boston Phoenix*. September 4, 1973.

———. "Mark Frechette's 'Personal Act of Revolution.'" *Boston After Dark*. September 11, 1973.

Mekas, Jonas. "Films." *Avatar*. February 1968.

Mercuri, Sal. "Head Held High: The Velvet Underground Featuring Doug Yule." *The Velvet Underground Fanzine*. Volume 3, Fall/Winter 1994.

Micciche, S. J. "Bridgewater Holds Colony of Lost Men." *Boston Globe*. February 20, 1963.

Milano, Brett. *The Sound of Our Town*. Beverly, MA: Commonwealth Editions, 2007.

Miller, Neil. *Banned in Boston*. Boston: Beacon Press, 2011.

Mills, Paul. "An American Avatar: Mel Lyman." *Fusion*. April 16, 1971.

Mills, Peter. *Hymns to the Silence: Inside the Words and Music of Van Morrison*. New York: Bloomsbury Academic, 2010.

Moore, Gary. "Spaceship Interview Given via Ouija Board." *Boston Herald American*. March 26, 1978.

Morris, Dee. *Boston in the Golden Age of Spiritualism*. Stroud, UK: History Press, 2014.

Morrison, Van. Liner notes. *The Authorized Bang Collection*. Van Morrison. Legacy Records, 2017.

MTV News Staff. "Van Morrison Guided by Voices?" MTV News. May 8, 1996.

Mungo, Raymond. *Famous Long Ago*. Boston: Beacon Press, 1970.

Murphy, Jeremiah V. "Avatar Explains Its Side." *Boston Globe*. December, 1967.

Murray, Tom. Orpheus Review. *Broadside of Boston*. September 1968.

Myers, Ted. *Making It: Music, Sex & Drugs in the Golden Age of Rock*. Minneapolis: Calumet Editions, 2017.

Neuman, Scott. "On Anniversary of Apollo 8, How the 'Earthrise' Photo Was Made." NPR. December 23, 2013.

"New England Merchant's Bank Robbery." FBI File. September 11, 1973. Declassified December 21, 2010. Requested by Sean Maloney. Published at MuckRock.com.

Newsweek Staff. "The Bosstown Sound." *Newsweek*. January 29, 1968.

Nicholson, Louise. "Reviving the Regionalists: Thomas Hart Benton at the Metropolitan Museum." *Apollo Magazine*. October 10, 2014.

No Direction Home. Directed by Martin Scorsese. Paramount Pictures. 2005.

Norris, Rob. "I Was a Velveteen." *Kicks Magazine*. 1979.

O'Brian, Dave. "The Sorry Life and Death of Mark Frechette." *Rolling Stone*. November 6, 1975.

O'Connor, Thomas H. *Building a New Boston*. Boston: Northeastern University Press, 1993.

Paglia, Camille. "Cults and Cosmic Consciousness: Religious Vision in the American 1960s." *Arion*. December 2003.

Paine, Katharine. "Commune's Image Belied Reality." *Boston Herald American*. March 26, 1978.

Pareles, Jon. "Borrowed Songs, with Exuberance." *New York Times*. April 30, 1996

Parker, Jim. "Breakfast with Ram Dass—Interview with Dr. Richard Alpert." *Drug Survival News*. May–June 1982.

Pearson, Jesse. "The Follies of Documentary Filmmaking." *Vice*. September 1, 2007.

Penn, Stanley. "Selling a New Sound." *Wall Street Journal*. May 27, 1968.

Penner, James. *Timothy Leary: The Harvard Years*. Rochester, VT: Park Street Press, 2014.

Pilati, Joe. "Fort Hill Commune Seeks Facts in Bank Holdup Death." *Boston Globe*. September 3, 1973.

Powell, Mike. "Pixies: Catalog Album Review." *Pitchfork*. April 25, 2014.

Ram Dass, Fierce Grace. Directed by Mickey Lemle. Lemle Pictures. 2001.

Reed, James. "The Jim Kweskin Jug Band Celebrates Its 50th Anniversary." *Boston Globe*. August 22, 2013.

Reed, John D. "Judge Convicts Two in Avatar Trial: 'What Justifies Words Like These?'" *Harvard Crimson*. December, 9, 1967.

———. "War on Hippies." *Harvard Crimson*. October 13, 1967.

Reed, Lou. "We Are the People." *Fusion*. 1971.

Riddell, Janet. "Negroes Call It 'Colonialism.'" *Boston Globe*. April 9, 1968.

Roberts, Andy. *Albion Dreaming: A Popular History of LSD in Britain*. Singapore: Marshall Cavendish Editions, 2012.

Rokeach, Milton. *The Three Christs of Ypsilanti*. New York: New York Review Books, 2011.

Rothman, David J. *The Discovery of the Asylum: Social Order and Disorder in the New Republic*. Revised edition. London and New York: Routledge, 1972.

Rotman, Alan B. "Gripe Time, People." *Broadside of Boston*. January 1968.

Sales, Bob. "Where Are the Listeners? A Journey from Fort Hill to Zabriskie to Cell 104." *Boston Globe*. September 9, 1973.

Sanchez, Theresa. "Ames Robey: Psychiatrist Argued DeSalvo Was Innocent." *Boston Globe*. October 13, 2004.

Scharpling, Tom, and Aimee Mann. "Interview with Aimee Mann." *The Best Show on WFMU*. December 1, 2009.

Selvin, Joel. *Here Comes the Night: The Dark Soul of Bert Berns and the Dirty Business of Rhythm and Blues*. Berkeley, CA: Counterpoint, 2015.

Sheahan, Denis. "Scientology . . . Lend-Lease Racket." *Women's Wear Daily*. August 7, 1968.

Sheehan, Henry. "Chevy Chase Is Fletching, Kvetching." *Boston Globe*. March 17, 1989.

Sherman, Marjorie. "Fleeting Glimpses of Selves on Screen Satisfied Bostonian." *Boston Globe*. June 20, 1968.

Sherman, Paul. *Big Screen Boston: From Mystry Street to The Departed and Beyond* Black Bars Publishing, 2008.

Shteamer, Hank. "In Full: Lewis Merenstein, Producer of *Astral Weeks*." hankshteamer.com. March 1, 2008.

Sides, Hampton. *Hellhound on His Trail: The Electrifying Account of the Largest Manhunt in American History*. New York: Doubleday, 2010.

Silber, Irwin. "What's Happening." *Sing Out!* November 1965.

Silver, David. "What's Happening, Mr. Silver?" *New England Scene*. August 1967.

————, and Mel Lyman. "Transcript of an Interview Between Mel Lyman and Dave Silver." *Avatar* #19. February 16, 1968.

Simels, Steve. Unpublished Chevy Chase Profile for *Rolling Stone*. 1989.

Sloss, David. "'What's Going On Here?': Louis Lyons and the News." WGBH Alumni. http://wgbhalumni.org. June 30, 2016.

Slung, Michele B. "Non-Psychedelic Reflections of Fort Hill." *Harvard Summer News*. August 20, 1968.

Smith, Huston. *Cleansing the Doors of Perception: The Religious Significance of Entheogenic Plants and Chemicals*. New York: Jeremy P. Tarcher/Putnam, 2000.

Smith, Joe. *Off the Record: An Oral History of Popular Music*. New York: Warner Books, 1988.

Smith, Roberta. "Bruce Conner's Darkness That Defies Authority." *New York Times*. June 30, 2016.

Snyder, Tom. "Norfolk, Massachusetts, Inmates/White House Transcripts." *NBC Evening News*. March 23, 1975.

Somma, Robert. "The Boston Sound Revisited." *Fusion*. December 1969.

————. Eponymous Album Review. *Fusion*, issue 8. April 1969.

Stuart, Sarah Payne. *My First Cousin Once Removed*. New York: Harper Perennial, 1999.

Sullivan, James. *The Hardest Working Man*. New York: Gotham Books, 2008.

Tarbi, Charles. "Drugs Cited in Student Sentence." *Boston Globe*. May 29, 1970.

Taylor, Robert. "Baba Ram Dass (the Former Richard Alpert, PHD) Shares His Experiences." *Boston Globe*. June 14, 1970.

The Boston Strangler. Directed by Richard Fleischer. 20th Century Fox. 1968.

The Dick Cavett Show. Season 4. Episode 69. April 6, 1970.

The Night James Brown Saved Boston. Directed by David Leaf. David Leaf Productions. 2008.

Theroux, Paul. "The Story Behind Thomas Hart Benton's Incredible Masterwork." *Smithsonian Magazine*. December 2014.

Thomson, Graeme. "Van Morrison." *Uncut*. May 2015.

Three Films. Directed by Jonas Mekas Films. 2013.

Tosches, Nick. *Hellfire: The Jerry Lee Lewis Story*. New York: Grove Press. 1998.

————. "Hipsters and Hoodlums." *Vanity Fair*. December 2000.

Traum, Happy. "Van Morrison: In Conversation." *Rolling Stone*. July 9, 1970.

Treaster, Joseph B. "Researchers Say That Students Were Among 200 Who Took LSD in Tests Financed by C.I.A. in Early '50's." *New York Times*. August 9, 1977.

Trustman, Alan. *Stories, Some of Which Are True*. Self-published. 2016.

———. "Who Killed Hollywood?" *The Atlantic*. January 1978.

Tudan, Jonathan Alan. *Lovers, Muggers & Thieves: A Boston Memoir*. Hawknest, 2008.

Uncredited. "After the Brawl Was Over." *Daily Times*. May 5, 1956.

———. "Alan Freed's Rock 'n' Roll Show Today Stood Up in Court." *The Times* (Shreveport, LA). May 8, 1958.

———. "Apollo 8: Christmas at the Moon." www.nasa.gov. December 19, 2014.

———. "Battle of Four-letter Words." *Time*. March 8, 1968.

———. "Bieberman Sentenced for Shipment of LSD." *Harvard Crimson*. December 6, 1966.

———. "Boston-Filmed 'Crown Affair' Premieres in June 19 Benefit." *Boston Globe*. June 2, 1968.

———. "Court Finds Lisa Bieberman Guilty of Violations of Federal Drug Laws." *Harvard Crimson*. November 18, 1966.

———. "Cult Leader's Early Years Were Spent on the Move." *Boston Herald American*. March 26, 1978.

———. "A Curious Story About Mrs. Lincoln Reiterated." *The New York Times*. Februray 23, 1872.

———. "DeSalvo Seeks $2-Million in 'Boston Strangler' Suit." *New York Times*. December 4, 1968.

———. "The Great Spook Temple Boston Town." *Fort Wayne Weekly Gazette*. December 26, 1895.

———. "He's Not the Boston Strangler. He Didn't Kill My Aunt." *The Guardian*. September 21, 2000.

———. "Incident in Harvard Square." *Boston Magazine*. January 1968.

———. "Many Religious Communes of Young People Are Under the Sway of Compelling Leaders." *New York Times*. December 14, 1969.

———. "*Moondance* Review." *Rolling Stone*. March 19, 1970.

———. "Myddle Class Review." *Billboard*. December 1965.

———. "Nation: Love-In in BossTown." *Time*. July 12, 1968.

———. "Review of *Zabriskie Point*." *Broadside of Boston*. March 1970.

———. "Rock 'N Roll Banned in Boston After Riot That Probably Never Happened." *New England Historical Society*. 2015.

———. "'Spring Sing' on Common." *Boston Globe*. April 12, 1968.

———. "The Two Sides of Titicut." *Boston Globe*. January 21, 1968.

———. "Van Blows It." *New York*. May 20, 1996.

Unterberger, Richie. *White Light/White Heat: The Velvet Underground Day by Day*. London: Jawbone Press, 2009.

UPI Staff. "Boston Curfew Plan Considered." UPI. June 28, 1968.

———. "Martin Luther King's Widow Responds to Suit." UPI. April 8, 1988.

———. "'Zabriskie Point' Star Is Held for Bank Robbery." *Wisconsin State Journal*. September 1, 1973.

Various. *Avatar*. Biweekly newspaper. 24 issues, Boston, June 9, 1967–April 26, 1968.

Vitellomarch, Paul. "Father of Rock Criticism Is Dead at 64." *New York Times*. March 31, 2013.

Vitti, Phillip M. *The Passage: Memoir of a Boston Undercover Cop in the 60's*. Bloomington, IN: AuthorHouse, 2012.

Von Schmidt, Eric, and Jim Rooney. *Baby, Let Me Follow You Down*. Amherst: University of Massachusetts Press, 2008.

Vrabel, Jim. *A People's History of the New Boston*. Amherst: University of Massachusetts Press, 2014.

Vronsky, Peter. *Serial Killers: The Method and Madness of Monsters*. New York: Berkley Books, 2004.

Walker, Beverly. "Michelangelo and the Leviathan: The Making of *Zabriskie Point*." *Film Comment*. September 1992.

———. "On the Set of *Zabriskie Point*." *The Real Paper*. September 12, 1973.

Walsh, Kenneth T. "How Robert F. Kennedy's Death Shattered the Nation." *U.S. News*. June 5, 2015.

"Wax! Crackle! Pop! Show #15: Jonathan Richman Celebrates Lou Reed's birthday!" Radio Valencia. March 3, 2014.

Weil, Andrew. *The Natural Mind*. Boston: Houghton Mifflin, 2004.

Weiss, John. *Life and Correspondence of Theodore Parker*. New York: D. Appleton & Company, 1864.

West, Kathy. *A Song for You: The Quest of the Myddle Class*. Bloomington, IN: Xlibris, 2011.

Wetlaufer, Suzanne. "'60s Commune Finds Affluence in the '80s." *The Sunday Enterprise*. August 4, 1985.

Whalen, Tom. *The Birth of Death and Other Comedies: The Novels of Russell H. Greenan*. Champaign, IL: Dalkey Archive Press, 2011.

What's Happening, Mr. Silver? Directed by Fred Barzyk. WGBH. 1967–1968. Episodes: "Mel Lyman and the Avatar," "Madness and Intuition," "Mysticism," "Magazine Show," "Reaction to Magazine Show," "McLuhan's Children,"

"Underground Films," "Double Channel Experiment," "Tisket A Tasket, David Silver Is in a Basket."

White, Laura. "She Gave Up Computers to Play Drums in Band." *Boston Herald Traveler*. September 27, 1967.

Williams, David R. "Letter to the Editor." *Rolling Stone* #100. January 1968.

Williams, Paul. Liner notes. *11PM Saturday*. The Bagatelle. ABC Records. 1968.

———. *The Map, or Rediscovering Rock and Roll*. And Books, 1988.

Wilton, John. "Last Week." *New York Avatar* #4. May 10, 1968.

Yorke, Ritchie. *Van Morrison: Into the Music: A Biography*. Charisma Books, 1975.

DISCOGRAPHY

Aerosmith. "Dream On" b/w "Somebody." Columbia Records. 1973.

Albert DeSalvo. "Strangler in The Night" b/w The Bugs, "Albert Albert." Astor Records. 1967.

Allan Kaprow. *How to Make a Happening*. Mass Art Inc. 1966.

Beacon Street Union. *The Clown Died in Marvin Gardens*. MGM Records. 1968.

Beacon Street Union. *The Eyes of the Beacon Street Union*. MGM Records. 1968.

Chamaeleon Church. *Chamaeleon Church*. MGM Records. 1968.

David Gude, Jackie Washington, Hedy West, The Greenbriar Boys. *New Folks*. Vanguard. 1961.

Earth Opera. *Earth Opera*. Elektra Records. 1969.

Earth Opera. *The Great American Eagle Tragedy*. Elektra Records. 1969.

Geoff & Maria. *Pottery Pie*. Reprise Records. 1968.

James Brown. *I Can't Stand Myself When You Touch Me*. King Records. 1968.

James Brown. *I Got the Feelin'*. King Records. 1968.

James Brown. *James Brown Plays Nothing But Soul*. King Records. 1968.

Jim Kweskin. *Jim Kweskin Lives Again*. Mountain Railroad Records. 1978.

Jim Kweskin. *Jump for Joy*. Vanguard Records. 1967.

Jim Kweskin. *Relax Your Mind*. Vanguard. 1966.

Jim Kweskin. *Richard D. Herbruck Presents Jim Kweskin's America Co-starring Mel Lyman and the Lyman Family*. Reprise Records. 1971.

Jim Kweskin and His Friends. *What Ever Happened to Those Good Old Days at Club Forty Seven in Cambridge Massachusetts*. Vanguard Records. 1968.

Mel Lyman Family. *Birth*. Transparency. 2002.

Mel Lyman Family. "The Lyman Family Children's Christmas Tape." Unreleased. Date Unknown.

Michel Legrand. *Thomas Crown Affair [Original Motion Picture Soundtrack]*. United Artists. 1968.

Orpheus. *Ascending*. MGM Records. 1968.

Orpheus. *Orpheus*. MGM Records. 1968.

Rick Philp and David Palmer. Petrucci & Atwell Demos. Unreleased. 1969.

The Apple Pie Motherhood Band. *The Apple Pie Motherhood Band*. Atlantic Records. 1968.

The Astral Projection. *The Astral Scene*. Metromedia Records. 1968.

The Bagatelle. *11 P.M. Saturday*. ABC Records. 1968.

The Barbarians. "Moulty" b/w "I'll Keep On Seeing You." Laurie Records. 1966.

The Lost. "Violet Gown/Mean Motorcycle." Capitol Records. 1967.

The Lost. *Early Recordings: Demos, Acoustic, Live 1965–1966*. Arf! Arf! Records. 1996.

The Lost. *Lost Tapes 1965–'66*. Arf! Arf! Records. 1999.

The Lyman Family with Lisa Kindred. *American Avatar*. Reprise. 1969.

The Modern Lovers. *The Modern Lovers*. Beserkley. 1976.

The Myddle Class. "Don't Let Me Sleep Too Long" b/w "I Happen to Love You." Tomorrow Records. 1966.

The Myddle Class. "Free as the Wind" b/w "Gates of Eden." Tomorrow Records. 1965.

The Remains. *The Remains*. Epic Records. 1966.

The U And I Band. The *U And I Band At Home*. No label. 1985.

The Velvet Underground. *Final V.U. 1971–1973*. Captain Trip. 2001.

The Velvet Underground. *Live at the Boston Tea Party*, December 12th 1968. Keyhole. 2014.

The Velvet Underground. *Loaded*. Cotillion. 1970.

The Velvet Underground. "Tea Party Bootleg Recordings: 12/12/68, 1/10/69, 3/13/ 69, 7/11/69." Unreleased.

The Velvet Underground. *The Velvet Underground*. MGM Records. 1969.

The Velvet Underground. *White Light White Heat*. MGM Records. 1968.

The Velvet Underground & Nico. *The Velvet Underground & Nico*. Verve Records. 1966.

Thomas Hart Benton. *Saturday Night at Tom Benton's*. Decca Records. 1942.

Ultimate Spinach. *Behold & See*. MGM Records. 1968.

Ultimate Spinach. *Ultimate Spinach*. MGM Records. 1968.

Ultimate Spinach. *Ultimate Spinach III*. MGM Records. 1968.

Van Morrison. *The Authorized Bang Collection*. Legacy Recordings. 2017.

Van Morrison. *Astral Weeks Live at the Hollywood Bowl*. Listen to the Lion Records. 2008.

Van Morrison. *Astral Weeks*. Warner Brothers. 1968.

Van Morrison. *Blowin' Your Mind!* Bang Records. 1968.

Van Morrison. *Moondance*. Warner Brothers. 1968.

Various. *Anthology of American Folk Music*. Compiled by Harry Smith. Smithsonian Folkways. 1952.

Various. *Festival: Newport Folk Festival 1965*. Vanguard. 1967.

Various. *New England Teen Scene*. Arf! Arf! Records. 1994.

Various. *Newport Folk Festival 1964—Evening Concerts, Vol. 1*. Vanguard. 1965.

Various. *Zabriskie Point [Original Motion Picture Soundtrack]*. MGM Records. 1970.

IMAGE CREDITS

Page 1, top left: courtesy of Michael Ochs Archives; top right: courtesy of MONTUSE /Dick Iacovello/https://www.facebook.com/diacovello; bottom: courtesy of the United Illuminating, Inc.

Page 2: All images courtesy of the United Illuminating, Inc.

Page 3, top left: courtesy of Murray Lerner, MLF Productions; top right, courtesy of David S. Wilson; bottom left; courtesy of the United Illuminating, Inc.

Page 4, top left: courtesy of Dick Weisberg; top right: courtesy of David Silver; middle: courtesy of Bruce Arnold Music/Orpheus; bottom left: courtesy of Ted Myers; bottom right: courtesy of John Sposato.

Page 5, top left: courtesy of David Bieber Archives; top right: courtesy of *Rolling Stone*; bottom left and right: courtesy of MONTUSE/Dick Iacovello/https://www .facebook.com/diacovello.

Page 6, top: courtesy of Michael Dobo/DoboPhoto.com; center: courtesy of Ken Wachsberger; bottom left: courtesy of *Rolling Stone*; bottom right: photo by Barry Savendor, 1968, courtesy of Charles Giuliano.

Page 7, top left: photo by Jeff Albertson, courtesy of UMass (Amherst) Department of Special Collections and University archives, W. E. B. Du Bois Library; center left and middle: photos by and courtesy of Ronn Campisi; center right: courtesy of Brandon Hodge, mysteriousplanchette.com; bottom right: photo by Andrew Browder, courtesy of Althea Greenan.

Page 8, top left: courtesy of Michael Dobo/DoboPhoto.com; bottom left: photo by Peter Simon, courtesy of PeterSimon.com; bottom right: courtesy of Liberation News Service.

INDEX